高等院校“十三五”规划教材——经济管理系列

商务沟通

(第二版)(双语)

张素红　〔澳〕卡洛琳·哈奇(Caroline Hatcher)　编著

清华大学出版社
北　京

内 容 简 介

本书内容主要包括两个方面：一是口头沟通，阐述了演讲、口头商务沟通、人际沟通及跨文化沟通等策略；二是书面沟通，主要包括如何撰写各类商务信函，如何构造写作的正面效应，如何运用翔实的事例使沟通更具说服力，如何撰写商务报告等。学生通过对本书内容的学习，可提高写作能力、策划能力，增强与他人沟通的能力，培养说服他人、影响他人的能力。

本书不仅可以作为高等院校本科"商务沟通""国际商务(英语)写作"等课程的教材，也可作为其他专业学生提高英语阅读能力、英语沟通能力的辅助阅读教材，还可作为从事管理工作的人员及企业内部沟通培训的参考书。

图书在版编目(CIP)数据

商务沟通：双语版：汉，英/张素红，(澳)卡洛琳 • 哈奇(Caroline Hatcher)编著. —2 版. —北京：清华大学出版社，2020.1(2023.12 重印)

高等院校"十三五"规划教材. 经济管理系列

ISBN 978-7-302-53801-1

Ⅰ. ①商… Ⅱ. ①张… ②卡… Ⅲ. ①商业管理－公共关系学－高等学校－教材 Ⅳ. ①F715

中国版本图书馆 CIP 数据核字(2019)第 217939 号

责任编辑：章忆文 李玉萍
装帧设计：刘孝琼
责任校对：周剑云
责任印制：杨 艳
出版发行：清华大学出版社
网 址：https://www.tup.com.cn, https://www.wqxuetang.com
地 址：北京清华大学学研大厦 A 座 **邮 编**：100084
社 总 机：010-83470000 **邮 购**：010-62786544
投稿与读者服务：010-62776969, c-service@tup.tsinghua.edu.cn
质量反馈：010-62772015, zhiliang@tup.tsinghua.edu.cn
课件下载：https://www.tup.com.cn , 010-62791865
印 装 者：三河市龙大印装有限公司
经 销：全国新华书店
开 本：185mm×260mm **印 张**：20.5 **字 数**：500 千字
版 次：2006 年 3 月第 1 版 2020 年 1 月第 2 版 **印 次**：2023 年 12 月第 4 次印刷
定 价：56.00 元

产品编号：083568-01

第二版前言

越来越多的组织在招聘时都强调“要有良好的沟通技巧”。企业呼唤管理人才，而管理的精髓则在于有效的沟通。但在实际工作和生活中，很多人在公众面前发言会紧张害怕；公司经理在百忙之中抽出时间，希望听听对商业计划书的理解，但员工却不知道该如何下手；由于表达能力较差，新产品发布会上的介绍不尽如人意；由于沟通方式不当，产品得不到消费者的认可；优秀的大学毕业生甚至在用人单位面前不知道如何推销自己。他们失去的不仅仅是一次机会，更是自己未来发展的机会。为解决这些问题，我们编写了本书。

本书是继 2006 年初版之后的第二版。第二版内容在第一版的基础上进行了不同程度的调整和修订，更新了相关案例、思考题等，同时也增加了“学习实践”环节。本书分为三个部分。第一部分为管理沟通基础(包括第一、二章)。第一章介绍商务沟通技能的重要性。第二章介绍沟通、商务沟通、正式沟通、非正式沟通等基本概念和特点，了解有效沟通的障碍，并可以通过不同途径克服障碍实现有效沟通。第二部分为口头商务沟通(包括第三至五章)。第三章介绍演讲的准备步骤，强调演讲中如何做到以听众为中心，实现沟通预期目标。第四章介绍不同文化背景下影响沟通反馈的行为模式和态度，培养个体差异在跨文化背景下如何影响沟通行为的意识，掌握有效管理跨文化交流的原则。第五章介绍通信技术在有效沟通中的作用，如何利用相关技术实现有效沟通目的。第三部分为书面商务沟通(包括第六至八章)。第六章介绍商务活动中写作的重要性、写作指导性原则，如何使写作通俗易懂。第七章介绍商务书信的格式和类型，如何在信函中表达“肯定”和“否定”，如何撰写商务沟通中的简短信函，如说服性信函、推销信函、备忘录等。第八章介绍提案、报告和商业计划书的构成和写作方法。

本书具有如下特点。

(1) 完整的内容结构体系。本书在内容上包括沟通的基本理论以及在不同情景中沟通的运用技巧。主要包括口头沟通和书面沟通。其中，口头沟通不仅包括演讲技巧，而且涉及跨文化沟通以及如何运用科学技术进行有效的演示。书面沟通包括一般的商务书信格式、各种信函的撰写以及推销信、商业计划书的撰写等。

(2) 理论与实践相结合。本书较为深入、系统地介绍了沟通理论，具有较强的理论性。同时增加了“学习实践”环节，强调理论与实践相结合。每章提供了相关案例、总结、讨论题和练习题，以帮助读者巩固和加深对各章节重点内容的学习和理解。

(3) 实用性。本书提供了一些来源于实践的沟通贴士和撰写模板，使读者在运用中有所参照。

(4) 跨文化体会。本书两位作者来自不同国家，有着多年的大学教学经验和实际工作经验，对不同沟通问题的理解角度不同。读者不仅能体会地道的英文写作，而且能够理解符合中国国情的问题解决方式。

本书采用双语编写，中英文对照。由金陵科技学院张素红教授与澳大利亚昆士兰理工大学教授卡洛琳•哈奇(Caroline Hatcher)合著而成(注：两位作者的简介见下页)。两位作者都有在不同国家学习、工作和生活的经历，对管理沟通尤其是跨文化沟通有着深刻的体会和丰富的经验。因此，本书不仅有着理论参考价值，而且也有实际指导价值。既可以学习地道的英文写作，也可以参考中文阅读，但我们不希望读者在阅读本书时跳过英文部分而直接阅读中文内容。如果真是这样，很遗憾，您将错过本书的许多精彩之处。

事实上，很多已经在职场拼杀多年的人并不擅长在公众场所表达自己的观点。因此，本书的读者不仅包括商务沟通专业的大学生，也包括那些希望提高自己的沟通能力、提高说服他人、影响他人能力的人。

本书的编写分工如下：第二、六、七、八章由张素红编写和翻译，第一、三、四、五章由 Caroline Hatcher 承担英文写作，张素红完成翻译工作。金陵科技学院吴迪老师对再版的部分英文内容进行了翻译。

非常难忘 2015 年，Caroline Hatcher 教授到金陵科技学院商学院，开展了为期近半年的学术研究与交流。在此期间，我又有机会和她在教学与科研方面进行深度合作。此书的再版也是我们相隔 10 年后再次合作的成果。非常感谢 Caroline Hatcher 教授，为她的敬业与认真而感动，她在腿部受伤且布里斯班今年遭遇寒冷的冬天时仍然坚持对此书进行修订。感谢金陵科技学院吴迪老师对再版部分英文内容的翻译与核对，感谢商学院张薇老师对本书再版提供了很多建设性修改意见，感谢商学院吴茜老师和刘源老师对书稿内容进行了核对。感谢身边所有关爱我的家人和朋友。

本书部分内容不完全是对英文的一对一翻译，两位作者共同参与对本书的结构及其内容的讨论。由于时间有限，再版最初的很多设想没能实现，甚是遗憾。由于作者水平有限，本书部分内容及翻译可能存在不足之处，还望读者批评指正。

编　者

2019 年 6 月

作者简介

张素红，金陵科技学院教务处副处长，教授，南京大学法学硕士，获澳大利亚国立大学 MBA 学位。主要研究方向为公共管理、人力资源开发与管理、商务沟通、跨文化管理等。曾在澳大利亚学习和生活多年，近年来主持和参加多项省、市级科研项目，发表多篇学术论文。

卡洛琳·哈奇(Caroline Hatcher)，澳大利亚昆士兰理工大学(Queensland University of Technology)布里斯班商学院荣誉退休教授(Emeritus Professor)，获得组织沟通专业博士学位，在商务沟通研究方面有着丰富的教学经验，尤其擅长跨文化沟通的口头沟通技巧，发表过多篇文章和著作，是 *Speaking Persuasively: The Essential Guide to Giving Dynamic Presentations and Speeches* 一书的作者之一，此书在澳大利亚、英国和美国出版发行。Caroline Hatcher 有着多年的大学工作经验，同时也有着多年的咨询、管理经验，主要咨询内容为沟通和组织变化管理等，也有着在英国、日本多年的工作和生活经历。

第一版前言

越来越多的公司在招聘时强调“要有良好的沟通技巧”。企业呼唤管理人才，而管理的精髓则在于有效的沟通。但我们看到的是：很多人在公众面前发言会紧张、害怕；公司经理在百忙之中抽出时间，希望听听对商业计划书的理解，但员工却不知道该如何下手；由于表达能力较差，新产品发布会上的介绍不尽如人意；因为沟通方式不当，产品得不到消费者的认可；优秀的大学毕业生甚至不知道在用人单位面前该如何推销自己……他们失去的不仅仅是这一次机会，而是自己未来发展的机会。正是在这种情况下，我们编写了本书。

本书的主要特点如下。

(1) 完整的结构体系。本书在内容上包括了沟通的基本理论以及在不同情景中的沟通运用技巧，分为口头沟通和书面沟通。口头沟通不仅包括演讲技巧，而且涉及跨文化沟通以及运用科学技术进行有效演示的方法。书面沟通包括一般的商务书信格式，拒绝函电和接受函电的撰写，以及推销信、商业计划书的撰写等。

(2) 理论与实践相结合。本书较为深入、系统地介绍了沟通理论，具有较强的理论性，同时又强调理论与实践的结合。书中不仅提供了体现主题的案例，而且在案例前提供了思考题，让读者带着问题有目的地进行阅读。章后的本章小结突出了该章的重点内容，帮助读者回忆、复习所学内容。大部分章后还提供了讨论题和练习题，帮助读者巩固和加深各章所强调的内容。

(3) 实用性。本书提供了一些来源于实践的沟通贴士和撰写模板，使读者在应用中有所参照。

(4) 跨文化的体会。本书两位作者来自不同的国家，有着多年的教学经验和实际工作经验，对不同沟通问题的理解角度较广。读者不仅能欣赏到地道的英文写作，而且能够学到符合中国国情的问题解决方式。

许多跨国企业将中国作为未来开发的主要市场，而中国企业面临的也是越来越激烈的世界性挑战。一方面，许多国内企业亟需了解国际商务沟通实务的人才；另一方面，很多人的英文水平还不能达到阅读英文原版教材的程度。因此，本书采用双语编写，先用英文写成，然后译成中文。这样，读者有很大的选择空间，既可以读到地道的英文，必要时也可以参考译文。国外有不少关于商务沟通或管理沟通的专著或教材，但它们的角度是从西方文化背景和价值观出发的，我们在编写过程中，根据中国国情，对一些理论加以修改，使其更适合中国读者。

据调查，很多人工作中面临最大的困窘是在公众场所进行发言。因此，本书的读者不仅包括本科生，也包括在企业或其他组织机构工作的人，还有那些希望在日常生活中提高自己与他人的沟通能力，提高自己说服他人、影响他人能力的人。通过对本书的阅读，读者可以从中得到一些启示，将沟通技巧运用到许多领域，对生活和工作都会有所帮助。

本书的第二、六、七、八、九章由张素红编写和翻译，第一、三、四、五章由卡洛琳·哈奇(Caroline Hatcher)承担英文写作，金陵科技学院张薇承担翻译工作。

在此，十分感谢 Caroline Hatcher 的合作，并十分敬佩她的敬业精神；感谢金陵科技学院商学院葛军院长对本书编写提供的大力支持；感谢所有在编写过程中给予我无私帮助的人，包括我的家人。

由于作者水平有限，书中尚有不足之处，还望读者批评指正。

张素红

2005 年 11 月

目 录

Part 1 Foundations for Management Communication

Part 2 Oral Communication in Business

Part 3 Written Communication in Business

第一部分　管理沟通基础

第二部分　口头商务沟通

第三部分 书面商务沟通

Part 1

Foundations for Management Communication

Chapter 1

Business Communication

Management Success

Study Case：Communication in the Workplace

Norm Fjeldheim credits much of the success in his career to learning and developing his business writing and reporting skills. As a leader in a leading company in the digital wireless communications industry, he relies heavily on these well-honed skills. In overseeing all aspects of Qualcomm's information technology, he interacts with people in a wild variety of positions including Qualcomm senior executives and board members, senior executives of customers and suppliers, and occasionally even the Department of Justice and FBI on Security issues. He also keeps his direct reports and customers informed and on track. By far the most important tools he uses daily for the majority of his work are Eudora, PowerPoint, and Word.

When asked about the most important class to take, he definitively answers "Business Communication". He says, "Even if you have great technical skills, your career will get stalled without good communication skills. In fact, the better your communication skills, the further you will go. While technology changes over time, being able to communicate well will always be valuable."

Norm Fjeldheim, Senior Vice President and CIO
Qualcomm

(Source: Kathryn Rentz, Marie E. Flatley, Paula Lentz, *Business Communication (Twelfth Edition)*, McGraw Hill, 2012, P1)

Analysis：Your work in business will involve communication—a lot of it—because communication is a major and essential part of the work of business. By improving your communication ability, you improve your chances for success.

1.1 The Importance of Communication Skills

Because communication is so important in business, businesses want and need people with good communication skills. Evidence of the importance of communication in business is found in numerous surveys of executives, recruiters, and academicians. Without exception, these surveys have found that communication (especially oral and written communication) ranks at or near the top of the business skills needed for success.

For example, NFI Research, a private organization who regularly surveys over 2000 executives and senior managers, found that 94 percent of members rank "communicating well" as the most important skill for them to succeed today and tomorrow. Employers in the United States surveyed for the National Association of College and *Employers' Job Outlook 2016* also cited "communication skills" at the top of the list. Employers rated "ability to verbally communicate with persons inside and outside the organization" and "ability to create and/or edit written reports" as number one in their top 10 highly prized qualities in job applicants. Recruiters who participated in *The Wall Street Journal*'s ranking of MBA programs and *The Bloomberg Recruiter Report* (*2015*) agreed communication skills were in short supply. They rated "interpersonal and communication skills, a teamwork orientation, personal ethics and integrity, analytical and problem-solving abilities, and a strong work ethic" as the most important.

Unfortunately, the business need for employees with good communication skills is all too often not fulfilled. Most employees, even after training in the University, can't meet the need. Effective communicators are, therefore, in high demand.

The authors of this book recognize the centrality of good communication to business, and we believe that learning about business communication and practicing the skills of speaking and writing right from the start of your career will lead not only to a fulfilling working life, but also to more opportunity and promotion. In other words, by putting business communication high on your agenda right from the start of your career, you will be setting yourself up for future success.

1.2 Writing about Business Communication

As authors, we take business communication seriously and we want you to do so. That is why we have carefully developed four threads running through each of the chapters to explore each of the topics. We have included the following contents in every chapter:

(1) An explanation of the theory that explains why what we suggest is a good idea.

(2) Examples of how business communication works in practice, using many case studies.

(3) Exercises and activities to challenge you to apply our explanations to particular situations.

(4) Guiding principles that you can test yourself when you apply your knowledge to new situations.

We cover many topics that will help you to be effective in a variety of situations where you must use communication skills in business. This ranges from internal communication, where you are working with members of your own organization to external communication where you are dealing with various stakeholders such as clients or potential clients, regulatory bodies and other organizations. The book also helps you with formal communication situations such as giving presentations, writing sales letters, business plans, and memos as well as informal communication situations such as online communication, handling conflicts and influencing others.

1.3 Why We Wrote This Bilingual Book

As China extends its global influence and moves to a more open economy, there is an ever-increasing need for ambitious business students to acquire the skills of world best practice, whether it will be used at home or abroad. By doing this, students can benefit from the collaboration of business communication specialists who bring knowledge of the East and West together. This book was written by authors from China and Australia, a significant trading partner of both the US and the Asian region. Our combined knowledge and advice will prepare you for many future challenges of business communication.

As writers, we also recognize the importance of ensuring that we write for you as the particular target market for this book. You will most likely see yourself in the picture below as we describe our audience:

(1) We have written this book for young Chinese bilingual who are learning or have learned English and may feel more confident when using an English text if they can confirm their understanding in a convenient manner by simply referring to the appropriate Chinese language section when they need to.

(2) We want the book to prepare our readers for business careers by exploring situations which apply to domestic business situations as well as situations where business is conducted in a multi-national environment, and more generally, to prepare readers to do business in an international environment. This means the readers want both local and international examples, as well as cross-cultural examples.

Do you fit this picture? If your answer is yes, this book is for you. It will prepare you to be an effective business communicator.

1.4 The Values Explored in This Book

The ability to relate to other people is an essential quality for a good manager. In fact, being social aware, having good communication skills, both spoken and written, and empathy with others are now regarded as critical to good leadership. US psychologist Daniel Goleman and his colleagues have popularized the significance of emotional intelligence as a fundamental competence for leaders and managers. Emotional intelligence consists of a number of abilities: the ability to monitor your feelings and emotions, the ability to monitor the feelings and emotions of others, and the ability to employ this information to guide your future thinking and action (Goleman, Boyatzis & McKee, 2002).

The fundamental task of emotionally intelligent leaders then, is to "prime good feeling in those they lead". This causes "resonance—a reservoir of positivity that frees the best in people". That is why we give a lot of attention to you, as a communicator, and to the audience in any communication situation discussed in this book. In fact, while all of the chapters in this book place the listener or reader at the heart of the communication interaction, Chapter 3 on persuasion and presentations, and Chapter 7 on effective business letters remind you persistently of the mantra of good communication: it's all about audience, audience, audience.

One of the qualities of emotional intelligence that helps you to communicate well with your audience is adaptability. This quality, along with your responsiveness to others, allows you to adjust your message to the circumstance or interaction style of your audience. This means listening carefully to the responses of others, recognizing their differing perspectives on issues and then adapting to meet their needs while sharing yours.

This textbook also continuously asks you to reflect on how to match your style and tone with those you are communicating with. And this is no easy task. You have many opportunities to put yourself to the test. For example, there are case studies where you can observe and judge effective and ineffective communication behaviors and there are exercises where you can put yourself to the test. There are also guidelines and tips such as simple, easy-to-remember acronyms to allow you to use good models of practice. These will help you as a template for your first forays into activities such as writing a sales letter, or developing a business plan. One example used in the book is an approach to cross-cultural encounters: PLACE—prepare, listen, adjust, communicate and enjoy! Keeping an acronym like this in mind can smooth an encounter. You will find many more!

Most importantly, this book is grounded in a commitment to ethical communication at all times. This is demonstrated throughout the book by guidance that suggests that a respectful, open and honest communication style will be most effective and admirable.

On many occasions when you read this book, you will notice the suggestion to be strategic in your use of particular communication patterns. For example, in situations where you wish to persuade others, we are offering guidance and insight which could be used to manipulate others. However, your responsibility is to use this knowledge ethically and to always stay within the bounds of good and reasonable practice.

1.5 Does Experience Bear Out These Claims

Many successful leaders of both large multinational corporation and small companies regularly cite their people and the management of them as the reasons for their success.

Carly Fiorina, former CEO of Hewlett Packard (HP) from 1999 to 2005 believes that the job of the leader is "to set the frame, to set the people free" and the Virgin Atlantic Airways' CEO Richard Branson agrees. For example, Richard Branson, when asked about what is important in starting up a business, claimed: "I think you have to be passionate. Not just in it to make a lot of money." This followed his answer that it is "people, people, people" who are the three most important things in starting up a business. Closer to home in China, Jack Ma of Alibaba Group advises young entrepreneurs to learn from and listen to more experienced managers as they develop their careers.

In an article "*On the Challenge of Management*", other leaders reinforce this view that communication, passion and managing and responding to people effectively are the essential core competence of business.

- Business Council of Australia's CEO asserts that: "I don't do things unless I can be passionate about them" and rates people skills as the key managerial skills for success.
- Ella Bache's CEO Karen Mathews asserts that: "good leaders possess a raft of traits, including honesty, an ability to listen, entrepreneurship, intuition, compassion… And what makes a great leader is they know when to call on the different qualities."
- Internet trading company CMC's CEO David Trew advises: "You have to be passionate about business and about your role because passion is a strong driving force that will bring about other positives for the business."

Good business practitioners are clear about the role of communication, emotional intelligence, and soft skills in business.

1.6 Myths of Communication

There are many myths about communication, and it is always important to recognize that myths are not always a good reflection of reality. As you read the book, we are sure that you will agree with us that the myths listed below misrepresent both the many difficulties and challenges and also the opportunities of effective communication. Consider these:

- Communication is easy.
- If we can just communicate, we can agree.
- Natural and spontaneous expression facilitates communication.
- Communication equals to information given.
- A good professional relies only on cold hard facts to achieve his purpose.

ACTIVITY FOR LEARNING

Choose one or two of the Communication Myths listed above. Think of examples from your experience where you noticed that the myth reflects, or more likely, does not reflect your experience. Why?

As teachers, researchers, and business consultants with many years' experience, we are sure that, after you read this book, reflect on your own experience and practice the strategies that we have proposed, you will agree with us that being a good business communicator, you will take all of the knowledge, emotional intelligence, and strategic effort and skills that you can bring to the tasks ahead of you. Good luck with the challenges. We know that you will be rewarded tenfold if you can become an excellent business communicator!

Chapter 2

The Challenges for Communication in the New Century

LEARNING OBJECTIVES

On completing this chapter, you should be able to:

- Understand the conceptions of communication and business communication commonly used and referred to in this book.
- Understand that communication can be divided into formal communication and informal communication.
- Recognize the barriers to effective communication.
- Know that effective business communication can be achieved by using the major components in the process of communication.
- Understand the trends and challenges for business communication in the future.

Study Case：Columbia Disaster Communication Failures

In 2003, the Columbia space shuttle disintegrated on re-entry, resulting in the deaths of all seven crew members. The independent research team investigating the disaster found communication problems to be the root causes of the accident. The researchers concluded the organizational barriers prevented effective communication of critical safely information and restrained communication of professionals.

The report identified the following communication problems:

(1) Communication flow between managers and subordinates: Managers did not heed the concerns of the engineers regarding debris impacts on the shuttle. Throughout the project, communication did not flow effectively up or down from program managers.

(2) Circulation of information among teams: Although engineers were concerned about landing problems and therefor conducted experiments on landing procedures, the concerns were not relayed to managers or system and technology experts who could have addressed the concerns.

(3) Communication sources: Managers received a large amount of their information from informal channels, which blocked relevant opinions and conclusions from engineers.

(Adapted from Columbia Accident Investigation Board, Report of Columbia Accident Investigation Board, Volume 1, August 2003, http://www.nasa.gov/columbia/home/CAIB_Vol1.html.)

Analysis：As we see in the above case, good communication is worth every minute it takes and every penny it costs. Poor communication can cost billions of dollars. However，cost of poor communication are not just financial. Not all communication costs are so dramatic. When communication isn't as good as it could be, your organization pay a price in wasted time, wasted effort, lost goodwill, and legal problems.

2.1 About Communication

2.1.1 Communicating in organizations

Attaining your complete career objectives without good communication skills is unlikely. However, you can achieve much for your organization and yourself by using the full range of your communication abilities. "Employment Opportunities!" advertisements in international publications such as the *Wall Street Journal*, *National Employment Weekly*, dozens of Internet job sites now available, and elsewhere regularly call for "excellent presentation skills, well-developed writing abilities", and "interpersonal communication strengths" as primary requirements for management positions at all levels. Recent surveys published in *Harvard Business Review*, *Business Week*, and *Fortune* point to communication skills as one of the most important determinations for upward career mobility across industry.

Walk through the halls of contemporary organizations—no matter whether it's a small start-up entrepreneurial firm, a Fortune 500 global giant, a state government office, or a not-for-profit organization and what do you see? You see managers and other employees reading reports, reading and drafting email messages, attending meetings, conducting interviews, talking on the telephone, conferencing with subordinates, holding business lunches, reading mails, dictating correspondence, and making presentations. In short, you see people communicating.

An organization is a group of people working together to achieve a common goal, and communication is a vital part of that process. Indeed, communication must have occurred before a common goal could even be established. And a group of people working together must interact; that is they must communicate their needs, thoughts, plans, expertise, and so on. Communication is the means by which information is shared, activities are coordinated, and decision making is enhanced. Understanding how communication works in business and how to communicate competently within an organization will help you participate more effectively in every aspect of business.

What do we mean by communication? Early communication theorists set up a model of communication that consisted of the source of the message, the transmission of the message and the receiver of the message. On reflection, this model assumes that communication is a linear process: a message is sent and received, and communication is achieved. We all know intuitively that this is not quite how communication works. As a useful model, this is a too-simple perception of what is a more complex process.

Today, you have to answer several questions about communication because of the continual changes in the way business operates:

(1) You need to achieve personal and professional goals with the communication tools. But which communication abilities really matter for a fast-track professional?

(2) Which communication skills will matter most for you in the years ahead?

(3) How do you make sure you are preparing for the future, not the past?

(4) How can you accommodate the new and emerging communication lessons and technologies?

(5) How do you deal with the ethical issues that are bound up in virtually all communication relationships?

Skilled communicators share in the give-and-take of ideas and feelings. Even when they give speeches, communicators notice responses from their audiences. The speaker alone can only make speech noises. The audiences alone can only wait to hear or see something. Together, they can communicate in the mutual activity of making thoughts and feelings common to the group or interaction. Mere speaking is a one-way activity, while communication involves common (communal) interests shared by all parties involved in the communication.

2.1.2 The components of communication

Communication is the process that occurs between participants as they send and receive messages—sometimes through spoken or written words and sometimes through such nonverbal means as facial expressions, gestures, and voice qualities. Figure 2.1 illustrates the communication model which consists of five components: stimulus, filter, message, medium, and destination. Ideally, the process ends with feedback to the sender, although feedback is not necessary for communication that has taken place.

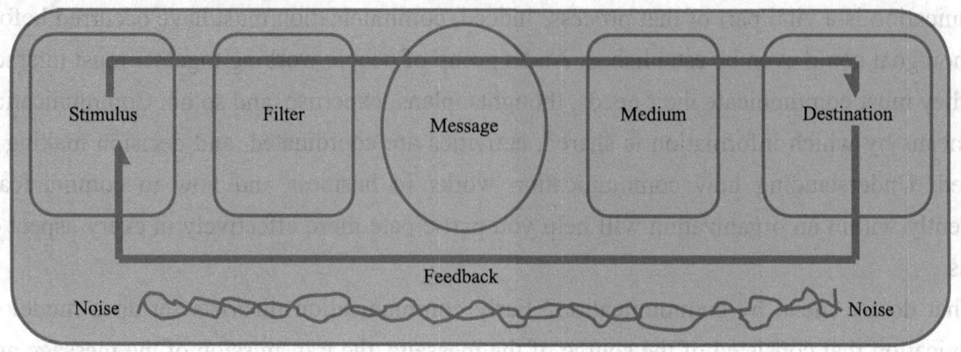

Figure 2.1 The Communication Model

(Source: Ober S, Newman A. 商务沟通[M]. 7版. 北京：清华大学出版社，2013.)

1. The stimulus

Step 1: A stimulus creates a need for communication.

In order for communication to take place, first there must be a stimulus, an event that creates within an individual the need to communicate. An internal stimulus is simply an idea that forms within your mind. External stimuli come to you through sensory organs—your eyes, ears, nose, mouth, and skin. A stimulus for communication in business might be an email message you have just read, a bit of gossip you have heard over lunch, or even the hot air generated by an overworked heating system. You respond to the stimulus by formulating a message: a verbal message (written or spoken words), a nonverbal message (non-written and non-spoken signals), or some combination of the two.

2. The filter

Step 2: Our knowledge, experience, and viewpoints act as filters to help us interpret (decode) the stimulus.

If everyone had the same perception of events, your job of communication would be easier; you could assume that your perception of reality was accurate and that others would understand your motives and intent. Indeed, each person has a unique perception of reality, based on his or her individual experiences, culture, and emotions at the moment, personality, knowledge, socioeconomic status, and a host of other variables. Each variable acts as a filter in shaping a person's unique impressions of reality.

3. The message

Step 3: We formulate (encode) a verbal or non-verbal response to the stimulus.

The extent to which any communication effort achieves its desire goal depends on how well you construct the message (the information to be communicated). Success at communicating depends not only on the purpose and content of the message but also on how skillful you are at communicating, how well you know your audience (the person or persons you are communicating with), and how much you hold in common with your audience.

4. The medium

Step 4: We select the form of the message (medium).

Once the sender has encoded a message, the next step in the process is to transmit that message to the receiver. At this point, this sender must choose the medium, that is, the means of transmitting the message. Oral messages might be transmitted through a staff meeting, a personal conference, a telephone conversation, a voice mail, or even such informal means as the company grapevine. Written messages might be transmitted through a memorandum, a report, a brochure, a bulletin board notice, an email, a company newsletter, or an addition to the policies and procedure manuals. And nonverbal messages might be transmitted through facial expressions, voices, gestures or body movements, or in written documents through layouts or images.

5. The destination

Step 5: The message reaches its destination and, if successful, is perceived accurately by the receivers.

The message is transmitted and enters the sensory environment of the receiver, at which point control passes from the sender to the receiver. Once the message reaches its destination, there is no guarantee that communication will actually occur. We are constantly bombarded with stimuli, and our sensory organs pick up only part of them. Even assuming your receiver does perceive your message, you have no assurance that it will be interpreted (filtered) as you intended. Your transmitted message then becomes the source, or stimulus, for the next communication episode, and the process begins anew.

2.2 The Role of Communication in Business

2.2.1 Communication on jobs

Communication—oral and written, verbal and non-verbal—goes to both internal and external audiences. Internal audiences are other people in the same organization: subordinates, superiors and peers. External audiences are people outside the organization: customers, suppliers, distributors, unions, stockholders, potential employees, trade associations, special interest groups, government agencies, the press and the general public.

People in organizations produce a large variety of documents. Table 2.1 lists a few of specific documents produced at Ryerson, a company that fabricates and sells steel, aluminum, other metals, and plastics to a wide variety of industrial clients and has sales offices across the United States, Canada, and China.

All of the documents in Table 2.1 have one or more of the three basic purposes of organizational writing: to inform, to request or persuade and to build goodwill. In fact, most messages have multiple purposes. When you answer a question, for instance, you are informing, but you also want to build goodwill by suggesting that you are competent and that your answer is correct and complete.

Table 2.1 Internal Documents Produced in One Organization

Types of documents	Description of documents	Purpose(s) of documents
Transmittal	Memo accompanying document, telling why it's being forwarded to the receiver	Inform; persuade readers to read documents; build image and goodwill
Monthly or quarterly report	Report summarizing profitability, productivity, and problems during a period; used to plan activity for next month or quarter	Inform; build image and goodwill (report is accurate, complete; writer understands company)
Policy and procedure bulletin	Statement of company policies and instructions (e.g., how to enter orders, how to run fire drills)	Inform; build image and goodwill (request is reasonable; writer seeks glitters of company)
Performance appraisal	Evaluation of an employee's performance	Inform；persuade employees to improve
Memo of congratulation	Congratulations to employees who have won awards, or have been promoted	Build goodwill

(Source: Locker K O, Kienzler D S. *Business and Administrative Communication*[M]. 10th ed. NewYork: McGraw-Hill, 2013.)

2.2.2 Internal and External Communication

Internal communication means communication that takes place within an organization. This is the communication among the business employees that is done to create, implement, and track the success of the business's operating plan. Internal communication takes many forms. It includes the ongoing discussion that senior management undertakes to determine the goals and processes of the business. It includes the orders and instructions that supervisors give employees, as well as oral exchanges among employees about work matters. It includes reports that employees prepare concerning sales, products, inventories, finance, maintenances, and so on. It includes the email messages that they write in carrying out their assignments and contributing their ideas to the business.

External communication refers to the kinds of communication between one organization and outside institutions and persons, including clients and potential clients, service and product providers, and professional bodies. Indeed, an organization can't exist or run its business by itself without communicating with other organizations or individuals. Look at Table 2.2 below.

Table 2.2 External Documents Produced in One Organization

Types of documents	Description of documents	Purpose(s) of documents
Quotation	Letters giving price for a specific product or service	Inform; build goodwill (price is reasonable)
Claims adjustment	Letters granting or denying customer request to be given credit for defective goods	Inform; build goodwill
Job description	Description of qualifications and duties of a job, used for performance appraisals, salaries, and hiring	Inform; persuade good candidates to apply; build goodwill (job duties match level, pay)
Annual report	Report to stockholders summarizing financial information for a year	Inform; persuade stockholders to retain stock and others to buy; build goodwill

(Source: Locker K O, Kienzler D S. *Business and Administrative Communication*[M]. 10th ed. New York: McGraw-Hill, 2013.)

2.2.3 Formal communication and informal communication

Both internal communication and external communication can be divided into two kinds: formal communication and informal communication.

Formal communication refers to communicative activities like a business talk, a speech, a presentation, a business letter, etc. The characteristics of formal communication are seriousness, exactness and expectation that the communication is regarded by the organization as speaking for the organization and that what is said is official. This often requires a suitable design and good preparation. You need to collect as much information as you can for the purposes of this type of communication. Also you need to pay careful attention to the way you present this type of communication. During the process of communicating, some different opinions may occur because people differ from each other in their perceptions or have different objectives. So, excellent communication skills are needed and expected in order to solve any problems that may arise or to achieve an agreement about the issues covered.

When formal communication is carried out in a written form, it needs even greater effort and precision as what is written on the paper forms a record of the interaction. The tone, the structure, the words and phrases should be noticed because these factors affect the outcomes of formal communication directly. In formal communication, you have to take full responsibility for whatever message you want to send.

Informal communication, on the other hand, refers to the ways that employees connect with each other, both within and across businesses without official constraints of business rules such as procedures. Figure 2.2 below illustrates several of the variables that we think distinguish formal communication from informal communication. At the heart of what we term informal communication is its unstructured nature. Conversations take place at the time needed, perhaps with only some of the participants really required, and about the topics at hand. Informal person to person interaction allows the building of relationships. None of those characteristics—timing, participants, or agenda—are scheduled in advance. Moreover, during its course, the communication changes to take into account the participants' current interests and understandings. In this sense, informal communication is truly interactive, with all participants in the communication being able to respond to what they perceive to be the current states of affairs, including the communication up until that point and their perception of the other participants' reactions to it. Through this feedback mechanism, informal communication can be more effective than formal channels, as participants in the conversations elaborate or modify what they have to say in order to deal with someone else's objections or misunderstanding. Additionally, many "off the record" comments are made, the language is more colloquial and often less guarded, and no record of the interaction is necessarily kept. One way to formalize the communication is to ask for a summary of the interaction after the event. This then changes the communication into a more formal form.

Formal	Informal
-Scheduled in advance	-Unscheduled
-Arranged participants	-Random participants
-Participants in role	-Participants out of role
-Preset agenda	-Unarranged agenda
-One-way	-Interactive
-Simplified content	-Rich content
-Formal language & speech register	-Informal language & speech register

Figure 2.2 The Formality Dimensions of Communication

(Source: Kraut R E, Fish R S, Root R W, et al,. Informal communication in organizations: form, function, and technology. S. Oskamp & S. Spacapan (Eds)[C]. *Human Reactions to Technology: The Claremont Symposium on Applied Social Psychology*. Beverly Hills: Sage Publications, 1990.)

ACTIVITY FOR LEARNING

(1) Think of a time when you needed to use formal communication in your organization (perhaps your university). Now compare this with your informal communication within the organization.

(2) Consider the differences in your language choices, styles and channels of communication.

1. Formal internal communication network: direction of flow

Within the organization, information may be transmitted from superiors to subordinates (downward communication), from subordinates to superiors (upward communication), among people at the same level on the organizational chart (horizontal communication), and among people in different departments within the organization (cross-channel communication). These four types of communication make up the organization's formal communication network. We'll use part of ABC Company's organizational chart, as is shown in Figure 2.3 to illustrate the directions of communication.

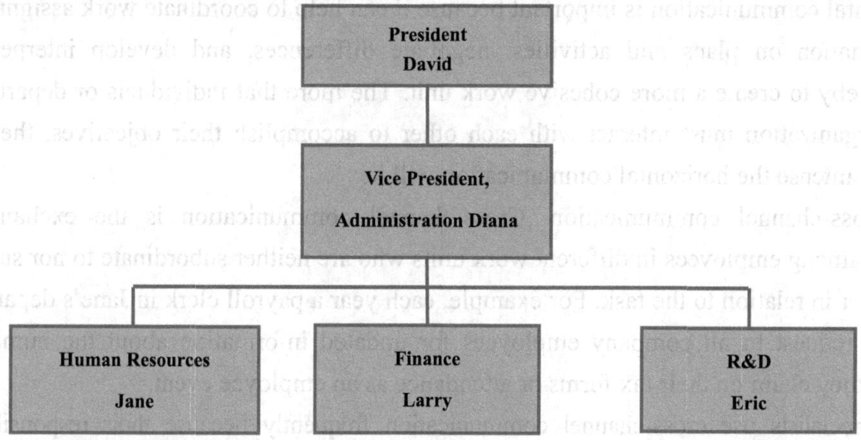

Figure 2.3 Part of the Formal Communication Network of ABC Company

(1) Downward communication. In most organizations, the largest number of vertical communications move downward from someone of higher authority to someone of lower authority. For example, at ABC Company (see Figure 2.3), David sends an email message to Diana about a computer report; Diana, in turn, confers with Eric. Through written and oral channels, information regarding job performance, policies and procedures, day-to-day operation, and other organizational information is communicated.

Higher-level management communicates with lower-level employees through such means as websites, emails, memorandums, conferences, telephone conversations, company newsletters and videos. One problem with written downward communication is that management may assume that what is sent downward is received and understood. Unfortunately, that is not always the case.

(2) Upward communication. Upward communication is the flow of information from lower-level employees to upper-level employees. In Figure 2.3, for example, Jane sends a monthly status report to the president regarding human resource action for the month, and Diana responds to David's memo regarding a computer report. Upward communication can take the form of emails, memorandums, conferences, reports, suggestion systems, or union publications, among others.

Upward communication is important because it provides higher management with the information needed for decision making. It also cultivates employee loyalty by giving employees an opportunity to be heard, to air their grievances, and to offer suggestions. Finally, upward communication provides the feedback necessary to let supervisors know whether subordinates have received and understood messages that were sent downward.

(3) Horizontal communication. Horizontal communication is the flow of information among peers within the same work unit. For example, the administration division holds a weekly staff meeting at which the three managers (Jane, Larry, and Eric) exchange information about the status of their operation.

Horizontal communication is important because it can help to coordinate work assignments, share information on plans and activities, negotiate differences, and develop interpersonal support, thereby to create a more cohesive work unit. The more that individuals or departments within an organization must interact with each other to accomplish their objectives, the more frequent and intense the horizontal communication will be.

(4) Cross-channel communication. Cross-channel communication is the exchange of information among employees in different work units who are neither subordinate to nor superior to one another in relation to the task. For example, each year a payroll clerk in Jane's department sends out a request to all company employees for updated information about the number of exemptions they claim on their tax forms or attendance as an employee event.

Staff specialists use cross-channel communication frequently because their responsibilities typically involve many departments within the organization. They lack line authority to command those with whom they communicate, so they must often rely on their persuasive skills, for instance, when the human resources department encourages employees to complete a job-satisfaction questionnaire.

2. Informal communication network

The informal communication network is the transmission of information through non-official channels within the organization. Carpooling to work, waiting to use the photocopier, jogging at noon, eating in the cafeteria, or chatting at a local meeting—whenever workers come together, they are likely to hear and pass on information about possible happenings in the organization.

The complexity of this information network, especially in larger organization, cannot be overemphasized. Typically, it is really not a single network but a complex relationship of smaller networks consisting of certain groups of people. Known as the grapevine in management literature, this communication network is more valuable to the company's operations than a first impression might indicate. Certainly, it carries much gossip and rumor. Even so, the grapevine usually carries far more information than the formal communication systems, and on many matters, it is more effective in determining the course of an organization. Skillful managers recognize the presence of the grapevine, and they know that the powerful people in this network are often not those at the top of the formal organizational hierarchy. They find out who the "talk" leaders are and give them the information that will do the most good for the organization. They also make management decisions that will cultivate positive talk.

2.2.4 Business communication

An Insider's Perspective: Intuit

Like any highly technological business, software giant Intuit—developer of such popular financial and tax preparation products as QuickBooks, Quicken, and Turbo Tax, —thrives on creativity and innovation. Realizing that employees at all levels have the potential to help improve processes and performance, company officials have determined that the best way to maintain corporate growth is to foster a corporate culture of continual learning. Thus the practice of "learn-teach-learn" was born.

With learn-teach-learn, Intuit's managers learn about ideas and potential improvements from employees, who are encouraged to share freely; develop a plan of action and teach the employees about the plan; then gather more from employees' responses. Vice President of Human Resources Jim Grenier says that such back-and-forth communication produces good ideas. "It's not about a consensus culture", he says. "You're looking for more input from employees, as well as learning from the best 'wheel-makers' both inside and outside the company… so you can make better decisions. Employees know that we are serious about asking for their feedback, and we listen and we do something about it."

Another way Intuit solicits input from employees is through an annual survey that examines their attitudes on a wide range of company practices. Following the survey, managers get additional feedback in "skip-level" meetings with subordinates of those who report directly to them. Since implementing the survey in 2000, Grenier notes, annual employee turnover at Intuit has been cut in half.

(Source: Ober S, Newman A. 商务沟通[M]. 7 版. 北京：清华大学出版社，2013.)

The definitions of business communication vary. So it is hard to find a specific description for business communication. However, business communication does have its specific applications, which differ to a certain degree from other forms of communication. Business communication includes elements like dynamic and multi-channeled processes, internal communication, external communication and a form of organization. So, we can define business communication as a dynamic, multi-channeled process, which covers internal as well as external communication for a given organization.

An organization may be set up to be different departments according to their specific products/services. This arrangement is called departmentation by product. Each department can work independently. Another common arrangement is to set up different departments in terms of their different functions. In this case, it would be easier for people to handle problems occurring in their work. No matter what kind of organizational arrangement that has been established, managers should always be able to get all the information required before they make any decisions or make an appraisal.

Business communication is regarded as dynamic because it is always changing with the changing business and other factors coming from the internal and external environments. Business never remains static.

Another important feature of business communication is that it is multi-channeled. For example, business people may wish to get in touch with each other over the phone, by sending emails or faxes to each other, or face-to-face. Also, they sometimes prefer to choose the channel of telephone or video conference to discuss important issues if members of the group are geographically dispersed. Multi-channeled business communication is highly advantageous for business people to achieve their business targets effectively and efficiently.

2.2.5 External Communication Network

The importance of external communication to a business is becoming increasingly clear. Because the success of a business depends on its ability to satisfy customers' needs, it must communicate effectively with those customers. But businesses also depend on each other in the production and distribution of goods and services. Coordinating with contractors, consultants, and suppliers requires skillful communication. In addition, every business must communicate to some extent with a variety of other external parties, such as government agencies and public-interest groups. Some external audiences for today's business are illustrated in Figure 2.4. Like internal communication, external communication is vital to business success.

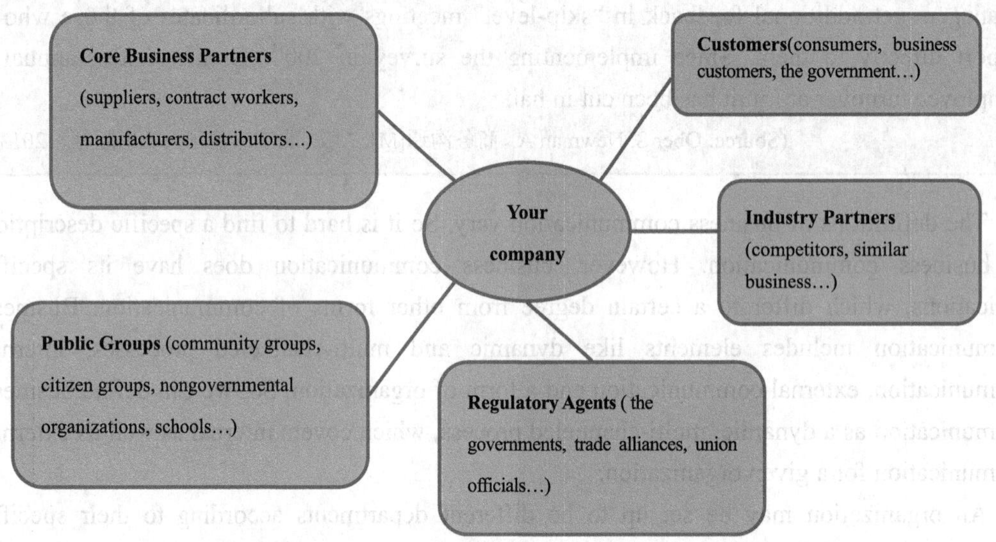

Figure 2.4 Likely External Audiences for Today's Business

(Source: Rentz K, Flatley M E, Lentz P. *Lesikar's Business Communication*[M]. 12th ed. New York: McGraw-Hill, 2012.)

Today, many companies spend a large sum of money each year on advertising because advertising is one popular way to promote products or raise a company's profile. If a company is not satisfied with the advertisement's effect, it will drop the advertising agency or replace it with another one. That is the reason why Coca-Cola abandoned Madison Avenue and chose Creative Artists to be their new advertising agency in 1992. They claimed that Madison didn't deliver new high impact advertising that really appealed to the consumers. Advertising plays an important role in building an image either for a product or for an organization. Businesses today are critically concerned with building their brand and reputation and business communication plays an important part in that process.

Another example of external communication is the recent US Masterfoods Mars and Snickers poison scare in Australia when US Masterfoods (Australia) decided to recall all Mars and Snickers bars products back from the marketplace nationwide. As a response to the poison scare, the company president Weston-Webb used live press conferences, hotlines and advertisements to communicate with the public to assure them that Masterfoods cared. Following the scare, they then used advertisements again, to inform Mars bars lovers that their products were back and safe. All these forms of communication can be classified as external.

Another important aspect of external communication is the individuals who are involved, like consumers and shareholders. People do not always represent organizations, but just themselves. Individuals today tend to be more concerned with the quality of service. Many companies are making consumer satisfaction as their target, and are striving towards this goal. Motorola can be cited as a typical example. Each year, Motorola spends nearly $200 million on quality education for their employees in order to minimize defective products. Moreover, the company executives visit their customers to learn about their opinions and needs for the products. They also conduct quality surveys and analyze the customers' complaints in order to achieve what they called "total customer satisfaction".

2.3 The Barriers to Effective Business Communication, and How to Overcome Them

Communication plays a major role in employer-employee relationships in firms. It also affects the relationships in the management team. Although effective communication does not guarantee success of a business, its absence usually assures problems. A communication problem may soon become a crisis or it may linger on for years.

More specifically, communication influences the effectiveness of the hiring and training of employees, motivation of employees, providing daily instructions, performance evaluations and the handling of discipline problems. These are the obvious roles of communication.

Communication also affects the willingness of employees to provide useful suggestions. For employees to feel that they are a part of the business, there needs to be effective and continuous communicators. In fact, for employees to make the important evolution from "workers" to "working managers", it requires effective communication between supervisors and employees.

Employees typically are hesitant to state their goals, their concerns and their disappointments. Of course, an employee may be a complainer and share views to the point where the supervisor silently begs for less "communication". Much more common is the need to better understand what an employee is "really thinking".

However, considering the complex nature of the communication process, your message may not always be received exactly as you intended. Sometimes your messages will not be received at all; at other times, they will be received incompletely or inaccurately. Some of the obstacles to effective and efficient communication are verbal; others are nonverbal. As is illustrated in Figure 2.5, the barriers can create an impenetrable "brick wall" that makes effective communication impossible.

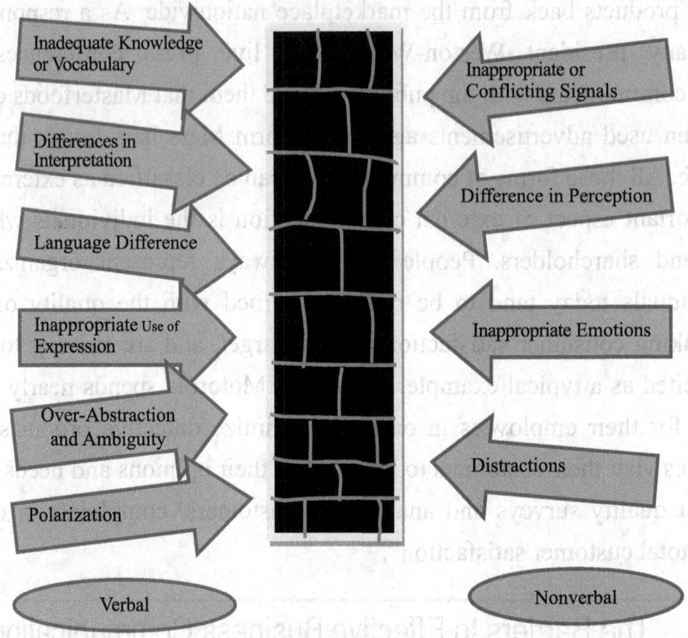

Figure 2.5 Verbal and Nonverbal Barriers to Communication

(Source: Ober S, Newman A. 商务沟通[M]. 7 版. 北京：清华大学出版社，2013.)

2.3.1 Verbal barriers

Verbal barriers are related to what you write or say. They include inadequate knowledge or vocabulary, differences in interpretation, language differences, inappropriate use of expressions, over-abstraction and ambiguity, and polarization.

1. Inadequate knowledge or vocabulary

Before you can even begin to think about what you will communicate, you must first of all, have the idea; that is, you must have sufficient knowledge about what you want to say. Regardless of your level of technical expertise, this may not be as simple as it sounds. Assume, for example, that you are Larry, manager of the finance department at ABC Company. Dave, president of the company, has asked you to evaluate an investment opportunity. You've completed all necessary research and are now ready to write your report. Or are you?

Have you analyzed your audience? Do you know how much the president knows about the investment so that you'll know how much background information to include? Do you know how familiar David is with investment terminology? Can you safely use abbreviations like NPV and RRR, or will you have to spell out and perhaps define net present value and required rate of return? The answers to such questions will be important if you are to be objective, informative and accurate in writing the report.

2. Differences in interpretation

Sometimes senders and receivers attribute different meanings to the same word or attribute the same meaning to different words. When this happens, miscommunication can occur. Every word has both a denotative and connotative meaning. Denotation refers to the literal, dictionary meaning of a word. Connotation refers to the subjective, emotional meaning that you attach to a word. For example, the denotation meaning of the word plastic is "a synthetic material that can be easily molded into different forms". For some people, the word also has a negative connotative meaning—"cheap or artificial substitute". Most of the interpretation problems occurred because of the personal reactions suggested by the connotation meaning of a word. The problem with some terms is not only because that people assign different meaning to the term but also because that the term itself might cause such an emotional reaction that the receiver is "turned off" to any further communication with the sender.

3. Language differences

In an ideal word, all managers would know the language of each culture with which they deal. International business people often say that you can buy in your native language anywhere in the world, but you can sell only in the language of the local community.

To ensure that the intended meaning is not lost during translation, important documents should first be translated into second language and then retranslated into English.

4. Inappropriate use of expressions

Expressions are groups of words whose intended meanings are different from their literal interpretations. Examples include slang, jargon, and euphemisms.

Slang is an expression, often short-lived, that is identified with a specific group of people. Business, of course, has its own slang, such as 24/7, bandwidth, hardball, and window of opportunity. Jargon is the technical terminology used within specialized groups such as IT professionals or accountants; it has sometimes been called "the pros' prose". Do you know the meaning of some common computer terms, such as FAQ, JPEG or management terms like strategic fit? As with slang, the problem is not in using jargon—jargon provides a very precise and efficient way of communicating with those familiar with it. The problem comes either in using jargon with someone who doesn't understand it or in using jargon in an effort to impress others. Euphemisms are inoffensive expressions used in place of words that may offend others or suggest something unpleasant. Sensitive writers and speakers use euphemisms occasionally, especially to describe bodily functions. Common examples in English are that a person has "passed away" instead of describing him as "dead"; or "moved on" to describe someone who has been fired or left the company.

5. Over-abstraction and ambiguity

Abstract words are necessary in order to communicate about things you cannot see or touch. However, communication problems arise when you use too many abstract words or when you use too high a level of abstraction. The higher the level of abstraction, the more difficult it is for the receiver to visualize exactly what the sender has in mind. For example, if you are talking about the costs of a project, you need to give examples of what you mean by "very expensive".

Ambiguity arises when a word has several meanings and it is not clear which meaning you are suggesting.

6. Polarization

At times, some people act as though every situation is divided into two opposite and distinct poles, with no allowance for a middle ground. Of course, there are some true dichotomies. For example, you might assume that a speaker either is telling the truth or is lying. In fact, what the speaker actually says may be true, but by selectively omitting some important information, he or she may be giving an inaccurate impression. Is the speaker telling the truth or not? Most likely, the answer lies somewhere in between. Likewise, you are not necessarily tall or short, rich or poor, smart or dumb. Competent communicators avoid inappropriateness either/or logic and instead make the effort to search for middle-ground words when they best describe a situation.

2.3.2 Nonverbal barriers

Not all communication problems are related to what you write or say. Some are related to how you act or present the communication. Nonverbal barriers to communication include inappropriate or conflicting signals, differences in perceptions, inappropriate emotions, and distractions.

1. Inappropriate or conflicting signals

Suppose a well-qualified applicant for an administrative assistant position submits a resume with a typographical error, or an accountant's personal office is in such disorder that she can't find the papers she needs for a meeting with a client. When verbal and nonverbal signals conflict, the receiver tends to put more faith in nonverbal than verbal signals because nonverbal messages are more difficult to manipulate than the verbal code. Another fact is that when we say one thing, for example, that we are pleased to meet someone—but our action, posture, or expression suggests something contradictory, others will usually believe what we do rather than what we say.

2. Differences in perceptions

Even when they hear the same speech or read the same document, people of different ages, socioeconomic backgrounds, cultures, and so forth often form very different perceptions. Because each person is unique, with unique experiences, knowledge, and viewpoints, each person forms a different opinion about what he or she reads and hears. Some people tend automatically to believe certain people and to distrust other people. For example, when reading an email from the company president, one employee may be intimidated by the president and he or she accepts everything the president says, whereas another employee may have such negative feelings about the president that he or she believes nothing the president says.

3. Inappropriate emotions

In most cases, a moderate level of emotional involvement intensifies the communication and makes it more personal. However, too much emotional involvement can be an obstacle to communication. For example, excessive anger can create such an emotionally charged environment that reasonable discussion is not possible. Likewise, prejudice, stereotyping, and boredom all hinder effective communication. Such emotions tend to create a blocked mind that is closed to new ideas, rejecting or ignoring information that is contrary to one's prevailing belief.

4. Distractions

Any environmental or competing element that restricts one's ability to concentrate on the communication task hinders effective communication. Such distractions are called noise(see Figure 2.1). A study conducted at the University of London found that "an average worker's functioning IQ falls 10 points when distracted by ringing telephones and incoming emails". Examples of environmental noise are poor acoustics, extreme temperature, uncomfortable seating, body odor, poor telephone connections, and illegible photocopies. Examples of competing noise are other important business to attend to, too many meetings, and too many reports to read.

2.3.3 Other barriers to communication

Any one of the components of the communication process can become a source of barriers to communication. You need to identify if you have any of these problems in order to improve your communication skills.

1. Muddled messages

Effective communication starts with a clear message. Contrast these two messages: "We will have a meeting tomorrow morning." "We will have a meeting at 9 a.m. tomorrow morning." Only one word(9 a.m.) makes the second message clearer than the first one. Such a muddled message can be a barrier to communication because the sender leaves the receiver unclear about the intent of the sender. The receiver has to assume what the message could be. But how does a message sender know that the message is clear rather than muddled? Feedback from the receiver is the best way for a sender to be sure that the receiver has a correct understanding of the message.

ACTIVITY FOR LEARNING

(1) Choose the right medium to achieve your purpose.

(2) You have to announce a temporary hold on non-essential stationery spending in your department. How do you communicate this?

Here are some examples of where the communication medium was wrong.

An advertising campaign on local radio would be a highly ineffective way of reaching the desired audience if the message was complex and really intended for a narrow niche audience. One company sent an email to tell a staff member that he or she was fired.

Using a variety of channels and an appropriate medium helps the receiver understand the nature and importance of a message. For example, using a training video on cleaning practices helps new employees grasp the importance placed on their health. The video can be watched several times and is formal enough that employees recognize that the company spent resources to produce it. This signals the importance of the topic to employees. A birthday card to an employee's spouse is more sincere than a request to the employee to say "Happy Birthday" to the spouse. Employees recognize this.

2. A distracting environment

Create a good environment in which to communicate. There's nothing worse than trying to communicate your message to a group of people who cannot "hear" you.

The reasons of their inability to "hear" you might be as follows.

(1) Your voice is not being strong enough.

(2) Too many others are talking in the room at the same time.

(3) Too many phone calls are coming into their office while they are trying to read your report.

(4) Their minds are full of other pressing matters.

(5) They are supposed to be somewhere else at that moment.

(6) Their Internet connection is slow.

(7) The room's air-conditioning is not working and the room is hot and stuffy.

There are of course some possible distracting reasons why your receivers cannot or will not attend to your business communication. The point is to do whatever you can, whilst acknowledging that this might be next to nothing, to reduce the number of distractions your chosen audience might be subjected to.

3. Socio-psychological barriers

Recognize the way social and psychological differences can interrupt and distort communication. The attitudes and opinions, place in society and status consciousness arising from one's position in the hierarchical structure of the organization, one's relation with peers, seniors, juniors and family background—all these deeply affect one's ability to communicate both as a sender and a receiver. Status consciousness is widely known to be a serious communication barrier in organizations. It leads to psychological distance, which further leads to breakdown of communication or miscommunication. Often it is seen that a person high up in an organization builds up a wall around himself or herself. This restricts participation of the less powerful in decision-making. In the same way, one's family background formulates one's attitudes and communication skills.

4. Dealing with barriers to good communication

(1) Language. This includes both the words and the use of them by different groups, including the jargon that professional groups use.

(2) Technical content. Communication is a process between people. Information is not equal to communication.

(3) Not recognizing the receivers' needs. Starting out with the recognition that listeners are listening with one question on mind: What's in it for me?

(4) Inadequate feedback. Feedback is the oil that makes the process smooth and flow. Without it, communication runs inefficiently and ineffectively.

(5) Emotional interference. When emotional issues are at the forefront of interaction, they need to be addressed before proceeding to rational discussion.

(6) Degree of knowledge and expertise of both senders and receivers. The knowledge level of interactant must always be considered.

(7) Lack of trust/honesty. Without trust, communication falters.

(8) Cultural differences. Adjustment and recognition of the value of diversity can smooth all cultural differences.

(9) Poor listening skills. We spend about 45% of our time listening, so it is a skill of extreme importance and we need to be active listeners.

(10) Hierarchy. Recognizing that hierarchy restricts honesty and makes individuals defensive is the first step in managing it effectively to achieve good communication.

The barriers to effective business communication are many, but with care and attention, the majority of them can be overcome. The fewer barriers, the greater chance that your business communication will be heard, understood, and your "most desired action" (MDA) that you wish them to take will actually occur.

2.4 Criteria for Effective Messages

Channel Choice Affects Message Success

"It's (sic)① official, you no longer work for JNI Traffic Control and u (sic) have forfeited (sic) any arrangements made." Can you imagine getting such a text message? The Sydney employer was sued over this inappropriate choice of a communication channel for

① 英文原文中使用了很多不适合在正式文书中使用的字母或单词。例如用“u”代替“you”。

firing an employee. In setting the matter, the commissioner went further in stating that email, text messages, and even answering machines were inappropriate for official business communication. Or what about being notified by text message of an overdue bill? While some might think of that as a service, others regard it as invasive and inappropriate.

Historically, the importance of channel choice has been disputed, with some arguing that it is simply a means for transmitting words and others arguing that the chosen channel is, in itself, a message. However, today most people realize that the appropriate choice of communication channel contributes significantly, along with the words, to the success of the message. While early research in media richness provides guidelines for understanding when to use very lean (printed material) to very rich (face-to-face) channels, more recent studies as well as new technologies and laws have added new dimensions to this theory. Not only are there no clear-cut rules or guidelines, but the smallest change in context may lead to different choices.

In selecting a channel, a communicator needs to weigh several factors. Some of these include the message content, the communicator's levels of competency with the channels, the recipient's access to the channel, and the recipient's environment. Appropriate choice of communication channel helps people communicate clearly and improve their productivity and personal relationships.

(Source: Rentz K, Flatley M E, Lentz P. *Lesikar's Business Communication*[M]. 12th ed. New York: McGraw-Hill, 2012.)

Good business and administrative communications meet five basic criteria: it's clear, complete, and correct; it saves the audience's time; and builds goodwill.

(1) **It's clear.** The meaning the audience gets is the meaning the communicator intended. The audience doesn't have to guess.

(2) **It's complete**. All of the audience's questions are answered. The audience has enough information to evaluate the message and act on it.

(3) **It's correct**. All of the information in the message is accurate. The message is free from errors in spelling, grammar, word choice, and sentence structure.

(4) **It saves the audience's time.** The style, organization, and visual or aural impact of the message help the audience to read or hear, understand and act on the information as quickly as possible.

(5) **It builds goodwill.** The message presents a positive image of the communicator and his or her organization. It treats the receiver as a person, not a number. It cements a good relationship between the communication and the receiver.

2.5 How to Solve Business Communication Problems

When you are faced with a business communication problem, you need to develop a solution that will both solve the organizational problems and meet the psychological needs of the people involved. Here are some suggestions that you can consider.

2.5.1 Understand the situation

What are the facts? What can you infer from the information you're given? What additional information might be helpful? Where do you get it?

Other important questions are as follows.

(1) **What's at stake—for whom?** Think not only about your own needs but also about the concern your boss and your audience will have. Your message will be most effective if you think of the entire organizational context, and the larger context of shareholders, customers, and regulators. When the stakes are high, you'll need to take into account people's feeling as well as objective facts.

(2) **Should you send a message?** Sometimes, especially when you're new on the job, silence is the most tactful response. But be ready for opportunities to learn, to influence, to make your case.

(3) **What channel should you use?** Paper documents and presentations are formal and give you considerable control over the message. Emails, texts, social media such as phone calls, and stopping by someone's office are less formal. Oral channels are better for group decision making, allowing misunderstandings to be cleared up more quickly, and seem more personal. Sometimes you may need more than one message, in more than one channel.

(4) **What should you say?** Content for a message may not be obvious. How detailed should you be? Should you repeat information that the audience already knows? The answers will depend on the kind of message, your purpose, audiences, and the corporate culture.

(5) **How should you say it?** How you arrange your ideas—what comes first, second, and last—and the words you use to shape the audience's response to what you say.

ACTIVITY FOR LEARNING

(1) Use the Six questions for analysis to analyze your audience, your purpose, and the situation.

(2) Try to imagine yourself in the situation, just as you might use the script of a play to imagine what kind of people the characters are.

Kitty O. Locker (2005) suggests using the six questions to analyze your audience, your purpose and the situation in her book *Business and Administration Communication* (6th Edition). They are as follows.

(1) Who is (are) your audience(s)? What characteristics are relevant to this particular message? If you are writing or speaking to more than one person, how do the people in your audience differ?

(2) What are your purposes in writing or speaking?

(3) What information must your message include?

(4) How can you build support for your position? What reasons or readers' benefits will your reader find convincing?

(5) What objective(s) can you expect your reader(s) to have? What negative elements of your message must you de-emphasize or overcome?

(6) What aspects of the total situation may affect the reader's or listener's response? The economy? The time of the year? Morale in the organization? The relationship between the reader and the writer? Any special circumstances?

2.5.2 Brainstorming solutions

Problem solving usually starts by gathering knowledge. What are the facts? What can you infer from the information you're given? What additional information might be helpful? Where could you get it? What emotional complexities are involved? This information will usually start to suggest some solutions, and you should brainstorm other solutions. In all but the very simplest problems, there are multiple possible solutions for any problems. The first one you think of may not be the best. Consciously develop several solutions. Then measure them against your audiences and purposes: Which solution is likely to work best?

Making the Most of Your Brainstorming

Matt Bowen, president of the Aloft Group Inc. marketing and PR agency, has advice on running a successful brainstorming meeting.

(1) Identify a clear, concrete goal before you start. That allows you to establish some boundaries for ideas—about practicality or cost, for example—and helps you keep your brainstorming session focused.

(2) Let everyone involved in the meeting know what the goal is ahead of the time. That gives everyone a chance to have ideas ready when they come to the meeting. Set limits on meeting size and duration. Bowen recommends limiting a brainstorming meeting to one hour, with no more than five to seven participants. An hour is enough time for a focused discussion, and it's easier for everyone to participate and be heard in a small team.

(3) Let the ideas flow freely. Bowen recommends practicing active listening skills that encourage people both to share their ideas and to build on each other's ideas.

(4) Brainstorm with a diverse team. The best ideas come out the teams made up of people with very different perspectives. Remember that there are no bad ideas; any ideas, however impractical, might inspire the best solution, and spending time weeding out weak ideas can stifle creativity.

(Source: Spors K K. Productive brainstorms take the right mix of elements[N]. *Wall Street Journal*, 2008, 7-24:B5.)

2.6 Trends and Challenges in Business and Administration Communication

Both business and business communication are changing. Some trends in business, government, and non-profit organizations affect business and administrative communication: a focus on quality and customer's needs, entrepreneurship and outsourcing, teams, diversity, globalization, legal and ethical concerns, balancing work and family, and the rapid rate of change and technology.

2.6.1 Focus on quality and customer's needs

Communication is at the center of focus on quality and customer's needs. Brainstorming and group problem solving are essential to develop more efficient ways to do things. Then, these good ideas have to be communicated throughout the company. Innovators need to be recognized. And only by listening to what customers say—and listening to the silences that may accompany their actions—can an organization know what its customers really want.

2.6.2 Entrepreneurship and outsourcing

Since the 1980s, the number of businesses in the United States has risen faster than that of the civilian labor force. In China, with the growth of the economy and the support of government policies, more and more people have become entrepreneurs of their own companies. The role of these kinds of private companies is very important for the development of the economy. Some established companies are trying to match the success and growth rate of start-ups by nurturing an entrepreneurial spirit within their organizations.

Some businesses have been forced to become entrepreneurial because of outsourcing. Outsourcing means going outside the company for products and services that once were made by the company's employees. Companies can outsource manufacturing, customer services and accounting. So, outsourcing makes communication more difficult and more important than it was when all jobs were done in-house. It is harder to ask questions, since people are no longer down the hall. And it's easier for small problems to turn into major ones. Communication is the lifeblood of organizations whether large or small.

2.6.3 Teams

To produce quality products while cutting costs and prices in order to attain the core competence for the companies, more and more companies are relying on cross-functional teams. Collaborative work capitalizes on the different perspectives, experiences, ideas, styles, and strengths each individual contributes. The prevalence of cross-functional teams puts a premium on learning to identify and solve problems, to share leadership, to work with other people rather than merely delegating work to other people, to resolve conflicts constructively, to negotiate arrangements effectively to the team's satisfaction, and to motivate everyone to do his or her best job. At the heart of all these processes is good communication.

Successful group work requires thoughtful up-front planning and attention to all the processes to deliver effective teamwork. For example, while it is critical to maintain cohesion, care must be taken to avoid the tendency for groups to put such a high premium on an agreement that they directly or indirectly punish dissent. This is called groupthink and is just as dangerous for group outcomes as constant conflict is. The conversational style also needs attention. As organizational relationships change and become more democratized and decreasingly hierarchical, conversational patterns of the organizations will change and the meaning you give to them will change with this: so, pay attention to conversations, showing interest, politeness and appropriateness.

2.6.4 Diversity

China has traditionally maintained a stable, relatively homogenous working population. However, this is changing as China looks to the rest of the world for business and increasingly invites countries like the US, Japan, and Germany, to seek entry to China's marketplace. Women, people of different ethnicities, and immigrants have always been part of the workforce in the world. *Business Week* reports that two-third of all industries already operate globally or are in the process of doing so. An increasing share of profits comes from outside the headquarters' country. Otis Elevator's largest market is in China. McDonald's earns more than 62% of its income outside the US, and almost 98% of Nokia's sales are outside its home country. Diversity in the workforce comes from many sources:

- Gender.
- Race and ethnicity.
- Regional and national origin.
- Social class.
- Religion.
- Age.
- Sexual orientation.

• Physical ability.

Helping each worker reach his or her potential requires more flexibility from managers as well as more knowledge about intercultural communication. And it's crucial to help workers from different backgrounds understand each other.

Treating readers and listeners with respect has always been a principle of good business and administrative communication. The emphasis on diversity simply makes it an economic mandate as well.

2.6.5 Rapid rate of change

As the twenty-first century begins, the world is in a constant state of change, and no organization in the world can escape the effects of operating in a continually dynamic, evolving landscape. The forces of change are so great that the future success, indeed the very survival, of thousands of organizations depends on how well they respond to change or, optimally, whether they can actually stay ahead of change.

It is widely acknowledged that change—from such forces as globalization, relentless technological advances, unprecedented competition, political upheaval, and the opening of new markets—exerts constant pressure on organizations of all sizes and types. As a result, these organizations are beginning to adapt, restructure and change in response to evolving developments in the world.

The successful implementation of change requires a carefully designed strategy implemented with a thorough understanding of the organization's culture and its key players. Changing the way an organization operates is tough. You can spend a lot of money on new software, redesign your business processes, and offer training, but, will this guarantee change? No. You also need effective communication throughout the organization.

Effective communication is a lot more than just giving people regular updates. People are naturally resistant to change, and you've got to sell them on the benefits of it. To communicate (i.e., sell) the change, do what any good marketing manager would do. Define segments and then develop key messages for each segment.

Develop a strategy around the best medium for reaching everyone—newsletters, email, workshops, brownbag lunches, etc. —and how often people will need to be reached. To reach larger audiences consider setting up monthly presentations with a forum for questions and answers.

No matter which media you choose, it is critical to communicate regularly but be sure to establish a schedule that you can keep. Also, for those people who are on the front lines driving the change, provide talking points on a weekly basis. This will allow them to provide consistent messaging and to speak with one voice.

As you implement your strategy, be aware that communicating is a two-way process. Once your information goes out, it becomes just as important to collect, analyze, and synthesize what comes back. Interviewing people and encouraging feedback must be a part of your rollout. Only by getting thorough and candid feedback will you identify problems and learn where to adjust the process.

2.6.6 Development of technology

Technology is a form of communication. However, people still do the communicating. This means that having the means to communicate (the technology) is only the first step in the process. Meaning must be generated between those creating the messages and those understanding them. Just as information does not mean communication, neither does using technology mean that communicating is occurring.

Intranets are very useful resources which give everyone in an organization access to information inside the organization through web pages. All this can work relatively smoothly using common computer and Internet tools, such as word processing software and email programs.

One of the most discussed items coming out of the events of the terrorist attacks around the world since the attacks in the USA on September 11, 2001, is the need for effective internal communication. Many companies have become very concerned about what systems and policies are in place to inform employees within the organization about what is going on during a crisis event, provide instructions on what actions to take, and locate employees to make certain they are safe.

Internet technology needs to be part of the comprehensive plan for employee and leadership communication in case of large-scale internal or external crises. The Internet-based communication management system described earlier can play a key role because of its ability to launch new sites quickly and the ability to control access to any site. An internal-only site can be launched to keep employees informed and a different site can be launched exclusively for the management team.

Extranets are the way to save time and money and improve quality for companies through Web pages to provide information on products/services for customers or suppliers. Internet connections and smartphones allow employees to work at home rather than commute to a certain office, with telecommuting being one positive solution to peak hour commuting. Fax and email make it easy to communicate across oceans and time zones and tele- and video-conferencing on WeChat for example make it possible for people on different continents to have a meeting without leaving their home towns or offices.

With the development of technology in recent years, many people prefer these ways of working, without the limitations of time and zones, to communicate throughout the world. Information technology makes it available to achieve this target for the people. However, information overload often occurs within this increased information-rich environment, when messages arrive faster than the human receivers can handle them. In the information age, time management depends, in part, on being able to identify which messages are important and which can be relegated to the trash button.

Summary

Communication helps organizations and people to achieve their goals. The ability to write and speak well becomes increasingly important as you gain promotion in an organization.

Internal communication goes to people inside the organization. External communication goes to audiences outside: clients, customers, suppliers, stockholders, the government, the media and the general public. All forms of business represent the organization and so are very important.

The SENDER-RECEIVER model of communication is recognized as one of the most commonly recognized models, originally developed by Berlo. Communication involves several major components in this process. They are a sender who has a message for a receiver, sent along channels chosen by the sender. However, communication occurs not just in a sender or a receiver, but in the space between them. Together, the participants make meaning from the various codes used in the situation, from the words to the non-verbal expressions.

You must overcome many barriers when communicating. One tool to help you is "The Six Questions" technique to analyze your audience, your purpose, and the situation and other ways in order to achieve an effective communication.

Both business and business communication are changing. Some trends and changes in business, government and nonprofit organizations affect business and business communication. These include: quality issues and customer needs; entrepreneurship and outsourcing; teamwork; the diversity of the workforce; the rapid rate of change; and the development of new communication technology.

All these barriers to communication and changes in the environment challenge us and make it increasingly hard to be effective in our business communication tasks.

Questions for Discussion

(1) Why is it necessary to master the medium of your communication? What common communication media do business people regularly use?

(2) In what ways does quick access to information both benefit and challenge business communicators?

(3) What are the key differences between upward and downward communication?

(4) What kinds of new communication technologies do you look forward to using? How might you prepare yourself to use them effectively?

(5) Explain why some business people resist using audio or video teleconferencing, even

though the technology can save them time, travel, and the money. Also, explain how, in your opinion, such resistance can be overcome.

Exercises

Organize several small groups in the class. Each group chooses and represents an organization that you have studied. Now, ask yourself the following questions:

(1) What channels of communication are the most important in your organization?

(2) What documents or presentations do you create? Are they designed to inform, to persuade, or to build goodwill? A mixture? Are there any other reasons to communicate in business?

(3) Who are your most important audience within the organization?

(4) Who are your most important external audience?

(5) What are the challenges of communicating in this organization?

Part 2
Oral Communication in Business

Chapter 3

Winning Hearts and Minds Through Effective Presentations

LEARNING OBJECTIVES

On completing this chapter, you should be able to:

- Recognize the importance of persuasive skills as a successful employee and manager.
- Understand the role of the audience in all interactions especially persuasive ones.
- Understand the different sorts of persuasive appeals that you can use to lead your audience to your point of view.
- Know the steps in preparing to present to individuals and groups.
- Know how to structure an effective presentation to win hearts and minds.

Study Case：How Executive Feel about Graduates' Communication Skills

The Conference Board, along with Corporate Voices for Working Families, the Partnership for 21st Century Skills, and the Society for Human Resources Management, asked several executives to indicate the skills they felt very important for new graduates to have in the workplace. The top five skills were oral communication(95.4%); teamwork/collaboration(94.4%); professionalism/work ethic(93.8%); writing communication(93.1%); and critical thinking/problems solving(92.1%).

The executives were also asked to rate graduates' skills in the above areas as "excellent" or "deficient." Interestingly, when rating four-year graduates, 46.3 percent of the respondents gave an "excellent" rating to graduates' skills in information technology application (which was 11th on the executives' list of important skills, with 81.0%), but only 24.8 percent gave an "excellent" rating to graduates' oral communication skills (first on the list). Written communication, writing in English, and leadership skills appeared on the "deficient" list.

(Source: The Conference Board, Are they Really Ready to Work? Employers' perspectives on the Basic Knowledge and Applied Skills of New Entrants to the 21st Century U.S. Workforce, The Conference Board, 2006,Web , 30 June 2009.)

Analysis： The results of this study encourage us to keep working to improve our communication skills. This chapter and several others in this book provide many useful strategies and tips for doing so.

3.1 The Gentle Art of Persuasion

Employees come in all shapes and sizes, from young employees just entering the workforce to senior leaders and managers. However, one thing that successful leaders and managers have in common is that they have the ability to present their ideas in a persuasive way that excites and engages those around them. Kevin Thomson, the former president of the International Association of Business Communicators claims that there are a range of benefits of being a persuasive person who demonstrates:

- passion at work.
- excellence in customer service.
- enthusiasm for quality products, and a spirit of innovation through capacity to motivate people to develop ideas and products.

Many young people such as the readers of this textbook know that, personally, they are passionately committed to success but find themselves struggling to communicate this passion as they prepare to take their place at work. Persuading others to accept your ideas is a significant challenge in the contemporary workplace. As a significant dimension of all levels of leadership competency, all employees, not only managers, must persuasively communicate ideas and manage relationships with others (Goleman, Boyatzis & McKee, 2002).

New and young employees need the important skill of being persuasive. Many times every day all employees are called upon to use this skill to get their work done effectively. Communicating well and being persuasive are often said to be ways of behaving that "natural leaders" are born with. Is there any evidence for this claim? Undoubtedly, many great speakers have learned at an early age from their parents about the importance of engaging language, the use of powerful arguments and how to look and sound confident. However, the authors' experience in training 1 000 students and business professionals suggests that shy and doubtful learners can become effective and successful speakers. For example, one of our trainees learned the techniques of storytelling and emotional connection with his organization and confirmed to us that it has changed his entire image as CEO of a large hospital. Another, a quiet undergraduate student started to enjoy giving presentations once she learned and applied some of the communication skills.

You will find that most of the skills needed to be a good communicator are easy to learn and will come even more easily if you practice every day. Also, the ability to be a persuasive communicator ensures that all your other skills, such as good financial and human resource management and decision-making are enhanced, because others can:

- clearly understand your reasoning and your commitment to your ideas and to them.
- trust that you have the answers they need to commit to your goals and to make them their own.
- feel the excitement and passion needed to put ideas into action.
- understand the implications of your ideas for them.

3.2 Persuading Others

As Carly Fiorina, one of the US Republican Party hopes for the 2016 US Presidency, and former CEO of Hewlett-Packard recommends: the job of the leader is "to set the frame, to set the people free" (Trinca, 2000). We can see from her statement that being a persuasive communicator is a subtle art, but one that you can learn. Effective persuasion allows listeners to see and connect with your vision and then to decide to act in the direction that you are guiding them towards. The effective use of the art of persuasion allows your audience (whether they are a large group, a small group or even an individual) to create an effective picture in their minds of where you want them to go and how to get there. In other words, being an effective persuasive communicator prepares you to be an effective employee, and later in your career, a successful manager and leader.

So, this chapter provides you with helpful guidelines for developing the skills of a persuasive communicator. First of all, we will outline some key elements of persuasive communication, and provide some examples of effective communication inspiring leaders have used to engage with and mobilize their listeners. These guidelines suggest some useful directions for developing your own persuasive skill.

To do this, Professor Lee Newman, Dean of the IE School of Human Sciences and Technology in Madrid, Spain, suggests that all business professionals need to be "behaviorally fit"—a set of behaviors so well-tuned that they compare with the fitness of a well-trained athlete who goes to the gym every day (Newman L, 2015). Just imagine if you took on the challenge of a work-out plan every day focusing on your communication behaviors such as persuasion and listening, your behavioral fitness will make you an outstanding communicator who will be on track to become a successful leader and manager.

3.3 Getting to the Heart and Soul of Persuasion

The persuasive leaders that you know most likely have created their positive image with a great deal of hard work and strategic thinking. They are also experienced hands at doing so with integrity. After all, we put our trust in those we admire rather than in those who promise more than they can deliver. Models of outstanding communication such as Bill Gates of Microsoft, Jack Ma of Alibaba, Richard Branson of the Virgin Group, Angela Merkel, Chancellor of Germany are inspirations to us.

But what does it mean to be persuasive? While many people think of persuasion as a moment in time when someone tries to encourage another to do what they want, to send a message, we want to propose a much broader way to think of persuasion.

Persuasion occurs when one or more people are involved in both one-off and on-going activities or interactions (such as conversations, presentations and interviews). These interactions create, modify, reinforce or even change the beliefs, attitudes, intentions, motivations or behaviors of others. This process can be two-way, with speakers and listeners engaging with each other to develop their ideas together. Speakers can increase their persuasive impact if their listeners get involved during the interaction.

Being persuasive requires that you are able to put your ideas together in such a way that you get the attention of your listeners, you impress them with your knowledge and communication, and build their commitment by engaging them emotionally with your ideas—you win their minds and hearts.

Developing this skill is just like developing your financial or athletic skills. You must learn techniques and strategies to succeed. Nonetheless, because persuasive communication is often subtle and behaviour-shaping, you have a particular responsibility to ensure that you consider the outcomes for all stakeholders and do not use your knowledge of how language persuades others to manipulate those around you.

Kenneth Burke, the father of modern rhetoric, challenged us long ago to remember: You persuade a man (or even a woman) only in so far as you can talk in his language, by speech, gesture, tonality, order, image, attitude, idea, identifying your ways with his. Yet, many speakers still start out with a focus on what they want to say. Listeners, on the other hand, start by asking: what's in it for me?

3.4 Audience, Audience, Audience

Taking the audience as the starting point of any communication is a revolutionary idea, but it is a surprisingly difficult task for speakers to begin with. This idea of framing or organizing a message from the point of view of the audience is one important step when you are getting ready to win the hearts and minds of your listeners. If you wish to be truly influential, you need to be aware of whom you are talking to and adapt to their needs. How your listeners are thinking and feeling should always determine how you are going to approach them. There are four golden principles about creating messages that are right for your audience, linked to the situation you are in and the characteristics of the people who will receive and engage with the message.

3.4.1 Principle 1: The situation itself is critical

If you have the chance to pitch a new idea to your team, it will really matter how the audience feels about the situation:

- Is this an innovation launch where new ideas are expected?
- After a long and heated debate about ideas or processes, will some staffs members ultimately be forced to change their behavior?
- Will you get five minutes or many weeks to persuade your team?
- Will the item be on the end of an agenda or the beginning? Or, is the meeting entirely devoted to the issue?
- Is this communication with an individual, a small group, or a large group?

The situation will be one important factor that determines how you should approach an issue and will require that you adjust your content accordingly.

3.4.2 Principle 2: The frame of mind of your audience really counts

You will need to consider whether your listeners oppose or agree with your ideas or are neutral or new to the ideas. You also need to consider their values and attitudes. For example, if you are speaking to a group of young entrepreneurs, you know that they will have a different set of values from some older Chinese listeners.

The real test of an effective message is not what the speaker thinks is important. Rather, understanding how the audience is thinking about an issue is critical to your success. Respecting their perspective on things that will affect them and then building your argument around these perspectives will lead to successful persuasion.

3.4.3 Principle 3: The preferences of your audience for certain types of communication are important

Peter Thompson, in his useful book, *Persuading Aristotle*, created a simplified template for thinking about this issue. Many people have, at some time, completed a simple test to determine how they communicate and make decisions. What Thompson has done is to take this step further by considering how to adapt your communication to suit differing communication styles of your listeners.

For example, imagine that you are talking to an "auditor" in Figure 3.1. An auditor person has a high preference for details, careful outlining of the issues and proceeding slowly. A listener with IT or financial and accounting interests may have this approach as his work usually requires attention to detailed information. You, on the other hand, might like to talk "big picture" ideas and proceed quickly through your topics, searching out new directions as you go. Students of HR and marketing may well be "communicators" or "shakers" and even "sharers". By considering your listener's needs, you will do better to adapt to your audience's pace, their information requirements, their tone and even their emotional state.

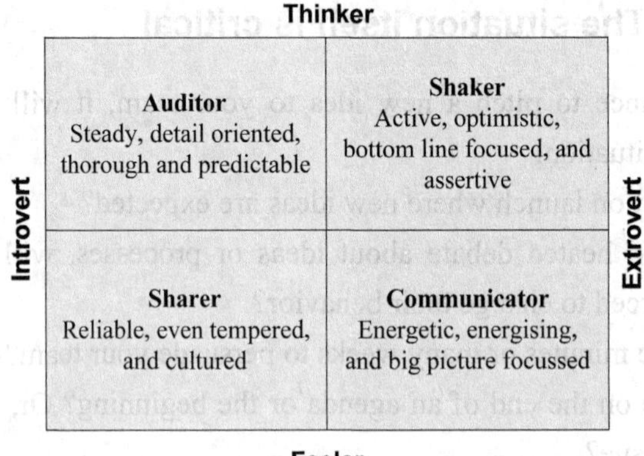

Figure 3.1 Adapting Communication Styles to Different Listeners

(Source: Thompson P. *Persuading Aristotle*[M]. Sydney: Allen & Unwin, 1998.)

This model is useful because awareness of the communication needs of those listening to you gives you a map to help you diagnose which adaptations or adjustments of your natural communication will improve your persuasive powers and so increase your chance of success. If you know that your audience has a variety of types in the group, the challenge is to build strategies to suit all these differing groups. Your versatility will increase your likelihood of success. Practicing different ways to approach a topic is one example of how you can become behaviorally fit. By preparing a message for an auditor with its detail and thoroughness and then changing that approach to persuade a shaker who wants a quick decision and outcome, you can do your own behavioral workout, fine-tuning your choice of content, language and style. For example, if you wanted to persuade your manager to allow you to take 3 days leave for a family wedding, how would you adapt your approach for an auditor, or a shaker or a communicator described in Figure 3.1?

3.4.4 Principle 4: The demographics of your audience are an important consideration in sizing up how and what to communicate

Considering the age, gender, educational experience, and socio-economic and cultural background of your audience is an excellent way to find signposts that will signal what matters, what does not, what "hot buttons" or special trigger responses that listeners have and what will be interesting and useful to them.

Young employees will often have different priorities from older staff members, and styles of communicating need to be shaped by these issues.

When Jack Ma, owner of the globally admired Alibaba Group addressed a group of young entrepreneurs about *how to be successful in life in 2015* , he gave advice and spoke passionately and honestly and disclosed much of how he felt about the importance of living life to the full, of learning and letting go of past mistakes and looking forward. His speech inspires many young Chinese listeners to live their dreams.

Giving examples of a particular point after you have made a claim and the use of a more or less formal style of communication are two ways that you adapt to your audience. Another example is the preference for a "no collar workplace", with its informal dress codes, or moving jobs often. These behaviors are popular amongst younger generation professionals. Dressing like this or changing employers often may not be appreciated by older Chinese business people. For the younger generation, these behaviors represent ambition and a drive for success. For older Chinese, these behaviors may represent disrespect for authority and lack of loyalty. Or you need to use international examples for a young audience, but you should stick to examples of Chinese companies for an older more conservative and most likely less outward looking audience. Adapting to the audience is essential to get you to your persuasive goal.

3.4.5 Developing a persuasive argument

The Greek philosopher, Aristotle, is as famous in the West as Confucius is in China. Confucius developed a code of good living and effectiveness for working in a bureaucracy. As long as two thousand years ago, Aristotle played a similar role in the West. Along with his views on philosophy, Aristotle created a set of concepts to help explain the ways through which people are persuaded.

Aristotle understood that there are three different sorts of appeals that are used to persuade others.

Ethos refers to the credibility or believability of the speaker. Speakers are more effective as persuaders if they are believed by listeners to be credible sources. The speaker's background experience, current titles, reputation for honesty and relationship management, personal style, warmth, passion and confidence all contribute to this credibility. Listeners are immediately skeptical of speakers if their credibility and credentials are not readily apparent through what they say and how they say it.

Pathos refers to the emotional appeals made by the speaker to listeners, listeners respond with emotion to the ideas of others. When citizens are reminded by their government that they should be proud to be Chinese or French, the dominant appeal is to pathos. For this type of persuasion to be succeeded, strong emotional appeals to the citizen's love of country and pride are crucial to the success of the communication. Other appeals are to ambition, security, and social responsibility.

Logos refers to the logic of the speaker's argument. Listeners can be convinced by clear reasoning, along with facts, statistics, and other forms of evidence, to accept a speaker's argument.

3.5 Building Credibility (Ethos)

Just as you must consider your audience's characteristics in shaping your message, you are equally dependent on your audience to determine your credibility or ethos. There are three primary dimensions that determine whether a listener considers you to be believable. Extensive communication research suggests that listeners make their judgment based on a combination of assessments of your expertise, trustworthiness, and the goodwill or sense of caring that you generate (McCroskey & Teven, 1999).

Attention to demonstrating expertise, or even the expertise of others on whom you rely to make your claims, is a critical pathway to achieve credibility for many audiences. Remember that most contemporary young workers desire to work with talented peers, and are seeking challenge and opportunity. Whether you seem informed, qualified, competent or experienced will shape how people hear and engage with your messages.

Equally, the sense of your personal integrity, often generated over time rather than in the moment of encounter, and a sense that you care, understand and have the interests of the listener at heart all play a critical role in the believability of the message. Interestingly though, it seems that your credibility has more significance in an interaction when listeners are less involved in an issue than when they are already involved. In the case of listeners who are already involved and think the issue is important, the strength of the arguments themselves is the most important (Gass & Seiter, 2003). For example, when you are attempting to persuade your colleagues to try a new idea, technique or new product and they know little about it, one of the important pathways through which your listeners make a judgment is to decide whether they trust your knowledge and expertise.

Being persuasive requires considerable strategic focus on your part and is never a simple process. Consequently, you need to demonstrate that, over time, you are trustworthy, knowledgeable and committed. You need to signal that moving forward together with your audience is your desired outcome.

A number of secondary dimensions also affect credibility. Much of this credibility is achieved not so much by what you say, but by how you communicate non-verbally. How extroverted, composed or confident-looking and sociable you are contributes to the way an audience perceives his interaction with you. One way to think about this relationship is to think of the level of "immediacy" or the way that your non-verbal behavior suggests warmth, closeness, friendliness and involvement with those with whom you are communicating. A large degree of separation between you and others could be either physical or psychological, but your listener's sense of this separation or closeness will determine the way they "hear", connect with and interpret your message.

Another way in which you develop credibility is through your presentation style. Both what you say and how you say it matter. The ways that you use your body and voice form important "codes" that allow others to make sense of your message. For example, if you fidget and look nervous, these actions give clues to your listeners that make them feel that maybe you don't know what you are talking about, or that you are not telling the truth, or that you are too inexperienced to trust. These non-verbal communication codes are understood by our listeners at a very unconscious level. Research has often shown that listeners believe the non-verbal codes more than the verbal codes, when there is a contradiction between them. So, even if you are telling the truth, the audience may walk away with some doubts and uneasy feelings about you and your ability to deliver on your promises. These codes form a very powerful part of the communication between a speaker and a listener.

These codes include messages through:

- eye contact.
- the types and range of gestures you use.
- the vitality of your facial expression.
- the passion of your voice.
- the energy your body gives out.
- the stillness which suggests that you are composed and relaxed in the discussion.

You might like to go back to Chapter Two to reflect on these different and important non-verbal codes where they are described in more detail.

Great communicators like the former US president Barack Obama, Jack Ma of Alibaba, and the famous Steve Jobs of Apple understand and use this knowledge every time they interact. The versatility of their facial expressions, tone of voice, eye contact and vocal warmth and energy provides an excellent model for those wishing to achieve communicative effectiveness. This is a secret code that everyone understands but which is hard to master.

ACTIVITY FOR LEARNING

Watch and listen to speakers such as Jack Ma, or any other outstanding speakers on the Internet. Read the description of who the audience is and identify 3 different ways that the speaker is targeting the particular audience.

A good guiding rule on managing non-verbal behavior is that one of the best ways to build rapport is to mirror the non-verbal behaviors of the audience. Your upper body, in particular, is your expressive core, and adds powerfully to your communication. However, Anthony Robbins, a very famous US-based master of persuasion who trains business speakers in the West and is popular on the speaking circuit, gives this advice in his best-selling book *Unlimited Power*. Robbins suggests that one good place to start to build rapport is with the voice. Robbins offers this advice (Gass & Seiter, 2003):

Mirror his(or her) tonality and phrasing, his(or her) pitch, how fast he (or she) talks, what sort of pauses he (or she) makes, his (or her) volume. ... People feel that they have found a soul mate, someone who totally understands ... Who is just like them.

It is nonetheless important to remember here that learning the strategies is just the first step in being a good communicator. As non-verbal communication specialist Edward Sapir suggested, non-verbal codes are both elaborate and secret (Sapir, 1927). We can often detect subtle messages about the integrity of their meaning and the truthfulness of the speaker, both consciously and unconsciously.

If the speaker is insincere, we will often come away less convinced of the argument than if our reading of the non-verbal communication instills us with confidence. In sum, non-verbal strategies need to harmonize with the verbal message and support the relationship between the speaker and listener. Managing this balance during presentations effectively must not be confused with trying to manipulate or deceive an audience.

Direct and sincere eye contact is a critical part of persuasive behavior. Many studies have demonstrated that those who engage in more eye contact, use pleasant facial expressions and use gestures, such as gesturing to emphasize a point, achieve more agreement and acceptance than those who look away and use limited facial expression.

In all, knowing what an audience needs to know, finding ways to mirror their thinking while leading them forward to imagine a new way to think about an idea, and giving a sense of direction are all part of the broad repertoire of skills that you need to succeed in your career.

3.6 Winning Hearts Through Winning Words (Pathos)

Great communicators also understand the power of language to shape the way audiences respond. By helping listeners to see and feel the power of your ideas, you increase your chance to be persuasive. Some presentations rely almost entirely on pathos. One famous example that still moves listeners when they view the media footage is African American civil liberties leader, Martin Luther King's "I have a dream" speech. King was leading an US movement to give equal rights to white and black citizens, such as to ride on a bus or enter shops and hotels equally with white Americans. It was delivered at a rally of over 200 000 civil libertarians in 1963 in Washington, D.C. Martin Luther King appealed to the sense of justice in all Americans and roused those civil rights' devotees who attended the rally to fight unceasingly for black rights. His ability to use the language of leadership in such a powerful way certainly contributed both to the improvement of civil rights for African Americans. We cannot underestimate the power of emotion.

We have never forgotten a student's presentation on the dangers of drinking and driving in which the speaker described an accident in which she was involved. This student described in great detail how the accident suddenly happened. She then described what she did after leaving her own car. She told us, in a quiet and deliberate way, that she and her two friends ran to the car of the other driver in the accident. They were confronted by absolute stillness and silence. The other driver was sprawled across the wheel, his face pressed on the windscreen and his eyes staring out at them. They felt paralyzed by the horror of the moment. She managed to bring that horror to her audience as well, and to use that emotion to heighten our rejection of the practice of drinking and driving. Those images were just as powerful without pictures, because her language choices tapped our emotions and unsettled our thinking by requiring us to imagine that horrible scene. This then led to us being challenged to think about the consequences that we might cause if we drink and drive, and to raise guilt in anyone in the audience who has ever driven after drinking alcohol.

The use of metaphors and analogies can often stimulate new ideas and emotional responses. For example, you might describe the audience's company as "flying like a bird" on the international market, and the listeners' pride in their company's achievements will be aroused. The effect of repetition and rhythm to add clarity and focus and the role of stories in making abstract concepts into real and meaningful experiences are all useful tactics when using pathos to build an argument.

A story about one successful young entrepreneur who took a small start-up company to international success is given a more powerful emotional appeal if you tell the story so that the young entrepreneur lives in a town in China that you live in or a famous city in China at least. You should give concrete details about him. For example, his name is Wei and you describe where he comes from, how old he is and some details about his success. It might even be a "rags to riches" story. By referring to Wei on several occasions during the speech, your audience imagines this person and connects with him through admiration of his achievements.

Look for the balance of persuasive appeals that is required in all successful presentations, but remember to add appeals to emotion. Appeals to pride, to self-esteem, to ambition, loyalty or perhaps even to fear, both verbally and visually, will enhance and support your message.

3.7 Winning Minds Through Reasoning and Evidence (Logos)

Reasoning and use of evidence are also strong persuaders. The more you develop strong reasoning to assert your ideas, support your view with facts, and the more you back these up with detail, the more chance you have of persuading your listeners to agree with you. You should never speak in abstractions without referring to specific examples or case studies to support your point of view. One of the best ways to learn about the use of evidence and reasoning is to watch an effective persuader in action.

Some of the best examples of clear and logical argumentation come from the financial reporting cycle each year, when CEOs and their Boards must report to their shareholders. Shareholders are keen to get the best returns from their investments, so the Board must be able to explain clearly why they make decisions and how this has affected the financial returns.

Mixing your appeals to achieve success

Many best-selling books, such as *Inside Steve's Brain*, by Leander Kahney, have written about leadership and communication and the effective use of language to develop appeals to pathos and logos. Books like this offer useful advice. Observing examples of the strategies of good communicators serve the purpose here of exploring the impact of the combination of all three appeals: sound reasoning and evidence, credibility appeals and appeals to emotion through effective language choices.

One outstanding communicator, mentioned earlier in the chapter, who recognizes and uses the power of many of these appeals is Carly Fiorina, former CEO of the technology giant, Hewlett-Packard (HP). Indeed, Fiorina combines all three appeals: ethos, pathos and logos (McCarthy, Hatcher, 2003). She has been presented, in the media, as a tough corporate warrior, with the will to accomplish the almost impossible (as her strategy of achieving a merger between technology giants Hewlett-Packard and Compaq in 2002 suggests).

Fiorina also presents an image as a charismatic leader and communicator. Jeff Christian, the head-hunter who interviewed Fiorina for her position at HP described her, in an interview, as "incredibly captivating" and one HP director claimed that Fiorina was seen as a "very courageous leader" by employees despite fear about the merger between HP and Compaq that she led.

Carly Fiorina devotes a great deal of her energies to communicating with her various stakeholders in her business life and her political followers during 2016. Throughout her earlier time at HP, she placed a high priority on talking to stakeholders, initially travelling to offices all over the world, making endless presentations at various industry conventions, to customers and other stakeholders. Fiorina's perception of communication is worth noting. She told Helen Trinca, a journalist for the *Australian Financial Review* in 2000 that: Effective leadership requires an understanding that you don't own people, and you can't control people. They must want to, they must choose to be in the company of others, oriented towards a particular mission. That means, in my view, using communication vehicles really creatively.

In 2002, Fiorina promised to reinvent HP in three years, setting out to transform Hewlett-Packard's slipping profits and world-wide image. One of Fiorina's key strategies was to create strong images of what HP wished to achieve at the time, binding together dimensions of its past history and culture with a strong new image of a company which claimed to be inventing the future while being socially responsible. She regularly drew upon the powerful mythology of the founders of Hewlett-Packard "Bill (Hewlett) and Dave (Packard)" in her internal communication because these iconic and popular figures still mattered to many of the staff at HP. The image of the old garage still appears around the organization, eliciting images of spontaneity and natural backyard inventiveness. This idea is built on the fact that, when the original owners of Hewlett-Packard, Bill Hewlett and Dave Packard first started their business, they worked in an old garage in their back garden. This allowed her to draw upon the strength of what has traditionally been called HP's "garage culture".

However, Fiorina took another important step in her argumentation by using the idea of HP's tradition of invention and linking it to the new technologies. This helped her to link the past and future.

Many of Carly Fiorina's speeches still address the importance of businesses' leading change to improve society, and of course, the appeal to pathos is obvious. However, Fiorina's understanding of effective persuasion is demonstrated when she ensures that she weaves a strong and clear thread of logic through this seemingly emotional message. For example, when addressing an education and technology conference in 2002, she argued strongly that we (HP) must contribute—not just for our shareowners, not just for our customers, not just for our employees but for our communities as well.

Fiorina then moved on quickly to point out that: "This is of course, an issue of enlightened self-interest, as much as it is about business or philanthropy. Education is the single most important lever for increasing economic prosperity. It is the single most effective lever, the most important lever for growing a diverse, highly skilled workforce."

It is also interesting to note her use of repetition of words and the structure of phrases to reinforce her message in the examples above.

Aristotle believed that the most effective persuasive presentations have a mix of ethos, pathos, and logos—of credibility, emotion, and logic, and he believed that the mix should be balanced. You must be like the cook who follows a recipe carefully. Sometimes a recipe requires a little of an ingredient like chilli or soy sauce and sometimes you must pepper the dish with chilli to get the correct taste. Of course, knowing the occasion and the audience will help you to determine the correct mix.

ACTIVITY FOR LEARNING

Watch and listen to speakers such as Carly Fiorina, Jack Ma, or some other outstanding people you admire on the Internet.

- Write down some of the images they use.
- Note the powerful words they repeat to add impact to their message.
- Follow the arguments they make that support their key messages.
- Identify which gestures look powerful and the co-ordination of words and gestures by the speaker.
- Notice their use of voice to signal sincerity, or confidence, or connection with the audience.

A conscious and careful mix of logical arguments, imaginative language and images, appeals to the heart and appeals to credibility can engage your listeners by helping them to see things in a different light. Studying successful speakers such as Carly Fiorina or Richard Branson, CEO of Virgin Airlines as well as local Chinese speakers, and the structure, language choices and themes that they use can provide inspiration for any one wishing to find ways to develop their persuasive skills.

3.8 Preparing to Present

Now that we have considered some important strategies for developing a persuasive argument, let's work on getting ready to deliver.

3.8.1 Step 1: Be mentally prepared

See yourself sitting calmly in the room of your presentation and breathing deeply and freely. Now you are standing confidently and walking to the front of the room, you look purposefully out and smile at your audience before you begin.

This is the image you must keep with you at all times. You know that most people, faced with the idea of presenting to listeners, feel real fear. You are not alone! It is also comforting to know that you can overcome fear if you prepare for it. If you are prepared, listeners will not, cannot, hear your heart beating or feel your palms sweating; if you are focused on the purpose of your message and your desire to communicate that message, and if you appear confident, you will be assured of making contact with your listeners.

In the earlier section of this chapter, we considered your audience and their characteristics. At this stage of your preparation, you should make an educated guess about your listeners and how they think and feel. You have now to prepare to know everything to know about the speaker, and you have to prepare to know yourself. Let's begin that preparation.

1. Recognize your strengths

Begin by recognizing your strengths. Reflect on when you communicated well with others. What aspects did you do well? We are sure that, if you are fair with yourself, you will realize that you could write a long list of your strengths and capabilities. For example, most people win over others with a warm smile. So, relax and smile, and you will feel good. Imagine yourself standing in front of your listeners and smiling before you begin to speak. If you breathe deeply, and smile, and think about building a good relationship with your audience, you always have a good beginning (unless, of course, you want to set up a serious atmosphere).

It is highly likely that you know your topic well and can speak easily on it in conversation. If the topic is a new and challenging one, make sure that you have researched and become familiar with it. Ask the experts for advice, discuss the topic with friends, visit the organization's website, or visit the library and search for that information which will most interest your audience.

2. Consider your weaknesses

It is also useful to list your fears. Are those fears rational and worth worrying about? If your answer is yes, are there ways in which you can remove them?

If you are worried about making mistakes, always keep in mind that you will always make some mistakes in a presentation, but if you forgive your small mistakes as a normal part of communication and ensure that you have other strong qualities, your audience will remember you with warmth and interest, and value your expertise and directness.

If you appear confident, you will build the confidence of your listeners and if you appear enthusiastic and passionate about your ideas, you will also build a strong relationship with them. To do this, you must be capable of clearly recalling memories of the best and strongest images of yourself as a speaker.

3.8.2 Step 2: Plan your material

How will you establish your credibility? Does your experience, expertise or research, or title, or relationships with others suggest that you are credible?

Be sure to select only the best points to fit the time you have.

Be sure to identify 2 or 3 key messages that you wish to share. For each message, you may have several key points that support your key messages.

Also, think carefully about the best arrangement for your ideas.

Now, you can think about the best words and phrases to develop your points. Consider the suggestions in the section above on choosing language and images and facts and figures to excite and interest your listeners.

3.8.3 Step 3: Practice your presentation

If you now practice speaking those phrases onto your smart phone, you can watch and listen to your presentation and this will help you to remember useful words and images when you speak to listeners. Remember, a video or audio recording is useful for the speaker just as the computer is for the writer. You can use this strategy to make the drafts of your presentation, just as a writer makes drafts of a text on the computer.

3.8.4 Step 4: Bring your presentation together

Finally, you must work on the introduction, conclusion and the links which hold your ideas together. These links can be thought as the "glue" that holds a presentation together.

1. The introduction

Once you have developed a well-structured body for your presentation, you can start to work on your introduction and conclusion. The introduction is very important because it is often the aspect of the presentation which causes the audience to decide whether you are worth listening to. It must function to get each listener's attention and to give listeners direction. You are giving your audience a map of the whole presentation.

In some situations, if you and your topic have not been introduced to the audience beforehand, the introduction will have to perform the function of revealing the details of your topic and showing that it is worth listening to. You may also need to establish your credibility early in your presentation and ensure that the listeners know a little about you. Finally, it is critical to build rapport or emotional connection in this early part of the presentation. This is your chance to make the audience feel that you are likeable and to present the "human face" of your ideas. In summary, then, there are five functions of the introduction that you need to achieve:

- get your listeners' attention.
- outline the topic.
- establish your credibility.
- give your listeners direction and so provide a map of what you will be talking about.
- build a relationship with the audience—a connection between you and the audience.

Remember that a speaker must "grab" the attention of the audience at the beginning of a presentation. Be daring, and be prepared to do the work to compel your listeners to pay attention to you. There are many means of getting your listeners' attention:

- tell them why and how your topic relates to them.
- capture them with a quotation.
- make a striking statement.
- ask them a rhetorical question (such as "Who knows?" "Researchers have come up with some surprising findings?").
- tell them a story which explains an idea in the presentation.
- tell them a joke about the topic—always make sure that humor is relevant to the topic.
- give them a shock by quoting surprising statistics.

Whatever you do, add detail to make your statements concrete through as many of the senses as you can, and carry your listeners along with you. Obviously, the listener's action is a potentially effective device if you, and they, can handle it effectively. This might include asking your audience members to raise their hand in agreement or asking a question that needs an answer from the audience.

Here is an example of this technique.

Imagine the presentation we heard from one student speaker who began with a role play of three people eating dinner.

Suddenly one of them falls to the floor, obviously having a heart attack, while the others sit stunned. The speaker, a nurse in the organization, comes forward and asks who of us in the room can help this man because the other people sitting at his table do not know how to do. Most of us are forced to confront our ignorance of first aid and the helplessness we would face in this situation. The shock and reality of the role play motivates us to listen doubly carefully to the speech and her message to attend a first aid course as a matter of urgency.

You do need to think carefully about the appropriateness of any attention grabbing strategy. One speaker recently made global headlines and was condemned by the bank he was consulting to, the global community and Chinese workers from around the country when he used an attention seeking device in training.

If you are concerned about the creative difficulty of coming up with such a daring introduction, or, if you are worried about the personality required for achieving such a dramatic effect, remember that, for the sake of originality, it is worth learning that the risk is worth taking. However, any of the strategies listed above could be successful, if you plan appropriately and carefully for the needs of the audience and the specific situation, and you present the introduction with flair and polish.

2. The conclusion

The conclusion to any speech should be punchy, concise and clearly summarize your key ideas and messages. Make sure that your conclusion is not too long because once you have signaled that you are in the concluding stages of a presentation, listeners want you to finish quickly and clearly. A conclusion for a ten-minute presentation should be no longer than thirty to fifty seconds.

For example, in a presentation to their organization to motivate the employees to offer good service, the speaker talked about the importance of reputation in building customer loyalty. The conclusion included three good reasons to offer good service, and then a punchy, concise reminder that:

Reputation markets are winner-take-all events, so we must care for our reputation in the market-place if we want to be a successful company.

Of course, if you are capable of it, there is nothing that compares to the crescendo or drawing the audience's emotions to a high pitch at the end: it is incomparable as a conclusion to a motivational presentation. One famous conclusion is the final stages of American civil libertarian Martin Luther King's now famous "I have a dream", which was discussed earlier. King wanted to inspire hundreds of thousands of people to take up the fight for the civil rights of African American citizens, so that they could go on buses and be treated equally with all white Americans. In a passionate voice, he concluded(Thompson, 1992):

When we allow freedom to ring—when we let it ring from every village and every hamlet, from every state and every city—we will be able to speed up that day when all of God's children, black men and white men, Jews and Gentiles, Protestants and Catholics, will be able to join hands and sing in the words of the old Negro spiritual, "Free at last! Free at last! Thank God almighty, we are free at last!".

Notice how carefully King structured these final words of the speech to lift the emotions and commitment of the audience. Notice the use of repetition and the use of structuring into three-part messages—"black men and white men, Jews and Gentiles, Protestant and Catholics" or "Free at last! Free at last! Thank God almighty, we are free at last!" He also used his voice by lengthening the word "free" to inspire them through this important non-verbal code. Martin Luther King had the ability to make a speech which was both inspiring and coherent.

ACTIVITY FOR LEARNING

Listen to Martin Luther King's "I have a dream" speech on the Internet.

3. The glue

Let us now look at those techniques which will help you to achieve coherence or the holding together of your ideas in your presentation like that achieved in the earlier examples: the glue.

What do we mean by the glue? The metaphor of "glue" helps us to imagine the sticky adhesive qualities of the many connective words that you need to make a coherent presentation. The parts of your presentation must be glued/connected/woven together to clearly lead your listeners through your ideas, to your intention and key messages. There are four aspects of the glue you need to understand and must learn to use: signposts; transitions; internal previews and internal summaries.

(1) **Signposts.** We have just given you an example of signposting in the previous sentence—"four aspects". These are simple, helpful directions for the listener. Other examples are: "There are three key issues to be considered. Firstly… Secondly… and finally..."; or "The most important point to consider is…"; or "For example, …". You can also use simple questions such as: "Why is this important?"; or "How can we solve the problem?". Signposts show the listener where you are up to, and where you and they are headed; they help the listener to know where, on the map of your speech, you are focused. In other words, they point out the organizational pattern of your speech as it happens.

(2) **Transitions.** Transitions are the links that you build for your listeners from one part of your presentation to the next: "Now that we have explored…"; or "Let us turn to…"; or "We

have focused so far on..., so it's time now to discuss...". These links help the listeners to understand the relationships of parts of the presentation to each other, and of each part to the whole. Transitions are, therefore, very important to orientate listeners to your map of ideas or the strategic and practical arrangement of your topic and speech.

(3) **Internal previews and summaries**. Internal previews and summaries give the listeners a similar opportunity to the one they enjoy when they can look back over what they have read, or skim forward to find out what they are going to cover in the next paragraph. Provide these previews and summaries within each major part of your presentation. The principle to use when deciding what to say is: you should say what you are going to say in this particular part, say it, and then summarize what you have just said.

The difference between listening and reading is that listeners cannot go back to what you have said earlier. If they miss it or forget it, that idea is lost to them. So, repetition is very important in oral presentations. This is a simple but critical thing to remember if you want to succeed in giving presentations.

An internal preview invites the listener to know what is coming by previewing the way ahead, just as a movie preview encourages you to go to the movie. An internal summary invites the audience to pause for a moment while the speaker restates what has been said so far by summarizing the earlier points.

For example, we have outlined a simple map of a structured presentation: ① the introduction; ②the body, which consists of clearly marked points in clearly marked parts; ③the conclusion, and holding the good structure together; ④the glue, which consists of signposts, transitions, internal previews and internal summaries.

Summary

Becoming an effective presenter is a critical skill for all those who wish to succeed in their working lives. This chapter has emphasized four important aspects of effective presentations.

- All presentations should be guided by the mantra: It's all about audience, audience, audience!
- Every presentation should develop a persuasive argument for accepting the ideas presented (including both content and non-verbal elements).
- Every presentation must use a careful preparation strategy.
- Every presentation needs a carefully planned structure, a well developed introduction, subtly but clearly developed links or "glue", and a high impact memorable conclusion.

If you work carefully on all of these aspects, you can become a memorable and effective presenter. You will be able to leave your audience with a strong memory of your ideas and a commitment to them, using the same strategies that excellent speakers such as Jack Ma, Martin Luther King, Carly Fiorina, Steve Jobs and speakers whom you have personally admired have used. Having read this chapter, you have, at your disposal, many guidelines for delivering an effective presentation.

Questions for Discussion

(1) What are the golden principles of creating messages? Why is each of them important?

(2) Consider the different communication styles. Which of the four main styles is your dominant style? Compare this with others in your discussion group.

(3) Consider the different codes of non-verbal communication. Which ones are most important for you when you are listening to a speaker? Can you recall a time when you were aware that you were listening to or observing the non-verbal communication more than the words themselves? When and why?

Exercises

(1) Write down one sentence that tells your audience that you are credible—is it your knowledge about the subject, your experience, your title or role in your organization, your attitudes and values? Keep this sentence in mind the next time you are preparing a presentation.

(2) Develop a metaphor or image that helps to explain one of your ideas. For example, effective communication in business is the "lifeblood" of an organization. Think of a metaphor to describe your favorite subject at university or your best friend. Eg.: a best friend might be "a helping hand".

(3) Go back to the opening pages of this chapter. Can you find examples of signposts, transitions, internal previews and internal summaries?

While it is easier to go back and find these in written documents, such as this chapter, the function is just as important as in an oral presentation.

Examples to look for:

Signpost

Firstly, secondly, etc.

Principle 1, Principle 2

Transitions, previews, summaries

In the earlier section of this chapter, we considered your audience and their characteristics (*Summary*). You have, by now, made at least an educated guess about your listeners and how they think and feel about the context of this presentation, and you have thought about persuasion for your context. You have now to prepare to know everything there is to know about the speaker; you have to prepare to know yourself (*Preview*). Let's begin that preparation (*Transition*).

Chapter 4

Cross-Cultural Management and Business Communication

LEARNING OBJECTIVES

On completing this chapter, you should be able to:

- Understand some of the patterns of behavior and attitudes of different cultures that shape communication responses.
- Understand the way cultures learn to see their behaviors as "normal".
- Develop awareness of your own culture's patterns of behavior.
- Develop awareness of how individual differences affect communication behavior in cross-cultural settings.
- Understand how English as a second language affects communication in cross-cultural settings.
- Learn some principles for managing a cross-cultural interaction effectively.
- Develop some cross-cultural communication (CCC) strategies to handle specific situations such as conflicts, formality, face-saving, learning, giving and receiving, feedback.

Study Case：Marketing Disney to China

Only six months after Hong Kong Disneyland opened, Disney officials were scrambling to understand why attendances was so low at the new park. They turned for answers to Chinese travel agents who book tours. Some of these agents believed Disney officials had not tried to understand the local market and Chinese cultures.

After the disappointing start at the Hong Kong park, Disney officials were anxious to learn and ready to make changes. Using the travel industry feedback and other market research, Disney developed a new advertising campaign. Original ads had featured an aerial view of the park; new TV spots focused o people and showed guests riding attractions. A new print ad featuring a grandmother, mother and daughter showed that Disney is a place where family can have fun together.

Disney also worked to make visitors more comfortable inside the park. At an attraction offered three different languages, guests gravitated toward the shortest line—usually the line for English-speaking guests. Now, three separate signs clearly mark which language will be used to communicate with the guests in that line.

Greater use of Mandarin-speaking guides and materials helps guests better enjoy shows and attractions. Also, additional seating was added in dining areas because Chinese diners take longer to eat than do Americans. Disney is hoping such changes will attract more guests to the Hong Kong park.

(Source: Merissa Marr ad Geoffrey A. Fowler , "Chines Lessons for Disney." *Wall Street Journal*, 2006, June 12, B1, B5.)

4.1 Understanding Our Cross-Cultural Behaviors

Managers and employees all over the world share one important quality. They need to be able to work with others to achieve business outcomes. This is particularly true in the twenty-first century, where almost every employee is a part of a team, whether working with those of other cultures directly face-to-face, or being a part of a global or cross-country team connected via the Internet. One of the biggest challenges, and also one of the greatest opportunities, is that people across the world have many similarities as well as differences. Individuals working together might be similar or different not only because of their age, gender, first language, second language, expertise and educational background, but also because of their life experiences and cultural backgrounds. Our background provides us with a very specific experience of life, driven by a set of values and attitudes as well as a set of norms of behavior considered appropriate by our national group.

4.2 Cultural Concepts and the Differences between Chinese and Foreign Business Communication Practice

4.2.1 Power and relationships

A very well-known researcher, Geert Hofstede, who spent a lifetime studying how culture affects our behavior, considers that culture is composed of many elements which can be classified into four different categories. They are:

- the symbols we use, including our language.
- the heroes we hold dear, such as our ideal types of people.
- the rituals that we perform, including the celebrations we have and everyday events such as business meetings.
- the values we believe in, such as our broad feelings about what is good or bad, rational or irrational, and normal or abnormal.

Taken together, this is what is meant by culture.

Geert Hofstede likened culture to computer software. He suggested that culture is a collective mental programming of the mind which distinguishes members of one category of people from another. In fact, Geert Hofstede wrote a now very famous book entitled *Cultures and Organizations: Software of the Mind* (1991) to share his extensive research about national culture and how it affects business practice. It is no wonder then, that when cultures meet, they often find it difficult to understand each other. To continue the metaphor of computer software, meeting someone from another culture might be as difficult as getting Microsoft Word to talk to a Microsoft Excel spreadsheet!

Hofstede's work can help us to understand how cultures are similar and how they differ. He used his role in the technology giant, IBM, to identify a number of dimensions that seem to differentiate people along the lines of culture. Using employees and managers in 53 different national subsidiaries, Hofstede and his co-researchers identified the following dimensions that make cultures similar to and different from each other.

Hofstede Identified 5 Dimensions of Cultural Approach

(1) Power distance—the degree of inequality among members of a population of a country that they see as normal and acceptable. This ranges from relative equal to extreme unequal.

(2) Individualism—the degree to which members of a population of a country act as individuals rather than as a collective. This ranges from extreme individualism (or independence of individuals) to extreme collectivism (or interdependence of members of a group).

(3) Masculinity—the degree to which members of a population of a country value "masculine" values such as assertiveness, performance, success and competition over "feminine" values such as warm relationships, co-operation, caring, connection, and service. This ranges from "tender to tough" (Hofstede, 1991).

(4) Uncertainty avoidance—the degree to which members of a population of a country prefer working in familiar, structured versus unfamiliar, unstructured situations. This ranges from relatively flexible to extremely rigid, from high levels of innovation to resistance to new approaches.

(5) Long-term orientation—the degree to which members of a population of a country value building long-term relationships, being careful with money, and perseverance over a "short-term orientation" where the population responds negatively to respect for tradition.

Hofstede described these dimensions on a continuum or scale from a high degree of each dimension to a low degree of each dimension, so countries can be compared with each other.

We now live in a global society where cultures continuously interact in a mediated way via television shows, the Internet, music, the social media and email, and face-to-face through travel to other countries, education abroad, and business ventures such as multi-national companies. In the twenty-first century, cultures are no longer shielded from each other by geography or time.

Changing Times at Disney

One company that has ventured into countries around the world with its very culturally specific product is Walt Disney Co., with its famous Disneyland product. Theme parks designed to lure visitors to meet their fantasy characters face-to-face after a lifetime of reading about them in fairytales and seeing them in movies and TV programmes have gradually spread across the world. The first Disneyland was built by company founder Walt Disney in Anaheim, California in 1955.

Since then, other parks have been built in Orlando and Tampa in Florida. Much-loved Mickey Mouse, Donald Duck and Sleeping Beauty have survived cross-cultural encounter, but many of the aspects of Disneyland have been gradually modified to suit the new host cultures. For example, a new site in France, just outside Paris, opened in 1992. Originally named EuroDisney, the name was changed to Disneyland Paris in 2002, because according to the then CEO Michael Eisner, the word "Euro" suggested only ideas of "business" and "currency" to the French, not the glamour that it had been intended to suggest. Many lessons were learned by the company as it continued to make losses throughout the 1990s. A number of the ways that food is served have been modified to suit French tastes in Disneyland Paris. Wine, an essential requirement of French cuisine is now served after an initial ban, and some adjustments to staff rules and extra training have been included to harmonize employment relations. New sites in Tokyo in 1983 and later in Hong Kong have benefitted from this willingness to respect cultural differences.

The opening of Shanghai Disney in 2016 demonstrates how behavioral flexibility is the key to successful cross-cultural communication and management. Current CEO, Bob Iger described Shanghai Disney as "authentically Disney, distinctly Chinese". He claimed that 70% of the rides are original and 4 of the 6 Lands are newly conceived. Much-loved characters such as Mickey Mouse, Donald Duck and the princesses are all featured throughout the theme park. However, Main Street, a cultural reminder of early US town life and a core feature of previous parks, has become Mickey Avenue. Also, Frontierland, another US cultural record of the early days of US pioneering history has become Treasure Cove, a more globally recognizable phenomena based largely on successful films such as *Pirates of the Caribbean*. Tomorrow Land has also been updated to reflect a more contemporary figure called Tron. A fourth significant change is the addition of a Chinese themed "Garden of the Twelve Friends" in which characters such as Remy from *Ratatouille* and Tigger from *Winnie the Pooh* are performed as Chinese Zodiac animals and the setting includes a Wandering Moon Teahouse. Walt Disney Co. has changed its behaviors very considerably from the days when they promised that every Disneyland throughout the world would be identical.

As you can see from this case study, when businesses and their employees accommodate our similarities and our differences, sensitive cross-cultural management can bring great success.

Indeed, as you are reading this book, you will be engaging globally with the authors from China and Australia who worked together to create what you are learning. So, our collective knowledge and some values are inevitably going to be global. Therefore, we must always avoid using generalizations about cultures to stereotype others. Hofstede's dimensions are really just good guides as to what we should be careful about when dealing with other cultures. This knowledge is like a set of signposts to alert us so that we can keep going on the pathway of effective communication.

To give you an example of the differences that you might expect, let's compare China, Japan, the United States, United Kingdom and Sweden. Remember, all these descriptions are on a relative scale—that is, the approaches of these countries are compared with each other on a continuum.

ACTIVITY FOR LEARNING

Study Table 4.1 below to reflect on the differences between China and some other countries with whom you might communicate in business.

Table 4.1 Comparison of Cultural Dimensions of 5 Countries from Across the World

Country	Power distance	Individualism/ Collectivism	Masculinity/ Femininity	Uncertainty avoidance	Long-term/ Short-term orientation (LTO)
China	High	Low individualism	Moderate masculinity	Moderate	High LTO

Country	Power distance	Individualism/ Collectivism	Masculinity/ Femininity	Uncertainty avoidance	Long-term/ Short-term orientation (LTO)
Japan	High	Low individualism	Very high masculinity	High	High LTO
United States	Moderate	High individualism	Moderate masculinity	Low	Moderate LTO
United Kingdom	Moderate	High individualism	Moderate masculinity	Low	Moderate LTO
Sweden	Low	High individualism	Low masculinity	Low	Moderately high LTO

(Source: Hofstede G. *Cultures and Organizations: Software of the Mind*[M]. 1991, Sydney: McGraw-Hill. Hofstede G. Cultural constraints in management theories[J]. *Academy of Management Executive*, 1993, 7(2) :81-94.)

4.2.2 Context and communication

Another important way through which to understand communication across cultures is by recognizing the way people from different cultures consider that they should use information. Edward Hall has explained the way this happens by describing cultures as "high context" or "low context". High context cultures, such as China, Japan and many other Asian cultures assume that the knowledge needed to interact is carried by the culture and the people of an in-group interacting together, so this information need not be made explicit in their words. Words and word-choice become very important as few words are used. Typically, a high context culture will be collectivist and relational.

On the other hand, cultures such as the US, Australia and the United Kingdom are low context cultures and ideas are made explicit to make meaning clear amongst those interacting. These differences in use of ideas and words can have a large impact on how people understand each other. Low context cultures typically have members who work things out independently and also expect to have many relationships but fewer intimate ones by whom they are supported. For example, if a Chinese and an Australian employee were communicating, the Chinese employee may expect the Australian to understand that the young Chinese employee is offended by a direct conversation about a disagreement with a senior leader. The Australian, by contrast, would expect to lay out the points of disagreement very clearly and directly. Usually, it is only when someone breaks the rules that you expect, that you notice differences.

There are numerous other frameworks based on national culture, but these two by Hofstede and Hall provide useful points of reference when approaching a cross-cultural situation.

4.2.3 Business practices

As this is a book about business communication, it is also important to recognize that business practices themselves are also part of the dynamics of cross-cultural management.

Countries also vary in their styles and approaches to do business. Sensitivity to practices like management strategies and business planning, who speaks at meetings, or even who attends meetings, uses of business letters, the design of annual reports and other documents, and the political and cultural influences on negotiation are all integral to success in cross-cultural communication. One example of the need to deal carefully with the business approaches of other countries is the need to respect the different financial requirements of Islamic banking. Many countries in the Middle East such as Saudi Arabia and Bahrain, as well as Pakistan and Sudan, and countries closer to China such as Malaysia and Indonesia practice Islamic banking where no interest is allowed to be paid on financial products. Later chapters in this book will take up many of these differences that need to be accounted for in interaction. The important point here is to recognize that not just national culture but business culture and the connected communication practices all play a part in a successful cross-cultural encounter.

4.2.4 The role of individual differences in shaping cross-cultural encounters

Recent researchers have cautioned that we need to take the complexity of cross-cultural encounters into account. To avoid "sophisticated stereotyping" based on the above dimensions (Osland & Bird, 2000), we need to recognize the ways individuals make choices on how to engage with others. Even within a culture, there is considerable variation in interaction style.

ACTIVITY FOR LEARNING

(1) Observe 2 class members and 2 family members. Note their similarities and differences when the interaction takes place.

(2) Are there differences linked to age, gender, and experience of using social media and others?

Ganesh (2015) and Holmes (2015) warn against relying on formulas such as Hofstede's and Hall's dimensions alone. They argue that the differences such as gender, age, and access to travel, interaction with foreigners such as on the Internet through social media, and experience in virtual teams in business and education also affect the way we interact cross-culturally. This personal experience makes the rules more complex and adaptive in the twenty-first century. Recent studies of the evolution of the use of business English in China suggest that young Chinese professionals are communicating more directly than Hofstede's or Hall's model would suggest.

These less rigid boundaries do seem understandable as a global culture emerges rapidly, particularly for the younger digitally literate generations. Many boundaries are moving and changing as geography and time become less relevant. Another example of this exposure and globalization of culture is the huge popularity of Korean New Wave music, fashion and television drama across many countries in Asia. Cultural adaptation in ways of viewing life and particularly celebrity lifestyles makes communication across these cultures less risky and less likely to be difficult for the younger generations. Equally, opportunities to interact via the Internet provide both a safer environment and a more gradual and potentially democratic way for users of English to communicate.

4.2.5 The role of English as a second language in shaping cross-cultural encounters

In addition to understanding how individuals bring their life experiences to a cross-cultural encounter, note that the role of first language and English as a second language is increasingly being recognized as an important element in these dynamics. English as first language speakers have some advantages in encounters with those speaking English as a second language. This may lead to power imbalances in the communication.

However, bilingual speakers have two windows of opportunity to understand cross-cultural dynamics. It is important to acknowledge language difficulties and to have the confidence to ask clarifying questions and to alert speakers from other cultures when they are breaking cultural rules. Even when both parties are using English as the common language, the choices of "which" English words and the tone of the message will be strongly driven by cultural patterns of the speaker's or the writer's first culture. For example, as authors, we noted the importance of metaphor in annual reports from China and the limited use of metaphor in Australian business reports.

In order to strengthen the employee communication internationally, IBM has launched a global consistent English language policy and dedicated training programs for all employees, requiring them to use English at work, whether they are in Japan or are UK based employees. Dedicating significant resources to such a project demonstrates the value of good cross-cultural management to successful business outcomes in the estimation of IBM.

4.3 How to Handle Cross-Cultural Communication Effectively

Now that we have recognized some of the pitfalls of dealing with the dynamics of cross-cultural communication, it's time to develop some strategies to allow you to communicate well in the situation. The diagram below (Figure 4.1) demonstrates the dynamics of a cross-cultural encounter. Each of us brings our cultural values, attitudes and behaviors to the situation. The overlapping part of the two circles represents the high risk part of the encounter, when you and your communication partner are dealing with aspects that challenge either one or both of your deeply held cultural patterns.

For example, when a Korean person meets a person from Australia, a moment of high risk is deciding what to call each other. The Australian may go straight to give names and say: "Hi, my name is Jack." Because Koreans live a high power-distance culture where formality is high, this will be a difficult moment. The Korean finds it difficult to be called by his first name, which is reserved only for close family members and friends, and would prefer Mr. Park or Mr. Kim to be comfortable. For Jack and Mr. Park, this cross-cultural interaction can cause some tension because competing rules are at play here. However, if Jack and Mr. Park handle this complexity competently, they can have a smooth and successful encounter. Some Koreans who have studied overseas have adopted an English name to deal with just such an issue. This adaptive behavior demonstrates that not just national cultural patterns are at play here, but also the choices individuals make to deal with such challenges.

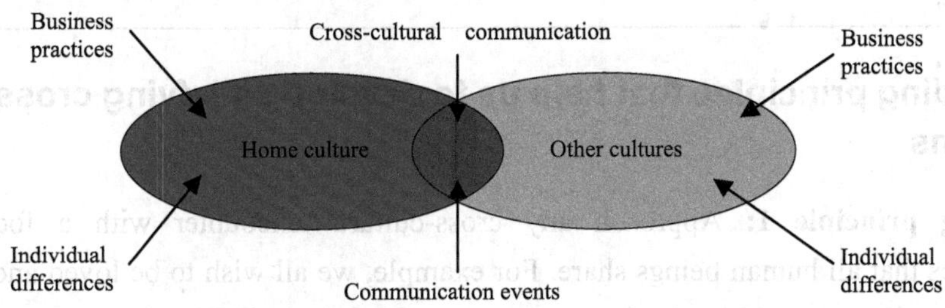

Figure 4.1 The Dynamics of Cross-Cultural Communication

The first step in this process is to reflect on your home culture. Understanding your own culture, what it sees as normal, and how various behaviors are interpreted is an important step in the learning process. Good cross-cultural communicators are self-reflective. The ideal cross-cultural interaction recognizes that both speakers will need to adjust their behaviors. The "third" space, shown in Figure 4.1 in a dark colour, is a negotiated space between the speakers.

ACTIVITY FOR LEARNING

Answer the following questions about your home culture.

Think about your culture—a cultural inventory. Work in groups of two or three, reflect on how your culture communicates in the following situations. Make brief points about each.

(1) Establishing a relationship: Meeting (e.g. purpose, authority relationships, who speaks and decides, typical topics, forms of address).

(2) Engaging (talking and silence, turn-taking, good manners).

(3) Handling conflicts (attitudes, techniques).

(4) Other observations.

(5) Describe one advertisement that you feel tells something significant about your cultural values and what it says about your culture.

(6) Describe one advertisement that you feel tells you about another culture and what it says about that culture.

(7) Tell one story that reflects how your culture operates (from the home, leisure or workplace).

(8) Check back on Table 4.1 once you have developed your set of rules. Compare this set of rules with another country in the table.

(9) What differences do you notice between your self-assessed behavior and the dimensions in Hofstede and Hall?

(10) What other aspects (many described above) could explain your identified differences of behavior? Age, language?

Remember, you may have to reflect very carefully on what rules govern your behavior. Rules are "automatic"—that is, it seems natural to do this. It is usually when a rule is broken that we notice—because we often react by assuming that the rule violator did it deliberately. Rules have a sort of "moral force" and our response to an infringement or breaking of a rule is often strongly felt.

Some guiding principles that help us to develop satisfying cross-cultural interactions

Guiding principle 1: Approach any cross-cultural encounter with a focus on the commonalities that all human beings share. For example, we all wish to be loved and liked. Our differences in culture may determine how we express that love or liking.

Guiding principle 2: Be alert to your responses to infringements of what seems "normal" to you. Most often, if you feel surprised or shocked by some behavior, it is because what they are doing seems "normal" to your communication partner but not to you. It's now time to think about those differences in culture listed in the beginning of the chapter.

Guiding principle 3: Be careful not to stereotype people according to their culture. The cultural dimensions are guides to general patterns of behavior, not rules to which every person subscribes. Their life experience may allow them to make different choices and take on other behaviors. We are sure that you know a Chinese person who seems to react differently to most others. All cultures have some people who do not conform to the normal rules of their culture.

Guiding principle 4: If you need to develop a working relationship with someone from another culture, spend time getting to know that person and observe their behavior and interactions carefully. This will give you clues to your similarities and the differences you have. For those from cultures like the US, this means taking extra time to build a relationship with an other culture. As a Chinese member of an interaction with a US partner, it may seem perfectly normal to you to spend time to build this relationship, but to many US partners, this is considered a waste of time. Don't be offended if a Western partner seems to want to get straight to work. You may have to adjust to this approach, and meanwhile continue to provide opportunities for interaction. Once again, you are in a high risk zone early in the interaction.

Guiding principle 5: After you have established trust with your cross-cultural partner, openly and honestly discuss and agree to some rules of interaction for your partnership. This creates the "third space" described and visualized in Figure 4.1 above. This may involve conversations about saying "yes" and "no" for Japanese partners, building relationships through social interaction for Chinese partners, rules about hierarchy and handling lines of authority for Korean partners, and individual and group responsibilities for US partners.

ACTIVITY FOR LEARNING

Read the following case study. What are the three situations that the Korean employee might find it difficult to deal with, considering the Australian approach to communicating via email?

See if you can apply the ideas that you have learned so far in this chapter to detect issues.

What issues would you, as a Chinese employee, need to consider in your interactions with the Korean employees?

Online Communication between Koreans and Australians

There are many multi-national corporations operating all over the world. One study of the way Koreans and Australians use email to communicate about their business demonstrates that behavioral patterns for specific cultural groups tend to be the same, regardless of whether people are face-to-face or using technology to communicate. The Koreans in the study were formal, conscious of power and status, showed respect for seniors, tended to build a relationship first, and were not direct. The Australians, on the other hand, were relatively informal and friendly, unconcerned about status, expected to work on a first name basis with most others, and were direct in their requests. However, the study also found that both groups learned to adapt to each other over time. They adjusted their level of formality and developed more openness over time.

(Source: Kim H S , Hearn G, Hatcher C, et al. Online communication between Koreans and Australians[J]. *World Communication*, 1999, 28(4): 48-68.)

4.4 Learning about and Respecting Other Cultures

Some important differences in the way many Western and Eastern cultures approach a communication problem have been identified. These include the handling of conflicts, rituals and celebrations, handling relationships by managing face and embarrassment, and learning approaches and receiving feedback. Of course there are many more situations to learn about, but learning about these issues will provide a good basis for your future experimentation with cross-cultural encounters.

4.4.1 Handling of conflicts

Cultures such as Japan and Thailand generally avoid conflicts at all costs. They are keen to maintain harmony, feel uneasy when a conflict arises, and try to avoid interpersonal conflicts. In some organizational research, Thais have been found to seek to maintain smooth relationships and to communicate indirectly and politely, and business professionals seek to resolve conflicts collaboratively if a conflict arises. Japanese communicators are similarly keen to avoid conflicts and maintain a harmonious, polite communicative environment.

This approach to disagreement and even argumentativeness is in strong contrast with cultures such as the US and Australia. In highly individualistic cultures such as the US and Australia, being argumentative, for example, at a meeting, is strongly valued, when that behavior is compared with how Thais and Japanese conduct their interactions.

Speaking out, disagreeing and arguing through an idea publicly and logically is seen as a positive behavior of a successful business person in many western cultures. Some researchers, such as Avtgis and Rancer (2002), have studied how argumentative behavior is valued, and can demonstrate that some countries value argument more than others. For example, Australians value being more argumentative and verbally outspoken more than those from the United States.

This argumentative behavior can be rather shocking to more harmonious cultures like many Eastern cultures, while, from the Western perspective, not speaking out is seen as agreeing or as simply being weak or passive. Avtgis and Rancer found that, when compared with the Japanese, those from the United States, Australia and New Zealand were more argumentative and were likely to hotly debate issues in public situations like meetings. This difference in cultural styles can lead to major misunderstanding between groups.

Be prepared to adapt to the conflict handling style of your partner: harmony or heated debate must be met with an appropriate response.

4.4.2 Rituals and formality

Cultures like China, Japan and Korea based on Confucian ethics and values have a strongly ritualistic approach to business entertainment and meetings. While there are definitely many rituals in western cultures such as those of the US and UK, the approach is generally more informal and tends to give more choices to individuals as to how to celebrate, entertain, and conduct meetings. One ritual that Westerners have learned from the East is the use of business cards or "meishi" in Japanese terms. This was a convention of interaction practically unknown in the West until the 1990s. In countries like the US, the UK and Australia today, having a business card has come to be expected.

Westerners are often taken by surprise by the drinking rituals at business dinners so common in countries like China and Korea. Moni Lai Storz, author of *Dancing with Dragons: Chopsticks People Revealed for Global Business*(1999) suggests that these rituals are part of the aesthetic or artistic qualities encouraged by Confucianism, with its emphasis on beauty and ritual.

Here is an example of the cross-cultural tensions inherent in one such ritual.

In the United States, no one would be surprised by the way of "going Dutch" when going out for a meal, i.e. each pays for his own food.

What surprises those American business people (and other westerners as well) when they come to China is the hospitality shown by their Chinese counterparts, as they are often treated with dinners of eight or ten courses, sometimes even more than that. Some of them could not help but exclaim "What a banquet!" meaning they enjoyed the food very much. However, after the dinner, some would give another comment: "What a waste!" which can hardly be heard by those Chinese hosts.

Here is where a cultural misunderstanding occurs. What those Americans and other Westerners have seen is the result—a dinner given in their honor; what they have not seen or perhaps would not bother to inquire about is the impact of teaching from an ancient Chinese sage—Confucius. He once said "What a pleasure to have friends coming afar." In the eyes of the Chinese, those Americans and other westerners are like what had been described by Confucius as "friends coming afar".

(Source: 徐宪光. 商务沟通[M]. 北京：外语教学与研究出版社，2003.)

ACTIVITY FOR LEARNING

Recognize that your cross-cultural partners may be unfamiliar with many of your rituals. This does not suggest that they are poor communicators. You should help them to enjoy their new cultural experience. Alternatively, if some of those rituals are missing on your own international trips or in interactions, don't be nervous of new rituals. Be honest, ask questions and clarify what is unclear. People are usually delighted to share their special knowledge about their cultural traditions. Your questions are like compliments to them. Relax and enjoy the new experience. Being flexible and adaptable is the sign of a good cross-cultural communicator.

4.4.3 Managing face and embarrassment

In many Eastern cultures, such as Korea, Japan and Thailand, politeness is seen as an important virtue. Therefore, being polite by maintaining formality and ensuring that all rituals are performed according to rank is very important. By doing this, the social group can ensure that "face" will be maintained for everyone and thus harmony will be ensured. The idea that a person's public image or "face" is rather fragile and precious is somewhat strange to many Westerners. This does not mean that people from the US or the UK find it acceptable to be embarrassed by others, but rather that unless the embarrassment is strong, they often laugh off an embarrassing moment or event, or even tell stories later about the situation. As people from individualistic cultures, they are less formal and more strongly confident, relying less on others to approve them than in eastern cultures.

This difference of attitude towards "face" can cause many cultural misunderstandings.

Because Westerners do not necessarily recognize how easily this public image of a person can be harmed, their verbal and informal strategies to communicate can be seen as impolite and cause offence and even be considered disrespectful.

ACTIVITY FOR LEARNING

While you will always expect your "face" to be respected, try to be flexible, recognizing that people generally try to do the right thing in a situation. A blunder or error on their part which reduces your "face" is most likely unintentional miscommunication. Reflect on each cross-cultural encounter after it occurs. What could you do differently the next time?

4.4.4 Learning approaches and receiving feedback

Your first experience of training outside your home country or by a foreign trainer can be a daunting one, especially if moving from an eastern to a western culture. Table 4.2 below summarizes some of the key differences that you might find. You can easily see how many of the qualities that have already been mentioned about eastern cultures like China, Japan, Thailand, and Korea, and western cultures such as the US, the UK, Germany, Scandinavia, and Australia are clearly listed here. No wonder training and giving feedback is such a challenging task when trainers work with those from other cultures. They must be masters of both their content and their training style to satisfy their listeners.

Table 4.2 The Difference of Training Methods and Learning Approaches Between Western and Eastern countries

Anglo-Saxon training methods and learning approaches	Eastern training methods and learning approaches
Participation	Listening/rote learning
Risk-taking	Non-risk-taking
Questioning	Answering/taking copious notes
Trial and error	Certainty/authority of the expert's knowledge
Peer-centred	Teacher-centred
Egalitarian	Hierarchical
Individualistic	Collectivistic
Assertive	Non-assertive
Challenging	Accommodating
Controversial	Non-controversial
Argument/debate	Agreement
Informal/casual	Formal/ritualized

(Source: Storz M. *Dancing with Dragons: Chopsticks People Revealed for Global Business*[M]. Melbourne: Global Business Strategies, 1999.)

Remember, of course, that there are many transnational styles of communicating and individual differences in the delivery of training. Nonetheless, generally speaking, the authors have noted these contrasting patterns below during delivery of training. We note that individual differences and the role of English as a second language often play important roles in shaping participation, risk-taking, and questioning for both western and eastern nationals.

ACTIVITY FOR LEARNING

If you are being trained by a foreign or Western trainer, or asked to give feedback, make an effort to speak up, ask questions, and don't be afraid to ask for clarifications or voice your opinion if you find some observations and claims surprising. You will gain more from your learning this way, and your class will be able to reflect on similarities and differences as you and your trainer both adjust to each other's needs in your cross-cultural encounter.

4.4.5 Avoiding misunderstanding in cross-cultural business communication

Avoiding misunderstanding in cross-cultural communication takes commitment to be flexible in your approach to others and open and reflective about the ways you communicate. Do not be defensive but always observe and think about your communication in a cross-cultural interaction, so that you can recognize both when the communication is working well and when miscommunication is occurring. The key to good communication in every situation is to listen and watch non-verbal communication carefully.

As a simple device to help you enjoy your cross-cultural communication, try the PLACE technique.

Prepare—learn all you can about the new culture and people who you are going to encounter.

Listen—listen to and observe carefully the signals (both verbal and non-verbal) that you are receiving.

Adjust—adjust your approach to suit your cross-cultural partner and be flexible so that you respond quickly to divergent messages or messages that you did not expect.

Communicate—communicate positively, mirroring the style of your partner, reflecting their pace and how they are communicating whenever possible.

Enjoy—Enjoy the opportunity to experience the diversity of values, attitudes and ideas that a cross-cultural experience can bring. Diversity creates innovation and helps to bring partners together in successful business.

Summary

Whether you intend to live in China or to work overseas, you will be involved in cross-cultural communication. This is a critical part of your employee or management role and you need to develop skills to work with and manage a diverse range of people who populate our globe. Being cross-culturally competent requires a range of skills from being open and inquisitive to learning about other cultures, to heightened careful listening in cross-cultural interactions, to reflection on how your own culture works and what your culture and other cultures see as normal. Added to this, the communicatively competent person has also practiced on many occasions. They are behaviorally fit just like a good athlete trying to win a race. Most likely, the communicatively competent person has mis-communicated on many occasions and learnt from their mistakes without feeling that they have let themselves down. In other words, to be an effective cross-cultural communicator is a process of trial and error, with each experience and the information you have gathered from the interaction adding to your ability to create smoother and more effective interactions in the future. Overall, you are versatile, adaptive and knowledgeable. Cross-cultural communication is an essential and challenging tool of every effective business professional.

Questions for Discussion

(1) Discuss any differences that you have noticed between Chinese ways and foreign ways of the following issues: power-distance; decision-making and risk-taking.

(2) How do you feel when approaching a foreigner?

(3) What strategies can you use to communicate with a person from another culture? Share your experience of dealing with someone who is different from another culture? How did you react?

(4) What is your opinion about the case study of foreigners and their attitude to wards Chinese hospitality? Having now read this chapter, how might you deal with this?

Exercises

(1) Compare the cultural dimensions of China with another country (see Figure 4.1). If you were doing business with someone from another country, such as Canada or Japan, develop a list of 4 issues that you might need to be careful about, when approaching that person.

(2) Describe one situation where someone from China might react differently from someone from the United States. Use your experience from television, the Internet, email, travels, business or education abroad as the basis for that comparison.

Chapter 5

Getting the Best from Communication Technologies in Business

LEARNING OBJECTIVES

On completing this chapter, you should be able to:

- Understand the benefits and challenges of evolving communication technologies.
- Recognize the risks of ineffective use of tools such as email and SMS messaging systems, smart phones, social media and Internet-based videoconferencing and threats to communication when using supporting technology.
- Get the best out of emails, Internet videoconferencing, social media and mobile phones in business communication.
- Understand the role of communication technologies in effective communication.
- Know how to use supporting technology for effective presentations.

Study Case：I see What You're Saying

At the 1964 World's Fair in Brooklyn, AT&T introduced the picturephone, claiming that within a few years millions would embrace the device and society would be forever changed. Today, more than 50 years later, that has not yet happened, partly because of cost and partly because of the shaky video of the tiny screen and the out-of-sync audio. Another reason is psychological, having to do with the privacy.

As Kurt Scherf, a market researcher says, "People do not want to have to worry about combing their hair or changing out of their pajamas just to answer the phone." In fact, a study by AT&T found that people took an average of 11 rings to answer a videophone call—perhaps because they were tidying up their desk or personal appearance before answering.

Also, it is unlikely that you will be able to multitask—such as sifting through e-mail, folding laundry, or scanning the newspaper—while talking to someone who is watching your every move.

However, for telecommuters, grandparents with faraway grandkids, and anyone who wants to establish or maintain a long-distance personal relationship, the newer videophones may provide an acceptable substitute for face-to-face conversations.

While webcams have been around for years, their images are small and jerky. Plus, both parties have to be sitting in front of a computer to communicate. Because videophones have their own monitors, they can be used from anywhere. And the quality is such that visual cues such as eye contact, smiles, nods, winks, blushes, and other nonverbal communication appear natural and true.

Telephone plays vital roles in business. No wonder, then, that communicating effectively by telephone is a critical managerial skill, one that becomes increasingly important as the need for instantaneous information increase. Your telephone demeanor may be taken by the caller as the attitude of the entire organization. In this chapter, we will learn how to communicate effectively by use of the technologies.

5.1 The Opportunities and Challenges of Communication Technology Use

The evolving development of Internet-enabled technologies, such as tablets, iPads, smart phones, social media systems such as Tencent's WeChat and QQ, software programs such as Microsoft Office, and mobile apps have changed the way we communicate. We can now work with those in the office next door as well as those in an office on the other side of the world. We can now communicate through various media on the Internet: via email, video and audio conferencing, social media and SMS. We also can connect with others through many supporting platforms, such as language translation, data bases, voice and visual images and graphic displays.

These technologies are readily available, while the use of them is both an opportunity and a danger. This chapter provides some guidance towards the using and misusing of communication technologies. It will cover effective business communication via one to one and group interaction and in virtual teams, through the very important business tool of the world-wide web, social media channels of communication, smart phone use, email and the use of technology to enhance your presentations.

5.1.1 The history of our communication technologies

Before we start to consider the rules that might guide us on using communication technologies, a reminder of their quick pace of change will alert us to why getting the best use from them can be challenging. While businesses have been using the written and spoken words for centuries and have developed many agreed patterns of behavior for their use in business, many communication technologies are so comparatively new that they have been absorbed into our business practice like experiments without guidelines. With the convergence of technologies such as smart phones and world-wide web, SMS, WeChat and tablets, many of the differences between public and business communication and personal communication are often difficult to separate. This poses particular challenges for professional business communication, reputation, communication overload and security.

Figure 5.1 provides a brief historical overview of technology firsts. You may be surprised by how quickly communication technologies have evolved.

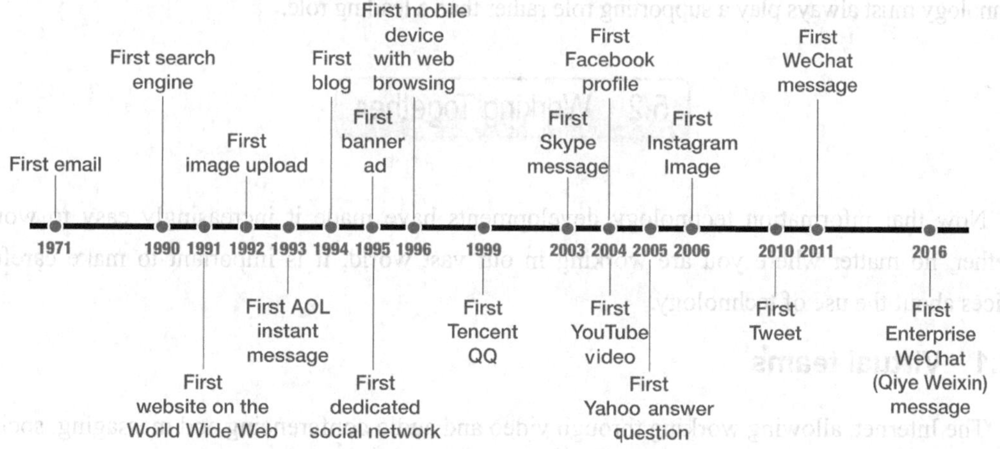

Figure 5.1 Timeline: Communication Technology Firsts

5.1.2 Principles of communication and professionalism

The easy availability of evolving and new technologies can lead to both good use and their misuse as business communication. No matter how many technologies we have at our disposal, it is important to remember that the principles of effective communication remain the same. They could be summarized in 10 simple ideas.

(1) Good communication is all about audience, audience, and audience.

(2) An effective business communicator develops a professional identity and reputation that instills confidence in those with whom he is communicating.

(3) A professional communicator ensures that there is a clear separation between his personal and business identity, and communication.

(4) A good communicator is always working on building a relationship between himself and the readers/viewers/listeners.

(5) Communication is like watching television serials where each new message builds on those that have gone before it.

(6) A good communicator grabs and maintains the attention of his readers/viewers/listeners.

(7) Key messages must always be clear.

(8) Too much information clutters a message.

(9) A good communicator always structures his messages to help the readers/viewers/listeners understand the ideas.

(10) A good communicator is above all a good listener who monitors feedback to adapt his messages.

With these principles in mind, any use of communication technology must therefore be strategic and support effective communication rather than show off the wonders of the technology. Just as there are leading and supporting actors on a stage, there are appropriate roles for the sender, that is, the human source of ideas, and the technology such as the machines and software that are used as a helper. Technology must always play a supporting role rather than a leading role.

5.2 Working Together

Now that information technology developments have made it increasingly easy to work together, no matter where you are working in our vast world, it is important to make careful choices about the use of technology.

5.2.1 Virtual teams

The Internet, allowing working through video and audio conferencing and messaging, social media and email, is at the disposal of the 21st century teams. In the past, it was likely that communication amongst employees dispersed across local, national and international offices was infrequent, confined often to an annual conference or occasional training sessions. Now, virtual teams of employees working in different locations, whether they are in different cities, different regions or in different countries, can communicate on a regular basis. This means that business-to-business and department-to-department communication occurs not just among leaders, but also among employees at every level, and in increasingly frequent and varied ways.

5.2.2 Digital Convergence

Digital convergence—linking mobile phones and Internet services such as websites, social media and message systems and payment systems.

With the increasing use of e-commerce in China, the role of websites is increasingly important as a window to the services, culture and branding of companies. Careful choices must be made about the image a company projects, user-friendly access, and coordination with other communication technologies like social media and email to drive customers to the site. All these need to work together to achieve successful business outcomes. China leads the world in its use of online shopping, followed by India and Singapore in Asia. Equally, poor communication choices can damage the reputation of an organization when instant complaints can be shared on social media.

A recent report by Tencent Inc., creator of social media platforms WeChat (discussed in more detail below under Social Media) and QQ, reported that 30% of China's on-line shoppers make impulsive purchases and that product recommendations in social media are more persuasive than traditional advertisements.

The digital convergence of smart phones with such services as WeChat payment supports the role of surfing the Internet where customers have almost endless choices. The glue that holds business strategies together is excellent business communication to capture attention, guide and structure purchasers' experience to achieve the outcomes sought by businesses. Intranet sites for organizations are also an increasingly important part of business communication strategies. They allow employees to seek out the information they want quickly and easily and communicate internally, they are empowered, and efficiency is achieved.

Airbnb

One innovative organization that uses both its Internet and its intranet to bring its users together is the global online accommodation service Airbnb. Airbnb has been so successful that it is possible to search for accommodation in many countries and diverse cities and rural locations throughout the world. The company relies on small private operators to provide reasonable-cost accommodation for travellers in their homes, in units or in stand-alone houses. Airbnb has structured its user-friendly service through its website and messaging service to allow customers to find their own accommodation from the extensive range offered, to negotiate bookings and arrival arrangements, and to provide feedback on the service offered. This feedback is cumulative and determines the "star" rating of any accommodation based on quality, location and host's enthusiasm. All this information then provides later customers with details that allow them to make decisions. Additionally, Airbnb also allows operators to provide feedback on customers on its intranet site. The feedback is then published for other operators to ensure that quality customers are welcomed in the future. So the reputation of both operators and customers is important. This almost instant assessment of operators and customers ensures that quality communication and behavior are achieved to suit both customers and operators. The reputation of Airbnb is powerfully enhanced.

In all these circumstances above, attention to coordinating internal and external business communication is critical to the success of the 21st century businesses.

5.2.3 Social media—WeChat

The most popular Chinese social media, WeChat, developed by Tencent, has been chosen by the Chinese government for its citizens and has continued to grow and develop since its introduction in 2011. With 700 million monthly users in 2016 (Tencent Research Report, WeChat Impact Report), social media such as WeChat plays a critical role in connecting people and sharing information and ideas in a continuous and free-flowing way, mostly not mediated by journalists, governments and organizations.

By providing text-messaging, hold-to-talk voice messaging, broadcast (one-to-many) messaging, video-conferencing, videogames, sharing of photographs and videos and location as well as its payment system, WeChat creates opportunities for employees to solve business problems as well as keep in touch with family and friends.

Research conducted by Tencent (Tencent Research Report, WeChat Impact Report, 2016) highlights the growing importance of WeChat in the everyday lives of its users. Currently, WeChat users are reported to:

- Spend more than 100 RMB per month on WeChat (70% of users).
- Watch WeChat news more than both news websites and TV combined.
- Open WeChat more than 10 times per day (61% of users).
- Check Moments each time when they open WeChat (61.4% of users).
- Work in corporations (40.4%).

WeChat offers speedy, efficient communication for business and private use. The 3 top reasons for using it, according to Tencent's study, are value (usefulness), interest and emotional connection. This is both strength and a potential danger.

Tencent (and many businesses) recognized the potential risks of mixing private and business use, and in 2016, introduced the more secure service for business, WeChat Enterprise. Evidence of the risks to business of the lack of separation between public and private life is that 72% of official accounts have been registered through a business entity (Tencent Research Report, WeChat Impact Report, 2016). The core reasons for businesses to operate accounts are to:

- Increase internal management and communication efficiency.
- Make system management improvements.
- Enhance corporate efficiency.

In order to increase internal communication and cooperation, the range of opportunities available throughout WeChat must be used carefully and strategically.

Guidelines for Effective Use of WeChat

(1) Ensure that you consider whether your messages are professional or private in nature. The appropriate tone and style are critical to success in every case.

(2) If for business, ensure that your language choices and information are suitable to protect the reputation and security of your business. Avoid slang.

(3) If private, remember that messages that are sent on WeChat represent you over time. Each message accumulates an image of you and so your reputation is at risk each time you press send.

(4) Be selective when deciding to whom to send your messages—to a group or an individual. As with email, receivers can experience overload if they are bombarded with too much information.

(5) After writing a message, read through it from the reader's perspective to ensure that you are clear and concise and do not cause offence.

5.3 Using Email Communication

5.3.1 Principles

World-wide email use also continues to grow at a healthy pace. A 2015 research report (The Radicarti Group) on email and mobile email use suggests that the number of email users in 2015 was 2.6 billion, with an anticipated 2.9 billion by 2019, this being over one third of the world's population. This means that now we can often resolve issues quickly with our ability to quickly connect with colleagues in our office, and all over the nation, and indeed the world. It has also increased pressure on employees and managers to read large numbers of emails daily, to find answers to requests and problems more quickly than previously, and to spend a significant proportion of the day online.

There are many advantages of using email. It is fast, relatively cheap and often makes others accessible to us where we would previously have found difficulty connecting. We are also accessible to others. Accessibility increases our sense of empowerment because it provides a communication channel to share ideas and opinions with people across the organization, not just with an immediate line manager. For example, Richard Branson, CEO of the Virgin Group (airlines, music stores and numerous other service businesses) is proud to claim that he receives about 70 letters (via email) each week from his staff and that he responds (often via an electronic newsletter) to their suggestions and concerns.

However, this accessibility is both an opportunity and a challenge. With accessibility can come information overload. This is because email writers are able to use the copy/paste functions of their software to send large amounts of unedited text to many people, can add an email address very easily to a list and can also confuse the somewhat less formal qualities of email with conversation.

Also, with an increasing use of mobile phones to access emails, many users read even less of their longer emails as it is difficult to do so on a mobile phone. All of these tendencies lead to problems for the sender and the reader. Large amounts of text on the screen can be difficult to scan for the significant information, and key points are often simply 'not read' past the first few lines, and even worse, some emails are never opened.

The case below is about a series of emails used for planning and laying out the details of two upcoming events that a small team of university and business people were arranging for a training program for the employees in a company. Here it is.

Letter 1

July 10

Dear Mr. Chen,

Ann and I met today to finalize the mentor program for our August event. Everything is organized.

As for the September 13 event, can you and the rest of the committee organize the speakers and invite them? I'm sure Mr. Wei will get the invitation ready. If we know by August 1, I can overview it, or if not, you can give the final approval.

If you organize the September event, I will do the August 23 event—I'm waiting on a confirmation from the Employee Club.

Mary

Letter 2

July 15

The response

Mary,

Thank you for all of your hard work. The mentoring program looks to be progressing really well. I will call a committee meeting early next week to plan the speakers for the September event and will hopefully have the names of yourself and Mr. Liu.

Thank you once again.

Mr. Chen

August 2

Mary received another email from Mr. Chen expressing concern that she (Mary) had not yet made arrangements for the September 13 event. Mary emailed Chen saying that she was puzzled by this response. Mary then resent her original exchange emails above.

Letter 3

August 10

Mr. Chen,

I am forwarding the emails from our exchange of early July.

I will organize for invitations to be sent today.

Regards!

Mary

Mary then received this response from Mr. Chen.

Letter 4

Mary,

Obviously, I did get this email and in the very hectic work and life balance that I am trying to cope with, I have not taken the detail from this email. I am willing to admit that this is my mistake.

Mr. Chen

ACTIVITY FOR LEARNING

Can you see what happened here? Clearly, Mr. chen was busy at the time that he received the first email in July and simply overlooked all but the first sentence outlining the arrangements for the first event. He did not read carefully enough to notice Mary's request to organize the September meeting.

This is the communication challenge of email. With so many emails coming at us, we often don't give priority to the details of them or attention they deserve. This means that we have to think about whether email is the right medium for the specific task and whether we can adequately communicate the significance and meaning of the message to the recipient.

Remember that we remember up to 70% of what we see and hear, but only 10% of what we read.

Therefore, the challenges of the writing of email are as follows:

- Email contains limited non-verbal codes.
- Making the key messages stand out can be difficult.
- Email does not allow immediate feedback and clarification like face-to-face communication does.
- Email is sometimes not read because of reader overload or inattention.
- Email communication lacks the richness of sensory inputs that face-to-face communication has. We only see it.
- Even the addition of emoticons such as a smiley face does not make email a rich source of communication.
- Email is sometimes not delivered to the intended reader because of technical difficulties.

5.3.2 When should I not send an email

There are many subjects that are too sensitive to discuss over email mainly because misinterpretation could have serious consequences. Some topics that should generally be discussed outside of email are:

- Disciplinary action.
- Conflicts about grades or personal information.
- Concerns about fellow classmates/workmates.
- Complaints.

When it appears that a dialogue has turned into a conflict, it is best to suggest an end to the swapping of email and for you to talk or meet in person.

5.3.3 Guidelines for effective email for business communication

(1) Make a conscious choice to use an email. Consider whether email is the right medium for the particular message. Perhaps a phone call or letter might be more effective.

(2) Use a clear, striking seeking subject line that gives the reader a good reason to notice and then want to read the email.

(3) Keep your email focused on the specific purpose.

(4) Develop a clear structure for the email. For example, number or letter the points for reference in replies and use headings to help scanning. Also, leave a space after each key aspect to help the reader.

(5) Have a concluding paragraph with action required of the reader listed.

(6) Write in a somewhat formal style that is business-like. Some personalization is appropriate but remember that email is considered an official medium in many countries and subject to legal constraints in a court of law. An email also represents your organization and so reflects on it as well as on you. So, avoid any defamatory or offensive messages.

(7) Use emoticons with care.

(8) After writing an email, read through it from the reader's perspective.

(9) Think about all of the audiences who might receive the email via a "cc" or to whom it

may be passed on.

(10) Proof your email before sending.

(11) Let a difficult message sit for at least 24 hours before you send it. Sometimes, just writing the email helps you to reduce your annoyance with a situation and it may be that, 24 hours later, you wish to tone down your message.

5.4 Balancing the Use of Smart Phones and Face-to-Face Communication

Mobile telephone use is increasing, and, like email communication, makes us readily accessible to clients and co-workers. Care needs to be taken to communicate professionally for business when on your phone, making a shift away from the informal and personal styles using abbreviations and slang commonly acceptable in private communication. Because messages send via smart phones are often short and omit detail, you also need to follow up at a suitable time with clear, more detailed information to ensure that your clients or fellow employees are clear on your message.

While mobile phones are very useful, they can also be disruptive. It is very important to be aware when it is or is not appropriate to use your mobile phone. For example, think carefully about whether your current conversation is less or more important than a phone-call you receive during the conversation. Unless you are sure that the phone-call is more important, consider the damage to your relationship with a current conversational partner when you interrupt the conversation to take a call.

Some Guidelines for Mobile Phone Use

(1) Consider whether face-to-face or mobile phone use is the best option for the communication event.

(2) Switch off your mobile phone or mute when attending a meeting or a presentation.

(3) Never answer a call at the meeting table. Always move to a quieter place, but preferably leave the call until the meeting or presentation is over.

(4) Do not check your mobile phone for calls during a conversation. Give those in the room full attention while you are together.

(5) When calling, always check first that the recipient of your call is able to and willing to speak. E.g. after the greeting, ask: "Is this a suitable time to speak with you?"

(6) Use the active listening strategy of summarizing what you have agreed before finishing the call.

5.5 Developing Effective Presentations

5.5.1 Principles and guidelines

The first section of this chapter discussed the many and varied ways to communicate with your audience when you have the challenges of being unable to interact face-to-face. Using communication technology can be a most effective and efficient way to communicate. However, we need to keep in mind at all times that if we have been asked by the audience to present our ideas face-to-face, the alternative of simply delivering a technology dominated presentation (such as a written report or a set of PowerPoint slides) is not the preferred option of the audience. They want you to talk to them about your ideas or proposals. They want a presentation where your interpersonal qualities will be evident. This may be because they need to understand you and the personality of your company and the people in it, or because they want the chance to ask you questions and get clarifications of ideas. Either way, the most important part of this type of presentation is you, not the technology.

5.5.2 Misusing technology

Presenters must not allow these potentially helpful tools, the technologies available to us, to divert us from what we are trying to achieve—good communication. The wonders of technology must not drive our communication. It will undoubtedly support and probably even influence and shape some aspects of our communication. But being aware that the new technologies are our servants but not our masters should act as a brake to keep control of how we use them.

Some of the most difficult decisions to make, when preparing presentations, are choices about which of the many exciting aids to use. One option is to use them all. The result will probably be to provide a barrage of ideas and possibilities, but the message will most likely be lost because the key messages are not clear. For example, the authors once watched a presentation where the speaker decided to use video footage and played it while talking to the audience. Of course, as an audience, we were unsure whether to listen to the speaker or watch the video. My response was to switch to the speaker most of the time, but suddenly I would see something interesting on the screen and start watching it, missing the points being made by the speaker! Such a missed opportunity for the speaker.

Despite these warnings, we are not suggesting that a technology-focused presentation is not useful. There are many occasions when this type of presentation will be the perfect choice. It is simply a matter of determining what the purposes and the objectives of your presentation are and then using the technology to support your personal presentation style and purpose.

5.5.3 Using technology effectively

Generally, your personal credibility is central to an effective presentation. You have the opportunity to bring your personality to the presentation because a "faceless" idea, covered by technology, may give the listeners a sense of unease and disconnection from you and your ideas. Instead, you want to bring the "hot" body to the presentation, not the "cold" technology. So, careful planning is very useful.

> One of the very interesting examples of effective communication technology choices was about the media tycoon Rupert Murdoch of Foxtel and Sky television. Rupert Murdoch, Chairman and Chief Executive of News Corporation, one of the largest media empires in the world, launched his five-year plan for his corporation. This speech was delivered live in London and transmitted via satellite to New York, Los Angeles and Sydney.
>
> Murdoch used the capabilities of our new technologies extensively. He clearly understood, though, that while he had the expertise and resources of his innumerable media institutions at his disposal, the credibility of his organization rested on him, not on a faceless institution. He responded to this knowledge by giving an imaginatively constructed and well-planned presentation. He was supported by a large video screen forming a backdrop (in fact, in Sydney his image was relayed to two full-size screens).
>
> The presentation outlined his plans for the next five years. The speech was introduced by a sophisticated, highly theatrical audio-visual presentation of the exciting possibilities for the future.
>
> Murdoch also interviewed a famous science fiction writer, Arthur C. Clarke, as part of the presentation. Murdoch wanted to demonstrate that he was a trailblazer and visionary thinker like his hero sci-fi writer Arthur C. Clarke who was ahead of his time in imagining new technologies.
>
> (Source: McCarthy P, Hatcher C. *Speaking Persuasively: The Essential Guide to Giving Dynamic Presentations and Speeches*[M]. Sydney: Allen & Unwin, 2002.)

Communication technologies add impact to your presentation and maintain audience concentration if used effectively. A study by the US-based Wharton School has found that the supporting technologies that you use can directly influence how your audience perceives you. You will be perceived as more professional than those who do not use such supporting aids, if you are careful in your choices. Complementing your speech with visual aids seems to be well worth the effort, according to this research. The Wharton School research claims that people remember:

- 10 percent of what they read.
- 20 percent of what they hear.
- 30 percent of what they see.

- 70 percent of what they see and hear.

With this research in mind, here are some tips on a range of strategies to make the most of what you want to say. Technologies such as electronic presentations using Microsoft PowerPoint and others on the market, images available from the Internet and of your own creation, videos developed by others and of your own productions, and audio recordings such as music can add strong interest to your presentations.

5.5.4 Deciding when to use visual support

There are some specific times when visual aids help you to explain your ideas and times when they distract the audience.

Here are some tips to help you to decide if you need visual support.

(1) Complex information can be easier to understand and remember if your oral presentation is supported by visual patterns and text.

The human mind cannot take in details in the way a computer can. Graphs, lists and tables can help the listeners to visualize the patterns while your voice focuses on the key arguments. Remember though, that it is not enough to just show the graphs or images. You need to direct your listeners' attention to the aspects of the graphs or image that are important to the argument.

(2) All good presentations have a theme or an image that reflects the important message. Create a visual display of the theme or image. For example, you may use a theme like "partnering with our clients" and place it on the footer of every PowerPoint slide along with your business's logo. Or, one slide may carry an image of your special "team" approach to do business. It could be an image of an outstretched hand or a scene from a team meeting.

Sometimes it is really quite difficult to describe some ideas by words. An image can instantly draw attention to an idea and repetition can be a subtle persuasive device to emphasize a point.

(3) Photographs, videos and soundtracks help you to bring the outside world into your audience's view. Photographs, videos or soundtracks from real places and events can help the audience to visualize the issues, the complexities and the challenges. The audiences love short, high-impact videos and clear photographs. The Internet is a wonderful source for these resources. Be sure to acknowledge any sources that you use.

Relationship building can be strengthened when your audience relaxes and laughs with you. Humor adds to your immediacy (or strength of personal impact on the audience) and you may find an illustration or a cartoon that will help you to draw attention to the challenges ahead, for example, in a humorous way.

5.5.5 Desktop presentation software

One of the most impressive developments in computer technology is the introduction of many new software packages. These help you to create a professional look for your visual aids.

For example, Microsoft PowerPoint is a frequently used software package, designed to give you the opportunity to create text, color graphics, matching diagrams and graphs, and clip art with a unified theme. However, there are many other software packages in the evolving communication technology market. For example, the new drone technology and its innovative software are adding new and exciting ways to incorporate images of people and places to bring national and international communities together.

You have a great deal of flexibility with this type of software because you are able to develop a number of slides or sequences for a particular audience and then you can alter the screens or change the sequence to suit another audience with different needs. For example, for some audiences you might want to add a number of tables and graphs because you know that they are a technical group who would not be satisfied without seeing survey results. Another audience, less technically oriented, might prefer just to see a summary of those results. You can delete and substitute and even change the background to suit the audience without starting all over again.

Visual support packages such as PowerPoint can assist the speaker to further extend their information-sharing by integrating support material into a presentation. For example, you can add hyperlinks to Internet sites, visit a particular site to show how a service or product works, and then return to your main screen and so create a seamless professional presentation.

With the aid of this sort of software, you can set up a slide show that can be timed to match your oral message, or set to run continuously if you are doing a product demonstration. However, we advise you to avoid this feature unless you are absolutely confident that your timing will be perfect. It leaves no room for error if your timing goes astray, and often leaves the speaker looking a little silly and the listeners confused because the text does not match the speaker's ideas.

Being determined to keep your sights on the communication of the message to the audience in front of you as the driving force of the presentation. One feature of these packages that can be misused is the automatic organizer template. In the case of PowerPoint, it is called "Auto Content Wizard". This feature attempts to think for you and is designed to help you to create a structure for your presentation by giving a range of speech outlines to get you started with a presentation.

We recommend that you avoid this type of template feature of packages and focus on developing your own outline with detailed attention to the specifics of your situation, your listeners, and your purpose. By using someone else's solution to your problem, your own creativity will be limited and you are more likely to miss thinking about your special audience for the presentation. Allowing technology to drive your presentation is rather like getting on a bus and hoping that the driver will tell you where to get off.

Audience "paralysis" is a grave danger when using this sort of software to support your presentation. If you have too many slides and/or too much text, you will put your audience to sleep. Avoid making the rhythm of a slide presentation too regular and too full of information. If you speak for 2 minutes on each slide for example and without any slides to emotionally connect the audience, your audience will lose concentration.

On the other hand, if you think creatively about different ways to share your ideas—through images, text, and sound—you will keep your audience interested. Change the pace, and add variety by incorporating activity (perhaps a handout or a question and answer section). If you help your audience to understand your ideas and engage them emotionally, you will create the sort of impact that will lead them to remember what you have said.

5.5.6 Music, visuals and voice-over

Music can provide a touch of magic to a presentation or remind the audience of some popular or familiar idea. Voice-overs and music can add to your message to provide variety and support to your own voice. A piece of music at the start or finish of a presentation can help you grab the attention of the audience and give focus to your ideas. For example, using a voice-over with gentle background music during a product display can draw in even the really lazy listener.

Always be careful to keep any audio or visual support short and relevant. An audience can quickly lose interest if they think that you are showing them more than they need to see or hear. Audiences don't like to waste their time.

5.5.7 Tips for visual and audio support

Tips for visual and audio support are as follows.

(1) Be selective. Keep it short.

(2) Keep any support material as simple and uncluttered as possible.

(3) Always discuss the aspects of your slide or image; don't just show it and hope the listener will fill in the details.

(4) Choose a few powerful aids rather than aiming for a complex visual presentation that takes your energy and the audience's focus away from your message.

(5) Make sure that your videos are short and relevant. Two-to-three-minute videos highlighting the key points are more effective than longer ones.

(6) Videos to set the scene or to explain a key point are very powerful.

(7) Become familiar with the facilities in a venue so that you can use them effectively.

(8) Rehearse your presentation with all your planned aids. Practice with all the aspects to avoid surprises such as a website hyperlink problem that you are not expecting.

(9) Check hyperlinks immediately before the presentation to ensure the link is available on the day.

(10) Have a contingency plan in case of technology failure. Keep control of the situation and your nerves if things go wrong with the technology, and remember that your message is the driving force of the presentation, not the other way round. The audience come to hear you, not your slide show or video. So, know your material well.

There are also some useful general guidelines for developing effective text, videos and graphs.

(1) Keep your visual aids truly visual. Large chunks of text are distracting to the audience. Limit your text to three or four points at most with short sentences or phrases.

(2) Keep fonts and layout consistent.

(3) Remember that a picture is worth a thousand words. Graphs and images focus your audience on the key ideas and you can use them to simplify the key messages. Keep them as simple and as attention-seeking as you can.

(4) Be consistent with color. Develop a color and pattern theme for each presentation. If you are creating a simple chart, use only about three colors: one for background, one for headings and highlighting, and one for the text itself. For graphs, use no more than five colors. Too much color is distracting and confuses the eyes. Use dark colors on a light background or vice versa.

(5) Use software features to animate graphical information, building data piece by piece. This will tell a story and so help your audience to focus on the key messages.

Careful, creative and effective use of communication technology has the potential to enrich your presentations and give impact to your messages. The tips above are important reminders of how to get the best out of this age of technology innovations.

ACTIVITY FOR LEARNING

Plan a presentation about a topic you feel confident about. Do your audience analysis (see Chapter 3). Make the plan for one identified audience. Once you have finished this plan, choose another audience— for example a more senior group or different professional group. Repeat the audience analysis. Adapt the speech to meet the different needs of the second audience. Compare the two speeches. Have you met the needs of each audience?

Read the case study below to learn how one team develop a presentation that tells their story effectively, using communication technology.

A team of traffic planners were preparing for a conference presentation on a bridge development project where an old decaying bridge and a new bridge stood side by side. They had proposed an innovative solution to a traffic problem, a solution which was good for traffic but also maintained the local community's desire to keep a special fishing and recreation spot around the old bridge. The team wished to share this innovative strategy through a presentation to other engineers and planners.

They started out with 23 text slides and 3 photographs for a 20-minute presentation.

We helped them to improve their use of supporting technology, using the guidelines listed above. Here are the questions we asked the team to help them to choose wisely.

(1) What do you really want to say here—what are your key messages?

(2) What level of detail do you need for the audience?

(3) How will you show the audience from all over the country what the site is like and what the issues are?

(4) How will you show them that the solution worked?

Using these questions as a framework, the team gradually clarified their goals. They determined that they needed to somehow show that the site had a history that needed to be maintained, that the traffic problem was quite challenging, and that the community interests needed to be served while keeping costs reasonable.

They came up with two themes of "balancing community and traffic needs" and "managing costs". With these two themes in mind, they looked for ways to show the history of the site, the complexities of the traffic situation and the technical aspects of building the solution. They found a 1935 press announcement and a photograph from a local paper about the old bridge and used visual images of the old and current bridge with traffic displays from a report they had written. These images became the central drivers of the presentation.

The team then worked through their original 23 text slides, selecting the detail they needed to support their key arguments, reducing the text on each slide to conform to the rules about the number of points and amount of text per slide, and placing a few key points on the images to increase impact.

The final strategy was to use the photograph of the successful design as both the opening and the closing slide to give the presentation a sense of unity.

The result was a presentation with 19 slides, 10 of which were images to help explain their ideas and reinforce their arguments, rather than just lists of points on a screen. The conference presentation went very well for the team, and many of the audience told them how much they had enjoyed the presentation.

Summary

Now that so many communication technologies are available to every business person, the challenge is to use them well rather than indiscriminately. It is true that these technologies should enhance good communication. However, communication technologies are only technologies, only when people use technologies properly, they will give full play to its function. Communication technologies are not a substitute for effective communication planning. There is no guarantee that a particular communication technology will help. It is up to you, as a strategic communicator, to ensure that you are clear about what you want to say, that you choose the right technology for the situation, and that the technology is used to help you to communicate in the most effective way possible to the audience that you are speaking with. Technology should be your servant, not your master!

Questions for Discussion

(1) What are some of the advantages of using technology for your presentations?

(2) What are the dangers of using technology for your presentations?

(3) Describe the best and most high-impact use of technology that you have seen in a presentation. Why was it effective?

(4) Discuss the advantages and disadvantages of email communication. Describe a time when you used email and it was successful. Explain why.

(5) Discuss the advantages of using WeChat to communicate in business. Which type of WeChat service could be useful? Why? For whom?

(6) What is your preferred communication technology? For private use? For business use? Why?

Exercises

Using a presentation topic that has been set for your class, plan a presentation that uses images, text and a short video or audio track. Write a series of questions about your presentation, like the ones above in the case study on the traffic presentation and based on the guidelines provided.

Now check whether your technology choices match the goals that you have set.

Part 3
Written Communication in Business

Chapter 6

Guidelines for Management Communication Writing

LEARNING OBJECTIVES

On completing this chapter, you should be able to:

- Understand the importance of writing in business.
- Understand some guidelines for writing.
- Know how to make your writing easy to read.

Study Case：When Words Hurt

In the summer of 2006, a large, midwestern state university was gearing up to host the first national Special Olympics, a competition featuring people with intellectual disabilities. Visitors would be arriving from all over the country, and the small university town wanted to put on its best face for the crowds. The student newspaper created a 14-page, full-color visitors' guides to the town and inserted it into the campus paper. Unfortunately, they named it "(Name of Town) for Dummies" after the popular book series.

The editor-in-chief quickly apologized for the insensitive word choice, while the newspaper removed the inserts and replaced them with reprinted publications featuring a new headline.

(Adapted from Lisa Rossi, "Olympics Section Goof Sends Paper Running," *Des Moines Register*, July 1,2006,1A,4A)

Analysis：Good business and administrative writing is closer to conservation and less formal than the style of writing that has traditionally earned high marks in college essays and term paper. In this chapter, we will learn how to write clearly and effectively.

With a net worth around $42 billion, Warren Buffett is ranked by *Forbes* magazine as the second richest person in the world, after Microsoft cofounder and Chairman Bill Gates. Buffett made his first stock purchase at the age of 11, but sold before the stock skyrocketed. This early lesson taught him to study hard and carefully to analyze potential investments. The result was the development of one of the world's largest holding companies, Berkshire Hathaway, Inc.

Although best known for his ability to pick stocks, Buffett was honored in 2006 by the National Commission on Writing for America's Families, Schools and Colleges for writing Berkshire Hathaway's annual report. Buffett writes: "One way or another, you have to project your ideas to other people. Writing isn't necessarily easy... But you get better and better at it, and I encourage everybody to do that."

6.1 The Differences Between Oral and Written Communication

Giving a presentation is in many ways very similar to writing a message contained in a letter or report. All of the chapters up to this point—on using "you-attitude" and positive emphasis, developing reader benefits, analyzing your audience, designing sliders, overcoming objections, doing research, and analyzing data—remain as relevant as when you plan an oral presentation.

Developing effective written messages allows you to:

- Present extensive or complex data such as financial data or statistics.
- Present many specific details of a law, policy, or procedure.
- Minimize undesirable emotions by clarifying issues.

- Develop a permanent record of the issues at hand.

Developing effective oral messages allows you to:

- Clarify your key topics and issues.
- Use emotion to help persuade the audience.
- Focus the audience's attention on specific points.
- Answer questions, resolve conflicts and build consensus.
- Modify a proposal that may not be acceptable in its original form.
- Get immediate action or response.
- Adjust your message to the needs of the audience quickly.

Oral and written messages have many similarities. In both, you should:

- Outline your clear goals.
- Adapt the message to the specific audiences.
- Show the audience how they would benefit from the idea, policy, service or product.
- Overcome any objections the audience may have.
- Use you-attitude and positive emphasis.
- Use visuals to clarify or emphasize material.
- Specify exactly what you want the audience to think or do.

An oral presentation needs to be simpler than a written message to the same audience. If the readers forget a point, they can turn back to it and reread the paragraph. With a written message, headings, paragraph indentations, and punctuations provide visual cues to help the readers understand the message and allow them to return to issues that they have forgotten or did not understand. The listeners, in contrast, must remember what the speaker says. Whatever they don't remember is lost. Even asking questions requires the audience to remember which points they don't understand.

6.2 The Importance of Skillful Writing

There are three primary reasons why this book places extra emphasis on writing. First, many experienced business people themselves tend to place writing skills ahead of other communication skills when asked what they seek in job applicants. Second, they seek strong writing skills in particular when considering whom to promote. Third, writing in a language other than your first language has particular challenges. So for you, as an English-as-a-second-language learner, writing is about not only language but also the style and tone appropriate to a business culture across national cultures. For example, in one study, a majority of the 305 executives surveyed commented that fewer than half their job applicants were well-versed enough in "global knowledge, self-direction, and writing skills" to be able to advance in their companies. As people move up, they do more and more knowledge work, and this work often requires the written forms of communication.

Another reason for our strong focus on writing is that, in some ways, it is more difficult to do well in writing than in other kinds of communication. Writing is what researchers call a "learning medium", which means that it does not offer the multiple information cues, feedback, and intense personal focus that face-to-face or even phone conversations offer. Writers essentially have no safety net; they can't rely on their facial expressions, body language, or tone of voice to make up for wording that isn't quite what they mean. The symbols used in writing—the alphabet, words, punctuation, and so forth—share no characteristics with the thing they represent (unless you count words that sound like the sounds they name, such as "buzz"). Capturing a complex reality by putting one word after another requires ingenuity, discipline, and the ability to anticipate how readers will be likely to react as they read.

ACTIVITY FOR LEARNING

Go back to Chapter 1 of this book. Examine the opening paragraphs which describe the skills and abilities that employers are looking for. Now, consider your current skills.

Write a sentence describing your skills as a writer. Go back to some of your recent writing and writing tests. Make a list of the skills that need improvement.

Identify the aspects of writing that you would like to improve. As you read through the rest of Chapter 6, and then Chapters 7 & 8, take special note of those areas and practice those skills especially.

6.3 The Costs of Poor Correspondence

Business Communication Lessons from Mars

The Mars climate orbiter spacecraft lost contact with NASA mission control just after it arrived at Mars.

A subsequent investigation revealed that the main problem was a minor software programming error caused by communication errors. Like many business projects, the Mars climate orbiter involved a wide range of people in a range of locations. The programmers who wrote the software that controlled the spacecraft's engines worked in Great Britain, and used metric measurements in their calculations, while the engineers who made the satellite's engines worked in the United States, and used a standard called English measurements. Both teams assumed that they were using the same measurement standards, neither team made any attempt to check, and no one else caught the error. With that failure, NASA lost a $125 million satellite and one year of effort, while gaining a major public embarrassment.

(Source: NASA MCO Mission Failure Mishap Investigation Board. Mars Climate Orbiter Mishap Investigation Board phase report[C]. 1999, 11-10.)

ACTIVITY FOR LEARNING

What does the case study tell you about the challenges of writing?

Developing good writing skills will add to your employability and attractiveness as a candidate for a successful business career. In the US, in 2004, a survey by the National Commission on Writing found that the ability to write is becoming an important requirement of a successful professional career. Two-thirds of salaried employees in large US companies have to write as part of their work. In fact, up to 80% of sectors assess the writing skills of applicants as part of the hiring process and almost half take writing skills into account when they decide whether or not to promote an employee.

The 2004 study shows that up to 70% of all professional employees prepare reports, memos and other correspondence. Unfortunately, the study also shows that firms have to spend 3–4 million dollars on training their staff to improve their writing skills. Clearly, companies value writing skills because they are important for business success.

When writing isn't as good as it could be, you and your organization pay a price in wasted time, wasted effort, and loss of goodwill.

6.3.1 Wasted time

First, bad writing takes longer time to read as we struggle to understand what we have been reading. Studies show that up to 97% of our reading time is typically taken, not in moving our eyes across the pages, but in trying to understanding what we are reading.

Second, bad writing needs to be rewritten. Many managers find that they spend a considerable amount of their time trying to explain to subordinates how to revise a document.

Third, ineffective writing may obscure ideas so that discussions and decisions are needlessly drawn out. People inside an organization may have different interests and values. But if a proposal is clear, at least everyone will be talking about the same proposed changes, so that differences can be recognized and resolved more quickly.

Fourth, unclear or incomplete messages may require the reader to ask for more information. If the writer is out of the office when the reader stops by or calls, even more time is wasted, for the reader can't act until the answer arrives.

6.3.2 Wasted effort

Ineffective messages seldom get results. A reader who has to guess what the writer means may guess wrongly. A reader who finds a letter or memo unconvincing or insulting simply won't do what the message asks.

6.3.3 Lost goodwill

Whatever the literal content of the words, every letter, memo, or report serves either to build or to undermine the image the reader has of the writer.

Part of building a good image is taking the time to write correctly. Even organizations that have adopted casual dress still expect writing to appear professional and to be free from typographical and grammatical errors.

6.4 Planning Your Writing

Even experienced business communicators sometimes fall prey to the "inspiration fallacy", that is, the belief that wonderful ideas for a business document will come at last to those who wait…and wait… to the last minute before beginning to write.

Managers who want to write well must also focus on planning as the essential first step for any writing project. When managers don't plan, the result is the writer's block—those agonizing minutes or hours when words simply won't "flow", usually because the planning process is missing in action. Alternatively, a lack of careful planning can lead to a disorganized and illogical document.

To avoid such problems, it is an essential step to plan your writing before you start, preferably in note form, but at least mentally. In your plan, six questions related to six key aspects of writing should be taken into account:

- Purpose—what are you trying to communicate?
- Audience—to whom are you writing?
- Exploration—what ideas should you consider?
- Outlines—how can you best arrange your ideas?
- Details and examples—how can you support your points?
- Action step—what do you want the reader to do next?

6.4.1 Purpose: What are you trying to communicate

In order to understand your communication purpose, you should understand the following communication checkpoints:

- What idea are you communicating?
- What do others expect you to accomplish with this communication?
- What do you want your audience to know after your communication?
- What do you want your audience to feel after your communication?
- What do you want your audience to do after your communication?
- What people, other than those in your audience, will be affected by your communication?
- Will this communication serve more than one purpose? Specify the various goals you want to achieve.

Communicating may have various purposes. You may wish to inform, to persuade or to describe your ideas. However, it is important to remember that even when you are describing something to a reader, your selection of ideas to leave in or out of the description and the types of words you choose to describe the ideas will have some persuasive elements in it.

To inform means that you are trying to explain something to your readers or to teach them something new. Writing like this covers many activities: an explanation about the millennium bug which bothered the computer users over the world, a new online procedure that your department is adopting, a report on the financial budget for the next fiscal year, a proposal for a merger between two companies, the opportunities that entrepreneurs in China now have to develop business links with international companies, a talk on the progress of a planned project, etc.

To persuade, on the other hand, means that one or more people are involved in both one-off and on-going interactions that create, modify, reinforce or even change the beliefs, attitudes, intentions, motivations or behaviors of others. Written communication where you will need to use your persuasive skills includes invitations, letters, reports and e-mails.

Writing with a persuasive purpose differs from information sharing in that it aims at changing the reader's beliefs, attitudes or behaviors, or moving them into taking some action. However, as one's beliefs, attitudes, or behaviors do not develop overnight, and you cannot expect the changes to take place all at once no matter how compelling the argument is. What a writer should think about is how to make the writing as persuasive as possible to achieve the most powerful appeal to the reader.

Just as information technology is causing a revolution in almost everything we do and think, so it is prompting an upheaval within organizations. The intellectual capital of an organization is now the pre-eminent source of wealth creation. New human management challenges arise from the demands of working with knowledge. For example, to use an organization's human capital well, a manager must learn to encourage new knowledge to come forward and manage knowledge he or she doesn't understand. To make the most effective use of structural capital such as networks and databases, organizations must free the flow of knowledge and people across traditional organizational boundaries and encourage all employees to share their knowledge.

——Frances Horibe

ACTIVITY FOR LEARNING

Read the case study above carefully. Note how powerfully the writer makes his argument. Notice especially:

(1) Powerful words and phrases.

- revolution; upheaval; pre-eminent source of wealth creation; free the flow of knowledge.

(2) Long and short sentences for impact.

(3) Closing with an action for the readers to complete.

- Encourage all employees to share their knowledge.

6.4.2 Audience: To whom you are writing

The audience for a message—the reader or readers—is often homogeneous: they have similar needs and attitudes. Often, the audience comprises just one person; but even when it doesn't, the audience usually consists of people with similar levels of expertise, background knowledge, and the like. Thus, you are usually able to, and should, develop your message to take account of the needs of your reader.

One way to analyze your audience is to call it a "market analysis". You are analyzing your audience as a market for your message. Once you have analyzed your market, you are ready to design your "product". That is to say, you are ready to tailor your message to your audience. Just as a manufacturer must design a product before deciding how to package the product, you must design your message before you can design your ideas package.

Figure 6.1 illustrates questions for audience analysis which you should consider so that you can have a clear analysis of the audience.

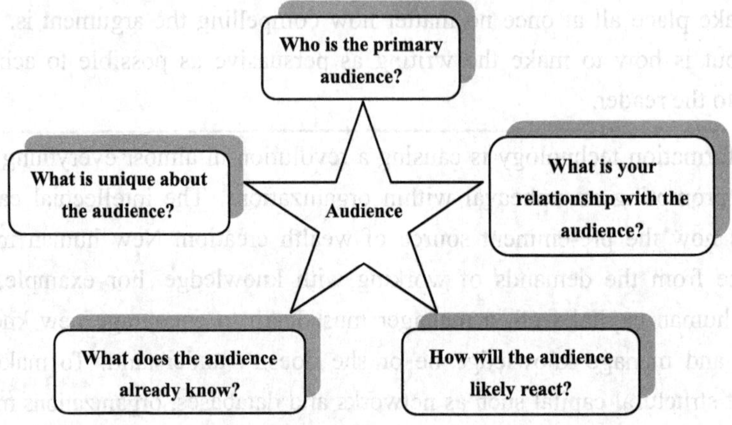

Figure 6.1 Questions for Audience Analysis

(Source: Ober S, Newman A. 商务沟通[M]. 7 版. 北京：清华大学出版社，2013.)

1. Who is your primary or main audience

For much correspondence, the audience is one person, which simplifies the writing challenge immensely. It is much easier to personalize a message addressed to one individual than a message addressed to many individuals. Sometimes, however, you will have more than one audience. In this case, you need to identify your primary audience (the persons whose cooperation is crucial if your message is to achieve its objectives) and then your secondary audience (those who will also read and be affected by your message). If you can't satisfy all of the audiences, try to satisfy the needs of the primary decision makers. Analyze your audience by asking the following questions:

- Who will be affected by what you write?
- What organizational, professional, and personal issues or qualities will affect the

audience's response to your message?

Though you should take time to analyze your audience early in the planning process, you should continue to think of your audience as you proceed through the rest of planning stage of writing and through the drafting and revising stages. Always be thinking about what kind of information will matter most to your audience and adapt your message accordingly. If you fail to meet your audience's needs, your message fails as well, and your professional image is compromised.

2. What is your relationship with the audience

Does your audience know you? If your audience doesn't know you, you will first have to establish your credibility by assuming a reasonable tone and giving enough evidence to support your claims. Are you writing to someone inside or outside the organization? If outside, your message will often be a little more formal and will contain more background information and less jargon than if you are writing to someone inside the organization. What is your status in the organization in relationship to your audience? Communications to your superiors are obviously vital to your success in the organization. Such communications are typically a little more formal, less authoritarian in tone, and more information-filled than communications to peers or subordinates. When you communicate with subordinates, be polite but not patronizing. Try to instill a sense of collaborating and of corporate ownership within your proposal. When praising or criticizing, be specific, and criticize the action—not the person. As always, praise in public but criticize in private.

3. How will the audience likely react

If the reader's initial reaction to both you and your topic is likely to be positive, your job is relatively easy. You can use a direct approach—beginning with the most important information and then supplying the needed details. If the reader's initial reaction is likely to be neutral, you may want to use the first few lines of the message to get the reader's attention and convince him or her that what you have to say is important and that your reasoning is sound. Make sure your message is short and easy to read and that any requested action is easy to take.

Suppose, however, that you expect your reader's reaction—either to your topic or to you personally—to be negative. This is a greater challenge. If the reader shows a personal dislike of you, your best stratagem is to call on external evidence and expert opinion to bolster your opinion. Show that other people whom the reader is likely to know and respect share your opinion or do as you are suggesting.

4. What does the audience already know

Understanding the audience's present grasp of the topic is crucial to making decisions about the content and the writing style. You must decide how much background information is necessary, whether the use of jargon is acceptable, and what readability level is appropriate. If you are writing to multiple audiences, gear the amount of detail to the level of understanding of the key decision makers (the primary audience). In general, it is better to provide too much rather than too little information.

5. What is unique about the audience

The success or failure of a message often depends on little things—the extra touches that say to the reader, "You're important, and I've taken the time to learn something about you." What can you learn about the personal interest or demographic characteristics of your audience that you can build into your message? Is the reader a "take change" kind of person who would prefer to have important information up front—regardless of whether the news is good or bad? What level of formality is expected? Would the reader be flattered or be put off by the use of his or her first name in the salutation? Have good things or bad things happened recently at work or at home that may affect the reader's receptivity to your message?

One of the most relevant demographic measures for writers is the literacy level of the audience. Unfortunately, even in advanced economies, you have to ask how well your audience can read and put information to use. In the United States, the answer may be "not very well".

The National Assessment of Adult Literacy (NAAL), conducted by the US Department of Education, found that 14% of adults had difficulty reading well enough to follow simple instructions (such as when to take medication), 12% struggled to use simple forms (deciding where to sign their name on a form), and 22% had trouble working with numbers. NAAL also found that 5% of adults were non-literate—their language skills weren't strong enough to participate in the assessment.

Overall, that translates into 30 million adults in the United States with "below basic" reading and comprehension levels, and another 63 million with only "basic" literacy level. For business writers, this poses a challenge. When composing a message for a broad audience of employees or customers, you may have to use short sentences, simple words, and clarifying graphics. What other techniques might you use to ensure that audiences with lower literacy levels can understand and use your message?

(Source: Kutner M, Greenberg E, Baer J. *A first look at the literacy of America's adults in the 21st century*[J]. National Center for Education Statistics: 2006, 28.)

6. Exploration: What ideas should you consider?

Once you have determined the purpose of your message and you have analyzed your audience, you are ready to design your message for your audience. This means that you must come up with the ideas that communicate your message to your audience. In many cases, this research can be informal—finding past correspondence; consulting with other employees or with outside advisors; getting sales records, warranties, websites, and product descriptions; and so forth. Such a personal investigation usually requires knowledge of your field of work, which is probably why you were assigned the problem. In other cases, you will do more formal research such as conducting surveys or an experiment. The experiment is a basic technique of science. Business uses experiments primarily in the laboratory, although experiments have some non-laboratory application in marketing. Surveys are more likely to be used in business, especially in solving marketing problems.

In some cases, you may use library and online research to find the information you need. Perhaps you have a good working knowledge of the techniques of research. To present facts from published sources in reports, you will need to use still other techniques: constructing a bibliography, citing references, quoting, paraphrasing, and so on. In any event, your task is to apply whatever research techniques are required to get the information you need for your problems.

The next major stage of the writing process is to interpret the information you've gathered. You had to interpret the elements of the situation to come up with your conception of the problem in the writing. You also had to interpret your data as you were gathering them to make sure that you were getting appropriate and sufficient information. But when your research is finished, you will need to come up with the interpretations that will guide the shape and contents of your writing. Your findings will need to apply clearly to the given problems in order to be viewed as logical solutions. But they will need to meet the reader's needs in order to be viewed as relevant and helpful.

7. Outlines: How can you best arrange your ideas?

Almost all professional business writers use some sort of outline early in the writing process. The business writer's outline is often like a rough working framework, which allows the writer to put the ideas into some logical sequence. A good one will show what things go together (grouping), what order they should follow (ordering), and how the ideas relate in terms of the level of generality (hierarchy).

1) Why should you need outline

If you use an outline, you will begin to write clearly because an initial written outline maps quite fully your main points and sub-points, placing them in order. Like builders following a blueprint, writers need clear outlines to write efficiently. When points in an outline are expanded to full or even partial sentences, much of the hard work of drafting is already over. The major phrases you've written in your outline grow into headings and topic sentences in the first draft. By filling in details, examples, definitions, and explanations, you quickly build an organized, coherent first draft.

2) Outline formulization

Once the topic is selected, the next thing to do is to formulize an outline under the topic. It is true that outlining takes time. However, you will find it pays off when you start your writing according to your formulized outline.

The outline usually starts with some rough ideas, i.e. ideas that have some relevance to the topic, yet are not well thought over or checked. However, such rough ideas are important in that they can give the writer a starting point to make a better version.

In constructing your outline, you can use any systems of numbering of formatting that will help you see the logical structure of your planned contents. If it will help, you can use the conventional or the decimal symbol system to mark the levels. The conventional system uses Roman numerals to show the major heading and letters of the alphabet and Arabic numerals to show the lesser heading, as illustrated here.

First One: *Conventional System*

Ⅰ. First-level heading

A. Second level, first part

B. Second level, second part

1. Third level, first part

2. Third level, second part

a. Fourth level, first part

(1) Fifth level, first part

Second One: *Decimal System*

1 First-level heading

1.1 Second level, first part

1.2 Second level, second part

1.2.1 Third level, first part

1.2.2. Third level, second part

1.2.2.1 Fourth level, first part

1.2.2.1.1 Fifth level, first part

Bear in mind that an outline is a tool for you, even though it is based on your reader's needs. Use it in any way that will help you write a good document such as a report or a letter.

Suppose you want to make an informative speech—to talk about electronic commerce. You have got some ideas to use such as Internet development, buying and selling over Internet, e-commerce and its safety, business online, etc. Very quickly you have jotted them down for fear of forgetting them. These ideas are what we call "original ideas".

The ideas you jotted down on electronic commerce are good ideas, but they are not sufficient to be made into an outline for good writing. What the writer should do now is to develop some new ideas on the basis of the very first two or three ideas, and then get them organized. In fact, such a process is more or less like rolling a snowball—starting with a handful of snow and it gets bigger and bigger as you roll it on.

Here is the example of expanded outline under the title of electronic commerce.

1 Introduction: the development of Internet and e-commerce

2 The advantage of e-commerce

2.1 Convenience—24-hour open service

2.2 More opportunities for comparing different shops and prices

2.3 More product selections

2.4 Buying and selling—both beneficial

3 Major concerns for consumers

3.1 Security

3.2 Privacy (the disclosure of one's personal information)
3.3 Dependability (service and quality)
3.4 Timeliness
4 Major concerns on the seller's part
4.1 Credit and fraud
4.2 Lack of regulations
4.3 The cost for Internet selling
5 The road ahead
5.1 Joint efforts by all sides concerned
5.2 Proper rules to be worked out
5.3 More education on e-commerce

(Source: 徐宪光. 商务沟通[M]. 北京：外语教学与研究出版社，2003.)

ACTIVITY FOR LEARNING

Select one topic you are interested in and formulize an outline under the topic. Consider if it is sufficient to be made into an outline for good writing.

8. Details and examples: How can you support your points

You need details, examples and stories to state and support your points clearly. Generally speaking, there are three roles of details and examples:

- To provide information.
- To verify an assertion.
- To illustrate an abstraction.

No message would be a convincing piece unless it contains enough facts or figures carefully selected by the writer for the purpose of supporting the subject and purpose. However, facts and figures ask for a careful selection on the writer's part. For example, when you are claiming compensation, you should supply enough evidence so as to make the intended receiver fully conscious of how reasonable and justifiable your claim is. Go back to Chapter 3 on persuasion to consider what makes an argument as persuasive as possible. Let us take a look at an example.

Dear Mr. Garden,

Thank you very much for your check dated September 7 for US$927.96. We have checked your account with this amount, leaving a balance of US$48.84.

The terms of sale, you will recall, were ROG76. Since you received the merchandise on August 12, you were entitled to a 5 percent discount only if the invoice was paid within ten days from that date. Unfortunately, these terms were not met.

Although I would like to make an exception in your case, Mr. Garden, I think you can understand that such an action would penalize those who are not accorded the same privilege.

You might be interested in the enclosed reprint of an article written by our new product research group, which appeared in the October *Plastics Engineering*.

Yours faithfully,

×××

(Source: Locker K O. *Business and Administrative Communication*[M]. 6th ed. 北京：机械工业出版社，2005.)

This letter to Mr. Garden is about his failure to meet the terms of sale for a purchase he made and to inform him that he is not entitled to a discount. The purpose is to inform the recipient of his financial responsibility for the transaction. This is not good news; however, to make the receiver be clearer about his responsibilities, the writer stated a number of facts and figures—from the money received to the money due, from the date when the merchandise was dispatched to the conditions for the discount when the invoice should be paid. To make his writing more emphatic, the writer also reminded the receiver of the potential problem of "special treatment" as a factor in the business ethics of the company. All these facts and figures have made the letter a very convincing and persuasive one.

6.5 Making Your Writing Easy to Read

Good business and administrative writing should be like a person talking to another person, even if a little more formally than in the spoken words. Unfortunately, much of the writing produced in organizations today seems to have been written by faceless bureaucrats rather than by real people.

Using an easy-to-read style makes the reader respond more positively to your ideas. You can make your writing easier to read in two ways. First, you can make individual sentences and paragraphs easy to read, so that skimming the first paragraph or reading the whole document takes as little work as possible. Second, you can make the document look visually inviting and structure it with signposts to guide the readers through it.

Kitty O. Locker (2005) gives the writers some advice on the ways to make their writing easier to read in the book *Business and Administrative Communication* (*6th Edition*).

She suggests the following:

- Choose words carefully.
- Tighten your written expression.
- Revise paragraphs carefully.

Here are some ways to make your writing easier to read.

6.5.1 Choose words carefully

Use words that are accurate, appropriate, and familiar. Accurate words are those that explain exactly what you want to say. Appropriate words convey the attitudes you want, express the tone you want, and fit well with the other words in your document. Familiar words are easy to read and understand.

How Big is "Huge"

When two people use the same words to mean different things, bypassing occurs.

A potential client told Lois Geller that he wanted a "huge" advertising campaign for his company. She spent three weeks preparing a proposal for a $50 000 advertising campaign. The client was horrified. It turned out that his budget for the whole previous year had been $10 000. To the client, a $5000 campaign would have been "huge".

(Source: Horowitz A. *Can you hear what I hear*[J]. Selling Power, 2001, 7/8: 70.)

To be accurate, a word's denotation must match the meaning the writer wishes to convey. Denotation is a word's literal or dictionary meaning. Most common words in English have more than one denotation. The word *pound*, for example, means, or denotes, a unit of weight, a place where stray animals are kept, a unit of money in the British system, and the verb *to hit*.

Coca-Cola spends an estimated $20 million a year to protect its brand name so that *Coke* will denote only that brand and not just any cola drink.

Problems also arise when writers misuse words. Read these examples:

The western part of Pennsylvania was transferred from Columbus to Philadelphia.

(Pennsylvania didn't move. Instead, a company moved responsibility for sales in western Philadelphia.)

Three major divisions of Stiners Corporation are poised to strike out in opposite directions.

(Three different directions can't be opposite each other.)

Words also have connotations. Connotation is the connected meaning that a word has. It entails how a word is usually used and in what context. For example, when using the word "pound" with a denotation of "hit", it would be inappropriate to use it to say "the woman pounded the little boy" unless she was hitting him with a big heavy log for example. The connotation of "pound" here is of a large, heavy type of hitting, not a quick smack or hit that a child would typically receive. This is the challenge in writing. The writer must achieve both the right denotation and the appropriate connotation to be effective.

Words are effective when their connotations, that is, their emotional associations or colorings, convey the attitude you want. A great many words carry connotations of approval or disapproval, disgust or delight. Words in the first column below suggest approval; words in the second column suggest criticism.

Positive word	**Negative word**
-assume	*-guess*
-curious	*-nosy*

-*cautious* -*fearful*
-*firm* -*obstinate*

6.5.2 As you write and revise sentences

Use active verbs most of time. "Who does that" sentences with active verbs make your writing more forceful and give the writing a sense of energy. This encourages the reader to continue reading your letter or report.

A verb is in active voice if the grammatical subject of the sentence does the action the verb describes. A verb is in passive voice if the subject is acted upon. Passive voice is usually made up of a form of the verb *to be* plus a past participle. Passive has nothing specifically to do with the past.

Passive voice can be past, present, or future:

were received (in the past)
is recommended (in the present)
will be implemented (in the future)

To spot a passive voice, find the verb. If the verb describes something that the grammatical subject is doing, the verb is in active voice. If the verb describes something that is being done to the grammatical subject, the verb is in passive.

Active Voice	**Passive Voice**
The customer received 500 widgets.	*500 widgets were received by the customer.*
I recommend this method.	*This method is recommended by me.*
The state agencies will implement the program.	*The program will be implemented by the state agencies.*

Using the active voice can also help the reader to imagine that he or she is going through the experience as they are reading about it.

Original sentence in passive voice: "*Eye exams and vision tests are covered in the plan.*"

Revised sentence in active voice: "*This plan covers eye exams and vision tests.*"

6.5.3 Tighten your writing

Writing is not wordy if the same idea can be expressed in fewer words. Unnecessary words increase word processing time, bore your reader, and make your meaning more difficult to follow, since the reader must hold all the extra words in mind while trying to understand your meaning.

Example:

Wordy: *Keep this information on file for future reference.*

Tighter: *File this information for reference.*

In order to develop tight writing, you should:

(1) Eliminate words that say nothing or which *duplicate* an idea.

Wordy: *I conducted this survey by telephone on Sunday, April 21. I questioned two groups of upper-class students—men and women—who, according to the student's directory, were still living in the dorms. The purpose of this survey was to find out why some upper-class students continue to live in the dorms even though they are no longer required by the university to do so. I also wanted to find out if there were any differences between male and female upper-class students in their reasons for choosing to remain in the dorms.*

Tighter: *On Sunday, April 21, I phoned upper-class men and women living in the dorms to find out ①why they continue to live in the dorms even though they are no longer required to do so, and ②whether men and women gave the same reasons.*

(2) Use gerunds (the-*ing* form of verbs) and infinitives (the *to* form of verbs) to make sentences shorter and smoother.

(3) Combine sentences to eliminate unnecessary words. Put the meaning of your sentence into subject and verb to cut the number of words.

Wordy: *The reason we are recommending the computerization of this process is that it will reduce the time required to obtain data and will give us more accurate data.*

Better: *Computerizing the process will give us more accurate data more quickly.*

(4) Divide long sentences with several ideas. First, you can vary sentence patterns in several ways. You can mix simple, compound, and complex sentences. Simple sentences have one main clause.

E.g.: *We will open a new store this month.*

Compound sentences have two main clauses joined with *and, but, or,* or another conjunction. Compound sentences work best when the ideas in the two clauses are closely related.

E.g.: *We have hired staff, and they will complete their training next week.*

We wanted to have a local radio station broadcast for the store during its grand opening, but the DJs were already booked.

Use these guidelines for sentence length and structure:

- Always edit sentence for conciseness. Even a short sentence can be wordy.
- When your subject matter is complicated or full of numbers, make a special effort to keep sentences short.
- Use longer sentences to show how ideas are linked to each other, to avoid a series of short, choppy sentences, and to reduce repetition.
- Group the words in long and medium-length sentences into chunks that the reader can process quickly.
- When you use a long sentence, keep the subject and verb close together.

6.5.4 As you write and revise paragraphs

Begin most paragraphs with topic sentences. A good paragraph has unity; that is, it discusses only one idea, or one topic. The topic sentence states the main idea and provides a scaffold to structure your document. Your writing will be easier to read if you make the topic sentence explicit and clear and put it at or near the beginning of the paragraph. When the first sentence of a paragraph is not the topic sentence, readers who skim may miss the main point. A good topic sentence forecasts the structure and content of the paragraph.

Hard to read (no topic sentence): *In fiscal 2012, the company filed claims for refund of federal income taxes of $3 199 000 and interest of $969 000 paid as a result of an examination of the company's federal income tax returns by the Internal Revenue Service(IRS) for the years of 2008 through 2010. It is uncertain that amount, if any, may ultimately be recovered.*

Better (paragraph starts with a topic sentence): *The company and the IRS disagree about whether the company is responsible for back taxes. In fiscal 2012, the company filed claims for a refund of federal income taxes of $3 199 000 and interest of $969 000 paid as a result of an examination of the company's federal income tax returns by the Internal Revenue Service (IRS) for the years of 2008 through 2010. It is uncertain if that amount, or any, may ultimately be recovered.*

When you're writing to a new audience or have to solve a particularly difficult problem, plan to revise the draft at least three times. The first time, look for content and clarity: Have I said enough and have I said it clearly? The second time, check the organization and layout: Have I presented my content so it can be easily absorbed? Finally, check the style and tone: Have I used you-attitude? Always finish with a spell-check.

As you revise, be sure to read the document through from start to finish. Read slowly and carefully, look at the text that is on the page, not just what you "expect" to see on the page. Read the text aloud may also alert you to errors. You may need to add transitions, cut repetitive parts, or change words to create a uniform level of formality throughout the document.

Tips for Writing Easy-to-Read Information

- Use friendly, simple language. Write in a conversational tone.
- Eliminate jargon when possible. If you can't eliminate it, define it.
- Use the active voice.
- Use short words and sentences.
- Limit your message to three to five main points. It makes your message easier to grasp.
- Use dot points to assist readers.
- Use black or dark-colored text on light-colored paper. Anything else can be hard to read.
- Use white space generously.
- Use a minimum 10-point serif font.
- Avoid using all capital letters.
- Keep your layout simple.

Summary

Written communication is a powerful tool in business and very different from oral communication. It is formal, leaves a permanent record of your ideas and intentions, allows you to strategically position your key message and offers no opportunity to adjust to the feedback of your reader. In that sense, it is a high risk form of communication. Written communication also has many similarities with oral communication in that it represents your image to others and allows you to influence the views of others.

This chapter has focused on written communication as a critical business skill. Poor correspondence and reporting will cost time and waste effort and could even lose goodwill for your company. So you need to consider the six questions related to six key aspects of writing when you are planning writing. You should focus on the purpose, the audience, the ideas and key messages of your written communication. You also need to make your writing easy to read. That is very important because the purpose of your writing is to send information and ask the reader or audience to take action based on your ideas. All good writing is clear, concise, uses words carefully, and structures paragraphs and sections to achieve the purpose: to share information and motivate appropriate action.

Questions for Discussion

(1) Why is it important to answer the question "To whom am I speaking?" before writing a letter or a memo?

(2) Explain the concept of *an outline* as a division process for structuring your ideas.

Exercises

(1) Assume you must write an email to your business communication professor, asking him or her to let you take your final examination one week early so that you can attend your cousin's wedding.

a. Perform an audience analysis of your professor. List everything you know about this professor that might help you compose a more effective message.

b. Write two good opening sentences for this message.

(2) Assume you are going to write a letter to your state representative about a proposed 6

percent increase in college tuition fees next year (you may make up any reasonable data).

a. Determine a specific purpose of your letter.

b. Brainstorm at least six facts, ideas, and questions you might want to raise in your letter.

c. Write the first part of the letter, and then share it with other students in your group.

Chapter 7

Correspondence

LEARNING OBJECTIVES

On completing this chapter, you should be able to:

- Understand the form and style of business letters.
- Identify the purpose and the reader.
- Understand how to adjust your style to the demands of the context.
- Know how to say "Yes" and " No" in the letters.
- Know how to write short forms of business communication, such as persuasive messages, sales letters, memos.

Study Case：Delivering Cancer News

Oncologists, doctors who specialize in treating cancer, have one of the toughest jobs when it comes to delivering negative news. These doctors often inform patients that they have a difficult battle to face or that there is almost no hope and death may be imminent.

Some medical schools now insist that students learn how to deliver bad news to patients, particularly those suffering from cancer. These medical programs have added classes where students learn to give the negative news through verbal and non-verbal forms of communication. Some of those schools also use role-playing with patient actors. The medical students have to inform the actors of an unwanted diagnosis and appropriately deal with the actor's response. Some studies suggest that the manner in which bad news is presented to a patient has significant effects on their overall health.

As an additional resource for doctors to be upfront with their patients, the American Society of Clinical Oncology has developed a booklet. It helps patients understand their options when they learn they have cancer. The goal is to help improving their quality of the life, maximize their remaining time, and plan for end-of-time care. The society believes that currently less than 40% of patients have conversations with their doctors about their options.

(Adapted from Dawn Sagario,"Doctors Learn to Convey Facts in Appropriate, Thoughtful Wat." *Des Moines Register*, October 17,2006, E1,E2; "Oncology Group Promotes Candor on End-of-Life-Care." *Des Moines Register*, February 8, 2011,6A)

Analysis：In a negative message, the basic information we have to convey is negative; we expect the audience to be disappointed or angry. Some jobs entail conveying more negative messages than others. Customer service representatives, employee relations personnel, and insurance agents all have to say no on a regular basis. Negative messages are a vital part of business and administrative communication. In this chapter, we will know different ways to construct the different parts of negative messages and how to improve the tone of the negative messages.

7.1 Writing for a Positive Effect

A Reply from Max Elliott

Dear Mr. Morley,

Your December 3rd complaint was received and contents noted. After reviewing the facts, I regret to report that I must refuse your claim. If you read the warranty brochure, you will see that the serving you bought is designed for light loads—a maximum of 800 pounds. You should have bought the heavy-duty product. I regret the damage this mistake caused you and trust that you will see your position. Hoping to be of service to you in the future.

To prepare yourself for this chapter, once again play the role of a small business manager, Max Elliott's superior. As you review Max's writing above, you see evidence of how his communication shortcoming affects your company's effectiveness as if it strives to compete. These messages go to the people inside and outside the company, they affect the human relationships that go far toward determining the success of the operation. Poorly written, insensitive message can produce serious negative reactions. Typical of Max's message is the letter above. You detect more than just the readability problem you saw in Max's message. The words are not polite. Instead of showing concern for the reader, they are blunt, tactless, and unfriendly. Overall, they leave a bad impression—the impression of a writer, and a business, unconcerned about the need for good human relationships. This chapter will show you how to avoid such impressions.

7.1.1 The Importance of clarity and a positive effect

Written communication within a business primarily requires clarity. Clarity is the primary goal for most of the writing you will do in business—especially your writing within the organization. Because much of this writing will concern matters that do not involve the readers personally, you will usually be able to communicate in a relatively matter-of-fact way. Your main objective will be to convey information, and you will want to do so quickly and accurately.

Good business writing especially to external audiences requires both clarity and the goodwill effect. When you want the message to be more personal, you will be concerned about more than just communication information. This will especially be the case when you communicate with people outside the organization and the major goal is to gain or to maintain a favorable relationship. Email messages or letters written by a company to its customers are examples of such communications.

One effect you should strive for in virtually any message is the goodwill effect. Wise business leaders know that the success of their business is affected by what people think about the business.

They know that what people think is influenced by their human contact with that business. The goodwill effect in messages is not desirable for business reasons alone. It is quite simply the effect most of us want in our relationship with people. The things we do and say to create goodwill are the friendly, courteous things that make relationships between people enjoyable. Such behaviors belong in business, in fact, they are a major and expected part of good business etiquette.

7.1.2 Emphasizing "You" more than "I"

Writing from the you-attitude is another technique for building goodwill in written message. You-attitude means focusing on the reader's interests, no matter what type of message you are preparing. You-attitude writing emphasizes the reader's perspective. It emphasizes you and your and de-emphasizes we and our, but it is more than a matter of just using second-person pronouns. It is fundamental to the practice of good business communication.

As a business writer, you must show empathy for your readers, particularly in documents such as personal letters. To show empathy in your letter, you must focus on your reader's needs more than your own needs. We will call this the "you emphasis" in business writing. The following two examples illustrate the difference between "I emphasis" and "you emphasis".

I am sending information on peripheral devices suited to the computer I sold you.

—*I emphasis*

You will receive complete instructions with details and capabilities and prices of optional additions suited to your new computer.

—*you emphasis*

Our policy prohibits us from permitting outside groups to use our facilities except on a cash-rental basis.

—*I emphasis*

Our policy of renting our facilities to outside groups enables us to make our full range of services available to your guests.

—*you emphasis*

7.1.3 Showing a warm, friendly tone

Parent, Child, or Adult

In the 1950s, psychologist Eric Berne developed a mode of people and relationships that he called "transactional analysis". It has proven to be so useful that it is still popular today.

At the core of this mode is the idea that, in all our transactions with others (and even with ourselves), people occupy one of three positions: parent, child or adult.

A parent is patronizing, spoiling, nurturing, blaming, criticizing, and/or punishing.

A child is uninhibited, freely emotional, obedient, whining, irresponsible, and/or selfish.

An adult is reasonable, responsible, considerable, and flexible.

Significant, the "self" that one projects invites others to occupy the complementary position. Thus, acting "parental" leads other to act "childish" and vice versa, while acting "adult" invites others to be adults.

In both internal and external business communication, strive for "adult-adult" interactions. Your courtesy and professionalism will be likely to elicit the same from your readers.

The tone of a business letter is very important to its success. The tone is the implied attitude of the writer towards the reader and the subject at hand. One way to emphasize the feeling of concern for the reader is to use a warm, friendly tone in your letter. Here, we suggest you to use two techniques to help you to convey a warm, friendly tone to your readers.

1. Focus on people more than on things

Concentrate on people as much as you can. In the following example, a supervisor tries to compliment an employee on a well-written report. Notice how the emphasis of the message falls on the document rather than the person and hence ends up sounding hollow and cold.

Version 1. *"Alternative in pension planning" presents four popular pension plans, each with advantages and disadvantages. The report evaluates the plans in relation to specific company needs. The report is clear and orderly.*

Notice how much better the following version sounds, when the supervisor focuses on the person instead of the product.

Version 2. *Thank you, Mary, for your good work in "alternative in pension planning". You have analyzed the four competing plans in a clear, orderly way — just what we need to help us choose the best plan for our company.*

When you concentrate on objects, your praise falls on the object instead of going to the person. Readers can hardly be expected to care when an object receives praise. When you move your emphasis to people, however, you create human warmth, and you get more positive responses.

2. Include feelings as well as facts

In addition to the focus on people more than on things, there is another way to heighten and emphasize your warm and friendly tone. That is, to include some of your feelings when you are telling your reader your facts. The following feelings would generally be inappropriate, however, in a business letter.

(1) Personal feeling about your personal life.

(2) Personal negative feeling about your company, your coworkers, your customers or anyone else with whom you work.

(3) Negative feelings towards your reader or any of your reader's associates.

(4) Intense emotions, such as love, hate, anger or fear.

Instead, you might include feelings of pride, respect, pleasure, or satisfaction.

Remember, be as personable in business writing as you would be in a face-to-face business meeting.

7.2 The Importance of Readable Format

Have you ever opened up a letter or a reading for a class, seen long, unbroken blocks of text, and dreaded jumping into the piece? Business readers are far too bombarded with messages to have patience with this kind of document. If you want your readers actually to read what you wrote and get your ideas and information, you must pay attention to an important element of any message: its physical format. Do not put off your readers with a daunting physical format.

The writer is responsible for making the important formatting decisions. Decades ago, you might well have been able to rely on a secretary or typist to format your documents for you. But widespread use of the personal computer, with its full-featured publishing capabilities, has placed the responsibility for readable formatting much more on the writer. Except for projects that will involve a graphic designer, you will make the key formatting decisions for your messages. What kind and size of type will you use? What kind of headings? Will you use any means of typographical emphasis? How about numbered or bulleted lists? Should the documents include such visual elements as logos, textboxes, pictures, or diagrams? Smart decisions on such matters will not only increase your readers' motivation to read but also enable them to quickly comprehend the main points and structure of the message.

7.3 Parts of Standard Business Letter

Today's business letters are expected to be friendlier than those impersonal business letters of the past. Both modern writers and readers know the importance not only of stating the message in a letter, but also of motivating the reader to understand the message and to act on it. In addition, modern business letters are much shorter than the business letters from the past. Modern business letters are also expected to be more attractive and more error-free than the letters used to be.

Now you are familiar with the overall tone and appearance that you should use in business letters, you need to explore each part of the letter and become confident of its use. The following are the individual parts of a standard letter, some of which you must include, some of which you should include, and some of which are optional.

- Letterhead (or return address) (must be included)
- Date (must be included)
- Inside address (of your recipient) (must be included)
- Subject statement (should be included)
- Attention line (optional)
- Salutation (must be included)
- Body (of the letter—your message)
- Complimentary close (must be included)
- Signature (must be included)
- Final notations (optional)
- Postscript (optional)

7.3.1 Letterhead

The letterhead displays the image your company wants to convey. Knowing who is writing helps your reader to decide whether to read what you have to say. The letterhead on business stationery always identifies the company, either by name, company logo, or both. The letterhead usually includes the address, city, state, and zip code of the company, along with one or more telephone numbers and a fax/cable/telex address code.

7.3.2 Date

Place the date of the letter two line-spaces below the return address and then leave two more line-spaces between it and the inside address. When you are writing a letter, keep in mind the following:

(1) Don't mix letters and numbers in the date (not Feb.2nd).

(2) Don't just use numbers (such as 8/21/16 or 9-27-16).

(3) Don't abbreviate the names of months that have only five or fewer letters (Standard abbreviations for Jan., Feb., Oct. are fine, though).

(4) Don't use unusual abbreviations or unusual sequences for the date.

7.3.3 Inside address

The inside address is the recipient's address. It is always best to write to a specific individual at the firm to which you are writing. If you do not have the person's name, do some research by calling the company or speaking with employees from the company. Include a personal title such as Ms, Mrs, Mr, or Dr. Follow a woman's preference in being addressed as Miss, Mrs, or Ms. If you are unsure of a woman's preference in being addressed, use Ms. Usually, people will not mind being addressed by a higher title than they actually possess. To write the address, use an appropriate style for the country that you are writing to. For international addresses, type the name of the country in all-capital letters on the last line. The inside address begins one line below the sender's address or one inch or 2.5 centimeters below the date. It should be left justified, no matter which format you are using.

Address your reader by his or her full professional name in the inside address. When you don't know the reader's name, use the job title both in the inside address and salutation. For example:

Director of Marketing
Victory Products, Inc.
300Buena Vista St.
Ft. Worth, TX 46839
UNITED STATES OF AMERICA

7.3.4 Subject statement

A subject statement briefly describes the topic of your letter. The subject line is a very important attention-getting opportunity for you to encourage your reader to see the letter as important for them to read. Make a clear, concise statement of the purpose of the letter. The subject line should always have two line-spaces above it and below it. It may be placed between the inside address and the salutation. In formal letters, instead of "Subject", business writers sometimes used the abbreviation "Re:".

7.3.5 Attention line

When you address your letter directly to the company, use the attention line to name a person, position, or the department whose attention you are calling to the message. The purpose of using the attention line is to ensure that the letter can be delivered to the right person or department directly. The attention line is usually placed after the inside address.

7.3.6 Salutation

In business letters, people address business correspondents as "Dear", even when our feelings for them are far from fond. The salutation should be addressed to the same person whose name appears on the first line of the inside address. If you don't know the name of the person to whom you are writing, use the job title in the inside address as the salutation.

Use the same name as in the inside address, including the personal title. If you know the person and typically address him by his first name, it is acceptable to use only the first name in the salutation (i.e., Dear Lucy). In all other cases, however, use the personal title and full name followed by a colon. Leave one line blank after the salutation.

If you don't know a reader's gender, use a nonsexist salutation, such as "To whom it may concern" or "Dear Sir/Madam". It is also acceptable to use the full name in a salutation if you cannot determine gender.

7.3.7 Body of your letter

The body of the letter contains the message you want your reader to receive. In order to grab your reader's attention at a glance, a layout can help you. Show clearly that your letter has a beginning, a middle and an end. The readers are able to perceive, at a glance, that the beginning of the letter will be easy because it requires the reading of only a sentence or two. Similarly, they notice that the ending is easy to read.

Keep all your paragraphs short (no more than 5～6 lines) in a business letter.

Having a checklist can help to ensure that you cover all the critical aspects of letter writing. In the book *Management Communication*, Arthur H. Bell & Dayle M. Smith suggest using the Six C's Checklist for a letter body.

(1) Complex: Include all the facts, arguments, examples and details you need to make your point.

(2) Coherent: Link your letter's points together in an organizational, logical way.

(3) Concise: Use the fewest words to express your ideas.

(4) Concrete: Use easy-to-understand words that give your reader specific pictures about your message.

(5) Convincing: Order the body of your letter logically so that your reader can understand and trust your message.

(6) Considerate: Use a warm and friendly tone to show that you care about your reader's

needs in the letter, looking at the message from your reader's point of view.

7.3.8 Complimentary close

This is the last chance to show regard for your reader. After the body of the letter, insert two line-spaces and write the complimentary close such as "Sincerely" or "With best wishes" that seems most appropriate to you. But how do you know when to use a warmer complimentary closing than "Sincerely" in a business letter? To a large degree, your feelings will guide you correctly. When you weigh those feelings, keep in mind the following comments when you have a business practice.

(1) A first letter to a new client or an unknown reader usually closes with a conservative ending such as "Sincerely". Warm personal regards in such an initial letter can be seen as insincere because the reader has no basis yet for judging your feeling.

(2) A business letter that begins with a first name such as "Dear Jenny" can have a warmer close than "Sincerely". In fact, "Sincerely" may make the reader feel that you have chosen a rather traditional, noncommittal closing for what may have been a warm and somewhat personal letter.

The complimentary close should be consistent with the salutation. For example:

(Formally)

Dear Sir(s)	*Yours faithfully*
Gentlemen	*Truly yours*

(Informally)

Dear Mr. Henry	*Yours sincerely*
	(*OR Sincerely yours*)

7.3.9 Signature

Your full name and professional title are typed beneath your signature. So your signature can have a personal flair—a hint regarding the personality of the signature. Also, it isn't always necessary to sign your name exactly as it is typed on the business letter. Remember: use a signature that pleases you and sign your letters naturally and confidently.

7.3.10 Final notations

Final notations often appear at the bottom of a business letter, and always below the signature and along the left-hand margin. Writers place these notations at the bottom of the letters so that these notations tell the readers to whom copies of the letter have been sent.

7.3.11 Enclosure

Enclosures simply record on the business letter the list of traditional items you have included with the letter. When the reader files the letter, the enclosure note stands as a record of pertinent related material that came with the letter.

7.4 A Note about Format and Font

When writing business letters, you must pay special attention to the format and font used. The most common layout of a business letter is known as block format. Using this format, the entire letter is left justified and single spaced except for a double space between paragraphs. Another format is known as modified block format. In this type, the body of the letter is left justified and single-spaced. However, the date and closing are in alignment in the center of the page. The final style is indented format. It is much like the modified block format except that each paragraph is indented instead of left justified.

The following shows examples of the different formats.

7.4.1 Block format

In this popular business format style, all parts of the business letter begin at the left margin. Paragraphs are separated from another by one or two extra line-spaces. This is a relatively modern-looking style and gives you an impression of being up to date. An example is as follows.

March 16, 2012

Mr. Huang
No. 65 Nathan Road
Kowloon
Hong Kong

Dear Mr. Huang:

The first paragraph of a typical business letter is used to state the main point of the letter. Begin with a friendly opening, then quickly go into the purpose of your letter. Use a couple of sentences to explain the purpose, but do not go into detail until the next paragraph.

In the second paragraph, state the supporting details to justify your purpose. These may take the form of background information, statistics or first-hand accounts. A few short paragraphs within the body of the letter should be enough to support your reasoning.

Finally, in the closing paragraph, briefly restate your purpose and why it is important. If the purpose of your letter is employment related, consider ending your letter with your contact information. However, if the purpose is informational, think about closing with gratitude for the reader's time.

Sincerely,

Lucy

7.4.2 Indented format

Three parts of the block format are moved to the center margin: the return address (if letterhead stationery is not being used), the date, and the signature block, including the complimentary close. Paragraphs are indented, usually five spaces. This common style is somewhat more traditional and literary in appearance than the block style. It requires more care and effort on the part of the writer, however, and partly for that reason is less popular in business today than the block style. An example is as follows.

March 16, 2012

Mr. Huang
No. 65 Nathan Road
Kowloon
Hong Kong

Dear Mr. Huang:

The first paragraph of a typical business letter is used to state the main point of the letter. Begin with a friendly opening; then quickly go into the purpose of your letter. Use a couple of sentences to explain the purpose, but do not go into detail until the next paragraph.

In the second paragraph, state the supporting details to justify your purpose. These may take the form of background information, statistics or first-hand accounts. A few short paragraphs within the body of the letter should be enough to support your reasoning.

Finally, in the closing paragraph, briefly restate your purpose and why it is important. If the purpose of your letter is employment related, consider ending your letter with your contact information. However, if the purpose is informational, think about closing with gratitude for the reader's time.

Sincerely,

Lucy

7.4.3 Modified block format

In this formation, elements of both the block format and the indented format appear. The return address (when not using letterhead), the date and the signature block are moved to the center margin. All other letter parts are placed along the left margin. Paragraphs are not indented.

The modified block is less common than block format and indented format, but it can be useful when the writer is trying to strike a modern look that still appears balanced on the page. An example is as follows.

March 16, 2012

Mr. Huang
No. 65 Nathan Road
Kowloon
Hong Kong

Dear Mr. Huang:

The first paragraph of a typical business letter is used to state the main point of the letter. Begin with a friendly opening; then quickly go into the purpose of your letter. Use a couple of sentences to explain the purpose, but do not go into detail until the next paragraph.

In the second paragraph, state the supporting details to justify your purpose. These may take the form of background information, statistics or first-hand accounts. A few short paragraphs within the body of the letter should be enough to support your reasoning.

Finally, in the closing paragraph, briefly restate your purpose and why it is important. If the purpose of your letter is employment related, consider ending your letter with your contact information. However, if the purpose is informational, think about closing with gratitude for the reader's time.

Sincerely,

Lucy

7.5 Saying "Yes" and "No" in a Letter

7.5.1 The prevalence of directness in business

Direct order is used in most business messages. That is, the message leads with its most important point and then moves to additional or supporting information. Communication is central to organized human activity. Especially in business, people need to know what to do, why, and how. They undertake any job understanding that they have a certain function to perform, and they need information to be able to perform it. Each business is unique in some ways, and each,

therefore, will have developed its own direct-message types—its preferred purposes, patterns, styles, and formats for these messages. Still, one can identify a certain basic plan for the direct message. Here is an example of poor structure that was used in an email, fax, or letter format. This letter's indirect and vague beginning slows reading.

> Dear Mr. Piper,
>
> We have seen your advertisement for 3 200 square feet of office space in *the Daily Journal*. As we are interested, we would like additional information. Especially, we would like to know the interior layout, annual cost, availability of transportation, length of the lease agreement, escalation provisions, and any other information you think pertinent.
>
> If the information you give us is favorable, we will inspect the property. Please send your reply as soon as possible.
>
> Sincerely

In order to create a direct writing, and for the reader to have a good understanding of what you really mean in the message, you need to follow the advice below.

Firstly, beginning with the objective. If you are seeking information, start by for asking it. If you are giving information, start by giving it. Whatever your key point is, lead with it. Put the key point up front. However, to put this point in context, you may need to lead with brief orienting information and then get to the real message. Then stop the first paragraph. Let the rest of the message fill in the detail.

Secondly, covering the remaining part of the objective. Complete the objective systematically—perhaps by listing or paragraphing. If you cover all of your objective in the beginning, nothing else is needed. If additional questions, answers, or information are needed, cover them systematically.

Lastly, ending with goodwill. End the message with some appropriate friendly comment as you would end a face-to-face communication with the reader. These final goodwill words will receive the best reader reaction if they are selected to fit the particular situation. Such general closes as "A prompt reply will be appreciated" and "Thank you for your time and consideration" are positive, for they express a friendly thank-you. And there is nothing wrong with a thank-you sincerely expressed here or elsewhere.

7.5.2 Format for "Yes" letters (sending positive message)

Sometimes, you will have to respond with a partial "no" to an order that you were unable to fill completely. Your readers look forward to hearing you say "yes" to orders, requests and invitations. When clients hear "yes", they value your company's participation in their own progress. You are letting them have their way rather than standing in their way.

When writing "yes" letters, a simple four-point plan should be used.

(1) Deliver the "yes" message as soon as possible in the letter. Reserve all the specifics and additional information for a later paragraph.

(2) Keep the "yes" message simple. Let the "yes" statement stand by itself without a clutter of conditions, comments and qualifications in the same paragraph. Don't spoil that moment.

(3) Tell the client exactly what you are saying "yes" to. Be specific. Especially in contractual matters and questions of credit, it is wise to spell out the exact commitment you are and are not making by your "yes" response.

(4) Sell your company's service, product, image, and the relationship.

1. Routine inquiries

The format of routine inquiries can be designed by the following steps:

First, routine inquiries appropriately begin by asking either of two types of questions: specific or general. First, it can be one of the specific questions to be asked (assuming that more than one questions need to be asked). Preferably it should be a question that sets up the other questions. For example, if your objective is to get information about the office suites described in the introductory situation, you might begin with these words:

Can you please send me additional information about the floor plan of the office suite that you advertised in Monday's Daily Journal?

In the body of the message you would include additional specific questions concerning the suites. Or, the opening question could be a general request for information. The specific questions would follow. This beginning sentence illustrates a general request:

Will you please send me a description of the features of the 3200-square-foot office suite advertised in Monday's Daily Journal?

Second, informing and explaining adequately. To help your reader answer your questions, you may need to include an explanation or information. If you do not explain enough or if you misjudge the reader's knowledge, you make the reader's task difficult. Where and how you include the necessary explanatory information depends on the nature of your message. Usually, a good place for general explanatory materials is before or after the direct request in the opening paragraph. Place the explanation anywhere it fits logically.

Third, structuring the questions. If the inquiry involves just one question, begin with it. If it involves more than one, make each stand out. Do this by: ①placing each question in a separate sentence. ②structuring the questions in separate paragraphs. ③ordering or ranking the questions by using words (first, second, third, etc.), numbers (1, 2, 3, etc.) or letter(a, b, c, etc.). This way, you make the questions stand out. ④using the question form of sentence. The questions that stand out are those written in question form: "Will you please tell me...?" "How much would one be able to save...?"

Last, ending with a friendly comment that fits the case. The goodwill ending described in the general plan is appropriate here, just as it is in most business messages. And we must emphasize again that the closing words do the most toward creating goodwill when they fit the situation. Remember to include important deadlines and reasons for them as well.

2. Routine replies

Routine replies provide the information requested in the original message or otherwise comply with the writer's request. Like the original request letters, they are organized in a direct organizational style, putting the "good" news—the fact that you're responding favorably with—up front.

Probably one of the most important guidelines to follow is to answer promptly. Your response should be courteous. If you appear to be acting grudgingly, you will probably lose any goodwill that a gracious response might have earned for you or your organization. Be sure to answer all the questions asked or implied, using objective and clearly understood language. The reader will probably be in a positive mood as the result of your letter, and you may consider either including some sales promotion if appropriate or building goodwill by implying such characteristics about your organization as public spiritedness, quality products, social responsibility, or concern for employees.

Often the writer's questions have been asked by others many times before, in such a situation, formal letter may be the most appropriate way to respond. A form letter is a letter with standardized wording that is sent to different people.

Tips for Routine Inquests and Replies

1. Routine inquests

(1) Present the major request in the first sentence or two, preceded or followed by reasons for making the request.

(2) Provide any needed explanation or details.

(3) Phrase each question so that it is clear, is easy to answer, and covers only one topic. Ask as few questions as possible, but if several questions are necessary, number them and arrange them in logical order.

(4) If appropriate, incorporate readers' benefits and promise confidentiality.

(5) Close on a friendly note by expressing appreciation, justifying any necessary deadlines, offering to reciprocate, or otherwise making your ending personal and original.

2. Routine replies

(1) Answer promptly and graciously.

(2) Grant the request or begin giving the requested information in the first sentence or two.

(3) Address all questions asked or implied; include additional information or suggestions if that would be helpful.

(4) Include subtle sales promotion if appropriate.

(5) Consider developing formal letter for frequent requests.

(6) Refer to any items you enclose with the letter, and insert an enclosure notation at the bottom.

(7) Close on a positive and friendly note, and use original wording.

(Source: Ober S, Newman A. 商务沟通[M]. 7 版. 北京：清华大学出版社，2013.)

Never Say "No"

In some cultures, it's rude to say no.

Japanese prefer to avoid direct confrontations. Changing the subject—even to something irrelevant—apologies, and silence are always preferable to saying no.

When Japanese businessmen write reject letters, they begin with buffers and offer reasons, apologies, and appreciation.

To avoid saying no, Czechs and Slovaks may say "We will see."

In Hungary, it is considered impolite to say "no" directly to a social equal or superior. Someone who doesn't want to do something may give a series of excuses, until the other person realizes that he or she should stop asking.

(Source: Azuma S. *Rejection Strategy in Business Japanese*[C]. Association for Business Communication Annual Meeting, Orlando: 1995, 11,1-4. Ruder C A, Richmond Y. *From da to yes: Understanding the East Europeans*[M]. Yarmouth: Intercultural Press, 1995.)

7.6 Delivering Bad News

Companies build goodwill, keep old customers and win new customers now not only by appropriate warmth in saying "yes" to orders, requests, adjustment letters, and credit applications, but also by their skill in saying "no" when they must.

Delivering bad news is one of the most difficult tasks a leader may be asked to perform. When employee and customer expectations do not match reality, dysfunctional behavior may result. To reduce the potential for dysfunctional behavior, bad news should be communicated openly and honestly, despite how difficult the news may be for the employees and customers to hear.

Sometimes it is necessary to refuse a person's request. Negative communications such as refusals, rejections, recalls, and apologies are hard to compose. Yet they are important. Good ones restore corporate reputations as well as customer and employee goodwill. Bad ones can lead to lawsuits. Corporate officers can be promoted or fired on the basis of a negative communication. Employees reporting negative situations are frequently penalized.

7.6.1 Negative message's purposes

A negative message always has several purposes:

1. Primary purposes

(1) To give the audience the bad news.

(2) To have the audience read, understand, and accept the message.

(3) To maintain as much as goodwill as possible.

2. Secondary purposes

(1) To maintain, as much as possible, a good image of the communicator and the communicator's organization.

(2) To reduce or to eliminate future communication on the same subject so the message doesn't create more work for the sender.

The advantage of the indirect order in refusal messages is illustrated by the following contrasting examples. Both refuse clearly. But only the one that uses the indirect order is likely to gain the reader's goodwill.

This is a bad email below because of its directness and negative language.

Subject: Your request for a donation

Ms. Cangelosi:

We regret to inform you that we cannot grant your request for a donation to the association's scholarship fund. So many requests for contributions are made of that we have found it necessary to budget a definite amount each year for this purpose. Our budgeted funds for this year have been exhausted, so we simply cannot consider additional requests. However, we will able to consider your request next year. We deeply regret our inability to help you now and trust that you understand our position.

Mark Stephens

The second example skillfully handles the negative message. Its opening words are on subject and neutral. They set up the explanation in the following sentences. The clear and logical explanation ties in with the opening. Using no negative words, the explanation leads smoothly to the refusal. Note that the refusal is also handled without negative words and yet is clear. The friendly close fits the case.

Subject: Your scholarship fund request

Ms. Cangelosi:

Your efforts to build the scholarship fund for the association's needy children are commendable. We wish you success in your efforts to further this worthy cause.

We at Pinnacle are always willing to assist worthy causes whenever we can. That is why every January we budget for the year the maximum amount we believe we are able to contribute to such causes. Then we distribute that amount among the various deserving groups as far as it will go. Since our budgeted contributions for this year have already been made, we are placing your organization on our list for consideration next year.

We wish you success in your efforts to improve the lives of the children in our city.

Mark Stephens

7.6.2 The parts of a negative message

Businesses must often say "no" to orders or inquiries. You must keep in mind that when you are writing a refusal letter, you can not only give negative responses to orders or inquiries, but also retain the customer's loyalty at the same time. At such time, use the following model in your letter saying "no" to the order.

(1) Begin with a positive buffer (perhaps a statement of application for the order).

(2) Go on to a clear statement of what you can and cannot provide.

(3) Include any explanation or qualification you feel will be helpful to the reader.

(4) Conclude with a statement of goodwill, appreciation.

1. Buffers

A buffer is a positive or neutral statement—not a negative one—that serves as a starting place for your negative response. Buffers allow the reader to feel comfortable with you before experiencing the discomfort of the no message.

To be effective, a buffer must put the reader in a good frame of mind, not give the bad news but not imply a positive answer either, and provide a natural transition to the body of the letter. The kinds of the statements most often used as buffers are good news, facts and chronologies of events, references to enclosures, thanks, and statements of principles.

To create effective buffers, you should:

(1) Choose a positive aspect of the subject at hand.

(2) Praise the reader for personal or professional qualities.

(3) Concentrate on special needs.

(4) Use time factors as explanations.

In using buffers, writers try to prepare the reader to receive the no response. Of course you cannot avoid disappointing the reader entirely. However, your effort to soften the blow of the negative response often builds goodwill that goes beyond the momentary disappointment.

2. Reasons

Avoid saying that you cannot do something. Most negative messages exist because the writer or the company has chosen certain policies or cut off points. Don't hide behind "company policy": readers will assume the policy is designed to benefit you at their expense. If possible, show how readers benefit from the policy. If they do not benefit, do not mention it at all.

Weak reason: *I cannot write an insurance policy for you because company policy does not allow me to do so.*

Better reason: *China Life Insurance Company insurance cars only when they are normally garaged at night. Standard insurance policies cover a wider variety of risks and charge higher fees. Limiting the policies we write gives China Life Insurance Company customers the lowest possible rates for auto insurance.*

If you don't have a good reason, omit the reason rather than use a weak one. Even if you

have a strong reason, omit it if it makes the company look bad.

The reason that hurts the company: *Our company is not hiring at the present time because profits are down. In fact, the downturn has promoted top management to reduce the salaried staff by 5% just this month, with perhaps more reductions to come.*

Better reason: *Our company does not have any opening now.*

Here is an example of successfully saying "no", while maintaining goodwill and productivity.

The Best Negative Is No Surprise

In the 1990s, Ford Motor Co. downsized, closing the venerable Thunderbird factory and laying off thousands of workers. Ford was able to do this without union strife—by talking about plans far advanced.

Ford's CEO and the United Autoworker's vice president met for breakfast every other month. Ford shared sensitive information and sought union input. When the Thunderbird factory closed, the union knew six months ahead of time. The union negotiated a hefty bonus for workers who moved to a Ford truck plant in another state.

According to industry analysts, Ford's honest communication about upcoming negatives not only averted costly strikes, but also contributed to its workers' high productivity during that period.

(Source: Sexton C. If Ford can do it, why can't GM[J]. *Business Week*, 1998, 7(29):36.)

3. Refusals

Deemphasize the refusal by putting it in the same paragraph with the reason, rather than in a paragraph by itself. Sometimes you may be able to imply the refusal rather than stating it directly.

Direct refusal: *You cannot get the insurance for just one month.*

Implied refusal: *The shortest term for an insurance policy is six months.*

Be sure the implication is crystal clear. Any message can be misunderstood, but an optimistic or desperate reader is particularly unlikely to understand a negative message. One of your purposes, in a negative message, is to close the door on the subject. You do not want to have to write a second letter saying that the real answer is "no".

4. Alternatives

Giving the reader an alternative or compromise, if one is available, is a good idea for several reasons:

(1) It can offer the reader another way to get what he or she wants.

(2) It can suggest that you really care about the reader and about helping to meet his or her needs.

(3) It can enable the reader to reestablish the psychological freedom you limited when you said no.

(4) It can allow you to end on a positive note and to present yourself and your organization as

positive, friendly and helpful.

An alternative allows the reader to react in a way that doesn't hurt you. By letting the readers decide for themselves whether they want the alternative, you allow them to reestablish their sense of psychological freedom.

5. Endings

The best endings look to the future. Here are some examples.

Good one: *Wherever you have your account, you'll continue to get all the service you've learned to expect from CHARGE_ALL, and the convenience of charging items at over a million stores, restaurants, and hotels in China and abroad—and in Shanghai, too, whenever you come back to visit.*

Avoid endings that seem insincere: *We are happy to have been of service, and should we be able to assist you in the future, please contact us.*

7.7 Getting the Tone Right in Negative Messages

Tone—the implied attitude of the author toward the readers and the subject—is particularly important when you want the readers to feel that you have taken their requests seriously.

Even the physical appearance and timing of a letter can convey tone. If the letter is accurately and carefully written and well laid out with all the necessary details, it suggests that you have taken the time to care about them. An obvious rejection letter suggests that the writer has not given much consideration to the reader's application.

It is important to remember that an immediate negative at the start of the letter suggests that the rejection didn't need any thought.

Avoid these phrases in negative messages as follows in Table 7.1.

Table 7.1 Avoid these phrases in negative messages

Phrases	Because
I am afraid that we cannot…	You are not fearful. Don't hide behind empty phrases.
I am sorry that we are unable…	You probably are able to grant the request; you simply choose not to. If you are so sorry about saying no, why don't you change your policy and say yes?
I am sure you will agree that…	Don't assume that you can read the reader's mind.

7.8 Persuasive Messages

Persuasion is the process of motivating someone to take a specific action or to support a particular idea. Persuasion motivates someone to believe something or to do something that he or she would not otherwise have done. Everyday, many people try to persuade you to do certain things or to believe certain ideas.

Your job in writing a persuasive message, then, is to talk to your readers into something, to convince them that your point of view is the most appropriate one. Such writing requires careful planning; you need to define your purpose clearly and analyze your audience thoroughly.

Remember the checklists for writing persuasive requests.

1. Determine how to start the message

(1) Direct plan—Use a direct organizational plan when:

—Writing to superiors;

—Your audience is predisposed to listen objectively to your request;

—The proposal does not require strong persuasion;

—The proposal is long or complete;

—You know your reader prefers the direct approach.

(2) Present the recommendation, along with a brief rationale, in the first paragraph.

(3) Indirect plan—Use an indirect organizational plan when;

—Writing to subordinates or colleagues;

—Writing to someone outside the organization;

—Strong persuasion is needed;

—The reader is initially resistant to your proposal;

—You know your reader prefers the indirect approach.

(4) Start by gaining the reader's attention.

(5) Make the first sentence motivate the reader to continue reading.

(6) Keep the opening sentence short, relevant to the message, and when appropriate, related to a reader benefit.

2. Create interest and justify your requests

(1) Develop the major part of your message to justify your request. Give enough background and evidence to enable the reader to make an informed decision.

(2) Use facts and statistics, expert opinion, and examples to support your proposal. Ensure that the evidence is accurate, relevant, representative, and complete.

(3) Use an objective, logical, reasonable, and sincere tone. Avoid obvious flattery, emotionalism, and exaggeration.

(4) Present the evidence in terms of either direct or indirect reader benefits.

3. Minimize obstacles

(1) Do not ignore obstacles or any negative aspects of your request. Instead, show that even considering them, your request is still reasonable.

(2) Subordinate the discussion of obstacles by position and amount of space devoted to the topic.

4. Ask confidently for action

(1) State the specific request late in the message, after most of the benefits have been discussed.

(2) Make the desired action clear and easy for the reader to take, use a confident tone, do not apologize, and do not supply excuses.

(3) End on a forward-looking note, continuing to stress reader benefits.

This persuasive memo uses the direct plan because the memo travels up the organization.

Persuasive Request Selling an Idea

MEMO TO: Elliott Lamborn, Vice President

FROM: Jenson J. Peterson, Marketing Supervisor

DATE: April 3, 20××

SUBJECT: Proposal to Reassign Employee Parking Lots

As one way of showing our support for the Ford Motor Company, which accounts for nearly half of our sales, I propose that the employee parking lots be to use by owners of Ford vehicles.

Begin with the recommendation, along with a brief rationale

During their visits, Ford personnel pass the employee parking lot and see that approximately 70 percent of our employees drive vehicles manufactured by their competitors. In fact, a Ford purchasing agent asked me last week, "How can you expect us to support you if you don't support us?"

Provide a smooth transition to the necessary background information

The purpose of this memo, then, is to seek approval to have our employee parking lot to use by Ford vehicles. The maintenance department estimates that it will cost about $500 to make the needed signs.

Repeat the recommendation after presenting most of the rationale

Our labor contract requires union approval of any changes in working conditions. However, Sally Marsh, our shop steward, has told me that she would approve this proposal if similar restrictions are imposed on the executive parking lot.

Neutralize an obvious obstacle

Since our next manager's meeting is on May 8, I look forward to being able to announce the new plan to them. By approving this change, Newton will be sending a powerful positive message to our visitors. We believe in the products we sell.

Close on a positive, confident note; motivates prompt action

(Source: Ober S, Newman A. 商务沟通[M]. 7 版. 北京：清华大学出版社，2013.)

An Ineffective Persuasive Request

January 13, 20××

Ms. Tanya Porrat, Editor
Autoimmune Diseases Monthly
1800 Ten Hills Road, Suite B
Boston, MA. 02143

Dear Ms. Porrat,

Subject: Request for You to Speak at the Multiple Sclerosis Congress:

I have a favor to ask—a rather large one, I am afraid. Having served as an editor of a professional journal myself, I know how busy editors are, but I was wondering if you would be willing to fly to Washington, D.C. on April 25 and speak at the closing banquet of our seventh annual congress.

The problem of course, is that as a nonprofit association, we cannot afford to pay you an honorarium. I trust that this is won't be a problem for you. We would however, be willing to reimburse you for air travel and hotel accommodations.

Our conference attendants would benefit tremendously from your vast knowledge of multiple sclerosis, so we're really hoping you'll say yes.

Just let me know your decision by March 3 in case we have to make other arrangements.

Please call me if you have any questions.

Cordially
May Lyon, Banquet Chair

(Source: Ober S, Newman A. 商务沟通[M]. 7 版. 北京：清华大学出版社，2013.)

Use a subject line that is too specific

Begin by directly asking for the favor, use me attitude language, and omit important information

Identify the obstacles in a selfish manner

Give a deadline for answering without providing any convincing rationale

Close with a cliché

This persuasive request uses the indirect plan because the writer doesn't know the reader personally and because strong persuasion is needed.

Effective Persuasive Request—Asking Favor

January 21, 20××

Ms. Tanya Porrat, Editor
Autoimmune Diseases Monthly
1800 Ten Hills Road, Suite B

Boston, MA. 02143

Dear Ms. Porrat,

Subject: Program planning for the Multiple Sclerosis Congress

"You have 1 chance in 1 000 if developing MS". That comment of yours in a recent interview in the Boston Globe certainly made me sit up and think.

Your knack for explaining medical facts would be of keen interest to those attending our annual congress in Washing, D.C. As the keynote speaker at our banquet at the Adams Hotel on April 25, you would be able to present your ideas to the 200 people present. You would be our guest for the banquet, which begins at 7 p.m., and your 45-minute presentation would follow at about 8:30 p.m.

We will reimburse your travel expenses. Although our nonprofit association is unable to offer an honorarium, we do offer you an opportunity to introduce your journal and to present your ideas to representatives of major autoimmune groups in the country.

We'd like to announce your presentation in our next newsletter, which goes to press on March 3. Won't you please call to let me know you can come. We will have a large, enthusiastic audience of medical researchers waiting to hear you.

Cordially

May Lyon, Banquet Chair

(Source: Ober S, Newman A. 商务沟通[M]. 7 版. 北京：清华大学出版社，2013.)

Open by quoting the reader, thus complimenting her

Intimate the request; provide necessary background information

Subordinate a potential obstacle by putting it in the dependent clause of a sentence

Close with a restatement of reader benefit

7.9 Sales letter

Sensitivity to the needs of the audience is very important in a sales letter. Potential customers need to know why they should buy the product or the service, donate to the charity, subscribe to the magazine, etc. The writer must provide clear information to help them understand what the letter is about.

Effective sales letters must influence the readers by truthfully presenting written information. If the letter is to influence the reader, it must demonstrate that the position or action it suggests serves the needs of the readers. The range of those needs is broad, and the readers often have many overlapping needs that the sales letter may address, such as the needs for

Money	*Health*
More free time	*Comfort*
Productivity	*Entertainment*
Importance	*Security*
Power	*Knowledge*
Attractiveness	*A desired skill*
Friends	*Reputation*

Market research is an effective way to test your market and understand your readers. Are they aware of their need for your product? If so, begin your sales letter by showing how your products meet their need. Are they unaware that your products can help them? If so, begin by reminding them in a sentence or two of a problem they may have experienced.

1. The steps of writing sales letter

Once you have analyzed the reader's needs and determined how much or how little to assume, you can begin a step-by-step planning process for each part of the sales letter. Here is an easy-to-remember way for the sales letter. It follows the letters **S-A-L-V-E-S.**

S—Spark the imagination and curiosity of the reader;

A—Announce the product or service;

L—List the advantages to the client;

V—Value the benefit that the client can get;

E—Express appreciation and goodwill;

S—Specify exactly what the client should do—and when.

Now, let's look at each stage in detail. This will help you to write a successful sales letter.

(1) **S**—Spark the imagination and curiosity of the reader. The introductory sentence used in the sales letter should get the reader's attention and help them to have a clear picture of the product or service, then guide them meaningfully to consider your worthwhile product or service.

You can spark your reader's imagination and arouse their curiosity by one of the following:

(i) "You can do something unique" as your first sentence for the reader. Few of us can resist reading on to find out what that "something" is.

(ii) You can drop an impressive name, if appropriate, and then associate the reader with that name.

The famous astronaut Yang Liwei, like you, knows the importance of regular eye examination.

(iii) You can mention local people, places, and events, if possible.

(2) **A**—Announce the product or service. In this section of the letter, announce the product or service in a frank and specific way. The reader has had his or her curiosity piqued in your opening sentences and now wants it satisfied. This portion should first advertise the product or service. Speak up for what you have to offer, naming it in specific terms. Where the space permits, provide a persuasive example or two.

(3) **L**—List the advantages to the client. What can attract the client is to know the advantages or the differentiations of the product or service. The client is concerned if his/her needs are satisfied by the product or service you offer. So, this section of the sales letter should convince the reader that your advertised claims in the second paragraph have practical applications. You have a chance to demonstrate the wide variety of needs your product or service can fulfill.

(4) **V**—Value the benefit that the client can get. This is the time to explain what kinds of value/benefit that the client can get from your plan.

(5) **E**—Express appreciation and goodwill. This is the time to thank the client for considering your ideas, to praise the reader's company, or to express goodwill. After all, the reader has faithfully followed the train of thought through the most of the sales letter so far. This compliment may seem to be unnecessary to you, but this is a high-interest item to the readers. Sometimes, the final sentences can matter most: the call to specific action.

(6) **S**—Specify exactly what the client should do—and when. Finally, tell the reader in a clear and specific way what you want him or her to do—and when—to bring about the advantages described earlier in the letter. Maintain the upbeat "Yes" attitude.

Specific action statements often consist of:

- an action verb (call, present, visit);
- a specific address and telephone number, a specific time (now, on or before);
- perhaps one final advantage if the reader does what you suggest.

By using the S-A-L-V-E-S approach, you can be sure to write a successful sales letter.

ACTIVITY FOR LEARNING

Try to use the method of S-A-L-V-E-S we have introduced above to write a sales letter. Consider if it can meet the reader's needs and to be a successful sales letter for your reader.

2. How to make your sales letter looks colorful and attractive

A Sales letter is an effective and efficient way to promote a product or service. However, most sales letters is regarded as rubbish and put into the rubbish bins by the clients for a number of reasons. Readers are often confused by a sales letter because they can't identify what it is that the letter is really asking and how they can benefit from the product or service being offered. It also takes the client a lot of time to read the sales letter. Therefore, paying attention to grabbing the attention of the reader and keeping it is very important.

Why is the fate of most sales letters so unlucky? One of the reasons is their boring, meretricious, tedious envelopes. So designing a unique envelope that can grasp the client's eyes is the first important step to reach your objective of getting the client to take notice. Here are some sentences that could be placed on the envelope that may urge the clients to open the sales letter and read it.

(1) Please pay attention! What's inside is about to change your life.

(2) Sample enclosed.

(3) Enclosed is the most unusual gift.

Maybe you are lucky because the clients are interested in reading the sales letter. You can take further steps to attract their attention.

(1) Enclose some baubles with the sales letter.

(2) Offer some largess such as a complimentary ticket. Everyone likes a free lunch.

(3) Have a special opening line with a question, an anecdote, or an interesting story. When you ask a question, most readers try to answer it and then keep on reading the rest of the letter.

In order to narrow the gap between the writer and the clients, some writers use words or sentences that are false and meaningless. The writers may want a closer relationship between them and the clients, but the result can go contrary to their wishes because trust is lost and their credibility is doubted by the reader. Don't use words like "revolutionary" "incredible" or "astounding" because they sound to be too exaggerated and reduce your credibility. This may even impact negatively on your relationship.

You should also be careful about the length of the sales letter. Some experts suggest that the sales letter should be within one page. Others argue that if the first page can grasp the eyes of the clients, you can make a deal with the reader at the third or fourth page. No matter what their opinions are, you should focus on what you can offer the clients rather than only on your product or service. Once you present your offers and advantages very clearly and completely, you can stop writing the letter.

Here is an example:

Read the following sales letter from Sandra Lanson of Floral Displays Inc. Using the advice given to you above, consider the qualities of good sales letters and decide if you think it is effective. Why or why not?

Complete Sales Latter Following the S-A-L-V-E-S

4982 Brooks, Suite 4 Toledo, OH 43606 (419)555-9046

April 10, 1999

Mr. David Jenkins
District Manager
Coleberry Financial Service, Inc.
324 Wall Avenue
Toledo, Ohio 69587

Dear Mr. Jenkins,

S Do you sometimes wish you could bring the park—trees, flowers, shrubbery—back to the office with you after lunch?

A Floral Displays, Inc. makes your wishes come true. We rent out and maintain gorgeous tropical plants for your office and reception area. For less than $2 per day, we can surround you in lush philodendron or hide you behind an elephant ear plant.

L Plants make business more pleasant and more profitable.

V Clients appreciate your thoughtfulness and admire your taste and they are in softening the bare edges of business life with lovely plants. Happy clients spend more, more often.

V Employee turnover is drastically reduced. Employees come to think of the office as an attractive, inviting place.

E Your reputation in Toledo as a leading financial services company can only be further enhanced by a modest investment in a more healthful, attractive and impressive office environment.

S Take a moment right now to call Marci (555-9049) for a free floral decoration analysis of your office. She will come at your convenience, finish her work quickly, then dazzle you with affordable decorating ideas. If you prefer, mail in the enclosed card for our latest color catalog of decorating ideas.

With best wishes,

Sandra T. Lansdon

Marketing Director

Enclosure: " Your Catalog Reservation" (return postcard)

(Source: Bell A H, Smith D M. *Management Communication*[M]. New York: Wiley, 2009.)

Checklist for A Sales Letter

1. Prepare

(1) Learn as much as possible about the products, the competition, and the audience.

(2) Select a central selling theme—your product's most distinguishing features.

2. Gain the reader's attention

(1) Make your opening brief, interesting, and original. Avoid obvious, misleading, and irrelevant statements.

(2) Use any of these openings: rhetorical question, thought-provoking statement, unusual fact, current event, anecdote, direct challenge, or some similar attention-getting device.

(3) Introduce the central selling theme in the opening.

(4) If the letter is in response to a customer inquiry, begin by expressing appreciation for the inquiry and then introduce the central selling theme.

3. Create interest and build desire

(1) Make the introduction of the product follow naturally after the attention-getter.

(2) Interpret the features of the product instead of just describe the futures, show how the readers will benefit from each feature. Let the reader picture owning, using, and enjoying the product.

(3) Use action-package, positive, and objective language. Provide convincing evidence to support your claims—specific facts and figures, independent product reviews, and so on.

(4) Continue to stress the central selling theme throughout.

(5) Subordinate price. State price in small terms, in a long sentence, or a sentence that also talks about benefits.

4. Motivate action

(1) Make the desired action clear and easy to take.

(2) Ask confidently, avoiding the hesitant "If you'd like to" or "I hope you agree that".

(3) Encourage prompt action.

(4) End your letter with a reminder of a reader benefit.

7.10 Developing successful memoranda

The memorandum (memo) is the important form of communication used to relay information within a company, club, or other organization. Second to the phone call, memos (whether sent as hard copy or email transmission) are the primary means of in-house communication in most businesses throughout the world. Memos covey queries, comments, replies, announcements, policy statements, statistical information, reminders, authorizations, and a host of other routine but vital communication.

The memo is a kind of in-house communication. Every word you write helps to create your business identity within your company. Though each of your memos may not actually be a "promotion ticket", your written work can drastically hurry or halt career advancement. Remember the research by the National Commission on Writing, quoted in Chapter 6, which suggested that up to half US companies take writing skills into account when promoting their staff. In China, most companies require high communication capability and skills for the candidates when they recruit new employees. Here are some principles that will help you to write a memo more effectively and efficiently.

(1) Use positive language. Positive language can achieve positive results in written communication.

(2) Effective in-house communication conveys the whole message, not a partial message.

(3) Style and form are as important in brief in-house communication as they are in longer documents sent out of the company.

The memo is usually concerned with only one topic. If you have more than two topics, write two memos. Not everything that can be said should be said in written form. Just as the word memo is short for memorandum, the message in memos should be brief and to the point.

Memos are not treasure maps. Never try to build a sense of suspense or intimacy at the expense of your message. Try to make your message clear and then add whatever social or personal remarks you wish to add warmth and intimacy. If writing to your in-house clients, maintain a polite attitude at all times. Use sentences like: "Thank you very much." Or "I am sorry that I couldn't..." or "I really appreciate it if..." and so on.

1. Memo format

Here is an example of a typical memo format. Remember, it is different from a letter because it is sent inside the organization only.

Memorandum

To: David J. Kaplan, President

From: Larry Hass, Public Relations

Date: June 3rd, 2016

Re: May meeting of Plant Safety Committee

As we agreed on March 30 meeting of the Environmental Impact Committee, we will meet again on May 12. I am requesting agenda items and meeting suggestions from each....

2. Summarizing the structure of order acknowledgements and other thank-you message

Acknowledgements are sent to let people who order goods know the status of their orders. Most acknowledgements are routine. They simply tell when the goods are being shipped. Businesses usually acknowledge orders with forms, but they sometimes use written messages. Acknowledgements can build goodwill.

One of the first thank-you messages you write will be the one for a job interview. Once you are employed, you may send thank-you messages after a meeting, when someone does a favor for you or gives you a gift, when you want to acknowledge others' effort that has somehow benefited you, when you want to thank customers for their business, or perhaps when someone has donated time or money to your organization or a cause it supports. The possibilities for situations when you might send thank-you notes are many, and sending a message of sincere thanks is a great way to promote goodwill and build your and your company's professional images.

To write an order acknowledgement or thank-you message, you can follow the suggestions below.

(1) Use the direct order: begin by thanking the reader for something specific (e.g., an order).

(2) Continue with your thanks or with further information.

(3) Use positive, tactful language to address vague or back orders.

(4) If appropriate, achieve a secondary goal (e.g., reselling or confirming a mutual understanding).

(5) Close with a goodwill-building comment, adapted to the topic of the message.

Summary

This chapter discusses the most important written communication forms and styles of business letters. By the words you choose, by the way you arrange them on the page, and even by the letterhead stationery you select, you create, for your reader, an image and impression of your company and yourself. The readers can identify whether your company is friendly, open, efficiently, organized and fair, based in large part on your letters.

For the short form of business communication, such as memos, executive summary and email, you still need to follow some professional techniques that are clear, accurate and persuasive. You should keep in mind:

(1) Not everything that can be said should be said in written form.

(2) Positive language can achieve positive results in written communications.

(3) Effective communication conveys the whole message, not a partial message.

(4) Style and form are as important in brief in-house communications as they are in longer documents sent out of the company.

Questions for Discussion

(1) Discuss the importance of using positive language to produce positive results.

(2) What strategy is the best in a message refusing a request when the reasons for the refusal are strictly in the writer's best interest?

Exercises

(1) Point out the shortcoming in the following email message from a sports celebrity declining an invitation to speak at the kickoff meeting for workers in a fund-raising campaign for a charity.

Subject: Your request for free lectures

Ms. Chung,

As much as I would like to, I must decline your request that I give your membership a free lecture next month. I receive many requests to give free lectures. I grant some of them, but I simply cannot do them all. Unfortunately, yours is one of that I must decline.

> I regret that I cannot serve you this time. If I can be of further service in the future, please call on me.
>
> Sincerely yours

(2) You work for an online mail-order company. It sells many novelties such as T-shirts with clever sayings, unique toys and games, and such household accessories as framed posters. Most of the employees are young, somewhat quirky, and very Internet savvy. Now consider the following email sent to everyone from the company president. Considering the advice in this chapter, what would be the main way to improve this negative announcement?

> It has become obvious to me that people are spending too much time doing social networking and not enough time actually working while on the job. From now on, you must do your networking (whether on MySpace, WeChat, QQ, or any other such network) on breaks or during other personal time. Anyone found using these websites on company time will receive an official reprimand.

Chapter 8

Proposals, Reports and Business Plans

LEARNING OBJECTIVES

On completing this chapter, you should be able to:

- Understand the importance of a proposal and a business plan.
- Understand the structures of a project proposal and a business plan.
- Know how to write a project proposal, a report and a business plan.

Study Case：Evidence to support superlatives in Business

Dave Lavinsky, a cofounder of Growthink, a professional consulting firm , advertises small business owners to draft their business plan carefully because investors will evaluate the potential of the business based on the intelligence shown in the plan.

Specifically, Dave advises his clients to provide evidences for superlatives (best customer service, finest quality) in the plan.

He advises business owners to cite third-party research or offer other concrete evidence when making superlatives claims. For instance, if a firm believe that the market for his products is growing exponentially, it should cite some independent research that validates this claim. Similarly, if a firm claim in the business plan that it has the best people working for it, the plan should include details of qualifications and experiences of the personnel to support the claim.

The practice of always supporting superlative claims in the business plan will increase a firm's fundraising chances by making it appear more credible in the eyes of the investors.

(Adapted from:Dave Lavinsky. "Business Plan Readers No Longer Believe the Hype." in BusinessWeek: Small Biz:Tips, March 20,2009. Http://www.businessweek.com/smallbiz/tips/archives/2009/03/business_plan_r. html.)

Analysis：In the workplace, much work is routine or specifically assigned by other people. But sometimes you or your organization will want to consider new opportunities, and you will need to write a proposal for that work. Generally, proposals are created for projects that are longer or more expensive than routine work, that differ significantly from routine work, or that create larger changes than does normal work. In this chapter, we will learn how wo write proposals effectively.

Making your case in a proposal or business plan may be your greatest opportunity to make a difference in business or create impact in your organization. Making a case requires all your persuasive skills as well your ability to demonstrate that you have the evidence to support your argument, phrased in the best possible language and with the clarity and accuracy that we have emphasized earlier in this book. Above all, you can only achieve an effective case if you do your audience analysis carefully, so that you will match the proposal or business plan with the people who will read it.

8.1 Writing a Proposal

8.1.1 About a proposal

Proposals come under many different guises. They range from casual, one-page memos to multiple-volume, lengthy tomes that are hundreds of pages long. Usually, a proposal is a document written by a person, business, or agency who wishes to perform a job or solve a problem for another person, business, or agency and receive funding or money for the proposed task. Despite the differences, all proposals have one thing in common: they all suggest performing or make a request to perform a particular task or project.

Quite often, proposals are written in response to a formal or casual request—a RFP (request for proposal). The government and funding agencies frequently publish formal RFPs. These RFPs appear whenever there is money to be distributed for research or when tasks need to be performed. Formal RFPs give the guidelines for the finished proposal, telling the proposal writers what need to be included in the proposal and sometimes outline the proposal's format. Proposal writers follow the guidelines and fill in the details and expenses of the job. Sadly, many worthy proposals fail because they do not follow the published guidelines of the RFP institution.

Proposals differ from most other business and technical writing in one important way—they deal with the future and with things and conditions that do not exist. Writing about what does not exist can be tricky. Further complicating the difficulty of writing proposals is the additional issue that proposals must be very convincing. Proposals must convince the reader that there is a situation or problem requiring attention, and that the proposal writer is the best person to solve the problem or repair the situation. A final issue that proposal writers must face is the idea that, more often than not, proposals are legally binding offers.

Proposals, then, have the following characteristics:

(1) Proposals deal with the future.

(2) Proposals must convince the reader that there is a problem and the writer can do something about it.

(3) Proposals must convince the reader that the writer is the best person to fix the problem.

(4) Proposals vary in length and formality.

(5) Proposals are often legally binding offers.

(6) Proposals, generally, fall into one of four types: research, research and development, planning, sales.

8.1.2 Project proposal

An unsolicited proposal differs from the solicited proposal in that the former typically requires more background information and more persuasion. Because the reader may not be familiar with the project, the writer must present more evidence to convince the reader of the merits of the proposal.

The proposal reader is typically outside the organization. The format for these external documents may be a letter report, a manuscript report, or even a form report, with the form supplied by the soliciting organization. If the soliciting organization does not supply a form, it will likely specify in detailed language the format required for the proposal.

When writing a proposal, the writer must keep in mind that the proposal may become legally binding on the writer and the organization. In spelling out exactly what the writer's organization will provide, when, under what circumstances, and at what price, the proposal writer creates the offer parts of a contract that, if accepted, become binding on the organization.

Proposals are persuasive documents, and all the techniques you learned about persuasion in correspondence apply equally here:

(1) Give ample, credible evidence for all statements.

(2) Do not exaggerate.

(3) Provide examples, expert testimony, and specific facts and figures to support your statements.

(4) Use simple, straight forward, and direct language, preferring simple sentences and the active voice.

(5) Stress reader benefits. Remember that you are asking for something, usually a commitment of money; let the reader know what he or she will get in return.

Obviously, having a good idea is not enough. You must be able to present that idea clearly and convincingly so that it will be accepted. The benefits of clear and persuasive writing go far beyond the immediate goal of securing approval for your current project. A well-written proposal increases both your visibility and your credibility with the reader and with the organization on whose behalf you wrote the proposal.

Although proposals vary in length, organization, complexity, and format, the following sections are typical:

(1) Background: Introduce the problem you're addressing and discuss why it merits the reader's consideration. Provide enough background information to show that a problem exists and that you have a viable solution.

(2) Objectives: Provide specific information about what the outcomes of the project will be. Be detailed and honest in discussing what the reader will get in return for a commitment of resources.

(3) Procedures: Discuss in detail exactly how you will achieve these objectives, include a step-by-step discussion of what will be done, when, and exactly how much each component or phase will cost.

(4) Qualifications: Show how you, your organization, and any others who would be involved in conducting the project are qualified to do so. If appropriate, includes testimonials or other external evidence to support your claims.

(5) Request for approval: Directly ask for approval of your proposal. Depending on the reader's needs, this request could come either at the beginning or at the end of the proposal.

(6) Supporting data: Include, as an appendix to your proposal, relevant, supplementary information that might bolster your arguments.

ACTIVITY FOR LEARNING

Read the following case and consider the advice of Richard Fulscher. Consider Richard Fulscher's assertion that the fundamental question the reader asks is: Why should I hire you over your competition and will you perform?

Effective business plans have all the right ingredients, in an easy-to-digest format. A proposal for new business is too often seen as the necessary drudgery to get the interview. But a great proposal is an excellent marketing weapon. It focuses on your team's presentation and separates you from mediocre firms.

I have reviewed hundreds of management/leasing proposals and most share the same mistakes as follows:

- Too little information—Submitting just a company brochure with a price quote.
- Poor writing—Pleasing to look at, but, after the first read-through, boring to read.
- Lack of marketing focus—Trying to be everything to everyone, but being nothing to no one.
- Too general and self-centered—Focusing on the company instead of addressing the prospect's needs and desires.
- Done too quickly—Offering trivial solutions and canned material instead of ideas that get results.
- No "sell"—Presenting just information rather than a persuasive argument for the company.

Prospects ask for proposals because they want to contrast companies, review their options, and compare solutions to their problems. They want to be convinced, reassured, and impressed. They want you to show your understanding of their problems, propose solutions, and demonstrate your capabilities. In short, they want to be sold. They want their most basic questions answered. "Why should I hire you over your competition and will you perform?" A great proposal provides all this information and more in a palatable format.

(Source: Fulscher R J. *A no-fail recipe: Winning business proposals*[J]. Journal of Property Management, 1996, 1-2(61): 62.)

Look at the example below. The solicited proposal seeks to persuade an organization to sponsor a workshop.

Dear Ms. Soule,

Subject: Proposal for an In-house Workshop on Business Writing

I enjoyed discussing with you the business writing workshop you intend to sponsor for the engineering staff at Everglades National Corporation. As you requested, I am submitting this proposal to conduct a two-day workshop.

Begin by identifying the purpose of the letter

Background

On September 4-5, I interviewed four engineers at your organization and analyzed samples of their writing. Your engineers are typical of many highly trained specialists who know exactly what they want to say but sometimes do not structure their communications in the most effective manner…

Thus I propose that you sponsor a two-day workshop that I will develop entitled "The Process of Business Writing".

Objectives

The workshop would help your engineers achieve these objectives:

(1) Specify the purpose of a message and perform an audience analysis.

(2) Determine what information to include and in what order to present it.

…

Procedures

The enclosed outline shows the coverage of the course. The workshop would require a meeting room with participants seated at tables, an overhead projector, and a chalkboard or some other writing surface.

My fee for teaching the two-day workshop would be \$2 000, plus expenses.

Qualifications

As you can see from the enclosed data sheet, I've had 15 years of consulting experience in business communication and have spoken and written widely on the topic.

Summary

My experience in working with engineers has taught me that they recognize the value of effective business communication and are motivated to improve their writing skills.

Best wishes.

Provide specific examples to show that a need exists

Suggest a reasonable solution

Tell exactly what the proposal should accomplish

Provide enough details to enable the reader to understand what is planned

Discuss costs in an open and confident manner

Highlight only the most relevant information from the enclosed data sheet

Show how the reader will benefit from the doing as asked

Close in a friendly, confident note

8.2 Writing a Report

8.2.1 Defining a report

Some people define reports to include almost any presentation of information, others limit reports to only the most formal presentations. We use this middle-ground definition: A business report is an orderly and objective communication of factual information that serves a business purpose.

As an orderly communication, a report is prepared carefully. Thus, care in preparation distinguishes reports from casual exchanges of information. The objective quality of a report is its unbiased approach. Reports seek to present facts. They avoid human biases as much as possible. The word communication in our definition is broad in meaning. It covers all ways of transmitting meaning: speaking, writing, using graphics. The basic ingredient of a report is factual information. Factual information is based on the events, statistics, and other data. Not all reports are business reports. Research scientists, medical doctors, students, and many others write them.

8.2.2 Short reports

1. Internal and External environment and purpose

Short reports are usually less than ten pages and can be read in one sitting. Business organizations of all sizes rely on these documents to learn what's happening (what has happened or will happen) in two worlds:

(1) The internal world: What are the employees working on? How is it going? What resources are being used, or which are required? In what ways is the company growing or shrinking? What problems need to be addressed?

(2) The external world: How is the company perceived by clients and the general public? What do clients want from the company? What's the company's competition, and how can it be met?

These issues and others are discussed by means of all communication channels within the company, including meetings, interviews, memos, and letters. However, a report often addresses these issues more thoroughly, and it's more formal than other forms of business communication.

The purpose of a report may be information (what is known about the topic), analytical (why circumstances have developed), persuasive (how readers should respond), or portions of all three. Because short reports are used for making decisions, they include enough evidence to support the options suggested in the report. Although short reports can refer to other written work, they should not just be cover letters of relatively disorganized collections of facts and figures.

2. Ten steps to write a short report

Step 1: Think about the W-O-R-M.

W(who/What)—Who will read the report? What are their interests? Their needs?

O(objective)—What is the objective of the report?

R(range)—What's the range of the report? How broadly should you describe and cover your topics? Do you want to interpret facts?

M(method)—What's the method of presentation in the report?

Step 2: Know what your audience wants. The report writer bears primary responsibility for knowing what the reader wants.

Step 3: Brainstorm about your topic.

Step 4: Research your topic. Once you have brainstormed your topic, you know what to look for in the piles of records and files heaped on your desk.

Step5: Arrange your major points. Think not only about what you want to say, but also about placing each aspect of your arrangement in its appropriate location.

Step 6: Write your rough draft.

Step 7: Revise your rough draft.

Step 8: Review the appearance of your rough draft.

Step 9: Prepare your final copy.

Step 10: Present your report advantageously.

8.2.3 Long reports

Consider the ingredients of a long report. First, it usually includes a number of prefacing pages called "front matter"—a title page, letters of authorization and transmittal, table of content and figures, sometimes even a preface and foreword, and usually an abstract or executive summary. The body of the report is usually 15 or more pages. Concluding matter includes appendixes, legal instruments (if any), endnotes, a bibliography, and perhaps a glossary and index. Few long reports in business number less than 20 pages, and most are considerably longer.

In many ways, long reports are extra-long versions of short reports. Review the elements of the short report, by checking the previous pages of this book. However, as they have few length restrictions, long reports can easily get sidetracked and confusing. So, it is very important to keep long report clear and readable. Pay particular attention to paragraph beginning and ending. Use these to provide summary introductions and conclusions as well as helpful transitions. Readers should not have to wade through several sentences before understanding your message and how it relates to surrounding paragraphs.

Follow the suggestions for writing style taught in previous chapters, and avoid "the ten fatal ills of business writing" shown below.

The Ten Fatal Ills of Business Writing

1. Anemic verbs (is, are, were, seems to be)

Not: *It is a policy of this company to promote creative thinkers.*

Instead: *This company promotes creative thinkers.*

2. Impotent verbs (passive constructions)

Not: *The account was handled carelessly.*

Instead: *Jack handled the account carelessly.*

3. Atrophy of the position of emphasis

Not: *There are two financial packages suited to our needs.*

Instead: *Two financial packages suit our needs.*

4. Distended sentence length

Not: *While seven of our managers at the midlevel range object to the idea of corporate offices, the majority of our senior staff are agreeable to the move as an opportunity to live in the sun belt.*

Instead: *Sevens midlevel managers object to moving our corporate offices. Our senior staff, however, welcome the move as a chance to live in the sun belt.*

5. Hypertrophy of the noun

Not: *The unification of companies will prove beneficial to the establishment of arrangements more conductive to solvency and profitability.*

Instead: *Merging our company will help solve our money problem.*

6. Slow sentence plus

Try to mix subject-verb-object sentence with other types.

For example: *Frustrated, Jerry wrote a scorching memo. (-ed beginning before the subject)*

7. Obese paragraph

Try "easy in and easy out", using very short paragraphs at the beginning and end of business letters, memos and short reports.

8. Noun clots

Not: *Please write a minoritiy's opportunity evaluation report.*

Instead: *Please write a report evaluating opportunities for minorities.*

9. Spastic repetitions

Not: *We received the benefits package. The benefits package provided for...*

Instead: *We received the benefits package, which provided for...*

10. Contagious prepositions

Not: *We ran an advertisement in a trade journal in May for a manager of the sales division at our* subsidiary *in Wisconsin.*

Instead: *"Sales manager" "Wisconsin subsidiary"(Combine prepositional phrases into adjective/noun combinations.)*

(Source: Bell A H. Nation's Business, 1984, (11))

8.3 How to Write a Business Plan

8.3.1 The importance of a business plan

"The business plan is a necessity. If the person who wants to start a small business can't put a business plan together, he or she is in trouble." Says Robert Krummer, Jr, Chairman of First Business Bank in Los Angeles.

The business plan becomes the point of departure for prospective investors to begin their due diligence in order to ascertain the various risks and potential of the venture: technology risks, market risks, management risks, competitive and strategic risks and financial risks.

Founders and investors try to set a code for their relationship and negotiation through various meetings and discussions. Issues that will be on the minds of all the parties constantly are as follows:

- Are these people intelligent?

- Can we have good cooperation within the time?
- Can they add value to the venture?
- Do they have the right management team?
- Are they honest?

The most valuable investors will see the weakness, even flaws, in how the market viewed the technology or service, the strategies, the proposed size and the structure of the financing and the team. By revealing themselves, the investors can bring the most insight and know-how to the venture, and add great value to the venture.

8.3.2 The plan is not the business

One of the best ways to define the blueprint, strategy, resource, and human resource requirements for a new venture is to develop a business plan. The vast majority of international companies of 500 fastest growing companies had a business plan at the outset. It is exceedingly difficult to raise capital from formal or informal investors without a business plan.

However, the plan doesn't mean the business. Some of the most impressive business plans never become great businesses. And some of the weakest plans lead to extraordinary businesses. Having a plan doesn't mean the business will be successful automatically. Unless the fundamental opportunity is there, along with the requisite resources and team needed to pursue it, the best plan in the world won't make much difference. On the other hand, the business plan can be thought of as a work in progress. The planning is a process, not just a plan. It can never be completed because it will be affected by many changing factors coming from the internal or external environment, such as capital, human resource, technology and potential risks and opportunities.

Figure 8.1 shows a business plan as part of a process. You can think about the advantages and disadvantages of the plan itself, measuring its value by its contents. However, it is even better to see the plan as part of the whole process of the result, because even a great plan is wasted if nobody follows it.

Planning is a process, not just a plan.

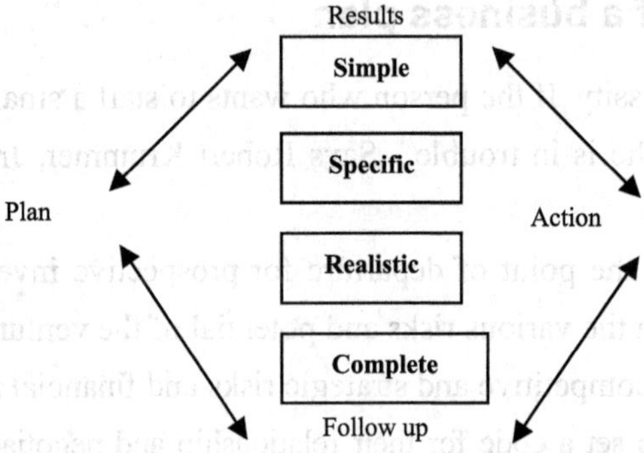

Figure 8.1 The Process of Planning

8.3.3 Preparing for a business plan

Despite the critical importance of a business plan, many entrepreneurs drag their feet when it comes to preparing a written document. They argue that their marketplace changes too fast for a business plan to be useful or that they just don't have enough time. But just as a builder won't begin construction without a blueprint, eager business owners shouldn't rush into new ventures without a business plan.

Before you begin writing your business plan, consider four core questions:

- What service or product does your business provide and what needs does it fill?
- Who are the potential customers for your product or service and why will they purchase it from you?
- How will you reach your potential customers?
- Where will you get the financial resources to start your business?

The team who will develop the business plan should believe the business they are considering has excellent market prospects and fits well with the skills, experience, personal goals and values. They need to know the most significant risks and problems involved in launching the enterprise, the long-term profit prospects and the future financing and cash flow requirements. They also need to know the demands of operating lead times, seasonality and facility location, as well as the marketing and pricing strategy needs.

1. Segmenting and integrating information

Organizing information in a way that it can be managed and be useful to the writing plan is a necessary step in order to have an efficient planning and writing. One effective way to organize information with the idea of developing a business plan is to segment information into different sections, such as one about the target market, a section about the industry, one about the financial plan and so on.

The order in which sections are developed can vary, but some sections can be developed simultaneously. For example, since the heart and soul of a plan lies in the analysis of the market opportunity, of the competition, and of a resultant competitive strategy that can win in the niche market, it is a good idea to start with these sections and integrate information along the way. And the financial and operations aspects of the venture will be driven by the rate of the growth and the magnitude and specific substance of the market revenue plans. These sections can be developed later.

2. Establishing action steps

Here is a guide to help you write the plan.

Step 1: Segmenting information (see Table 8.1). An overall plan for the project by sections needs to be devised and needs to include priorities, who is responsible for each section, the due date of a first draft, and the due date of a final draft. When you segment your information, it is vital to keep in mind that the plan needs to be logically integrated and the information should be consistent. It is best to assign the market opportunity section a high priority and begin work there first because of its importance to the whole plan.

Step 2: Creating an overall schedule. This process is to make the list of specific tasks that need to be completed, their priorities, which is responsible for them, when they will be started, and when they will be completed. It is helpful to break larger items into the small, manageable components and to include the components as a task. The list should be as specific and detailed as possible. Also the list needs to be examined for conflicts and lack of reality in time estimate.

Table 8.1 Segmentation Information

Section or Task	Priority	Person(s) Responsible	Date to Begin	First Draft Due Date	Date Completed or Final Version Due Date

(Source: Timmons J A, Spinelli S. *New Venture Creation: Entrepreneurship for the 21st Century*[M]. New York: Irwin McGraw-Hill, 2003.)

Step 3: Creating an action calendar (see Table 8.2). This is the process that combines the list of segments and the list of tasks to create a calendar. When combining the list to create a calendar, consider if anything has been omitted and whether you have been realistic in what people can do, when they can do it, and what needs to be done.

Table 8.2 An Action Calendar

Task	Week								
	1	2	3	4	5	6	7	8	9

(Source: Timmons J A, Spinelli S. *New Venture Creation: Entrepreneurship for the 21st Century*[M]. New York: Irwin McGraw-Hill, 2003.)

Step 4: Doing the work and writing the plan. During the process of writing the plan, adjustment needs to be made to the list and the calendar. As a part of this process, an attorney needs to have a review of the plan in order to make sure that it contains no misleading statements and unnecessary information and caveats, and also the document should be reviewed by an objective outsider.

8.3.4 Writing a business plan

When writing a plan, you should keep in mind that though one of the important functions of a business plan is to influence investors, rather than preparing a fancy presentation, you and your team need to prove to yourselves and others that your opportunity is worth pursuing, and to construct the means by which you will do it. Gathering information, making hard decisions and developing the plan come first. You should create a plan that outlines your goals, expected costs, marketing plan and exit strategy. A business plan is your road map for how you expect to succeed and how you'll measure success.

Here is the outline of a business plan. Read this outline carefully. It will act as a guide to help you with the development of your plan. When we first start to develop business plans, templates like this can save considerable time because they direct our attention to the essential elements that need to be covered. As we develop confidence, we can adjust and change the format.

Outline of a Complete Business Plan

Ⅰ. Executive Summary
- A. Description of the Business Concept and the Business
- B. The Opportunity and Strategy
- C. The Target Market and Projections
- D. The Competitive Advantages
- E. The Economics, Profitability, and Harvest Potential
- F. The Team
- G. The Offering

Ⅱ. The Industry and the Company and its Product(s) or Service(s)
- A. The Industry
- B. The Company and the Concept
- C. The Product(s) and Service(s)
- D. Entry and Growth

Ⅲ. Market Research and Analysis
- A. Customers
- B. Market Size and Trends
- C. Competition and Competitive Edges
- D. Estimated Market Share and Sales
- E. Ongoing Market Evaluation

Ⅳ. The Economics of the Business
- A. Gross and Operation Margins
- B. Profits Potential and Durability
- C. Fixed, Variable and Semi-variable Costs
- D. Months to Breakeven
- E. Months to Research Positive Cash Flow

Ⅴ. Marketing Plan
- A. Overall Marketing Strategy
- B. Pricing
- C. Sales Tactics
- D. Service and Warranty Policies
- E. Advertising and Promotion
- F. Distribution

Ⅵ. Design a Development Plan
A. Development Status and Tasks
B. Difficulties and Risks
C. Product Improvement and New Products
D. Costs
E. Proprietary Issues
Ⅶ. Manufacturing and Operation Plan
A. Operating Cycle
B. Geographical Location
C. Facilities and Improvement
D. Strategy and Plans
E. Regulatory and Legal Issues
Ⅷ. Management Team
A. Organization
B. Key Management Personnel
C. Management Compensation and Ownership
D. Other Investors
E. Employment and Other Agreement and Stock Option and Bonus Plans
F. Board of Directors
G. Other Shareholders, Rights, and Restrictions
H. Supporting Professional Advisors and Services
Ⅸ. Overall Schedules
Ⅹ. Critical Risks, Problems, and Assumptions
Ⅺ. The Financial Plan
A. Actual Income Statements and Balance Sheets
B. Pro Forma Income Statements
C. Pro Forma Balance Sheets
D. Pro Forma Cash Flow Analysis
E. Breakeven Chart and Calculation
F. Cost Control
G. Highlights
Ⅻ. Proposed Company Offering
A. Desired Financing
B. Offering
C. Capitalization
D. Use of Funds
E. Investor's Return
XIII. Appendixes

(Source: Timmons J A, Spinelli S. *New Venture Creation: Entrepreneurship for the 21st Century*[M]. New York: Irwin McGraw-Hill, 2003.)

Now it is time to examine the characteristics of various important elements of the business plan. You should use all the business communication knowledge and skills that you have learned in the earlier chapters, to make the document as clear, concise, appropriate in tone and persuasive as possible. After all, if you cannot articulate what it is that you intend to do, and if your plan cannot answer all the issues that the readers can think of, then your plan is not comprehensive and thorough.

1. Executive summary

The first section in the body of the business plan is usually an executive summary. The summary is short: about one or two pages. The summary states what the opportunity conditions are and why they exist, who will execute the opportunity and why they are capable of doing so, and how the firm will gain entry and market penetration.

The summary is important for those whose ventures are trying to raise or borrow money to develop the business. Many investors, bankers, and managers focus on the summary to determine quickly whether what the venture plan describes is of interest. Therefore, the summary may be the only section read unless it is appealing and compelling. You are likely missing the chance to present or discuss your business plan in person.

It is recommended that you pay careful attention to the summary. It usually contains the following details.

(1) **Description of the business concept and the business.** For example, Outdoor Scene, Inc. wanted to produce tents. The concept was "to become a leader in providing quality service, and on-time delivery in outdoors leisure products". Try to make your description 25 words or less.

(2) **The opportunity and strategy.** They refer to summarize what the opportunity is, and what the strategy is for entering to exploit it. The information should include an outline of the key facts, conditions, competitors' vulnerabilities, industry trends, and other evidence and logic that define the opportunity.

(3) **The target market and projections.** They refer to identify and briefly describe the condition of the industry and the market, who the primary customer groups are, how the product(s) or service(s) will be positioned and how you plan to reach and serve those groups. The information includes the structure of the market, size and growth rate for the market segments or niches you are seeking, your anticipated market share, the payback period for your customers, and your pricing strategy.

The next section outlines the context for the plan, including the industry, company, products or services to be offered.

2. The industry and the company and its product(s) or service(s)

Three major areas are usually considered in this section: the industry, the company and its product(s) or service(s). For the industry, briefly describe the current status and prospects for the industry in which the proposed business will be operated. Market size, growth trends and competitors need to be discussed in the plan along with any new products, new entrants and exits and any other trends and factors that could affect the venture's business positively or negatively.

As to the information about product(s) or service(s), try to describe some details about each product or service to be sold and the application of the product or service. Any unique features of the product or service should be emphasized and how these will create or add significant value. Also highlight any difference between what is currently on the market and what you will offer that will account for your market penetration.

As we mentioned earlier, the section on the market is the most important section in the plan. It is here that you will persuade your reader that you have a good chance of success.

3. Market research and analysis

Because of the importance of market analysis and as it is the basis of other parts of the plan, you are recommended to prepare this section before any other. This section will cover some details as follows:

(1) **Customers.** Try to discuss the targeted customers as well as the potential customers of the product or service, to show who and where the major purchasers for the product or service are in each market segment and indicate whether customers are easily reached and receptive. If you have an exciting business, explain your current customers and discuss the trends in your new business sales to them.

(2) **Market size and trends**. The task of this part is to explain the size of the current total market and the share you will have by market segment or by region for five years to describe the potential annual growth for at least three years of the total market for your product or service, and to review previous trends in the market. Some major factors that could affect market growth should be mentioned, such as industry trends, government policies and so on.

(3) **Competition and competitive edges.** It is now time to indicate who your key competitors are for your product or service in the market. Identify the assessment of the strengths and weaknesses of competitors, comparing competing and substitute products or services on the basis of market share, quality, price, performance, delivery time and other pertinent features. Discuss several key competitors and why customers buy from them and why customers leave them.

Also, this section needs to discuss the current advantages and disadvantages and differentiations of your product or service along with added value created by your product or service, in terms of economic benefits to the customers and to your competitors. Explain why you think your competitors are vulnerable and you can capture a share of their business.

Financial factors also need to be reviewed in the plan, such as financial position, resources, costs, and profitability of the competition and their profit trend.

(4) **Estimated market share and sales.** This part identifies any major customers who are willing to purchase or who have already purchased your product or service, discussing which customers could be major purchasers in future years and why. You should also estimate the share market of the market and the sales in units and dollars that you will acquire in each of the next three years based on the assessment of the advantages of the product or service, the market size

and trends, customers, the competition and their products and the trends of sales in prior years.

(5) **Ongoing market evaluation.** In this section, explain how you will continue to evaluate your target market in order to assess customer needs and to guide product improvement and new-product programs, plan for expansions of your production facility, and guide product/service pricing.

4. Marketing plan

The marketing plan explains how the sales projections will be attained. It covers the overall marketing strategy, pricing, distribution, promotion, advertising strategy and sales projections. It will focus on what needs to be done, how it will be done, when it will be done and who will do it.

(1) **Overall marketing strategy**. In this section, you need to describe the specific marketing philosophy and strategy of the company, giving the value chain and channels of distribution in the market niches you are pursuing; indicate whether the product(s) or service(s) will be introduced internationally, nationally or regionally and why. You must also explain any plans for the future, such as to obtain government contracts as a means of supporting product development costs and overhead.

(2) **Pricing**. You now need to discuss pricing strategy that includes the price to be charged for your product and service, comparing your pricing policy with those of your competitors. Explain how the price you set will enable you to get the product and service accepted, to maintain and increase your market share in the face of the keen competition and to produce profits.

Justify your pricing strategy and differences between your prices and those of competitive or substitute products or service in terms of economic payback to the customer and value added through newness, quality, warranty, timing, performance and so on.

Explain your pricing policy that covers the relationship of price, market share and profits. Include any discount allowance for prompt payment or volume purchases.

(3) **Sales tactics**. In this section, discuss the methods that will be used to make sales and distribute the product or service , including both the initial plans and longer-range plans for a sales force. Issues such as the value chain and the resulting margins to be given to retailers, distributors, wholesalers, salespeople and any special policies regarding discounts are also important. You also need to show how to build and structure a direct sales force and at what rate it will be built. If other media are used, such as email, magazine, newspaper, social media, or catalog sales, indicate the specific channels or vehicles, costs and expected response rates and yield from the various media and so on.

(4) **Advertising and promotion**. You should also describe the channels that the company will use to deliver the product(s) or service(s) to the customers. For consumer products, indicate what kind of advertising and promotional campaign is contemplated to introduce the product and what kind of sales aids will be provided. Present a schedule and approximate costs of promotion and advertising and discuss how these costs will be incurred.

5. Design a development plan

The next step is to design a development plan. This means to describe the information in detail about any design and development work and the time and the money required before a product or service is delivered. Such design and development might be the engineering work necessary to cover a laboratory prototype to a finished work, the design of special tooling or the identification and organization of employees, equipment and special techniques to implement a service business.

Development: Describe the current status of product(s) or service(s), indicating how to improve it to be marketable. Also, you need to explain the competence or expertise that your company has or will require to complete this development. Discuss any ongoing design and development work that can keep the product(s) or service(s) competitive so that customers' loyalty can be maintained.

This part of your plan simply outlines the steps you have taken toward developing your business and what remains to be done. Your stage of development section should cover the following:

(1) How will your product or service be made? Describe the workflow in the creation of your product or service.

(2) What are the problems that might occur in the development of your product or service? Have you created a checklist to ensure these problems are discovered?

(3) Who are your suppliers? Do you have alternate suppliers if one doesn't work out? What are their prices, terms and conditions?

(4) What quality control measures have you instituted?

6. Manufacturing and operation plan

Regardless of your type of business, you need to walk through the process of creating your product or delivering your service. This part of your business plan allows you to show an understanding of the process of manufacturing your product or delivering your service. This section should cover the following:

(1) What are the basic requirements for your business? Consider land, equipment, office space etc. If you own or need land, buildings or equipment, you should explain what worth it is or costs, how it is to be financed (e.g. bought or leased) and why it is vital to the success of the business.

(2) When can you start producing your product or service? How long does it take to produce a unit or a set number of units of your product?

(3) Where will you get the materials to produce your product/service? How much do they cost? Have you negotiated terms with suppliers?

(4) What factors can affect your anticipated time frame for production (e.g. rush orders, material shortages)?

(5) Will you make or buy the components necessary for the production of your product or service? Why?

(6) What will you do if the demand for your goods or services fluctuates? Have you conducted feasibility testing on your product (i.e. tested the process, prototyping and pricing)?

7. Management team

This part will cover the basic information first that includes how many employees the company has, how many managers, and how many of the managers are founders. Is your team complete, or are there gaps still to be filled? Is your organizational structure sound, with job descriptions and logical responsibilities for all the key members?

1) **Explain your organizational structure**

The organizational structure of a company is what you frequently see as an organizational chart, also known as an "org chart". If you have access to a graphic of an organizational chart, that works really well. If not, you can just use the text to describe the organizational structure in words, without a chart.

Make sure you explain how job descriptions work and how the main company functions are divided up. Are your organizational lines drawn clearly? Is the authority properly distributed? Do you have jobs that include responsibility without authority? Do your resources seem in line with your organizational needs?

2) **List team members and their backgrounds**

List the most important members of the management team, include summaries of their backgrounds and experience, using them like brief resumes. Describe their functions within the company. Resumes should be attached to the back of a plan.

3) **Discuss your management gaps**

You may have obvious gaps in management, especially in start-up companies, but even in more established companies. For example, a manufacturing company without a production manager has some explaining to do, and a computer company without service has some problems. It is far better to define and identify a weakness than to pretend it doesn't exist. Specify where the team is weak because of gaps in coverage of key management functions. How will these weaknesses be corrected? How will the more important gaps be filled?

4) **Other management team considerations**

Applicability depends on your company. Some questions that should be answered include: Do any managers or employees have "non-compete" agreements? Who is on your board of directors? What do the members contribute to the business? Who are your major stockholders? What are their roles in management?

8. Critical risks, problems, and assumptions

Every business has some degree of risk to it. It is important for you to think through and outline possible risks in your company. This will demonstrate that you understand the risks and, to the extent that you can, have made allowances for them. Detail how you plan to minimize or address the risks inherent to your business. Remember that the most important reason for writing a business plan is that it is an important tool to help you start and manage your business. Feel free to incorporate all identified risks within their respective sections of your business plan and make them clearly understood by any perspective reader of your business plan. For example, you can discuss human resource risks such as not being able to find skilled labour. Be honest about your risks and take them seriously because you can avoid many problems by thinking ahead.

Consider the following questions:

(1) What are the possible risks within your industry?

(2) What if the demand for your goods or services decreases?

(3) What if the number of competitors increases?

(4) What risks do you face in producing your product or service?

(5) What risks do you face with the marketing plan you have outlined?

(6) What human resources risks do you face? Consider your management team, advisors and your employees.

(7) What if your key employees quit?

(8) What if you run out of cash? Where else would you go?

(9) What if your major supplier has financial difficulties? Are there other suppliers?

(10) What, if any, environmental risks does your product or service face? Do they conform to environmental rules of the government, municipality, etc.?

9. The financial plan

The financial plan is basic to the evaluation of an investment opportunity and needs to present your best estimates of financial requirement. The purpose of the financial plan is to indicate the venture's potential and present a timetable for financial viability. It also can serve as an operating plan for financial management using financial benchmarks.

1) **Income statement**

An income statement shows your profit or loss for a particular period of time, detailing all revenues, expenses and other costs. As with the cash flow statement, it should be prepared on a monthly or quarterly basis to allow for proactive management of any changes. While a cash flow statement is used to monitor a business' cash position, the income statement is predominantly an accounting tool used to measure a business' performance.

Think about when you will achieve break-even for your business venture. That is the level of sales in either dollars or units where revenue equals total costs.

2) **Cash flow statement**

The old saying that "cash is king" is true. Simply put, without cash, your business can't operate. A cash flow statement is a reflection of how much money your business has at a particular point in time. If your cash inflows (collected revenue) exceed your cash outflows (disbursements), your cash flow is positive. If your cash outflows (disbursements) exceed your cash inflows (collected revenue), your cash flow is negative. Avoid the following common mistakes when preparing your income statement and cash flow statement:

(1) Projecting overly optimistic sales growth—most businesses grow gradually.

(2) Ignoring seasonality—is your business busiest in the summer or winter?

(3) Underestimating increases in expenses or cash outflows that come with an increase in sales.

(4) Assuming that collections will always be made in 30~60 days.

3) **Balance sheet**

A balance sheet is a snapshot of the financial state of your business at a particular point in time. It outlines your assets, liabilities and equity and helps you know the net worth of your business. A balance sheet should list current assets such as accounts receivable, inventory you have on hand, and your cash balance. It should also list fixed assets such as property, equipment, furniture and fixtures, and vehicles.

Current liabilities might include accounts payable and debts that you must pay within a year (suppliers & creditors). Long-term liabilities include long-term loans, like mortgages, equipment loans or loans you make to the business. Shareholder's equity is made up of permanent funds put into the business yourself or from someone who invests in your business for a share of ownership (capital stock) and retained earnings.

Here is a helpful set of Don't and Do to guide you on the path to a successful business plan.

Things not to do

(1) Don't have unnamed, mysterious people in the management team.

(2) Don't make ambiguous, vague, or unsubstantiated statements, such as estimating sales on the basis of what the team would like to produce.

(3) Don't describe technical products or manufacturing processes using jargon or in a way that only an expert can understand, because this limits the usefulness of the plan.

(4) Don't spend money on developing fancy brochures, elaborate slide show presentations and other "sizzle" —instead, show the "steak".

(5) Don't waste time writing a plan when you could be closing sales and collecting cash.

(6) Don't assume you have a done deal when you have a handshake or verbal commitment but no money in the bank.

Things to do

(1) Do involve all of the management team in the preparation of the business plan.

(2) Do make the plan logical, comprehensive and readable and as short as possible.

(3) Do articulate what the critical risks and assumptions are and how and why these are tolerable.

(4) Do identify several alternative sources of financing.

(5) Do spell out the proposed deal—how much for ownership and how investors will win.

(6) Do be creative in gaining the attention and interest of potential investors.

(7) Do remember that the plan is not the business and that an ounce of "can do" implementation is worth two pounds of planning.

(8) Do accept orders and customers that will generate a positive cash flow, even if it

means you have to postpone writing the plan.

(9) Do know your targeted investor groups (eg: venture capitalist, angel investment, bank, or leasing company) and what they really want and what they dislike, and tailor your plan accordingly.

(Source: Timmons J A, Spinelli S. *New Venture Creation: Entrepreneurship for the 21st Century*[M]. New York: Irwin McGraw-Hill, 2003.)

ACTIVITY FOR LEARNING

Here is a sample of Market and Marketing Strategy from Moot Corp Competition.

Compare this document with the elements of a Business Plan described earlier in this chapter. Beside each section, note to yourself, the role each element plays in the Business Plan. This will help you to develop your own strategy when the need to write a business plan arises.

Now visit www.businessplans.org or www.plans.com and review some more examples of effective business plans.

Summary

A business proposal describes ideas in such a way that they appear to fulfill the client's needs. Sometimes clients don't have a clear idea of their needs. In that case, the proposal must not only provide solutions, but also describe the problem.

The business plan, on the other hand, is more of a process and work in progress than an end in itself. The business plan is a blueprint and flight plan for a journey that you propose. It converts ideas into opportunities, articulates and manages risks and rewards, and articulates the likely fit and timing for a venture. A business plan answers the questions of what, who, where, why, when and how much. However, the plan is not the business. In fact, some of the most successful ventures ever were launched without a formal business plan or with one that would be considered weak or flawed. This does not mean that it is not useful. Often, the mere attempt to write a plan forces the planner to plan properly. When writing a business plan, try to avoid such problems as follows:

- The plan is too long—concisely written plans are preferred.
- Having little evidence from potential consumers that the business has merit.
- Competition is inadequately assessed.
- Sales expectations and projections are unreasonable.
- The plan demonstrates little operational knowledge.
- Financial assumptions do not match data in financial statement.
- Not providing for a realistic exit for investors.

Questions for Discussion

(1) Why should a proposal writer follow existing guidelines published by an organization requesting the proposal?

(2) What is a business plan, for whom is it prepared , and why?

(3) What should a complete business plan include? Make a list.

(4) Prepare an outline of a business plan tailored to the specific venture you have in mind.

(5) How can entrepreneurs use the business plan process to identify the best team members, directors, and value-added investors?

Exercises

Create an outline for a business plan to provide some products or service. Then write an executive summary, marketing research and analysis and marketing plan for the business plan.

第一部分

管理沟通基础

第 1 章

成功的商务沟通管理

引例：工作场所的沟通

诺姆·费尔德海姆(Norm Fjeldheim)将他职业生涯的成功大部分归功于他的不断学习商业写作和报告技巧。作为数字无线通信行业一家领先公司的领导者，他在很大程度上依赖于这些磨练得很成熟的技能。在对高通信息技术进行监管时，他与各种职位的人打交道，包括高通(Qualcomm)的高管和董事会成员，客户和供应商的高管，有时甚至与美国司法部(Department of Justice)和联邦调查局(FBI)就安全问题进行沟通。他还保持能获得直接报告和客户的知情，并进行跟踪。到目前为止，他每天大部分工作中使用的最重要的工具是Eudora、PowerPoint和Word。

当被问及他所上的最重要的课程是什么时，他明确的回答是“商务沟通”。他说，“即使你有很好的技术技能，如果没有良好的沟通技巧，你的事业也会停滞不前。事实上，你的沟通技巧越好，你的职业生涯就会走得越远。随着时间的推移，技术在不断变化，能够拥有很好的沟通技巧总是很有价值的。”

Norm Fjeldheim，高级副总裁兼CIO
美国高通公司(Qualcomm)

(资料来源：Kathryn Rentz, Marie E. Flatley, Paula Lentz，《商业沟通(第12版)》，McGraw Hill, 2012,p1)

引例启示：在商业领域的工作将会涉及沟通——很多的沟通——因为沟通是商业工作的一个主要和必要的部分。通过提高你的沟通能力，增加成功的机会。

1.1 商务沟通技能的重要性

沟通在商务活动中非常重要，因而要求人们掌握良好的沟通技巧。在大量来自高管、招聘和专业人士的调查中可以找到沟通在商务活动中非常重要的事实依据。同样，这些调查结果都说明沟通(尤其是口头沟通和书面沟通)技能被排在各种成功要素的最前列。

例如，NFI——一家私人研究组织最近通过对2000多个高管和高级经理的调查发现，94%参与调查的人将“良好的沟通能力”视为现在及未来事业成功最重要的技巧。通过国家联合大学对美国雇员的调查以及《2016年就业展望》对雇员的调查，一致认为“沟通技能”是求职者最重要的技能。在招聘中，雇主也将“能够很好地与组织内外进行沟通的能力”和“撰写及编辑书面报告的能力”列为求职者10个最重要的能力之一。参加了《华尔街日报》的工商管理硕士课程排名的招聘人员以及《2015年布隆伯格招聘报告》也认为目前沟通技能是十分缺乏的，他们认为“人际沟通技能、关注团队合作、个人道德和诚信、分析和解决问题的能力以及良好的职业道德”是最重要的。

遗憾的是，商务活动要求雇员拥有良好的沟通技能并不能完全实现。大多数雇员，甚至包括大学毕业生，都不能很好地进行沟通。现实需要大量的有效沟通者。

本书的作者们认识到良好沟通技巧对商务活动的重要性，并且确信通过学习商务沟通技能并将语言沟通与写作沟通技能付诸实践，不仅能成就令人满意的工作生涯，更重要的

是为将来的发展创造价值与机会。换句话说，如果初入职场就将商务沟通视为重要能力，则意味着为自己未来的成功铺平了道路。

1.2　商务沟通写作

本书的两位作者一致认为，我们要很认真地对待商务沟通，希望您也是如此。我们认真地通过如下四条线索来贯通每个章节并探讨每个主题。

(1) 介绍理论，并说明该理论的优点。

(2) 通过案例学习来说明理论在实际中的运用。

(3) 在特定情境下，对相关知识点进行练习和开展活动。

(4) 当面对新情况并需要运用知识进行解决时，文中的相关建议可以检验您的理解与运用能力。

本书包括了大量的主题，这些主题所涉及的内容是商务活动中都会用到的，具体包括在组织内部与同事进行的沟通以及与不同利益分享者的外部沟通(如客户、潜在客户、一般主体、社会组织等)所用到的内容。本书也能帮助大家进行正式沟通，如演讲、撰写推销信、商务计划、备忘录，以及一些非正式沟通，如网络沟通、处理冲突和影响他人等。

1.3　为什么要用双语写这本书

中国在走向世界，经济上会更加开放，经济类专业的学生迫切需要掌握一些好的实践技巧(无论这些技巧是运用在国内还是国外)。这样，学生可以从中西方优秀的商务沟通者合作的实践中受益。本书的作者来自于中国和澳大利亚，两国都是美国和亚洲国家主要的贸易伙伴。作者带来了有关东西方文化的知识，而这些知识的相互结合，可以帮助您为学习商务沟通面临的各种挑战做好准备。

作为作者，也认识到确定本书目标市场的重要性，我们这样描述目标读者。

(1) 本书是为能说双语的中国学生而编写的，他们正在学习英语或已经学习了英语，如果仅仅在需要时，通过参考恰当的中文部分便能够理解英文文本，他们会感觉更加自信。

(2) 我们期望这本书通过对那些国内商务及国际商务活动的介绍，能够为您的商务生涯尤其是国际环境下的商务活动做一些准备。也就是说，本书包括国内的实例和国际的实例，也包括一些跨文化的实例。

您的情况与这些相符合吗？如果是这样，这本书正是为您而写。它将为您着想，为您成为有效的沟通者而做准备。

1.4　本书中有价值的探索发现

作为一个出色的管理者，与他人交往的能力是最基本的素质。事实上，具有社会意识、拥有良好的沟通技巧(包括口头沟通和书面沟通)以及与他人的感情产生共鸣，对于一个优秀的领导者是十分关键的。美国心理学家丹尼尔·戈尔曼(Daniel Goleman)和他的同事扩展了情商的定义，认为情商是领导和管理者能力的基础，包括以下几种能力：控制自己感觉和情绪的能力、控制他人的感觉和情绪的能力、运用这些能力指导思维和行动的能力(Goleman，Boyatzis，Mckee，2002)。

那些情商高的领导们的基本任务是：为他领导的员工们营造舒适的心理环境——就像一种让人们自由发挥积极性的“水库”。而这也是我们同时关注作为沟通者的你，以及作为出现在本书中任何一种沟通情境中的听众的原因。事实上，本书中所有的章节都将听众或读者放在沟通互动的中心，第三章讨论劝说和演讲，第七章是有关有效商务书信的内容，这些内容不断地提醒你，良好沟通的“符咒”是：沟通关注的一切即是听众。

一种有助于和听众进行良好沟通的情商特性是适应性。这种特性，加上您和他人的共鸣，使您能够将所传达的信息适用于环境，或者适合于听众参与沟通的角色类型。这意味着认真关注他人的响应，认识到他们对问题的不同看法，从而在分享您的观点时，也能满足他们的需求。

本书不断要求您仔细思考：如何使沟通风格和语气适应于沟通对象，然而能做到这点并不容易。本书也提供了一些机会测试您的沟通能力。例如，通过案例学习，可以从中观察到有效的和无效的沟通行为，也可以通过一些练习进行自我测试。本书中也提供了一些学习原则和提示，如一些简单、容易记忆的缩写，可作为第一次撰写的参照模板，像撰写推销信或商务计划。其中一个例子就是：PLACE——准备(prepare)、听(listen)、纠正(adjust)、沟通(communicate)和享受(enjoy)。这是解决跨文化冲突的一个途径。记住这些字母组合，除了能够顺利地解决和面对沟通中遇到的各种情况，还会有更多的发现。

需要强调的是，本书提倡任何时候的沟通都必须体现道德特性。这个原则会贯穿本书的始末，而且尊重的、开放的和诚实的沟通才是有效的、值得赞赏的。

在阅读本书的过程中，可以发现一些有关特别沟通模式的建议是具有战略性的。例如，当希望说服其他人时，我们提出一些建议，告诉您哪些知识和技巧可以运用，而您的责任是有道德地运用这些知识，并且总是处于一种良好的和合理的实践过程中。

1.5 经验能证明这些观点吗

无论是国际大公司还是国内小公司，那些成功的领导人都视他们的员工和公司的管理为他们成功的原因。

卡莉·菲奥莉娜(Carly Fiorina)，1999—2005年任惠普(HP)公司的CEO。她认为，领导者的工作是“建立组织体系，让员工(在工作中)有一定的自由(度)”。维珍航空的CEO理查德·布兰森(Richard Branson)也赞同这种说法。例如，当理查德·布兰森被问到开创公司什么最重要时，他回答道：“我认为您必须有激情，而不是仅仅为了赚钱。”这样的回答也正回应了他之前回答的“人，人，人”是创建公司最重要的三个因素。中国阿里巴巴集团的马云也建议那些年轻的创业者在创业过程中要多从有经验的管理者那里学习相关的经验。

在文章“管理挑战”中，其他的领导者补充了这个观点，那就是沟通、热情、管理和有效地响应民众是商务活动最基本的核心能力。

- 澳大利亚商务理事会的 CEO 宣称："除非我对一件事充满热情，否则，我不会去做。"
- Ella Bache 公司的 CEO，卡伦·马修斯(Karen Mathews)认为："出色的领导者具有大量显著的特点，包括诚实、倾听的能力、企业家精神、直觉、同情心……他们的伟大之处在于知道何时运用自己不同的特性。"
- 互联网贸易公司 CMC 的 CEO，大卫·特鲁(David Trew)认为："您应该对生意和您的角色充满热情，因为热情是强大的驱动力，可以对商务活动产生积极的影响。"

出色的商务从业者非常清楚商务活动中沟通、情商和柔性管理技巧的重要作用。

1.6 沟 通 误 区

在沟通中有很多误区，而重要的是这些误区并不是对现实的真实反映。阅读本书时，我们确信您也同意下面列出的沟通过程中可能面临的一些认识误区。它们是：

- 沟通是容易的。
- 如果我们仅仅是沟通，我们就能达成一致。
- 自然的表达有助于沟通。
- 沟通等同于提供信息。
- 出色的沟通专家仅仅依赖于冰冷的现实来达到他们的目的。

学习实践

从上述所列出的沟通误区中选择一至两项。试从你的经历中举例说明，哪些误区对你产生或没有产生影响。为什么？

笔者作为有着丰富实际经验的教师、研究学者和商业顾问，我们相信，在阅读本书后，通过个人经历和在实践中运用我们提出的沟通策略，您也会同意：出色的商务沟通者要具备完成任务所需的广泛的知识、情商、战略性的技巧。面对挑战，祝您好运，我们确信，如果能成为卓越的商务沟通者，您将会得到巨大的回报。

第2章

新世纪商务沟通面临的挑战

【学习目标】

通过对本章内容的学习，你能够：

- 理解本书中提到的沟通和商务沟通的概念。
- 理解沟通可分为正式沟通和非正式沟通。
- 了解有效沟通的障碍。
- 把握沟通过程中的主要组成部分，实现有效沟通。
- 理解未来商务沟通的发展趋势和面临的挑战。

引例：哥伦比亚号灾难性的沟通失败

2003 年，哥伦比亚号航天飞机在重返大气层时解体，导致 7 名机组人员全部遇难。独立调查小组调查发现，通讯问题是造成本次事故的根本原因。研究人员得出结论，组织障碍阻碍了重要的安全信息的有效沟通，限制了专业人员的沟通。

报告指出了存在的下列沟通问题。

(1) 管理者和下属间的沟通：管理人员并没有关注到工程师关于碎片对航天飞机影响的担忧。在整个过程中，沟通信息并没有从项目经理那里有效地向上或向下进行传递。

(2) 团队间信息的传递：尽管工程师们担心着陆问题，因此进行了着陆程序试验，但这些问题并没有转达给本可以解决这些问题的管理人员或系统和技术专家。

(3) 沟通来源：管理者从非正式渠道收到大量信息，正是这些信息阻碍了工程师的相关意见和结论的传递。

(改编自哥伦比亚事故调查委员会，哥伦比亚事故调查委员会的报告，2003 年 8 月第一卷，http://www.nasa.gov/columbia/home/CAIB_Vol1.html.)

引例启示：正如上面的案例所示，良好的有效沟通所花费的每一分钟和每一分钱都是值得的。沟通不畅的代价可能是花费数十亿美元。然而，沟通不畅的代价不仅仅是经济上的，也并非所有的沟通成本都如此巨大。当沟通不尽如人意时，组织所付出的代价包括在浪费时间、浪费精力、失去商誉和法律方面的问题。

2.1 关于沟通

2.1.1 组织中的沟通

如果不具备良好的沟通技巧，您可能无法达到既定的职业目标。对沟通技巧的整合运用能够让您更好地实现组织目标及个人目标。我们在诸如《华尔街日报》《国家就业周刊》等杂志以及众多招聘网站上经常看到“就业机会来啦！”这样的招聘广告，这些广告无一例外地把“出色的演讲技巧，良好的写作能力”和“人际交往优势”作为申请所有层次管理职位的基本要求。《哈佛商业评论》《商业周刊》和《财富》的最新调查显示，沟通技能是职业升迁中最重要的决定因素之一。

在现代企业里，无论是初创的小型企业、世界 500 强巨头、政府机构，还是非营利组织，您看见了什么？您会发现，管理者和员工在阅读报告、起草邮件、参加会议、组织访谈、电话交流、与下属开会、商务用餐、阅读邮件、口述信件抑或演示文稿。简单来说，您发现人们在沟通。

组织是为了实现共同目标而合作工作的群体，沟通是整个工作过程的重要组成部分。事实上，沟通必然出现在共同目标确立之前，在一起工作的群体肯定会进行互动，也就是说，他们必须就其需求、想法、计划、专业知识等进行沟通。沟通是信息共享、协调活动和做出决策的重要手段。了解如何进行商务沟通及如何胜任在组织内部沟通，会让您更有效地参与各种商业活动。

沟通到底意味着什么？早期的沟通专家们提出了沟通模式，即包括消息发送者、消息传递者和消息接收者。这种模式认为沟通是线性过程：消息被传递和接收后，沟通就完成了。实际上这不是真正的沟通模式，这种模式将复杂的过程过于简单化了。

今天，随着商务实践活动的不断变化，我们需要回答关于沟通的几个问题。

(1) 你需要运用沟通工具达到个人目标和职业目标，但是哪种沟通能力对职业快速发展至关重要？

(2) 在未来几年里，哪种沟通能力对你最重要？

(3) 如何确定是在为将来做准备，而不是为过去做准备？

(4) 如何适应新出现的沟通理论和通信技术？

(5) 如何解决沟通中涉及的道德问题？

熟练的沟通者以给予和获取的方式分享观点和感觉，甚至当演讲时，他们也会注意听众的反应。单独的说话人自己仅仅是发出声音，单独的听众也仅仅是等待去听或看一些事情，这不是有效的沟通行为，只有两者结合才可以使沟通变成相互的行为，才能使想法和感觉在群体中传递或相互作用。单纯的讲话仅仅是一种单向行为，沟通涉及所有人的共同兴趣。

2.1.2　沟通的组成

沟通是发送和接收消息的过程，有时通过说和写来完成，有时也使用面部表情、手势和语调等非语言手段完成。图 2.1 展示了组成沟通模式的五个部分：刺激、过滤器、消息、媒介和终端。尽管反馈对于沟通来讲并不是必需的，但是在理想情况下，沟通过程伴随着发送者收到反馈而结束。

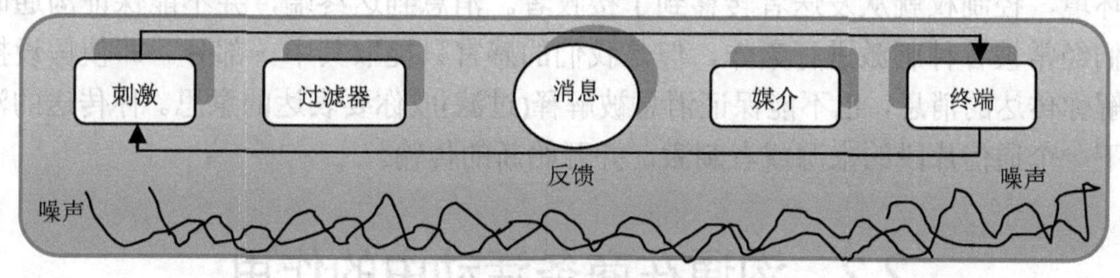

图 2.1　沟通模式

(资料来源：Ober S, Newman A. 商务沟通[M]. 7 版. 北京：清华大学出版社，2013.)

1. 刺激

第一步：刺激产生沟通需求。沟通，首先必须有刺激，即一个让个体产生沟通需求的事件。内部刺激只是在你头脑中形成的一个想法。外部刺激通过感官发生，包括眼睛、耳朵、鼻子、嘴巴和皮肤。商务交流中的刺激可能是您刚刚读过的电子邮件，午餐时听到的八卦，甚至是从温度过高的取暖设备释放的热气流。您用给出某种信息的方式对刺激予以回应：语言信息(书面或口头的话)、非语言信息(非书面和非口语信号)，或者两者相结合。

2. 过滤器

第二步：我们掌握的知识、经验和观点充当过滤器，帮助我们解释(解码)刺激。如果所有人对事件持有相同看法，你的沟通工作会相对容易；你可以假设你对现实的看法是正确的，其他人会理解你的动机和意图。事实上，每个人基于个人的经历、文化、情感、个性、知识、社会经济地位以及许多其他因素会对现实有独特的认知。每个因素在塑造个人对于现实独一无二的印象时都发挥了过滤器的作用。

3. 消息

第三步：形成(编码)对于刺激产生的语言或非语言上的反应。沟通能达到预期目标的程度取决于如何构建消息(需要被沟通的信息)。成功的沟通不仅取决于消息的内容和目的，还取决于巧妙的沟通技巧、对听众的(与你交流的某个人或一群人)了解程度以及你与听众的共同点有多少。

4. 媒介

第四步：选择传递消息的形式(媒介)。一旦消息发送者生成一条信息，下一步就是把消息传送给接收者。在这一点上，发送者必须选择媒介，即传输消息的手段。口头消息可以通过员工会议、个人会议、电话交谈、语音邮件等方式传播，甚至可以通过公司小道消息等非正式方式传播。书面消息可以通过备忘录、报告、宣传册、公告板、电子邮件、公司通信，或者政策的附加条款和程序手册来传递。非语言消息可以通过面部表情、语态、手势或者身体移动进行传播，或者通过书面报告中的格式或图像进行传播。

5. 终端

第五步：消息抵达终端，且能成功、准确地被接收者感知到。消息发出并进入接收者的感官环境，控制权就从发送者转移到了接收者。消息到达终端，并不能保证沟通确实发生。我们经常被各种刺激进行轰炸，但是我们的感官只提取其中一部分。即使假设接收者可以理解你传达的消息，也不能保证消息被解释(过滤)成你要表达的意思。你传送的消息于是成为下一个通信片段的来源或者刺激，并开始新的传输。

2.2 沟通在商务活动中的作用

2.2.1 工作沟通

内部和外部受众可以通过口头沟通与书面沟通、语言沟通与非语言沟通接收信息。内部受众是组织中的其他人，即下属、上司和同事。外部受众是组织外部人员：客户、供应商、分销商、工会、股东、潜在雇员、贸易协会、特殊利益集团、政府机构、媒体和公众。

人们在组织中会产生大量文件。表 2.1 列出了瑞尔森(Ryerson)公司制作的一些具体文档，这家公司生产并对行业客户销售钢铁、铝、其他金属和塑料，其销售网点遍布美国、加拿大和中国。

表 2.1 的所有文档都体现了组织写作三个基本目的中的一个或多个：通知、请求或说服，

以及建立友好关系。事实上，多数消息都有多个用途。例如，当你回答问题的时候，你在告知的同时也想通过其表明自身有能力、有远见且通过答案正确、完整来建立友好关系。

表 2.1　组织中产生的内部文档

文档种类	文档描述	文档目标
传递单	附带文档的备忘录说明了要传送给接收者的原因	通知；说服读者阅读文档；树立形象并建立友好关系
月度或季度报告	对阶段性收益率、生产率和问题进行总结的报告，用于下个月或下个季度活动计划	通知；建立良好形象和关系(报告是准确、完整的；撰写人对公司很了解)
政策和程序公告	公司政策或规章制度的文字陈述(例如：如何下订单，如何开展消防演习)	通知；建立良好形象和关系(要求合理；撰写人寻找公司的闪光点)
业绩评估	员工绩效评估	通知；使员工改进
祝贺信	对获得奖金和晋升的员工表示祝贺	建立友好关系

(资料来源：Locker K O, Kienzler D S. *Business and Administrative Communication*[M]. 10th ed. New York: McGraw-Hill, 2013.)

2.2.2　内部沟通和外部沟通

内部沟通是指组织内发生的沟通。这是以创建、实施和追踪企业经营计划而建立的企业员工之间的沟通。内部沟通需要多种形式。首先，它包括高级管理层关于决策目标和业务流程的讨论。其次，包括管理者给员工的命令和指示，还有员工之间关于工作问题的口头交流。再次，包括员工准备的有关销售、产品、库存、财务管理、维护等的报告。最后，包括员工们写的关于任务和对企业想法的邮件。

外部沟通是指组织与外部有关机构或个人之间的沟通，包括与客户和潜在客户间的沟通，与服务和产品提供者的沟通，以及与专业团体之间的沟通。一个组织不可能脱离与其他组织或个人的沟通而独自存在或运转。表 2.2 说明了企业外部沟通所传递的文档。

表 2.2　企业外部沟通所传递的文档

文档种类	文档描述	文档目标
估价单	为特定产品和服务定价	通知；建立友好关系(定价合理)
理赔书	授予或拒绝顾客对瑕疵品赔偿要求	通知；建立友好关系
职位描述	描述工作资格和职责，用于绩效考核、工资和招聘	通知；说服优秀求职者申请；建立良好声誉(工作职责和职级、薪水匹配)
年报	向股东报告年度财务信息	通知；说服股东保留股票并劝导其他人购买；建立良好关系

(资料来源：Locker K O, Kienzler D S. *Business and Administrative Communication*[M]. 10th ed. New York: McGraw-Hill, 2013.)

2.2.3 正式沟通和非正式沟通

无论是内部沟通还是外部沟通都可以分为两类：正式沟通和非正式沟通。

正式沟通是指商务谈话、发言、演示、商务书信等沟通活动。正式沟通的特点是它的严肃性、精确性和期望性，这种期望性是指正式沟通被组织认为是为组织代言，所说的内容是官方的。这种沟通常常需要适当设计和精心准备。这种正式沟通需要收集尽量多的信息，也需要认真选择沟通方式。因为人与人之间的理解会有差异或者目标会有不同，沟通过程中，可能会出现一些不同的意见。因此，为了解决出现的问题或为了就某个问题达成协议，需要卓越的沟通技巧。

当正式沟通以书面方式进行时，需要更大的努力和精确度，因为写在纸上的内容是沟通双方相互交往的记录。特别要关注写作的语气、结构、单词和短语，这些会直接影响正式沟通的效果。发送者要对正式沟通中所发出的任何一则信息负全部责任。

非正式沟通是指员工之间通过多种渠道进行的相互交流，这种交流不受组织中各种正式规则的约束，在组织内和跨组织进行。图 2.2 所列特征可以用来区别正式沟通与非正式沟通。非正式沟通最重要的特征是无规划性。如果需要交流，非正式沟通可以随时进行，甚至参与沟通的人中可能只有少数几个人才是沟通的真正参与者，沟通的主题也是信手拈来的。更进一步说，在沟通过程中，沟通方式等会随着参与者的兴趣与理解不同而变化。就这层意义而言，非正式沟通是完全互动的。沟通所有参与者都能认识到所谈论话题的目前状况并对其做出反应。通过这种反馈机制，非正式沟通比正式沟通更为有效，因为谈话的参与者为了应对其他人的反对或误解，会阐述或调整他们想要表达的内容。另外，沟通的内容不用记录，语言口语化且较随意，互动的沟通记录没有必要保留下来，这些都使得非正式沟通更为有效。将沟通正式化的一种方法是沟通发生后，做一份关于沟通内容的总结。

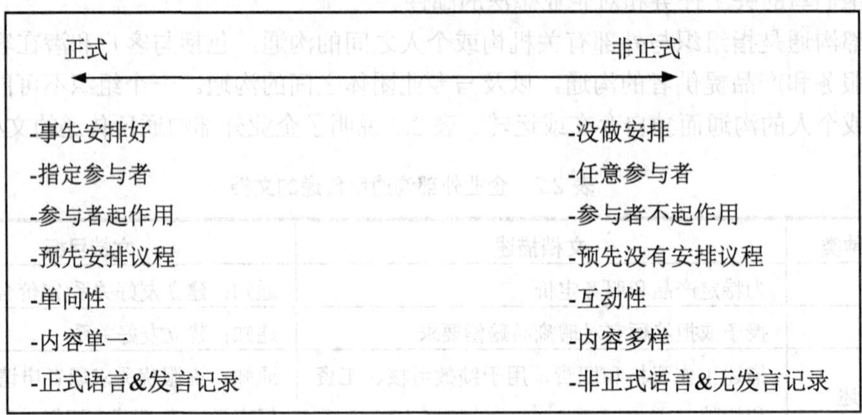

图 2.2 正式沟通与非正式沟通的维度

(资料来源：Kraut R E, Fish R S, Root R W, et al,. Informal communication in organizations: Form, function, and technology. S.Oskamp & S. Spacapan (Eds.)[C]. *Human Reactions to Technology: The Claremont Symposium on Applied Social Psychology*. Beverly Hills: Sage Publications 1990.)

学习实践

(1) 想象你在组织(或者你的大学)中需要进行正式沟通的情形，并且与需要进行的非正式沟通进行比较。

(2) 比较一下两者在语言选择、风格及沟通渠道上的不同。

1. 正式内部沟通网络：信息传递的方向

在组织内部，信息可以由上级传递给下级(下行沟通)，由下级传递给上级(上行沟通)，在组织架构中同级人员之间传递(平行沟通)，或组织内不同部门之间传递(跨渠道沟通)。这四种类型的沟通组成了正式沟通网络。我们将使用图 2.3 展示的 ABC 公司的部分组织架构图来说明沟通的方向。

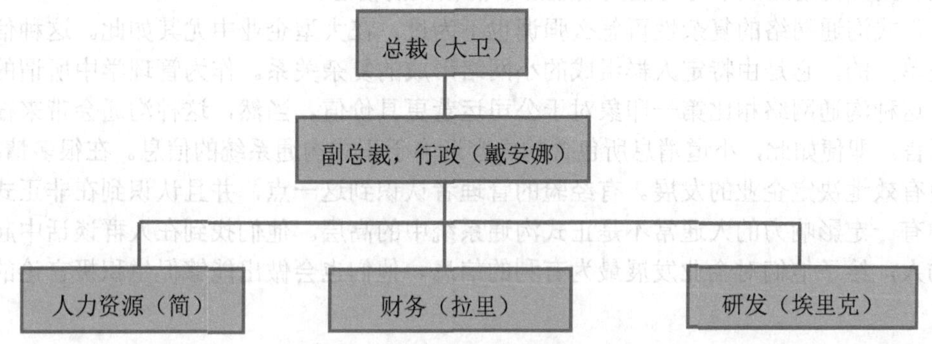

图 2.3　ABC 公司内部沟通网络框架

(1) 下行沟通。大多数组织中向下垂直沟通数量最多——即从上级到下级的信息传递。比如，在 ABC 公司中(见图 2.3)，大卫给戴安娜发送一封关于计算机报告的电子邮件；戴安娜又就其与埃里克进行商议。有关工作表现、政策和程序、日常运作的信息及其他组织信息通过书面和口语渠道进行沟通。

较高层次管理者与较低层次员工的沟通通过电子邮件、备忘录、会议、电话、公司新闻和录像等方式进行。书面下行沟通存在的一个问题是管理层认为下级会收到并理解所发送的信息，然而事实并非总是如此。

(2) 上行沟通。上行沟通是下级员工传递给上级员工信息。例如，在图 2.3 中，简将关于人力资源活动的月度状态报告汇报给总裁大卫，戴安娜对总裁大卫关于计算机报告的备忘录做出回应。上行沟通可以通过电子邮件、备忘录、会议、报告、建议系统或者内刊等形式进行。

上行沟通为高级管理层提供决策所需信息，所以很重要。这种沟通方式让员工有机会被倾听，从而培养了员工的忠诚度，让他们有渠道发泄不满并提出建议。上行沟通还提供必要反馈让上级了解下属是否接收到并理解了他们向下传达的信息。

(3) 平行沟通。平行沟通是在同一工作单元中同事之间传递信息。例如，行政部每周员工例会上三位经理(简、拉里和埃里克)就公司运营现状进行信息交换。

平行沟通之所以很重要，是因为这有助于协调工作分配、分享计划和活动信息、协商分歧及发展人际支持，从而创造一个更加团结的工作团体。组织内部个人和部门为了实现目标而进行的互动越多，平行沟通就越流畅、越强。

(4) 跨渠道沟通。跨渠道沟通是不同工作单元中员工的信息交换，他们不存在上下级关系。例如，简的部门的工资结算员每年都会给公司所有员工发送请求，让他们更新纳税申报单上的免税金额。

专家式员工的责任通常涵盖组织中很多部门，因此，他们会经常运用跨渠道沟通。他们没有对沟通对象的直接管辖权，因此，必须依靠自己的说服技巧，例如人力资源部门鼓励员工完成工作满意度调查问卷。

2. 非正式沟通网络

非正式沟通网络是通过组织内非官方渠道进行的信息传输。每当员工在一起的时候，比如拼车上班、等待使用复印机、午间慢跑、在餐厅用餐或者在局部会议中交谈时，他们很可能听到并传播组织中与可能要发生的事情相关的信息。

非正式沟通网络的复杂性再怎么强调也不为过，在大型企业中尤其如此。这种信息网络不是单一的，它是由特定人群组成的小网络形成的复杂关系。作为管理学中所谓的小道消息，这种沟通网络相比第一印象对于公司运营更具价值。当然，这种沟通会带来很多绯闻和谣言。即便如此，小道消息所包含的内容远多于正式沟通系统的信息。在很多情况下，它能更有效地决定企业的发展。有经验的管理者认识到这一点，并且认识到在非正式沟通网络中有一定影响力的人通常不是正式沟通系统中的高层。他们找到在人群谈话中起领导作用的人，给予他们对企业发展最为有利的信息。他们也会做出能够促生积极言论的管理决策。

2.2.4 商务沟通

内部人士的观点：Intuit 公司

像每一家高科技企业一样，软件巨头 Intuit(直觉软件)公司作为 QuickBooks、Quicken 和 TurboTax 等流行金融及税务筹划产品的开发者，依靠的是创造力和创新。意识到各级员工都有可能改进流程和绩效，公司高层决定保持企业发展的最佳途径是营造持续学习的企业文化。因此，“学-教-学”实践诞生。

在“学-教-学”理念的影响下，Intuit 公司的管理者了解员工的想法及潜在进步，鼓励他们自由分享；制订行动计划并教他们执行计划；并且从员工的反馈中得到更多信息，人力资源部副部长吉姆·格雷尼尔(Jim Grenier)表示这种来回沟通会产生好的想法。他说：“这不是一种共识文化，你在寻求员工更多的投入，同时向公司内外部最好的‘零件制造商’学习，这样会产生更好的决策。员工了解我们对他们的反馈会认真对待，我们倾听反馈并做一些行动。”

Intuit 公司另一种征集雇员意见的方法是通过年度调查来获得雇员们对公司营运的看法。调查之后，管理者会在越级会议上从直接对他们进行汇报的下属那里得到额外反馈。格雷尼尔指出，自 2000 年公司实施调查开始，Intuit 公司的离职率减少了一半。

(资料来源：Ober S, Newman A. 商务沟通[M]. 7 版. 北京：清华大学出版社，2013.)

对商务沟通的定义多种多样，很难找出一个对商务沟通的具体描述，但是商务沟通有其特定的应用范畴，而该范畴与其他沟通确实在某种程度上有所不同。商务沟通包括一些基本要素，如动态多渠道过程、内部沟通、外部沟通和组织形式。因此，我们可以把商务沟通定义为一种动态多渠道过程，它包括特定组织内部和外部的沟通。

当一个组织按照特定产品/服务来划分成不同的部门时，这种组织被称为“按产品划分部门”。每个部门可以独立运作。另外一种是按不同功能来划分部门。这种情况下，更容易解决工作中出现的问题。不论是哪种组织安排，在做出任何决定或评价之前，管理者都应大量收集所需的信息。

商务沟通之所以被认为是动态的，是因为它总是随着内部或外部环境的变化而变化，从不会处在静态之中。

商务沟通的另一个重要特征是它的多渠道性。例如，商务人士通过电话、发送邮件或传真、与对方面对面的交谈等多种方式相互联系。如果在不同的地点，有时他们也会选择电话或电视会议的形式讨论一些重要问题。多渠道沟通对于商务人士有效地达到商务目标具有非常积极的作用。

2.2.5　外部沟通网络

企业外部沟通的重要性是不言而喻的。企业的成功取决于是否可以满足顾客的需求，因此必须与顾客进行有效沟通。但是，企业在物质生产和分配上也是相互依赖的。与承包商、顾问和供应商协调都需要娴熟的沟通技巧。除此之外，每一个企业都会在某种程度上和一些外部组织沟通，比如政府机构和公共利益集团。图 2.4 阐述了当代商务中的外部参与者。和内部沟通一样，外部沟通对于企业的成功也是至关重要的。

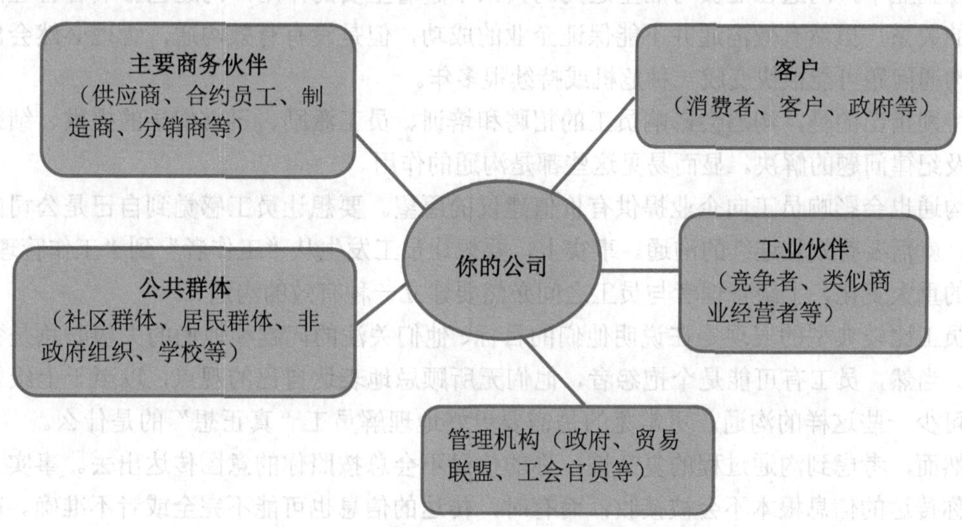

图 2.4　当代商务中可能存在的外部参与者

(资料来源：Rentz K, Flatley M E, Lentz P. *Lesikar's Business Communication*[M]. 12th ed. New York: McGraw-Hill, 2012.)

今天，很多企业每年在广告上投入大量资金，这是因为广告是推销产品或提高企业知名度的一种常用方法。如果企业不满意广告的效果，它会淘汰广告代理商或用另一家机构来取而代之。可口可乐公司在1992年放弃麦迪逊公司而选择创意艺人公司作为其广告代理商，其原因即在于此。可口可乐公司抱怨麦迪逊公司拿不出真正新颖、对消费者有吸引力的广告。广告对产品销售或企业形象的树立起着十分重要的作用。

另一个关于外部沟通的例子与美国玛氏食品有关。玛氏和士力架巧克力棒在澳大利亚遭投毒恐吓，故玛氏澳大利亚分公司决定从市场召回所有澳大利亚境内的玛氏巧克力棒。为了回应这一事件，公司总裁韦斯顿·韦伯(Weston-Webb)利用现场新闻会议、热线电话和广告与公众进行沟通，使公众相信玛氏食品的产品是受人喜爱的。紧接着他们又运用广告告知玛氏巧克力的爱好者们公司的产品是安全的。所有这些形式的沟通都可以认为是外部沟通。

在沟通中涉及的个人是外部沟通的另一重要方面，如与消费者或与股东之间的沟通。人们并不总是代表着组织，有时只代表他们自己。当今的个体消费者对服务质量尤其关注。很多公司将顾客满意作为他们努力的目标并向这一目标努力。摩托罗拉公司是一个典型的例子。为了将其不合格产品的数量降到最低，摩托罗拉每年在员工的质量教育上花费近2亿美元。此外，公司主管人员还走访顾客，以了解他们的意见及对产品的需求。他们还进行质量调查并且分析顾客的投诉，以达到他们所宣称的“顾客全面满意”的目标。

2.3 克服沟通障碍，实现有效沟通

在企业中，沟通在雇员与雇主之间的关系中起着主要的作用，沟通也影响各管理团队之间的关系。虽然有效沟通并不能保证企业的成功，但是没有有效沟通，管理必然会出问题。沟通问题可能很快变成一种危机或持续很多年。

特别指出的是，沟通会影响员工的招聘和培训、员工激励、日常指导的提供、绩效评估以及纪律问题的解决。显而易见这些都是沟通的作用。

沟通也会影响员工向企业提供有价值建议的愿望。要想让员工感觉到自己是公司的一部分，就需要有效且连续的沟通。事实上，要想让员工发生从“工作者”到“工作管理者”这样的重大变化，上级管理者与员工之间必然要建立一种有效的沟通。

员工比较典型的表现是在说明他们的目标、他们关注的问题和他们的失望时总是犹豫不决。当然，员工有可能是个抱怨者，他们无所顾忌地表达自己的观点，以至于上级管理者宁可少一些这样的沟通。更常见的是需要更好地理解员工“真正想”的是什么。

然而，考虑到沟通过程的复杂性，你的信息不会总按照你的意图传达出去。事实上，有时你传达的信息根本不会被接收；而有时，传达的信息也可能不完全或者不准确。高效且有效沟通中的一些障碍是语言上的，另外一些是非语言的。如图2.5所示，这些障碍会构成一堵难以穿透的“城墙”，使有效沟通变得遥不可及。

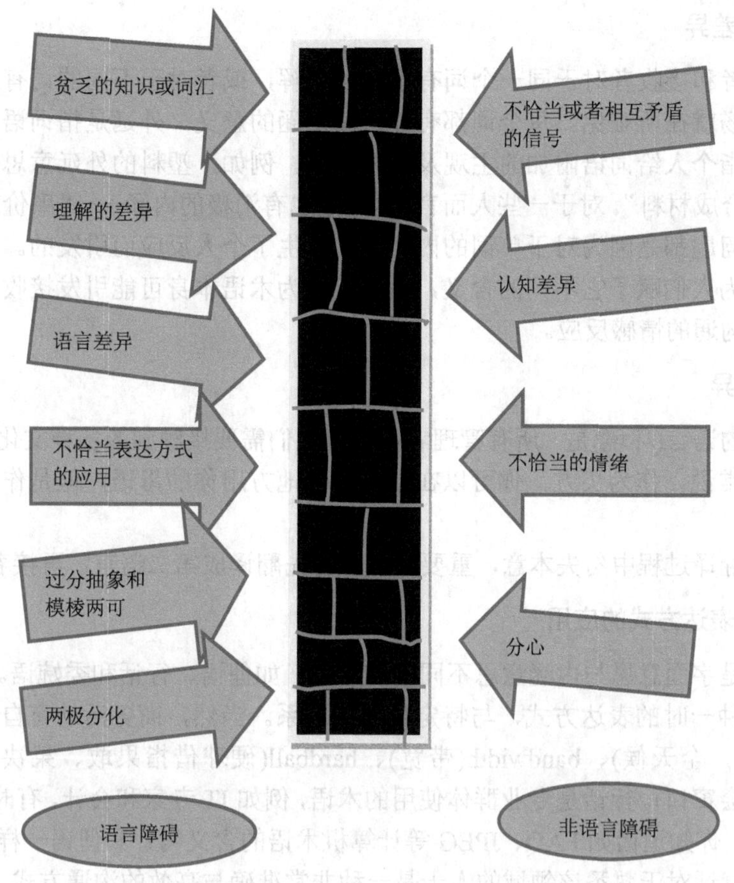

图 2.5　沟通中语言和非语言障碍

(资料来源：Ober S, Newman A. 商务沟通[M]. 7 版. 北京：清华大学出版社，2013.)

2.3.1　语言障碍

语言障碍与你的陈述和记录息息相关。它们包括贫乏的知识和词汇、理解的差异、语言差异、不恰当的表达方式的应用、过分抽象和模棱两可以及两极分化。

1. 贫乏的知识或词汇

在你开始想要沟通一个想法之前，首先必须有想法，也就是你对于想要说的主题有足够的知识储备。无论你的专业技术在什么层次，这都不像听起来那么简单。例如，假如(我们之前提到过的)ABC 公司财务部门经理拉里、公司总裁大卫，要求你评估一个投资机会，你完成了所有需要的研究，现在准备写报告就真的可以写吗？

你是否已经分析过你的听众？你知道总裁对这项投资有多少了解以便确定要在报告中包含多少背景信息？你知道大卫对投资术语的熟悉程度吗？你可以放心地使用术语，如净现值(NPV)和人民币存款准备金率(RRR)，还是必须阐明净现值和所要求的投资回报率？如果要客观准确地写报告，这些问题的答案很重要。

2. 理解的差异

有时发送者和接收者对于同一个词有不同的理解，或者对于不同的词有相同的理解。这样，沟通不畅就在所难免。每个词都有外延和内涵的意义。外延是指词语的字面和字典含义。内涵是指个人给词语附加的主观及情感意义。例如，塑料的外延意思是“可以塑造成不同形状的合成材料”。对于一些人而言，这个词也有消极的内涵——“廉价或伪造产品”。许多理解上的问题都是因为对于单词的内涵意义产生了个人反应而引发的。术语理解的问题并不仅是因为人们赋予它不同的含义，而且还因为术语本身可能引发接收者“拒绝”与发送者进一步沟通的情感反应。

3. 语言差异

一种理想的语言(环境)是，所有管理者都了解他们需要接触到的各种文化中的语言。国际商务人士经常说，作为买方，你可以在世界任何地方用你的母语，但是作为卖方，你只能说当地语言。

为确保在翻译过程中勿失本意，重要文档应首先翻译成第二语言，再接着翻译成英语。

4. 不恰当表达方式的应用

表达方式是字面意思与内涵意思不同的一组词，如俚语、行话和委婉语。

俚语是一种一时的表达方式，与特定群体相联系。当然，商务活动有自己的俚语，如24/7(每时每刻，全天候)、bandwidth(带宽)、hardball(硬球借指果敢、果决)、window of opportunity(机会窗口)。行话是专业群体使用的术语，例如IT专家和会计，有时候被称为“专业性的散文”。你知道诸如FAQ、JPEG等计算机术语的含义吗？和俚语一样，问题不是使用了行话——行话对于熟悉该领域的人士是一种非常准确与高效的沟通方式。问题是向不理解行话的人使用了行话，或是用行话来给别人留下深刻印象。委婉语是用无害的方式表达可能冒犯他人或者含义不好的事情。敏感的作家和演讲者偶尔使用委婉语，尤其是描述身体功能时。典型的例子是，英语中描述一个人去世，用“passed away”一词，而不是直接用“dead”；或者用“moved on”一词表达一个人被辞退或者离开公司。

5. 过分抽象和模棱两可

为更好地描述你不能看见或者触碰的东西，抽象词汇是很必要的。然而，当你使用太多抽象词汇或者过于抽象时会导致沟通问题。抽象程度越高，接收者就越难准确理解发送者心中的意思。

当一个词汇能表达几种意思，而又不清楚你所暗示的意思时，就会出现模棱两可的现象。

6. 两极分化

有时，一些人表现得好像每种情形都分为截然相反和不同的两极，没有中间地带。当然，这种二分法有时是对的。例如，一个人说的要么是真话要么是假话。事实上，说话人说的可能是真的，但是选择性地忽略掉一些重要信息，他或她就可能会给人留下错误印象。说话人有没有说实话？最有可能的是，答案在两者之间。同样的，你也并不是非高即矮、非富即贫、非智则愚。称职的沟通者应避免不恰当的“不是/就是”逻辑，并且努力去使用中性词汇描述事件。

2.3.2　非语言障碍

不是所有沟通问题都涉及你写什么或者说什么，有些问题与你的举止有关。沟通中的非语言障碍包括不恰当或相互矛盾的信号、认知差异、不恰当的情绪及分心。

1. 不恰当或者相互矛盾的信号

假设一位优秀的行政助理职位申请人简历上有排版错误，或者一位会计师的办公室乱得找不到与客户开会用的资料。当语言和非语言信号发生冲突时，接收者会倾向于接收非语言信号，因为非语言信息比语言信息更难处理。另外，当我们说一件事情的时候，比如我们很高兴认识某人，但是我们的行为、姿势或者表情暗示一些相反的东西，其他人通常会相信我们所做的而不是我们所说的。

2. 认知差异

即使听到同一个演讲或阅读同一份文件，不同年龄、社会经济背景、文化背景的人往往会形成不同的看法。因为每个人都是独一无二的，具有独特的经历、知识和观点，所以他们对读到和听到的东西会有不同的看法。有些人会不自觉地相信一些人，不信任其他人。例如，在阅读公司总裁电子邮件时，一名员工可能出于敬畏，接受总裁所说的一切。然而，另一位员工可能对总裁持有负面情绪，会不相信总裁的话。

3. 不恰当的情绪

大多数情况下，适度的情感参与可以加强沟通并使其更个性化。但是，过多的情感参与可能会造成沟通障碍。例如，过度愤怒能够使感情环境紧张，在这种情况下，理性沟通是不可能的。同样，偏见、成见、墨守成规和无趣都会阻碍有效沟通。这种情绪往往会让头脑封闭，回避新想法、拒绝或忽略与个人固有看法相悖的信息。

4. 分心

任何限制个人专注于沟通的环境或者竞争因素都会阻碍有效沟通。这些令人分心的事情被称作噪声(见图 2.1)。伦敦大学精神病学研究所研究发现，“当一位工人被电话和电邮分散注意力时，智商平均下降 10%”。例如：环境噪声有音响效果不佳、极端温度、不舒服的座位、体臭、电话连接不良和字迹模糊的复印件等；竞争性噪声有要参加其他重要业务、太多会议要开和太多报告要阅读。

2.3.3　其他沟通障碍

沟通过程中任何一个因素都可能成为沟通障碍。为了提高沟通技能，需要清楚地认识这些问题。

1. 混乱的消息

有效沟通从清晰的消息开始。比较一下这两条消息：“我们明天上午开会”“我们明天上午 9 点钟开会”，只多用了一个词就使第二条消息比第一条消息清楚得多。这种混乱的消息会成为有效沟通的障碍，因为接收者不清楚发送者发送消息的真正意图，而只好去猜测其意图。但是发送者如何判断信息是清楚的而不是混乱的呢？接收者的反馈是最好的验证办法，它可以让发送者确定接收者对消息的理解是正确的。

学习实践

(1) 选择正确的沟通媒介以达到沟通目的。

(2) 假设你针对部门一些不必要的办公用品花费，宣布必须采取临时的控制措施。该如何就这件事与其他员工进行沟通？

这里有一些沟通媒介选择错误的例子。

如果消息是复杂的，只是针对一定范围的听众，那么通过当地电台进行广告活动去赢得听众的方法是极其没有效果的。

选择多种渠道和适当的媒介传递消息有助于消息接收者对消息的内容和重要性进行理解。例如，利用录像对新员工进行清洁工作的培训，帮助他们理解和掌握关注健康的重要性。录像可以反复观看，形式是正式的，这样员工会认识到公司花费资源去做它的原因，也表明这个内容对员工十分重要。再如，一张送给员工配偶的生日贺卡远比让员工向他/她说声“生日快乐”要诚挚得多。

2. 环境中的干扰性因素

要给沟通创造良好的沟通环境，再也没有比将消息传递给一群人，但他们又不能够“听见”的情况更糟的了。

他们不能“听见”的原因可能如下。

(1) 你的声音不够洪亮。

(2) 房间内有太多的人同时在谈话。

(3) 他们在阅读你的报告时，办公室有太多打进来的电话。

(4) 他们脑子里装满其他更为紧迫的事情。

(5) 当时他们假定自己在其他某个地方。

(6) 办公室网络连接速度慢。

(7) 房间的空调坏了，室内闷热。

当然，还会有成千上万的干扰因素成为他们不能够或没有关注你的商务沟通活动的原因。最重要的是一定要尽量减少干扰听众的因素数量。

3. 社会心理障碍

社会心理的差异会阻碍和曲解沟通。一个人的态度和意见、所处的社会地位和身份意识的位置取决于其在等级组织结构中，以及与同事、年长者、年幼者的关系和家庭背景。所有这些深深地影响着一个人的沟通能力，不论这个人是信息发送者还是接收者。身份意识被广泛地认为是组织中严重的沟通障碍。它会导致心理上的距离，进而会引起沟通失败或沟通失误。我们常常看到组织中地位高的人在他或她的周围建立起一座“墙”，这座“墙”将限制那些权利较小的人参与决策。同样，一个人的家庭背景会影响其态度的形成和沟通技能的水平。

4. 良好沟通的其他障碍

(1) 语言。包括文字本身及其运用，也包括职业群体使用的专业术语。

(2) 技术含量。沟通是发生在人们之间的一个过程，信息并不等于沟通。

(3) 没有认识到接收者的需求。首先要明白听众在听时都会自问：“我能从中得到什么？”

(4) 不充分的反馈。反馈是润滑油，它使沟通变得流畅和通顺。没有反馈，沟通是不会有效率和效果的。

(5) 情绪干扰。进行理性的讨论前必须解决情绪问题。

(6) 发送者和接收者的知识和专业技术等级。必须始终重视沟通双方知识水平的相互影响作用。

(7) 缺少信任和诚实。没有信任，沟通就会迟疑不前。

(8) 文化差异。适应和认可多样性的价值观能够克服一切文化差异。

(9) 倾听水平低。我们要花费近 45%的时间去倾听，所以倾听是一种非常重要的技能，我们需要做一个积极的倾听者。

(10) 等级。等级限制了诚实，它使个体具有较强的自我防卫意识。认识到这一点的认识是达到有效沟通的第一步。

有效商务沟通的障碍很多，但是可以通过细心和关注将其克服。商务沟通的障碍越少，信息被听见、被理解、你的 MDA(最希望他们采取的行动)出现的可能性就越大。

2.4　有效沟通的标准

渠道选择影响消息(发送)成功

“正式通知，你将不在 JNI Traffic Control 工作，禁止参与公司各项安排。”恐怕你很难想象接收到这样一则消息(的心情)。这家悉尼用人单位因为使用不恰当的沟通渠道解雇员工而遭到起诉。为了解决这些问题，行政专员进一步说明电子邮件、短信，甚至自动答录机设置在正式商务沟通中都不够恰当。那么收到短信提醒的过期账单是否合适呢？有人认为这是正常服务，另外一些人认为这是具有侵略性且不恰当的做法。

历史上，渠道选择的重要性一直存在争议，一些人认为它们只是传递话语的手段，另一些人认为被选择的沟通渠道本身就是一种信息。不管怎样，现在大部分人意识到合适的沟通渠道选择加上语言，对成功传递信息十分重要。一项有关媒体丰富度的早期研究对于何时使用简洁(印刷材料)，何时使用丰富(面对面)的沟通渠道提出了建议，近期研究、新技术和法规给这个理论增加了新维度。不仅没有明确的规范和指导原则，连内容最细微的变化都会导致不同的选择。

在选择沟通方式的时候，信息传送者需要衡量几个因素，包括信息内容、信息传送者对于沟通渠道的驾驭能力、接收者信息渠道的获取以及接收者所处的环境。恰当沟通方式的选择能够使得人与人之间更准确地交流，从而提高效率并改善人际关系。

(资料来源：Rentz K, Flatley M E, Lentz P. *Lesikar's Business Communication*[M]. 12th ed. New York: McGraw-Hill, 2012.)

良好的商务和管理通信需要满足五个基本标准：清晰、完整、正确、节省听众时间、建立良好关系。

(1) **清晰**。听众获得的信息是发送者想要表达的内容，而不需要听众进行猜测。

(2) **完整**。听众所有的疑问都可以找到答案。听众有足够的信息进行评估并做出反应。

(3) **正确**。所有的信息都是准确的。没有拼写、语法、发音或者句型结构的错误。

(4) **节省听众时间**。信息的类型、组织结构、视觉或听觉的效果能够帮助听众读或听，理解并能快速做出反应。

(5) **建立良好关系**。信息展示了传达者以及所属组织的正面形象。它面对的接收者是人，而不是数字。它可以巩固传达者和接收者之间良好的关系。

2.5 如何解决商务沟通的一些问题

必须寻找一种途径解决商务沟通中出现的问题，它既能解决组织中出现的问题，又能满足沟通参与者的心理需求。这里有一些建议供考虑。

2.5.1 了解情况

事实的真相是什么？你能从得到的信息中推断出什么？还需要其他什么有用的信息？从哪里可以得到？

其他需要回答的重要问题如下。

(1) **基于什么样的立场和角度？**不仅要考虑自己的需求，而且需要关注你的老板和听众的需求。如果能基于整个组织环境，甚至包括股东、客户、监管者的更大的环境进行思考，信息将会是最有效的。当处在一个更高的立场，考虑客观现实的同时，也应当考虑人们的感受。

(2) **应当发出信息吗？**有时候，特别是刚入职场，沉默是最机智的回应。但是当有机会来学习，改变或者证明自己的时候，就不能再继续沉默了。

(3) **应当通过什么渠道(传递信息)？**纸质的文档和展示通常比较正式，并且更容易控制整个信息。电子邮件、短信、电话或者顺便到办公室拜访就没那么正式了。口头的方式更适合小组意见的决定，并且可以快速消除误会，以及更个人一些。有时你需要不止一条信息，并且需要通过不同的方式进行表达。

(4) **应该说些什么？**信息内容可能并不显而易见。应该具体到怎样的程度？需要重复那些听众已经知道的信息吗？答案取决于你所发信息的种类、目的、听众组成以及相应的企业文化。

(5) **通过怎样的方式进行表达？**如何组织自己的观点——哪个观点最先陈述，哪个其次，哪个最后，以及表达时所用的词汇都将影响听众对所表达观点的反馈。

学习实践

(1) 用下面提到六个问题的方法分析听众、沟通的目的和沟通环境。

(2) 把自己想象为剧本中所描述的某种情景中的角色，然后想象其他各种人物的性格。

基蒂·O.洛克(Kitty O. Locker，2005)在《商务和管理沟通》(第 6 版)一书中建议通过回答六个问题分析听众、沟通目的和沟通环境。这些问题如下。

(1) 谁是你的听众？特点是什么？如果写作或发言的对象不止一个，不同读者或听众之间有何不同？

(2) 写作或发言的目的是什么？

(3) 写作或发言应该包括什么信息？

(4) 如何针对你的立场建立支持体系？读者支持观点的原因是什么或他们的受益是什么？

(5) 对读者有什么期望？有哪些不利因素需要减少或克服？

(6) 在总体上有什么因素将会影响读者或听众的反应？经济因素？时间？组织中的士气？读者和作者的关系？其他特别的情况？

2.5.2 头脑风暴解决方法

信息收集通常是解决问题的开始。真相是什么？你能从现有信息中推断出什么？哪些额外信息是有帮助的？从哪里获取这些信息？受哪些主观因素的影响？这些信息通常会给我们提供建设性的解决方案，我们可以集中讨论其他方法。除了最简单的问题以外，其他问题都有多种解决方案。第一个想到的也许不是最好的，有意识地去发现更多的办法，然后对照听众和(发信)目标来衡量(分析)哪一种解决方案可能是最好的。

最大限度集思广益

Aloft Group 公司市场公关部经理马特·鲍文(Matt Bowen)针对如何成功地举行集体研讨会提出了自己的建议。

(1) 研讨会开始之前，明确一个清晰具体的目标。这样能够使你适当缩小讨论范围，如关于实用性或成本方面的内容，这能够使会议主题更集中。

(2) 提前让所有参会人员了解会议目标，这让他们在会议之前有准备好想法的机会。限定会议规模和持续时间。鲍文建议研讨会规模在 5～7 人，会议时间不要超过 1 小时。对于集中讨论 1 小时已经足够，而且小规模的分组会让每个人更容易参与讨论，每个人所提的意见也更容易被采纳。

(3) 让每位与会者自由发挥。鲍文建议锻炼倾听的技巧，(这种技巧)不仅鼓励大家分享想法，而且让每个人在他人思路的基础上进一步拓展。

(4) 团队多元化对于研讨会尤其重要，最佳解决方案往往出自由不同视野成员组成的团队。有一点需要记住，没有完全不好的想法，任何一个想法，不管多么不切实际，都有可能激发出最佳的方案，花时间清理一般方案简直就是扼杀创造力。

(资料来源：Spors K K. Productive brainstorms take the right mix of elements[N]. *Wall Street Journal*, 2008, 7-24:B5.)

2.6 商务和管理沟通的发展趋势及其面临的挑战

无论是商务活动还是商务沟通都在不断变化。一些来自贸易性的、政府的和非营利组织的变化趋势会影响商务活动和商务沟通：关注质量和消费者的需求、企业家精神和外包、团队、多元化、经济全球化、法律和道德关注、工作与家庭的平衡以及科技发展的速率。

2.6.1 关注质量和消费者的需求

有关质量和消费者需求的各种活动以沟通为中心。要达到沟通目的必须通过头脑风暴和团队解决问题来寻找更有效率的途径，然后集思广益得到的建议需要在整个公司内部进行沟通。创新思维需要被认可。只有倾听消费者的心声，聆听他们伴随行动表达的沉默，组织才能知道消费者的真正需求。

2.6.2 企业家精神和外包

从20世纪80年代起，美国商业数量的增长要比劳动人口数量的增长快得多。在中国，随着经济的增长和政府政策的支持，越来越多的人成为民营企业主。这些民营企业的角色对于经济的发展十分重要。很多知名公司通过在企业内培养企业精神，努力使其成功和其发展速度相一致。

一些商家因为外包的缘故被迫变成中间商。外包(外购)意思是曾经由企业自己员工生产的产品及服务现在由企业外部的组织进行生产。企业可以外包制造品、客户服务和财务项目。因此，外包项目使沟通变得比过去所有的工作都在企业内完成的时候更加困难，更加重要。要想提出问题很难，因为人们不再局限在大楼里上班，细小问题很容易变成主要问题。不论组织大与小，沟通是企业的生命线。

2.6.3 团队

企业为了获取核心竞争力，在降低成本和价格的同时还要生产出优质产品，越来越多的企业依赖于多职能的团队。合作性的工作利用不同的视角、经历、观念、风格及加强个体的奉献程度。多职能团队的流行要求高度重视学习发现和解决问题、共享领导能力、与他人一起工作而不是仅仅将某项工作委派给他人、建设性地解决冲突、为达到团队满意而有效地进行谈判、激励每个人去做好他或她的工作。所有这些过程的中心就是良好的沟通过程。

成功的团队要求事先有深思熟虑的计划和对过程的关注来进行高效率的团队工作。例如，维持团队凝聚力是十分关键的，必须十分谨慎地避免团队出现对协议持不同意见者的直接或间接的惩罚。这被称为群体思维，对于团队结局来说，它和连续的冲突同样危险。会话的风格同样需要关注。因为组织的关系在变化，变得更加民主化和等级逐渐减少，组织中会谈的模式将会改变，谈话的意义也会随着模式而改变。因此，会谈时要聚精会神，表现出你的兴趣、礼貌和有分寸的态度。

2.6.4 多元化

中国在过去很多年维持了一种传统的、稳定的、相对单一的劳动力人口。但是，随着中国经济向世界逐渐开放，逐渐邀请一些像美国、日本和德国等国家进入中国的经济市场，单一的劳动力人口的局面随着改革开放在改变。女性、有色人种和移民在世界上早已经是劳动力的一部分。《商务周刊》杂志报告说，三分之二的工业已经全球运营，或者在此过程中。逐渐增长的利益分享来自于总部所在国家以外的地方。奥蒂斯电梯公司最大的市场在中国，麦当劳公司的收入 62%来自于美国以外的国家，几乎 98%的诺基亚销售是在本土以外。劳动力的多元化来源有很多，比如：

- 性别；
- 民族和种族；
- 出生地和国籍；
- 社会等级；
- 宗教；
- 年龄；
- 性向；
- 身体能力。

帮助每个劳动者开发他或她的潜能，这要求管理者有更多的灵活性，也要求他们掌握更多的跨文化沟通的知识。至关重要的是帮助那些有着不同背景的工作者相互理解。

以尊敬的态度对待读者和听众是良好商务活动和管理沟通的一个原则，强调多元化也是使它经济化的要求。

2.6.5 变化迅速

21 世纪初期，整个世界处于动荡不安的变化状态之中，没有哪个组织能够摆脱不断动荡、进化环境的影响。变化的压力是如此之强，以至于数以千计的组织，未来的成功甚至生存决定于他们如何应对变化，或者最理想的是，他们是否能够走在变化的前列。

众所周知，一些变化，其动力源自经济全球化、科学技术的进步、空前的竞争、政治的巨变、新市场的开放，这些变化不断地给具有不同规模和类型的组织施加压力。结果是，为了适应世界的进化发展，这些组织开始去适应、重新建构和发生变化。

要想成功地应对各种变化，必须有精心设计的战略规划，其战略规划能够充分体现对组织文化和管理者的理解与认识。改变组织运行机制是十分艰难的，企业可以花费巨额资金研究开发新软件、重新设计业务流程、为员工提供培训，但是这些能保证应对变化吗？不能。企业需要的是贯穿于组织的有效沟通。

有效沟通不仅仅是经常地向人们提供最新资料。人们天生是抵抗变化的，应该以受益为基础推销这种变化。沟通(即推销)这种变化，像出色市场管理者所做的，将消费者进行分类，然后向每个类别发送主要信息。

围绕能够将信息传递给每个人的最理想的媒体制定战略——时事通信、电子邮件、工厂、午餐等——人们需要多久能够得到信息。面对大量的听众，考虑开展月度演讲，以及包含问题与回答的讨论。

不论选择什么媒体形式，重要的是沟通要有规律性，要制定一个能遵守的进度表。对于那些在第一线工作的人员来说，每个星期要提供话题，这样他们可以提供连续的信息和统一的观点。

执行战略时，要注意沟通是双向的过程。一旦信息发出，收集、分析、合成反馈的信息变得同样重要。与人们面谈，鼓励反馈是表达自己思想的一部分。只有得到彻底、公正的反馈，才能够发现问题所在，并知道需要在哪里进行调整。

2.6.6 科技的发展

科技是沟通的一种形式。但是，人们还是在进行沟通。也就是说，利用手段进行沟通是沟通过程的第一步。手段必须在发出信息和理解信息的人群中产生，正如信息并不意味着沟通，使用技术并不意味着沟通的发生。

企业内部互联网是一种很有用的资源，它能够通过网页让企业内的每一个员工得到有关企业的信息。所有这些相关工作在今天运用普通计算机和互联网工具，像文字处理软件和电子邮件一样可以简单、顺利地完成。

2001 年的“9・11”事件以后，人们讨论最多的问题之一是建立有效内部沟通系统的必要性。很多公司变得十分关心运用什么系统和政策去通知企业内部员工危机事件的进展如何，对如何行动提供指导，如何确定员工的位置以确保他们的安全。

为了预防大范围的内部沟通或外部沟通危机的发生，互联网技术是员工和领导之间广泛沟通计划的一部分。前面谈到的基于互联网技术的沟通管理系统起着主要的作用，因为它们能够迅速发布信息和控制信息发往的方向。内部网站可以让员工见多识广，不同的站点可以专门为管理团队服务。

外部网通过网页为消费者或供货商提供产品或服务信息，是企业节约时间和金钱，提高产品质量的一种有效方法。网络和智能手机使员工在家而不是在特定的办公室工作成为可能；远程办公可以积极地解决上下班高峰交通拥挤的问题；传真和电子邮件使跨地域和时间的沟通变得容易起来，电话和电视会议让不同地方的人们不需要离开家或办公室就可以参加会议。

随着近几年科技的发展，很多人更喜欢这种不受时间和地域的限制、实现全世界范围内沟通的工作方式。信息技术让人们实现这个目标成为可能。但是，当信息传递的速度超出人类对信息的把握能力时，在大量信息增长的情况下，会出现信息超负荷的状况。在信息时代，时间的管理部分取决于能够认识到哪些信息是重要的，哪些信息可以被归为垃圾信息。

本 章 小 结

沟通可以帮助组织和人们达到其目标，写作和演讲能力的好坏对你在组织内的升迁愈发重要。

内部沟通是组织内人们之间的沟通。外部沟通是与外部进行的沟通，包括与客户、消费者、供应商、股东、政府、传媒和普通公众进行的沟通。商务沟通中所有形式的沟通都代表公司，因此沟通非常重要。

沟通中的“发送者—接收者”模式被认为是一种最常见的模式，早期由伯洛(Berlo)发展。沟通过程中涉及几种主要的组成部分，即发送者、发送渠道和接收者。但是沟通不仅仅发生在信息发送者和接收者之间，也包括两者所处的外部环境，沟通者使用的一些代表不同含义的编码，从使用的字词到非语言的表达方式。

为了取得有效沟通，人们必须克服商务活动中的各种障碍，通过回答“六个问题”和其他方法分析听众、沟通的目的和情境。

商务活动和商务沟通每时每刻都在发生变化，商业、政府和非营利组织的发展趋势和变化会影响商务活动和沟通，这些变化趋势包括关注质量和消费者的需求、企业家精神和外包、团队、多样化、变化迅速、沟通科技的发展。

沟通中的所有障碍和环境的变化正在对我们形成挑战，而且使我们在商务沟通任务中保持高效变得愈发困难。

第二部分

口头商务沟通

第3章

用出色的演讲赢得听众的心声

【学习目标】

通过对本章内容的学习，你能够：

- 认识到劝说技巧对成功员工和管理者的重要性。
- 理解劝说过程中听众的地位。
- 理解劝说过程中可以使用的不同方法。
- 知道面对个人和组织演讲时的准备步骤。
- 知道如何构建有效沟通。

引例：管理层是如何看待毕业生的沟通能力

大会理事会以及工薪家庭之音、21 世纪技能伙伴和人力资源管理学会，要求几位高管提出他们认为新毕业生在工作场所拥有的非常重要的技能。高管们列出的五大技能分别是口头交流(95.4%)、团队合作(94.4%)、专业精神/职业道德(93.8%)、写作交流(93.1%)和批判性思维/解决问题(92.1%)。

高管们还被要求将毕业生在上述领域的技能评定为“优秀”或“不足”。有趣的是，在对四年制毕业生进行评级时，46.3%的受访者对毕业生的信息技术应用技能进行了“优秀”评级(在高管们重要技能清单中排名第 11，占 81.0%)。但只有 24.8%的人对毕业生的口头交流能力给予了“优秀”的评价(排名第一)。书面交流、英语写作和领导技能都出现在“缺陷”名单上。

(资料来源：会议委员会，他们真的准备好工作了吗？雇主对 21 世纪美国劳动力新进入者基本知识和应用技能的看法。会议委员会，2006 年，网络，2009 年 6 月 30 日)

引例启示：以上研究的结果激励我们不断地提高自己的沟通技巧。本章和本书中的其他几章提供了许多有用的沟通策略和技巧。

3.1 劝导说服的微妙艺术

从初入职场的年轻员工到高级领导者和管理者，职场中有各式各样的雇员，但是成功的领导者和管理者的共同点是他们有以劝导方式陈述自身观点并激励他人的能力。国际商务联合会前任主席凯文·汤姆森(Kevin Thomson)指出，成为一位劝说型人才将会受益匪浅，他们能够做到以下几点。

- 对工作充满激情。
- 为客户提供优质的服务。
- 热切地追求高质量产品，具有激励人们产生创意并开发产品的创新精神。

如这本教材的读者一样，许多年轻人都渴望成功。但是他们在实际工作中也认识到与他人沟通确有困难。在当下的职场中说服他人认同自己的观点确实是一个很大的挑战。领导胜任力的一个很重要的方面是：所有员工(不仅仅是管理者)都必须具有说服力地交流思想并处理好与他人的关系的能力(Goleman, Boyatzis, McKee, 2002)。

新员工和年轻员工需要具备重要的劝说性沟通技巧。工作中，员工每天会多次使用这项技能以高效完成工作。良好的沟通和说服能力被称为“天生的领袖”生而具备的行为方式。这一论断有什么证据？毋庸置疑，很多伟大的演说家从小就从父母那里学到了引人入胜的语言、有力论据的使用以及如何看起来、听起来很自信的重要性。然而，作者训练 1000 名学生和商务人士的经验表明，害羞和自我怀疑者能够成为高效且成功的演说家。例如，一名学员向我们证实，他学会了讲故事的技巧并知道如何与组织保持情感联络，(这些)彻底改变了他作为大型医院首席执行官的形象。另一名沉默寡言的大学毕业生在习得并运用一些沟通技能后，开始享受演讲的过程。

你会发现优秀沟通者必备的技能很容易通过学习掌握，如果你每天都坚持训练，这些将变得更加容易。此外，拥有说服性的沟通能力可以提高其他方面的能力，如财务管理能力、人力资源管理能力、决策能力等，因为其他人通过与你沟通后能够：

- 清楚地理解你的逻辑以及你对他们的承诺；
- 相信你所致力于的目标能够满足他们的需求；
- 感到实现目标需要振奋精神和激情；
- 理解观点的言外之意。

3.2　说 服 他 人

作为 2016 年美国总统大选共和党候选人和惠普公司的前首席执行官，卡莉•菲奥莉娜(Carly Fiorina)建议：领导者的工作是“确定组织结构体系，让人们自由工作”(Trinca, 2000)。我们从中可以看出，成为劝说型沟通大师是一种微妙的艺术，但并不是高不可攀，你也可以学会。高效地使用劝说性沟通技巧能够让听众(不论是大群体、小群体或是个人)在他们的头脑中形成一幅画，可以看到自己被希望带到哪里及如何抵达。换句话说，成为有效劝说型沟通者是使你成为高效员工，进而成为成功管理者和领导者的必要前提。

本章提供了一些有用的提高劝说型沟通技能的指导。首先概述劝说型沟通的关键要素，接着提供了一些激励型领导曾使用过的利用有效劝说来与听众建立友好的关系或动员听众的实例。这些指导为发展你自己的劝说技能提供了有用的建议。

为此，西班牙马德里 IE 商学院人类科学与技术学院教授李・纽曼(Lee Newman)建议，所有专业商务人士都需要“行为健康”，一系列协调优化过后的(商务)行为可以与每天去健身房训练的运动员的健康媲美(Newman L, 2015)。试想一下，如果每天都面临着制订诸如劝导与倾听的沟通行为计划的挑战，行为健康将促使你成为杰出的(商务)沟通者，继而成为成功的领导者及管理者。

3.3　获取劝说的灵魂

一些劝说型领导已经通过艰苦工作和战略思想树立了他们的正面形象。他们既有经验又诚实正直。毕竟，比起那些做出承诺却无法实现的人，我们更愿意相信那些我们所钦佩的人。如美国微软公司总裁比尔・盖茨(Bill Gates)、阿里巴巴的创始人马云、英国维珍集团首席执行官理查德・布兰森(Richard Branson)、德国总理安格拉・默克尔(Angela Merkel)以及中国周恩来总理的优异的沟通模式，可以给我们以启发。

什么是劝说呢？大多数人认为劝说的含义是某个人鼓励他人去做他们想做的事，即传达信息，但我们认为劝说应该覆盖更广泛的含义。当一个人或多个人参与一次性或连续进行的活动或者互动性活动(如对话、演讲或访谈活动)时，劝说即发生。这些互动活动能够形成、调整、加强，甚至改变其他人的信仰、态度、意图、动机或行为。该过程是双向的，演讲者与听众双方共同切磋，产生新的思想火花。如果听众参与互动，演讲者能够增强其劝说的影响力。

有说服力的沟通要求演讲者能够集中全力吸引听众的注意力，用知识和沟通技巧给听众留下深刻印象，用思想和感情与听众建立一种信任，即赢得他们的心声。

发展沟通技能，就像发展财务技能和运动技能一样，必须学会运用技术和战略获得成功。因为劝说性沟通总是很微妙，会受到人们行为的左右。因此，劝说者有一特殊的责任：确保已经考虑到所有利益相关者的利益，不要使用说服的手段来左右周围与你利益相关的人。

现代修辞之父坎尼斯·伯克(Kenneth Burke)建议：

你劝说一个男人(包括女士)时，要用他的语言，即说话、手势、音调、次序、形象、态度、观点尽量与他的一致。

然而许多演讲者仍以自己期望的演讲内容开场，没有考虑到听众的需求。听众不禁要问：所讲的内容对我有什么意义？

3.4 一切为了听众

任何沟通都把听众作为沟通起点是一个创新性的观点，但是对演讲者而言这样的开场却是相当困难的。希望赢得听众的心，很重要的一步是从听众的角度设计或组织沟通内容；希望沟通具有真正的感染力，也需要对自己讲述的对象有清楚的认识，了解他们的不同需求并尽量满足。如何进行演讲取决于听众如何思考和如何感知。关于如何建立既适合听众，又关系到你所处的情境及接收和参与信息的听众的特性信息，有以下四条黄金原则。

3.4.1 原则一：情境本身十分关键

如果有机会向团队成员提出新的建议，听众对情境的感觉真的十分重要。

- 新的观点是一种创新吗？
- 在经过长期的激烈辩论后，一些员工最终会被迫改变他们先前的行为吗？
- 你需要五分钟还是数周时间来劝说团队的其他成员？
- 主题出现在议程的结尾还是开头之处？或者会议的整个过程都在解决这个问题吗？
- 是进行个别沟通、小团队范围沟通，还是大团队范围内沟通？

以上的情景将决定如何解决问题，并要相应地调整自己的演讲内容。

3.4.2 原则二：听众的心境真的很重要

你需要考虑听众对自己的观点是赞同还是反对，或者是中立又或者他们对观点感到新奇。同样，你还要关注听众的价值观和态度。例如，如果演讲对象是年轻的企业家，他们的价值观有可能与一些中国的年长听众完全不同。

判定信息是否有效不是取决于演讲者自己对内容重要性的判定。理解观众是怎么想的是成功沟通的关键。要尊重听众对事物的不同观点，围绕这些主要观点进行讨论，这是通向有效沟通的途径。

3.4.3　原则三：听众对沟通风格偏好的重要性

彼得·汤普森(Peter Thompson)在《说服亚里士多德》(*Persuading Aristotle*)一书中创建了思考沟通风格的简单模式。许多人在完成简单测试后再决定选择沟通、决策的模式。汤普森在这个基础上，又进一步思考如何使自己的沟通风格适应不同听众的沟通风格。

例如，设想自己正在和图 3.1 中“倾听型”风格的人进行交谈。“倾听型”的人很注重细节，谨慎概述问题并缓慢推进。对于信息技术或者金融、会计感兴趣的听众通常在工作中需要注意详细信息，(因此他们)可能会用这种方法。但是，你可能更注重“全局”观点，讨论过程迅速，在进展过程中不断寻找新的方向。人力资源管理专业和市场营销专业的学生沟通风格可能属于“沟通型”和“激励型”甚至是“共享型”。通过了解沟通对象的需求，你将更好地适应听众的节奏、听众对信息的需求、听众的语气甚至情绪状态。

思维型

内向	倾听型 稳重，重细节，预见性强	激励型 积极，乐观，重原则，坚定自信	外向
	共享型 可靠，性情平和，有教养	沟通型 富有精力，使人充满活力，识大局	

感觉型

图 3.1　使沟通风格适应不同听众

(资料来源：Thompson P. *Persuading Aristotle*[M]. Sydney: Allen & Unwin, 1998.)

以上沟通模式十分有用，它似一幅图画，使你对听众的沟通需要有明确的认识，帮助判断如何调整沟通方式可以增强沟通的劝说力，从而增加成功的机会。如果你了解在一个群体里听众有多种类型，你面临的挑战是因地制宜、有针对性地选择不同策略。自己的多才多艺将提高成功的可能性。通过用不同方法完成一个主题的沟通可以体现你如何做到行为适应。你可以按照自己的行为模式，微调所选择的内容、语言和风格，为倾听型风格的人准备详尽全面的信息，然后改变方法去说服一个想得到迅速决定和结果的激励型风格的人。例如，如果你想说服经理允许你离开三天去参加家庭成员的婚礼，那么如何选用沟通方法去适用于图 3.1 中描述的倾听型、激励型和沟通型的不同风格？

3.4.4　原则四：听众人口统计的数据影响沟通的方式和内容

分析听众的年龄、性别、教育背景、社会经济文化背景，这是找到“路标”极好的方式，从中可以得知沟通内容哪些比较重要，哪些不重要，哪些内容是听众的“热点”，哪些又是他们反应的触发点，他们会对哪些内容感兴趣，哪些内容有用，等等。

年轻员工和年长员工在优先考虑的事情上存在不同，由此形成不同的沟通风格。

2015 年，在全球享有盛誉的阿里巴巴集团创始人马云为一群年轻企业家发表讲话，探讨如何在生活中取得成功。他的演讲诚挚而热情，并给大家提供了一些建议，同时强调尽情生活、学习并放下过去的错误，对未来充满期待的重要性。他的演讲鼓舞了许多中国年轻的听众去实现梦想。

陈述观点后就某一具体的点举例说明，并且使用比较正式的沟通方式是适应听众的两个方法。另一个例子是，很多人对“无领工作场所”非常喜爱，在这里你可以随意着装或工作。这种行为方式在年轻职业者中很流行，但是这种着装或频繁地更换工作不会受中国年长的商务人士的推崇。对于年轻人来说，这种行为方式被视为雄心、成功的动力，而对于中国的年长者，则意味着对权力的不尊重、缺乏忠诚。或者，为年轻听众可以选择国际方面的案例，对年长、传统的听众则使用中国公司的案例。选择适合听众的风格是实现说服目标的关键。

3.4.5 提高劝服能力

在西方哲学家里，古希腊的亚里士多德十分著名，就像孔子在中国家喻户晓一样。孔子为官僚机构制定了一套良好的生活准则和工作效率准则。早在两千多年前的西方，亚里士多德也扮演着类似的角色，他根据自己哲学上的研究观点，创建了一些概念来说明说服他人的几种方法。

亚里士多德认为，劝服他人有三种基本不同的要求，即道义、情感和理性。

道义是指演讲者的可信度。如果演讲者为听众所信任，他的说服力会更强。演讲者的个人背景、现有职务、诚实的信誉、人际关系管理、个人风格、诚恳、热情和自信都有助于形成良好的可信度。如果可信度没有通过所演讲的内容及演讲的方式表现出来，听众便会立刻怀疑演讲者。

情感是指演讲者向听众表现出的情感诉求，听众对演讲者的观点做出情感上的回应。当公民被政府提醒应该为自己是中国人或法国人而感到骄傲时，这里主要的吸引力是情感。这种劝说要想获得成功，对公民强烈的爱国情感、自豪之情的呼吁是沟通成功的关键。其他情感诉求包括雄心、安全和社会责任。

理性是指演讲者论证的逻辑性。听众为清晰的推理、事实、统计和其他形式的论据所折服，从而接受演讲者的论述。

3.5 建立可信度(道义)

正如构思演讲稿必须考虑演讲的听众一样，可信度或道义的建立也取决于听众。大量有关对沟通的研究表明，听众觉得演讲者是否可信主要取决于三个因素：听众根据演讲者的专业技能、可信度、信誉或者关怀感对演讲者做出判断(McCroskey，Teven，1999)。

在演讲中要充分证明自己的专业技术，甚至包括自己的观点是来源于他人研究的成果，这是为众多听众建立自己可信度的关键途径。切记，年轻的工作者都渴望与有才能的同伴共事，共同寻求挑战和机遇。演讲中自己的表现看起来是否见多识广、有资质、有能力或有经验，这些都会直接影响听众如何看待你的演讲内容。

同样，一个人正直品质的形成是经过长时间的而不是偶遇的一刹那。演讲内容的可信度关键体现在演讲中所表现的对人的关心、理解和发自内心的对听众的兴趣。然而有趣的是，演讲者的可信度在听众较少参与互动时比他们已经参与互动时显得更为重要。因为当听众已经参与互动时，他们会认识到互动内容的重要性，这时论证的力度才是最重要的(Gass，Seiter，2003)。例如，当你试图劝说同事去尝试新观点、新技术或者新产品，而他们对此知之甚少时，让你的听众作出判断的重要途径是他们对你的知识和专业相信与否。

劝说性沟通需要运用一定的策略关注你自身的部分，这个过程并不简单。因此整个演讲过程中要不断证明自己的诚信、渊博的知识和忠诚的品质，还要表明自己期望与听众共同达到沟通目的。

还有其他次要因素影响可信度。这种可信度的获取不是通过所讲的内容，而是在于如何运用非语言方式进行沟通。外向、镇静、自信、喜好交际都有助于与听众建立互动关系。思考这种关系的一种方法是表明“直接性”的程度，或者非语言行为体现的热情、亲近、友好，与沟通者打成一片。人与人之间的距离多数是物理上的或是心理上的，但听众与你的距离感或亲近感将决定他们如何“听”、如何互动以及如何诠释你演讲的内容。

其他提高可信度的途径是演讲风格的选择，说什么和如何说都很重要。身体和声音的使用方式会形成重要的“代码”，其他人通过这些“代码”理解信息。例如，表现得烦躁不安、紧张会暗示听众，让他们觉得或许你根本不懂演讲的内容，或所演讲的内容不真实，或者你根本没有经验，不值得信任。听众对非语言沟通代码的理解是无意的。研究显示，当语言代码和非语言代码相冲突时，听众更相信非语言沟通代码表达的信息。即使这时讲述的是真理，听众也可能会带着怀疑的心理走开，因为他们对你和你实现诺言的能力感到不信任。这些“代码”在听众和演讲者之间组成了沟通过程的重要部分。

通常这些“代码”的含义通过以下方式表达出来。

- 目光接触。
- 使用手势的种类和范围。
- 生动的面部表情。
- 富有激情的声音。
- 身体散发的能量。
- 一种沉静的状态，表明你在讨论中的沉着和放松。

你可以回顾第 2 章所讲述的这些不同的但重要的非语言代码，第 2 章讲述得更详细。

一些出色的沟通者，像美国前总统贝拉克·奥巴马(Barack Obama)、阿里巴巴的马云、著名的苹果公司的史蒂夫·乔布斯(Steve Jobs)等，每次互动时都理解并运用前面提到的有效方式与听众沟通。他们面部表情的丰富性、讲话的语调、目光的交流、温暖的声音及充沛的精力，为期望达到良好沟通效果的人提供了极好的沟通模式。这是每个人都能理解的秘密代码，但却难以精通和把握。

学习实践

通过网络观看或收听马云等较出色的演说家的演讲视频。分析听众特点，说明演说者针对不同听众采用的三种不同方法。

使用非语言行为的指导原则是：与听众建立一种和睦关系的最佳方式是真实地反映听

众的非语言行为。非语言表现力的核心是一个人身体的上半部分，它能强大地推动沟通的进程。但是，在西方从事商务演讲的培训工作并在业内颇享盛誉的著名劝说型大师安东尼·罗宾(Anthony Robbins)在他的畅销书《无限力量》(*Unlimited Power*)中曾经建议：建立和睦关系的良好方法之一是用声音。他建议(Cass，Seiter，2003)：

模仿听众的音调和措词，他的音高，说话的快慢，停顿的方式，他的音量……听众感到他们发现了心灵知己，一个完全能理解他们的人……就像他们自己一样。

学会使用非语言沟通策略只是成为沟通大师的第一步，其重要性不言自明。但是，正如非语言沟通专家爱德华·萨丕尔(Edward Sapir)所说，非语言代码既精致又隐秘，我们常常在有意无意、不知不觉中微妙地觉察出这些代码的完整性和演讲者所要表达的真实意义(Sapir，1927)。

如果演讲者表现得虚伪，听众常常更相信非语言行为带来的信息，而对演讲内容本身关注的较少。总之，非语言沟通策略的运用需要与语言内容相协调，并能维持演讲者和听众之间的和谐关系。演讲过程中需要有效地平衡语言沟通和非语言沟通之间的关系，并不等同于要应付、欺骗听众。

直接、真诚的目光交流也是劝说行为的关键部分。许多研究证明运用更多的目光交流、令人愉悦的面部表情和手势，如强调重点的手势，比那些东张西望、面部表情呆板的人能够获得更多认同。

总之，了解听众的需求，寻找出真实地反映听众思维方式的方法，同时引导他们用创新的思维去思考出新的方法，并指引他们的方向。所有这些，都是职业生涯想取得成功所要掌握的广泛技能。

3.6　通过有吸引力的言语赢得心声(情感)

优秀沟通者也懂得语言在听众对演讲内容做出回应时的作用。演讲的说服力通过帮助听众认识并感觉到观点的威力而增强。一些演讲的效果几乎全靠情感的因素。一个著名的例子是：当观看美国民权运动领袖马丁·路德·金(Martin Luther King)的演讲《我有一个梦想》的影像资料时，听众至今仍然会感动。他当时正在领导给予黑人和白人同等权利的运动，包括黑人能进入有白人的公交车、商店和酒店等。1963 年，华盛顿特区 20 多万自由主义者集会，马丁·路德·金呼吁全体美国公民要有正义感，激励那些民权献身者为黑人的民主权利进行不停息的斗争。他那充满情感的、震撼人心的讲演为改善黑人人权做出了杰出贡献。我们不能低估情感的力量。

我们清楚地记得一个学生所做的以酗酒驾驶的危险性为主题的演讲。演讲者描述了她亲身经历的事故。这个学生仔细地描述了事故是如何突然发生的，然后描述走出自己汽车后做的事。她从容地、不慌不忙地告诉我们，她和她的两个朋友冲向了事故中的另一辆车，他们面对的是死一般的寂静。另一辆车的司机四肢伸开，横卧在车轮下，他的脸伏在挡风玻璃上，眼睛直盯着他们。他们被那一幕惨象惊呆了。她设法将那一幕惨烈的情形描述给听众，并运用那种情感增强我们对酗酒驾车的强烈排斥。这些形象没有图片也一样震撼人心，因为她选择的语言触动我们的情感，要求我们去想象那可怕的一幕。这将引发我们去思考酗酒驾车会带来的结果，并且让那些曾经酒后驾车的听众心中产生犯罪感。

使用隐喻和类比常能激发听众产生新的观点和情感。例如，可以把听众的公司描述成在国际市场上“翱翔的飞鸟”，唤醒听众对公司已取得成就的骄傲；重复和韵律的使用也增强了内容的清晰度和重点，故事的运用使抽象的概念变得真实、有意义。这些都是运用情感进行论述的有效策略。

一个成功的年轻企业家创办了一家小企业并最终取得国际性成功，如果这名企业家和你一样来自中国的一个小镇或某一著名城市，则其更具情感吸引力。你可以向听众详细介绍他的情况，如他的名字叫魏、他来自哪座城市、他的年龄以及他成功的细节。这甚至可能是个“白手起家，终于致富”的故事。在演讲中多次提到魏的故事会使听众不断想象这个人，仰慕他已取得的成就。

成功的演讲的确要寻求各种劝说因素的平衡，但是还要注入感情的因素。用语言和视觉效果去唤起听众的自豪感、自尊心、雄心、忠诚甚至是恐惧，这将起到提高和增强演讲内容的效果。

3.7 通过论证和事实赢得心声(理性)

论证和事实也是较强的说服工具。论证越有力，事实论据越充分，支持观点的详细资料越多，听众赞同你的观点的机会也就越大。演讲不能没有具体的例子或案例作为论据来支持你的观点。学习如何运用论据、论证进行演讲，最佳方法之一是亲自观摩大师的演讲。

关于清晰和具有逻辑的论证的最好的例子来自首席执行官和他的董事会成员每年例行向股东们汇报时所出具的财务分析报告。股东们热衷于从投资中获得最大的回报，因此董事会必须解释清楚为什么做决定以及该决定将如何影响投资回报。

结合你的个人魅力来获得成功

许多畅销书，诸如利安德·卡尼(Leander Kahney)写的《撬开苹果》，提到领导能力与沟通及有效使用语言诉诸情感和理性。这类书(为沟通)提供很多有用的建议。通过研究优秀沟通者战略实例探索三种诉求组合，即合理的推理及证据诉求、公信力诉求以及通过选择有效语言来表达的情感诉求，所产生的影响。

本章之前提到的一位杰出沟通者，科技巨头惠普的前首席执行官卡莉·菲奥莉娜认可并运用诉求的力量。事实上，菲奥莉娜综合运用了三个诉求：精神、情感和理性(Hatcher，McCarthy，2003)。她在媒体面前展现了坚强的企业战士形象，用意志完成了几乎不可能实现的事实(从菲奥莉娜2002年建议实现科技巨头惠普和康柏的并购战略中即可看出这一点)。

菲奥莉娜同时展现了一位有魅力的领导者和沟通者的形象。猎头杰夫·克里斯汀(Jeff Christian)曾经采访过在惠普公司任职的菲奥莉娜，描述她为“非常迷人的(女性)”。此外，尽管存在对菲奥莉娜合并惠普和康柏公司的担心，但是一位惠普负责人声称菲奥莉娜仍被员工视为“无畏的领导者”。

2016 年，卡莉·菲奥莉娜投入大量精力与商务生活中的利益相关者及政治追随者进行沟通。早年在惠普的时候，菲奥莉娜把与利益相关者的对话放在优先级别，最初跑遍惠普位于世界各地的办事处，对客户和许多其他利益相关者做了大量的演讲。菲奥莉娜的沟通理念值得关注。她于 2000 年向《澳大利亚金融时报》(*Australian Financial Review*)的记者海伦·婷卡(Helen Trinca)讲述：“有效领导需要明白你不拥有任何人，也不能掌控任何人。面向特定任务他们必须期待并选择与他人合作。在我看来，这意味着具有创造力地使用沟通工具。”

在 2002 年，菲奥莉娜承诺三年内彻底改造公司，力求改变惠普利润渐少的局面，成为世界知名企业。菲奥莉娜的关键策略之一是创建惠普期望达到的企业形象目标，一种融入历史和创造未来同时有社会责任感的鲜明企业形象的文化。她在内部沟通时常常运用“比尔(Bill Hewlett)和戴维(Dave Packard)”这两位公司创始人的有力神话作为例子鼓励大家，因为这些偶像式的和备受欢迎的人物形象对众多惠普员工仍很重要。公司周围至今仍然保留陈旧的车库，意在引发员工自发性的想象和提供创造的自然氛围。这种创意起源于惠普的创始人比尔·休利特(Bill Hewlett)和戴维·帕卡德(Dave Packard)最初创办公司时，曾在后花园的旧车库工作。旧车库的存在，让菲奥莉娜充分利用了惠普“车库文化”作用的优势。

菲奥莉娜通过将惠普的创新传统与新技术紧密联系，使她自己的观点又迈进了一步。这样，她可以将过去和将来紧密连接。

菲奥莉娜的许多演讲都强调了商业发展对整个社会发展的重要性，当然，这里情感的吸引是演讲成功的因素。菲奥莉娜通过富有情感的内容表达出强大而清晰的逻辑，这充分证明了其对有效说服力的理解。例如，在 2002 年教育和技术会议上，她强调：“我们(惠普)必须努力——不仅为我们的股东，为我们的客户，为我们的职员，更为我们的社会。”

菲奥莉娜很快又指出：“当然，这是自我利益发展的结果，也是商业和慈善事业发展的结果。教育是唯一最重要的促使经济繁荣的杠杆，也是唯一的最有效的杠杆，是培养出多样化、高技能人才的最重要的杠杆。”

可以注意到在以上例子中，菲奥莉娜使用重复的词汇和短语加强内容的表达力度。

学习实践

通过网络观看或收听你所钦佩的比较出色的如卡莉·菲奥莉娜、马云等演讲者的演讲视频。同时：

- 记下他们所用的一些理念。
- 记录他们重复使用、能加深信息影响力的词语。
- 跟随他们讨论的节奏，注意其中支撑主要观点的部分。
- 辨别哪个手势看起来感染力强，演讲人语言和手势的协调使用。
- 观察他们如何通过声音传递诚意或者自信，与观众保持(情感)联系。

亚里士多德相信最有效的劝说演讲综合了道义、情感和理性，即可信度、感性和逻辑，并且三者必须均衡。你必须像严格按照菜谱的要求来烹饪一样。有时菜谱中需要添加一些调料，如辣椒、酱油，有时为了味道更美味，需要在盘中撒些胡椒粉和辣椒。当然，了解场合和听众会帮助你决定正确的搭配。

有意识、谨慎地将逻辑严密的论证、富有想象力的语言和图像、对感召力和可信度的吸引力等要素结合使用，能够吸引你的听众并使他们从不同的视角看待问题。向成功的演讲者如卡莉·菲奥莉娜、理查德·布兰森(维珍集团 CEO)和中国出色的演讲者学习，学习他们对结构的运用、语言和主题的选择，这些能为希望找到提高劝服技巧方法的人提供灵感。

3.8 准备演讲

前面已经介绍了一些进行劝说性论证的重要策略，现在可以着手为演讲进行准备。

3.8.1　步骤一：做好思想准备

在演讲室里镇静地坐着，自由地深呼吸。然后自信地站起来，走上讲台。开始演讲前，面带微笑，胸有成竹地看着观众。

你一定要自始至终保持这一自信的形象。许多人面对听众演讲时会感到很害怕。这是大部分人都会经历的。要知道，充分的演讲准备可以克服紧张的情绪。如果做了充分准备，听众不会也不可能听见你的心跳，也不会感受到你的手掌在出汗；如果精力集中在演讲的目的和内容上，表现自信，这证明你确实在与听众进行沟通。

在本章前面部分，我们建议要认真考虑听众及其特征。在准备阶段，至少必须对听众和他们的思考和感觉方式进行合理的预测。必须了解关于演讲者的全部信息，必须了解你自己。现在可以开始做这样的准备。

1. 明确自身优势

首先认识自身优势。回顾一下与他人一次愉快沟通的经历。哪些方面做得好？如果客观地思考，每个人都会发现能写出自己一长串的优点和能力。比如，大多数人会以热情的微笑争取他人。因此，放松和微笑，自己也会感觉良好。开始说话前，想象自己站在听众面前，面带微笑的样子。如果做深呼吸，面带微笑，心理期望和听众建立良好的关系，这样一定会有良好的开端(当然除非自己希望创建严肃的气氛)。

最好是非常了解谈话主题，这样可以在沟通时运用自如。如果话题比较陌生或具有挑战性，确保自己已做了一些研究且对内容很熟悉。可以向专家请教良策、和朋友讨论主题、访问组织者的网站或去图书馆搜寻一些让听众最感兴趣的信息。

2. 考虑自己的弱势

列出自己会担心的内容，这样做对演讲很有帮助。那些担心是理性的吗？值得担忧吗？如果答案是“是”，有什么方法能消除吗？

如果担心会出现错误，那么记着在演讲中难免会出现错误。但是如果原谅自己沟通中出现的小差错，把它看成沟通过程中的正常现象，并确保演讲拥有其他高品质，那么听众会用热情和兴趣记住演讲的内容，并以此评价演讲者的专业知识和直率。

如果演讲者表现得自信，就可以帮助听众树立对演讲的信心，如果演讲者对演讲内容充满热情和激情，也会有助于与听众建立良好的关系。要想做到这些，作为演讲者，必须保持最好、最强的状态。

3.8.2 步骤二：计划演讲材料

你将如何建立公信力？你的经验、专业知识、研究成果、职称或者与他人之间的关系能够表明你是可信的吗？

确定选择你最适合的时间点来表达重要的观点。

要确定想要分享的2～3个关键信息，每条信息中都有若干关键点支持主要的观点。

同时，仔细思考对将要表达的观点进行最佳安排。

现在，你可以考虑用最好的单词和短语来阐述个人观点。考虑前述内容中关于选择语言、图像、事实及数据来激发听众兴趣的一些建议。

3.8.3 步骤三：练习演讲

如果用智能手机来练习就能看见和听见自己的演讲，那样会帮助自己在演讲时记住一些有用的词汇和图像。切记：录像或录音对演讲者极其有用，就像计算机文字处理软件对作家的重要性一样。可以运用这些工具为演讲的内容拟草稿，就像作家在计算机上拟稿一样。

3.8.4 步骤四：将演讲连贯起来

最后，必须斟酌开场白、结束语和过渡内容，这些内容将一系列演讲观点贯穿起来。这些内容好似“胶水”，将演讲内容“粘贴”在一起。

1. 演讲开场白

一旦演讲正文的结构确定以后，可以着手准备开场白和结束语。开场白很重要，因为它常影响着听众做出是否值得去听演讲的决定。开场白必须能够吸引听众的注意力，给听众指明方向。你需要给你的听众一张演讲的“地图”。

某些场合，如果自己和演讲主题事先未曾介绍给听众，开场白必须向听众大致介绍演讲的内容，并说明演讲的价值所在。在演讲初始阶段建立一种信任，确保听众对自己有一点了解。最后，在开场白开始时要关注建立友好氛围的重要性。这样，可以让听众感到你是令人喜爱的，也可显示演讲的“人性化”。总之，开场白要有五个方面的作用。

- 吸引听众的注意力。
- 概述主题。
- 建立你的可信度。
- 给听众提供演讲“地图”，让听众清楚演讲的内容，有方向感。
- 与听众建立良好关系。

请记住：在演讲开场时演讲人必须抓住观众的注意力。要大胆，充分准备，促使听众注意听演讲。吸引听众注意力的方法如下。

- 告知听众演讲主题是什么以及如何与他们密切相关。
- 用引证俘获听众。
- 陈述要引人注目。
- 用反问句(例如：“谁知道？”“研究人员已经得到了一些令人惊喜的发现？”)。
- 借趣闻轶事阐述观点。
- 说一些与主题相关的笑话。
- 引用令人吃惊的数据。

不论怎么做，都要通过增加许多细节的表达，使陈述更为具体，让听众“跟着你走”。显然，如果作为演讲者的你能够有效地处理好与听众的关系，那么他们的行为会潜在地成为对你有用的“工具”。这包括要求听众赞同时能举手，或问一个需要听众回答的问题。

这种技巧的实例如下。

> 假想我们在听一个学生演讲，他是模拟三个人进餐的角色扮演活动中的一个。
>
> 突然他们中的一个跌倒在地上，心脏病突发，其他人坐在那儿吓呆了。一个单位的护士走上前问这里谁能帮助这个人，坐在餐桌旁的另外两个人已经不知如何是好。我们不得不面对自己急救知识的缺乏和对这种紧急情况的无助。角色扮演活动带给我们的震惊和事实促使我们仔细听她的讲解，并认同她所传达的信息：参加急救课程的学习是当务之急。

你需要认真思考恰当地吸引观众注意力的策略。一位发言者最近上了全球新闻头条，他遭到向其咨询的银行、国际社会及中国员工的谴责，原因是他在进行培训时使用了一种能吸引注意力的探头装置。

也许有人担心大胆开场的创新难度，或者担心达到一个戏剧性效果需要的个性，但是记住：因为创新去冒险是值得的。如果能合理、仔细地制订计划满足听众和目前情况的需求，演讲开场又光彩耀人、引人注目，上述的任一策略都能成功。

2. 结束语

任何演讲的结尾应该强劲有力，简练且清晰地总结演讲的主要观点。注意结束语不宜太长，因为一旦暗示将要进入演讲的结尾，听众希望能快速、清晰地结束演讲。10 分钟的演讲结尾不能超过 30～50 秒。

例如，一个公司的演讲内容是鼓励员工提高服务水平，演讲者谈到信誉对建立客户忠诚度的重要性时，结束语包含了提供良好服务的三方面理由，有力、精练地提醒道：

> 名声市场是胜者为王的市场，如果我们希望成为成功的企业，必须关心我们在市场上的名声。

当然，如果你有能力，演讲的结尾最好声势渐增，把观众的情感调到高潮。作为激励式的演讲，没有比这样的结束语更有影响力的。一个著名的结束语是美国自由主义者马丁·路德·金的“我有一个梦想”演讲的最后一段，这在前面的内容中提到过。马丁·路德·金期望演讲能鼓舞成千上万的人为美国黑人公民的权利而战斗，这样在公共汽车上可以与其他所有白人美国公民一样，受到公平的待遇。在充满激情的声音中，他总结道(Thompson, 1992)：

当我们让自由之声轰响，当我们让自由之声响彻每一个大村小庄，每一个州府城镇，我们就能加速这一天的到来。那时，上帝的所有孩子，黑人和白人，犹太教徒和非犹太教徒，新教徒和天主教徒，将携手同唱那首古老的黑人灵歌："终于自由了！终于自由了！感谢全能的上帝，我们终于自由了！"

注意他是如何精心策划了演讲的最后一段文字的结构，以升华听众的情感和投入的。注意使用重复，使用排比结构——"黑人和白人，犹太人和非犹太人，新教徒和天主教徒"或"最终自由了，最终自由了，感谢上帝，我们最终自由了！"他也运用他的声音延长"自由"一词，通过重要的非言语信号鼓舞听众。马丁·路德·金的演讲既令人振奋又有连贯性。

学习实践

通过网络听马丁·路德·金的著名演讲《我有一个梦想》。

3. 黏合剂

接下来看看那些有助于实现演讲连续性或像前面的例子一样能够在你的演讲中保持观念一致性的技巧：黏合剂。

黏合剂的意思是什么？"黏合剂"帮助我们将许多构成逻辑性演讲需要的内容黏成一个整体。演讲的各部分必须黏合/连接/编织在一起，清晰地引导听众接受你的观点，达到演讲的目的。需要理解和学会使用的黏合剂有四个方面：路标、承上启下段落、(内部)预览和总结。

1)　路标

前面已经给出了路标的例子，这些是对听众有帮助的、简单的引导。再如，"以下是需要考虑的三个重要方面。第一……第二……最后……"，或"最重要的是……"，或者"例如，……"，也可以用简单的问题，如"它为什么如此重要呢？"或"我们该怎样解决问题呢？"。路标向听众展示将去何方，现在停在哪个内容的标题上。路标也帮助听众了解演讲里所关注的内容。换句话说，路标表明演讲的组织模式。

2)　承上启下段落

承上启下是为听众建立的从演讲的一部分到另一部分之间的连接："现在我们已经探究了……"，或者"让我们转入……"，或者"目前为止，我们已经着重阐述了……，现在是该讨论……的时候了"。这些连接帮助听众把握演讲每一部分之间以及部分与整体之间的逻辑关系。所以承上启下对于把握演讲观点的全局思路和实用性地安排主题和演讲十分重要。

3)　预览和总结

预览和总结使听众有机会回顾已读过的喜爱的内容，或快速浏览下一段将要涉及的内容。在演讲的每一个主要部分提供预览和总结。在决定说什么时要注意：首先应该说明这部分将要说的内容，再详细说明具体内容，然后概括已介绍的内容。

听和读的差异是听众无法回顾他们已听到的部分。如果他们错过或忘记，他们就会错过这些观点。所以，重复在口头演讲中是非常重要的。如果希望演讲成功，切记这是件简单而又重要的事。

预览将使听众预知接下来的演讲内容，就像电影预告片会吸引你去观影一样。阶段性的总结是指演讲者让听众暂作停顿，重申刚刚讲过的要点。

例如，我们已经给出一个结构清晰的演讲的框架：①前言；②正文，包含有显著标记的段落；③结束语，这些将所有的部分连接成整体；④黏合剂，包含路标、承上启下段落、预览和总结。

本章小结

成为有效沟通者对于那些希望在事业上取得成功的人来说是关键性技能。本章强调了有效沟通的四个重要方面。

- 所有的演讲必须受一条准则支配：一切都是为了听众。
- 为了让听众接受演讲的观点，所有演讲应该有说服性的论证(包括内容和非语言因素)。
- 每次演讲应该有严谨的准备战略。
- 每次演讲需要有周密计划，精彩的开场白，巧妙而严谨的承上启下内容或“黏合剂”，以及让人难忘的结束语。

如果能够认真完成这些内容，你也能成为一名令人难忘的、有效的沟通者。使用马云、马丁·路德·金、卡莉·菲奥莉娜、史蒂夫·乔布斯那样优秀的演讲者和你所敬佩的演讲者的沟通策略，你也能够让听众对你的观点和承诺记忆深刻。读过本章，相信你已经掌握了许多有效演讲的指导原则。

第 4 章

跨文化管理与商务沟通

【学习目标】

通过对本章内容的学习，你能够实现以下目标。

- 理解不同文化背景下沟通行为模式和态度。
- 理解不同文化背景下“正常”的行为。
- 提高对自我文化行为模式的认知。
- 提高对个体差异在跨文化背景下如何影响沟通行为的认知。
- 理解英语作为第二语言如何影响跨文化沟通。
- 掌握有效进行跨文化交流的原则。
- 运用跨文化沟通策略处理一些特殊情况，如冲突、礼节、保全面子、学习、礼尚往来、反馈等。

引例：迪士尼市场营销在中国

在香港迪士尼(以前也称为迪斯尼)乐园开张六个月后，迪士尼的官员们迫切地想了解为什么新公园里的客流量如此之低。他们向预订旅游项目的中国旅行社寻求答案。其中一些代理商认为迪士尼的官员没有意愿对当地市场和中国文化进行了解。

在香港公园令人失望的开业之后，迪士尼的官员们急于学习并准备做出一些改变。迪士尼公司利用来自旅游业的反馈和其他市场的调查，开展了一项新的广告活动。最初的广告以公园的鸟瞰图为特色；新的电视广告聚焦于人们，并向游客展示相关区域的景点。一个新的平面广告展示了一位祖母、母亲和女儿，说明迪士尼是全家可以在一起寻找快乐的地方。

迪士尼还致力于让游客在公园里有更舒适的体验。在一个景点提供了三种不同语言的指示标牌，游客们往往被吸引到最短的纵队——通常是说英语的游客的纵队。现在，三个独立的标志清楚地标明了哪种语言将用于与该队的客人进行交流。更多地使用普通话导游和中文景点介绍，可以帮助客人更好地享受园内的表演节目和景点。此外，用餐区增加了额外的座位，因为中国人用餐的时间比美国人要长。迪士尼希望这样的改变能吸引更多的游客来香港迪士尼乐园。

(资料来源：Merissa Marr ad Geoffrey A. Fowler,“迪士尼的中国教训(Chines Lessons for Disney).”华尔街日报，2006 年 6 月 12 日, B1, B5.)

4.1　了解我们的跨文化行为

对于全球范围内的管理者和雇员来说，他们都应该具备的重要能力是与他人合作完成工作任务的能力。尤其是在 21 世纪，无论是与拥有其他文化背景的同事直接进行面对面交流，还是作为通过互联网连接起来的全球或跨国团队的一部分，每位员工都是团队的一分子。世界各地的人们有许多相似之处，同时也存在差异，因此与世界各地的人进行沟通既是最大的挑战也是最大的机遇。共同工作的个体会因年龄、性别、母语、第二语言、专业知识、教育背景具有相似性或不同之处，也会因为生活经验和文化背景而相似或不同。背景给我们提供了独特的生活体验，这种体验受到价值观、人生态度及本国人认同的行为规范的驱动。

4.2　文化内涵及商务实践中的中外差异

4.2.1　权力与关系

著名研究员吉尔特·霍夫斯塔德(Geert Hofstede)倾其一生研究文化如何影响我们的行为，他认为文化是由多种元素构成的，这些元素可以分为以下四类。

- 我们使用的象征符号，包括语言。

- 我们崇拜的英雄，如心目中的理想型人物。
- 我们的例行公事，包括庆祝仪式和商务会议等日常事务。
- 我们信奉的价值观，如对好与坏、理性与非理性、正常与反常的感觉。

这些(元素)结合在一起，就是文化的含义。

霍夫斯塔德将文化比作计算机软件。他认为文化是共同的心理程序，将不同类型的人群区分开来。事实上，霍夫斯塔德在 1991 年出版的《文化与组织：心理软件的力量》一书中阐述了自己对国家文化及其对商务活动的影响所进行的广泛研究，这本书至今仍十分出名。毫无疑问，每当不同国度的文化接触时，人们会发现要想相互理解很困难，就像 Microsoft Word 和 Microsoft Excel 这两款不同软件对话一样困难。

霍夫斯塔德的研究工作有助于我们理解不同文化间的相似与差异。在科技巨人 IBM 公司，霍夫斯塔德通过研究，确定了多种文化维度，并通过它区分了不同文化类型的人。通过对 53 个 IBM 国内子公司的雇员和管理人员的调查研究，霍夫斯塔德和其他研究员一起确定了下列产生文化差异的维度。

霍夫斯塔德认定的文化差异的五个维度

(1) 权力差距——一个国家的社会成员所能接受或认为是正常的不平等待遇的程度。权力差距范围从相对平等到极端的不平等。

(2) 个人主义——一个国家的社会成员表现个人行为而不是集体行为的程度。程度范围从极端的个人主义(或个人的独立性)到极端的集体主义(或群体的依赖性)。

(3) 价值观念的男性气质——一个国家的社会成员看重男性的程度，重视“男性气质”，诸如过分自信、行动力强、渴望成功、竞争性，而不重视“女性气质”，诸如良好的关系、合作性、同情心、人脉、服务性。程度范围从“温和到强硬”(Hofstede，1991)。

(4) 不确定性的规避——一个国家的社会成员对待工作环境的喜好程度，是愿意在熟悉、有组织的环境中工作，还是愿意在不熟悉、无组织的环境中工作。程度范围从相对灵活、高度创新到极端严格、反对创新。

(5) 长期导向性——一个国家的社会成员对建立长期关系的重视程度，是精打细算、不屈不挠，而不是“短期行为”，社会成员消极对待传统。

霍夫斯塔德从连续性或级别上对这些文化维度进行从高到低的等级描述，因此各国间的文化可以进行相互比较。

我们生活在一个全球化的社会，不同文化通过电视、互联网、音乐、社交媒体、电子邮件及到其他国家进行面对面的沟通、海外教育和跨国企业的商业投资等形式不断地相互影响。21 世纪，不同文化不会再因为空间或时间因素而被隔离。

迪士尼的时代变迁

一家公司凭借特定文化产品进军世界各地，这就是以迪士尼乐园闻名的沃尔特·迪士尼公司。迪士尼为吸引游客而设计了主题公园，这满足了游客们与曾经出现在他们阅读过的童话故事和看过的影视作品中的人物进行面对面交流的需求，并逐渐遍布世界各地。1955 年，公司创始人沃尔特·迪士尼(Walt Disney)在加利福尼亚州的阿纳海姆建造了第一座迪士尼乐园。

此后，在佛罗里达州的奥兰多和坦帕又建立了其他乐园。备受喜爱的米老鼠、唐老鸭和睡美人在文化碰撞中幸存下来，但是迪士尼乐园的很多部分逐步被修改以满足新的东道主国家的文化。例如，1992 年在法国巴黎市郊建造的新乐园最初命名为“欧洲迪士尼”，2002 年改为“巴黎迪士尼乐园”，因为据当时的首席执行官迈克尔·艾斯纳(Michael Eisner)称，“欧洲”这个词语对于法国人来讲只有“商务”和“货币”的意思，并未体现出它想要展现的魅力。20 世纪 90 年代的持续亏损让迪士尼公司吸取了很多经验教训。巴黎迪士尼乐园的食物为适应法国人口味做了一些修改，作为法餐必备的葡萄酒起初是被禁止的，后又重新提供。为使雇佣关系和谐，对员工守则和额外培训也作了一些调整。1983 年在东京以及此后在香港开设的新乐园则受益于这种尊重文化差异的意愿。

2016 年上海迪士尼的开园展示了行为的灵活性如何成为跨文化沟通和管理成功的关键。现任首席执行官，鲍勃·艾格(Bob Iger)描述上海迪士尼是“具有典型中国特色的真正的迪士尼”。他声称 70%的游乐设施是原汁原味的，但是六个乐园中有四个是新构想的。备受喜爱的米老鼠、唐老鸭和公主都是主题乐园的特色。但是，作为早期美国城镇生活的文化象征和以前主题公园核心特征的美国小镇大街，已经变为米奇大街。同样的，作为美国早期开拓史上另一个文化记录的“边城乐园”已变为“宝藏湾”。“宝藏湾”享有全球知名度，很大程度上得益于电影，如《加勒比海盗》的热映。“明日世界”也已更新为“创世纪”以反映明日世界。第四个显著变化是添加了以中国十二生肖为主题的“十二朋友园”，其中包括《料理鼠王》中的里米和《小熊维尼》中的跳跳虎以及中国主题餐厅“漫月轩”。沃尔特·迪士尼公司在它承诺世界各地的迪士尼乐园都是相同的那天起，就已经明显地改变了其经营行为。

我们从案例研究中发现，当企业和雇员适应了我们与他们的相似性和差异时，敏感的跨文化管理会带来巨大成功。

确实，在阅读本书的时候，你将和来自中国和澳大利亚的作者交流，他们共同合作编写了此书。所以，我们共同的知识和一些价值观将不可避免地全球化。因此，我们必须避免对文化使用一般化的方式来给别人留下刻板的印象。霍夫斯塔德的文化维度很好地指导我们当面对不同文化时需要注意什么。这种知识就像路标一样时刻提醒我们，使我们能够维持有效沟通。

下面举一个文化差异性的例子。让我们比较中国、日本、美国、英国和瑞典，所有这些描述都在相对尺度下进行，也就是说，所有这些国家的文化都是连续性地相互比较。

学习实践

学习表 4.1 中列出的内容，思考作为可能的商业合作伙伴，中国与其他国家在文化上的差异。

表 4.1　世界范围内五个国家的文化维度比较

国家	权力距离	个人主义/集体主义	男性气质/女性气质	不确定规避	长期导向/短期导向
中国	高等	低度个人主义	男性气质适中	中等	高等
日本	高等	低度个人主义	男性气质很高	高等	高等
美国	中等	高度个人主义	男性气质适中	低等	中等
英国	中等	高度个人主义	男性气质适中	低等	中等
瑞典	低等	高度个人主义	男性气质低	低等	中高等

(资料来源：Hofstede G,1991. *Cultures and Organizations: Software of the Mind*[M]. Sydney: McGraw-Hill. Hofstede G. Cultural constraints in management theories[J]. *Academy of Management Executive*, 1993, 7(2) :81-94.)

4.2.2　语境与沟通

另一个帮助我们理解跨文化沟通的重要视角是了解拥有不同文化背景的人使用信息的不同方式。爱德华·霍尔用“高语境”或“低语境”描述文化中所涉及的信息内容。中国、日本和其他许多亚洲国家文化是高语境文化，这种文化认为互动所需的知识是由群体中相互作用的文化和人传递的，因此信息不需要明确用话语表达出来。话语简短使得用词和用词选择变得非常重要。通常，高语境文化是集体性和相关性的。

相反，美国、澳大利亚和英国是低语境文化，需在互动中将想法清楚、明确地表达出来。这种在表达思想及用词上的差异对于人们相互理解有着很大影响。低语境文化中的人通常独立工作并期待与许多人建立关系，但是支持他们的至交却很少。例如，如果一位中国雇员和澳大利亚雇员进行沟通，中国员工可能希望澳大利亚员工明白，年轻的中国员工如果直接和上级领导表达意见分歧，这会是一种冒犯。相反，澳大利亚人希望能够直接、清楚地表达不同观点。通常当有人打破规则时，人们才会注意到差别。

除此之外，还有许多基于民族文化的其他准则，但是当遇到跨文化情境时，霍夫斯塔德和霍尔提出的这两点是很有价值的参考。

4.2.3　商业实践

由于这是一本关于商务沟通的书，所以认识到商业实践本身也是跨文化管理动态的一部分也很重要。

各国的商务风格和方式也有所不同。对商务实践的灵敏度，如管理策略和商务计划、会议发言人，甚至参会人员、商务信函的使用、年度报告及其他文档的设计以及政治文化对谈判的影响等，是跨文化交流成功不可或缺的部分。与其他国家进行商务活动需要谨慎处理的一个例子是尊重伊斯兰银行制度不同的财务需求。中东许多国家，如沙特阿拉伯、巴林、巴基斯坦、苏丹以及靠近中国的马来西亚和印度尼西亚，奉行伊斯兰银行制度，不允许对金融产品支付利息。本书在后面的章节中，将继续阐释商务互动中的差异。在这里，重要的一点是认识到不仅是民族文化，而且企业文化及相关的沟通活动，都是成功实现跨文化交流的一部分。

4.2.4 个体差异对跨文化交流的影响

最近的研究者们建议，我们需要考虑跨文化交流的复杂性。为了避免基于上述维度(Osland，Bird，2000)的“复杂刻板印象”，我们需要识别个人与他人交往的方式。即使在同一文化背景下，互动风格也有很大的不同。

学习实践

1. 观察两名同学及两个家庭成员，注意他们在互动时的相似和差异。
2. 他们是否存在年龄、性别、社交媒体使用经历和其他方面的差异？

加纳什(Ganesh，2015)和霍姆斯(Holmes，2015)告诫人们不要仅仅依赖像霍夫斯塔德和霍尔提出的那种维度准则。他们认为，如性别、年龄、旅行方式、通过互联网社交媒体与外国人互动以及在商务活动中的虚拟团队经验和教育经历同样影响我们的跨文化互动方式。21 世纪，这种个人经验会使规则变得更加复杂和具有适应性。近期对商务英语在中国的发展研究表明，中国的年轻职场人士的沟通方式比霍夫斯塔德或者霍尔模式所描述的更加直接。

因为全球性文化迅速崛起，不同文化之间的界限不再那样严格也是可以理解的，尤其是对于受数字文化影响的年青一代。随着空间和时间相关性的减弱，许多文化边界在移动和变化。另一个可以说明文化爆炸和文化全球化的典型例子是韩国流行音乐、时尚以及韩剧在亚洲许多国家非常流行。生活观念的文化适应，特别是名人的生活方式，降低了文化差异带来的沟通风险且易于被年青一代接受。同样，互联网带来的互动机遇为英语用户提供了更安全的沟通环境和更缓和、更民主的沟通方式。

4.2.5 英语作为第二语言在跨文化交流中的作用

除了了解个人生活经验对跨文化交流的影响外，还要注意母语和作为第二语言的英语在交往动态中变得日益重要。英语作为母语的人比那些英语作为第二语言的人具有一定优势，这可能会导致沟通中的权力失衡。

然而，双语者可以通过两个窗口去了解跨文化动态。重要的是承认语言的困难，有提出问题的信心，而且当其他文化背景的人打破文化规则时，注意提醒他们。即使双方都将英语作为共同使用的语言，对于选择哪些词汇及何种语调都受演讲者或者作者的第一文化模式所驱动。例如，作为本书作者，我们注意到在中国年度报告中隐喻很重要，而在澳大利亚的商务报告中，隐喻却使用得非常有限。

为加强内部员工间的跨文化交流，IBM 推出了全球统一的英语语言政策并为所有员工提供了专门的培训计划，要求员工不论是在日本还是在英国，在工作中都要使用英语。IBM 在此项目中投入大量资源，展示出优秀的跨文化管理对于商务成功的价值。

4.3　如何有效管理跨文化沟通

认识到不同文化相遇时会出现的不利因素之后，我们可以运用一些策略确保有效的跨文化沟通。图 4.1 展示了跨文化沟通的动态性。我们每个人带来不同的文化价值、态度、行为。图中两个圈的重叠部分代表文化交流的高风险部分，因为这时，你和沟通伙伴面对的是对一方或双方根深蒂固的文化模式的挑战。

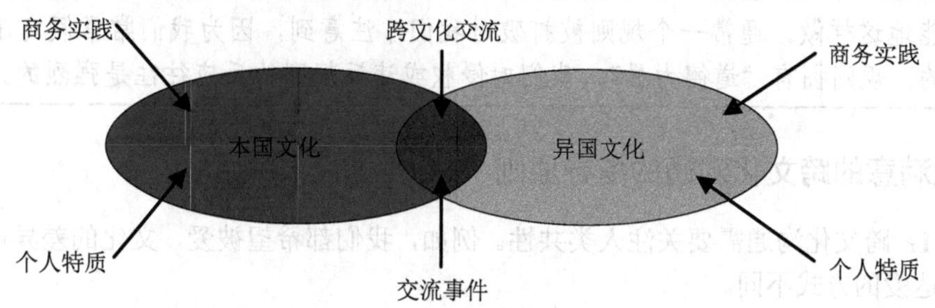

图 4.1　跨文化沟通的动态性

例如，当一名韩国人遇见一名澳大利亚人，如何称呼对方就是高风险事件。澳大利亚人会直接上前说出自己的名字："你好，我叫杰克。"因为韩国人生活在权力差距相差较大的文化中，注重正式礼仪，这将是个尴尬的场面。韩国人不习惯其他人直呼其名字，只有亲戚或好朋友才能这样称呼他们，他们更愿意被叫作朴先生或金先生。对杰克和朴先生来说，跨文化交流可能造成紧张气氛，因为交流中存在两种竞争性的规则。但是如果杰克和朴先生巧妙地处理了这个问题，他们的交流会很顺利、很成功。一些在海外留学的韩国人使用英文名来处理这样的问题。这种适应行为表明跨文化交流中不仅存在不同的文化模式，而且存在应对这种挑战的个人选择。

首先要思考本国的文化。了解自己的文化，分析哪些方面是正常的，如何理解不同行为，这是学习过程中很重要的一步。出色的跨文化沟通者都善于自我思考。理想的跨文化沟通认为，交流的双方都应调整自己的行为以适应对方的文化。如图 4.1 所示的"第三区域"描成深色，表示双方的协调空间。

学习实践

回答以下关于本国文化的问题。

思考你自己所属的文化——一份关于文化的清单，两人或三人一个小组，考虑在下列情形下你是如何进行文化交流的。对每个情形都简明地列出要点。

(1) 建立关系：会面(意图、权力关系、谁有话语权、典型话题、称呼方式)。

(2) 参与性(说话和缄默，轮流说话，举止得体)。

(3) 处理冲突(态度、技巧)。

(4) 其他观察。

(5) 描述一个广告，这个广告表达的是本国文化中重要的文化价值，并说说它表现了哪些方面。

(6) 描述一个广告，这个广告表达的是另一种文化，并说说它表现了哪些方面。

(7) 讲一个故事，能反映出本国文化是如何起作用的(从家庭、休闲或工作场所的方面)。

(8) 在建立了一套自己的规则后，回顾表 4.1，将这组规则与表 4.1 中另一个国家进行比较。

(9) 你注意到自我评估的行为与霍夫斯塔德和霍尔所提出的维度有哪些区别？

(10) 还有哪些方面可以解释你的行为差异？年龄、语言？

请记住，你必须慎重思考哪些规则支配你的行为。规则是无意识的，也就是说你近乎本能地这样做。通常一个规则被打破时我们才注意到，因为我们常常假定违规者是故意的。规则拥有“道德力量”，我们对侵权或违反规则的反应往往是强烈的。

实现满意的跨文化沟通的指导原则

原则 1：跨文化沟通需要关注人类共性。例如，我们都希望被爱，文化的差异可能决定了我们表达爱的方式不同。

原则 2：谨慎对待“反常”现象。往往沟通同伴做了件他们认为的平常之事，而自己却会因此感到震惊。这时就需要考虑章节开头列出的文化差异。

原则 3：注意不能仅根据文化形成刻板印象。文化维度是一般行为模式的规范，但不是每个人应遵循的规则。他们个人的生活经验会让他们做出不同的选择和行为。必然有这样一个中国人，他和大多数中国人在行为上有所不同。在任何一种文化中，都会有一些人不遵守自己文化中的正常规则。

原则 4：如果需要同来自异国文化的人发展工作关系，必须花时间了解这个人并仔细观察他的行为，这样才能了解你们之间的相似与差异。对于那些来自其他文化的人，比如美国，这意味着花费额外时间与其他文化建立关系。对于中国人来说，和某个美国人交往，花费时间建立友谊是正常的，但美国人则认为这样做是浪费时间。如果西方合作伙伴想直截了当进入主题，不要表现出不愉快，而是需要适应这种沟通方式，同时不断地加强交流。在沟通早期，双方处于高风险区域。

原则 5：在与来自不同文化的伙伴建立信任以后，坦诚地讨论，并达成沟通的默契。这就是图 4.1 所示的“第三区域”。这包括沟通时日本伙伴会说“yes”和“no”，中国伙伴通过社会交往建立关系，韩国伙伴的等级和权力分级规则，美国伙伴的个人责任和集体责任。

学习实践

阅读以下案例研究，就澳大利亚人通过电邮沟通的方法而论，哪三种情况会让韩国员工觉得难以处理？看看你是否可以应用在本章中学到的方法发现问题。作为一名中国员工，在与韩国员工的交流中，你需要考虑哪些问题？

韩国人与澳大利亚人之间的在线交流

世界各地有许多跨国公司。一项关于韩、澳之间商务来往邮件的研究表明，无论人们是面对面交流还是技术性远程交流，某一特定文化群体的行为模式趋于一致。研究还

发现，韩国人的交流比较正式，权力地位意识明显，尊重年长者，事先需要建立良好关系，表达含蓄。而澳大利亚人的沟通方式较随意、友善，不在乎地位，喜欢称呼对方的名字，表达直截了当。但研究还发现，双方之间会逐渐学会适应对方，逐步调整正式与非正式的程度，增强开放程度。

(资料来源：Kim H S , Hearn G, Hatcher C, et al,. Online communication between Koreans and Australians[J]. *World Communication*, 1999, 28 (4):48-68.)

4.4　了解并尊重其他文化

东西方不同文化在处理沟通问题的方式上的一些重要差异已经明确，包括冲突的处理、礼仪和庆典、关系的处理(面子和尴尬)、学习方法及接受反馈。除此之外，当然还有更多的内容需要了解，但了解这几个方面为跨文化沟通提供了良好的基础。

4.4.1　冲突的处理

一些国家如日本和泰国会不惜一切代价避免冲突，他们热心于维持和谐，一旦发生冲突便感到不安，力求避免人与人之间的冲突。一些研究表明，泰国人致力于维持和谐的关系，友好、间接地进行交流，商务人士间如果出现冲突会共同协作解决。同样，日本文化与泰国文化有点类似，日本人也尽量避免冲突，热衷于维持一个和谐、礼貌的沟通氛围。

这种对异议和争论的解决方式与美国人和澳大利亚人的做法截然不同。在高度个人主义的国家(如美国和澳大利亚)，人们喜好争辩。例如在会场上，美国人和澳大利亚人与泰国人和日本人相比更加重视辩论。

坦率地讲，在许多西方国家文化中，公开地据理力争、进行辩论被视为是成功商务人士的一种积极行为。一些研究员如 Avtgis 和 Rancer[①](2002)研究了争论行为的价值，证明一些国家尤其重视争论，例如澳大利亚人要比美国人更崇尚争论，更坦率直言。

许多拥有和谐文化的东方国家对这些争论行为感到相当震惊。然而，在西方人看来，如果不直言反对，则被视为认同或被看作是软弱或被动。Avtgis 和 Rancer 发现与日本人相比，美国人、澳大利亚人和新西兰人更为好辩，可能会在会议等公开场合展开热烈的辩论。文化风格的差异往往导致群体间的重大误解。

要尽量适应同伴处理冲突的风格：不论争论激烈还是平缓，必须运用适当的方式做出回应。

4.4.2　仪式和礼节

中国、日本和韩国的文化基础是儒家伦理和价值观，在商务宴请和会议方面都有一定的仪式程序。在美国和英国等西方国家中也有许多仪式，但通常不太正式，例如在如何庆祝、娱乐和召开会议方面人们一般有更多的选择余地。西方仪式中使用商务名片是从东方

① 此处为西班牙文，不翻译。

引进的，日本人称作 *meishi*，直到 20 世纪 90 年代，商务名片在西方国家才成为普遍的交往礼仪。在今天的美国、英国和澳大利亚等国家，使用商务名片已成为一种礼仪。

西方人对中国人和韩国人在商务宴请中饮酒的礼仪感到惊讶。莫尼赖(Moni Lai Storz)在《与龙共舞：全球商务揭秘之筷子民族》一书中指出这些仪式是儒家所提倡的美感、艺术感，是注重美感和礼节的表现。

下面这个例子说明了此种仪式中固有的文化间的冲突。

在美国，当外出吃饭时，没人会对“AA 制”，即每人都为自己的食物买单的做法感到诧异。

当那些美国商务人士(以及其他西方人)来到中国时，使他们大为吃惊的是他们的中国同伴所表现出的好客。他们经常享用八至十道菜的宴席，有时甚至比这还多。其中一些人禁不住惊呼：“好丰盛的宴会！”以表明他们很享用宴席上的饭菜。但宴席过后，其中一些人则会做出另一种评价：“真浪费！”当然这些话东道主是听不到的。

这里所出现的是一种文化误解。那些美国人及其他西方人士所看的是结果，即为他们举办了一桌酒席；他们所没有看到或是不屑了解的，是中国人的先贤“孔子”的教诲对后人的影响。他说过“有朋自远方来，不亦乐乎”。在中国人的眼里，这些美国人以及其他西方人就像孔子所描述的，是一些“远方的来客”。

(资料来源：徐宪光. 商务沟通[M]. 北京：外语教学与研究出版社，2003.)

学习实践

认识到你的跨文化合作伙伴可能并不熟悉你们的仪式，但是这并不表明他们是不好的沟通者，你应该帮助他们享受新的文化体验。另外，如果有些仪式在国际旅行或者与他人互动中漏掉了，不要对新仪式感到紧张。实事求是，不会就问，弄清楚不明白的地方，人们通常很乐意分享他们文化传统的专门知识。你的提问是对他们的赞美，所以放轻松并享受新的体验。灵活性和适应性是优秀跨文化沟通者的标志。

4.4.3 处理好“面子”问题和尴尬场面

在许多东方文化国度里，如韩国、日本和泰国，礼貌被认为是一项重要的美德。所以，通过保持庄重并按照等级完成所有仪式来表现礼貌，这一点非常重要。这样，社会群体能保证维护每个人的“面子”，从而维护了社会协调。许多西方人还没有清楚地认识到公众形象或“面子”是相当脆弱和珍贵的，但并不是意味着来自美国或英国的人会认为他们被置于尴尬的局面是可以忍受的。若非尴尬的局面很严重，他们都会对尴尬的时刻或事件一笑而过，并不放在心上，甚至事后作为谈话的素材。来自强调个人主义文化的国家的人对于正式的礼节要求不是太多，他们更为自信，更多地依靠自身力量而不是像东方文化中那样去依赖别人。

对于“面子”问题的不同看法会引起文化误解，因为西方人没有意识到个人在公众中的形象能够如此轻易地被破坏，他们运用口头和非正式策略进行沟通，这种沟通方式在东方文化的国度里常被认为是没有礼貌，是对别人的冒犯甚至被视为是失礼的。

学习实践

虽然人总是要“面子”，但是要认识到人们在特定情境下，通常都试图去做正确的事情。他们的一个疏忽或者错误让你失了“面子”，很有可能是无心之失。沟通发生后，回想每次跨文化交流，思考：下次会怎么做呢，会有所改变吗？

4.4.4　学习方法和接受反馈

第一次在国外接受培训或者接受外国培训师的培训经历可能会让人沮丧，尤其是从东方文化的国家进入西方文化的国家。表 4.2 总结了一些东西方文化存在的主要差异，列举出东方文化国家(如中国、日本、泰国和韩国)及西方文化国家(如美国、英国、德国、斯堪的纳维亚半岛国家和澳大利亚)的一些特点。毫无疑问，当培训师和来自异国文化的人们合作时，培训和提供反馈是富有挑战的。为了让学员满意，培训师必须是培训内容和培训方式方面的专家。

表 4.2　不同文化背景下的培训和学习方法

盎格鲁-撒克逊人的培训与学习法	东方国家的培训与学习法
参与	倾听/死记硬背
冒风险	不冒风险
提问	回答问题/做详尽笔记
反复尝试	坚信专家知识的权威性
以学生为中心	以教师为中心
平等主义	等级主义
个人主义	集体主义
自信	缺少自信
富有挑战	随和
争论的	不争论的
争论/辩论	一致性
非正式/随意	正式/奉行仪式主义

(资料来源：Storz M. *Dancing with Dragons: Chopsticks People Revealed for Global Business*[M]. Melbourne: Global Business Strategies,1999.)

当然，请记住，在培训过程中，有许多跨国沟通方式和个体差异。尽管如此，我们作为本书作者在培训实践中已经注意到这些不同模式。我们注意到，无论对于西方人还是东方人，个体差异和英语作为第二语言的因素在塑造个人参与、冒险和质疑方面都发挥重要的作用。

学习实践

如果你正接受外籍培训师或是来自西方国家培训师的培训，或者被要求提供培训反馈，要努力地发言、提问。如果发现培训师的观点和见解让人惊讶，要大胆要求进行详细的解释说明，或者发表自己的观点，你将从这种学习方法中获益。当你和培训师都在努力满足对方文化沟通的需求时，其他接受培训的人也会反思不同文化存在的相似和差异。

4.4.5 避免跨文化商务交流中的误解

为避免跨文化交流中可能出现的误解，要求沟通双方要采用更为灵活的方法，更为开放地对沟通的方式进行思考。不能在沟通中封闭自我，而要多观察、多思量，这样才能认识到何时沟通进行得顺利，何时出现了差错。任何情况下，良好沟通的关键都是倾听和仔细观察非语言交流方式所表达的信息。

下面介绍一个能尽情享受跨文化沟通乐趣的简单方法：PLACE 技巧。

准备(Prepare)——尽可能全面了解即将面对的异国文化和人群。

倾听(Listen)——仔细倾听和观察已接收到的信号(口头和非口头)。

调整(Adjust)——灵活地调整沟通的方法以适应跨文化沟通对象的要求，这样可以快速地对有分歧的或没有预料到的结果做出反应。

沟通(Communicate)——尽可能积极地进行沟通。适应对方的沟通风格，以及他们的步调和沟通方式。

享受(Enjoy)——享受跨文化交流带来的体验多样的价值观、态度和观念的机会。多样性产生创造力并带来成功的商务合作。

本 章 小 结

不论是打算在中国生活还是要去海外工作，都将会涉及跨文化沟通的问题。这是作为一名雇员和管理者必须拥有的重要能力，你需要提高这种技能，能够与来自全球各地的人们一起工作并管理他们。跨文化沟通能力包括许多技能，从开放、好问到学习异国文化，在跨文化沟通中聚精会神，认真思考本国文化如何起作用，以及本国文化和他国文化中的规范。另外，有沟通能力的人不会放过任何机会进行沟通练习。他们举止得体，犹如一名努力赢取比赛的优秀运动员。有较强沟通能力的人有些情况下也会出现沟通失误，但是他们毫不气馁地从失误中总结学习。换句话说，成为有效沟通者的过程是一个反复尝试的过程，每次从沟通中得到的经验和信息都增加了未来顺畅、有效的沟通的可能。总的来说，你多才多艺、适应性强且学识渊博。跨文化沟通是每个成功的商务人士都必须具备的、富有挑战性的工具。

第5章

在商务活动中运用最佳的沟通技术

【学习目标】

通过对本章内容的学习，你能够实现以下目标。

- 了解不断发展的沟通技术带来的益处和挑战。
- 认识到无效地使用如电子邮件、短信系统、智能手机、社交媒体和互联网视频会议这些工具时产生的风险及支持性技术对沟通产生的威胁。
- 在商务沟通中充分地发挥电子邮件、网络视频会议、社交媒体和移动电话的作用。
- 了解技术在有效沟通中的作用。
- 知道如何利用相关支持性技术做有效演示。

引例：当你说话时，我能看见你

1964 年在布鲁克林举行的世界博览会上，美国电话电报公司(AT&T)推出了可视电话(picturephone)，声称几年内将有数百万人接受这种设备，社会将永远改变。50 多年后的今天，这种情况还没有发生，部分原因是成本太高，部分原因是小屏幕上晃动的视频和音频不同步。另一个原因是来自心理上的，与隐私有关。

库尔特・斯彻夫(Kurt Scherf)，市场研究员认为，“人们不想仅仅为了接电话而梳头或换睡衣。”事实上，AT&T 的一项研究发现，人们平均电话响 11 下才来接听可视电话，可能是因为他们在接电话之前需要整理自己的办公桌或个人形象。

此外，你不太可能在与能够观察你一举一动的人进行交谈时，被发现自己同时处理多项事务——比如筛选电子邮件、叠衣服或浏览报纸。

然而，对于远程办公者、有远房孙子的祖父母以及任何想建立或维持远距离个人关系的人来说，新的可视电话可能是一种可以接受的面对面对话的替代品。

虽然网络摄像头已经存在多年了，但它们的图像又小又不稳定。另外，双方必须坐在电脑前进行交流。因为可视电话有自己的监视器，所以可以在任何地方使用。这种特质使得一些视觉，诸如眼神交流、微笑、点头、眨眼、脸红以及其他非语言交流等显得自然而真实。

电话在商业中起着至关重要的作用。毫无疑问，通过电话进行有效沟通是一项关键的管理技能，随着对即时信息需求的增加，这种技能变得越来越重要。您在电话中表现的态度可能会被来电者视为整个组织的态度。在本章中，我们将学习如何使用这些技术进行有效的沟通。

5.1 使用沟通技术面临的机遇和挑战

不断发展的互联网驱动技术，诸如平板电脑、iPad 系列产品、智能手机、腾讯微信和 QQ 等社交媒体系统、微软 Office 软件和移动 App 改变了我们的沟通方式。我们现在可以和隔壁办公室的人一起工作，也可以和世界另一端办公室里的人一起工作。我们现在可以通过电子邮件、视频和音频会议系统、社交媒体和短信等各种互联网媒体进行沟通。我们也可以通过许多支持平台与他人联系，比如语言翻译、数据库、影音图像和图形展示。这些技术容易被掌握，同时(对于这些技术的使用)既是一个机遇也是一个挑战。本章对于使用或不当使用沟通技术提供了一些指导。它将通过一对一、团队互动和虚拟团队，利用重要商业工具的使用，如互联网、社交媒体传播渠道、智能手机的应用、电子邮件和技术等增强演示效果，以达到有效的商务沟通。

5.1.1 沟通技术的历史

在开始考虑指导我们使用沟通技术的规则之前，意识到技术本身的快速变化将提醒我们对技术的充分使用具有挑战性。虽然企业使用书面和口头文字已有几个世纪且已形成许多在商业中约定俗成的行为模式，但是很多沟通技术相对较新，它们像没有实验指南的实验一样被吸收到商务实践中。随着智能手机、全球网络、短信、微信和平板电脑等技术的融合，公共沟通、商务沟通和个人沟通中的很多差异难以区分开来，这些对于专业性的商务沟通、良好声誉、沟通过量和沟通的安全性提出挑战。

图 5.1 提供了对各种技术开端简短的历史回顾，通信技术的发展之快可能会令你惊讶。

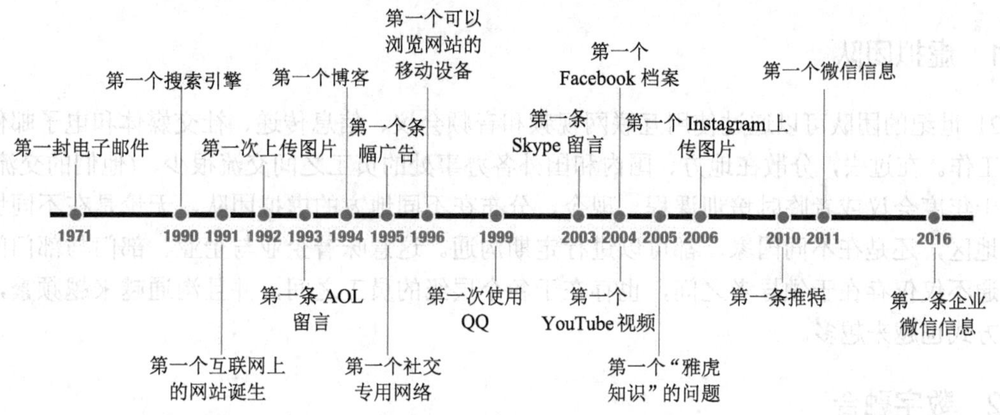

图 5.1　通信技术发展史时间轴

5.1.2　沟通和专业素质的原则

易于获得的社会进步以及新技术都可能导致沟通中正确或不恰当地使用各种沟通技术。无论我们使用多少技术，最重要的是记住有效沟通的原则是不变的，可概括为十条简单的原则。

(1) 良好沟通就是一切为了听众。

(2) 有效的商务沟通者具有职业素养和信誉，使被沟通者获得信心。

(3) 专业沟通者能确保个人和企业身份在沟通上有明显区别。

(4) 优秀的沟通者总是致力于与读者/观众/听众建立关系。

(5) 沟通就像是看电视剧，新信息总是建立在之前信息的基础之上。

(6) 优秀的沟通者能够抓住并维持读者/观众/听众的注意力。

(7) 关键信息必须清晰。

(8) 信息过量会让信息杂乱。

(9) 优秀沟通者会建构信息以帮助读者/观众/听众理解他所表达的观点。

(10) 优秀的沟通者首先是优秀的倾听者，他们能够通过反馈来不断调整所要传达的信息。

将上述原则熟记于心，任何通信技术的使用都应是有战略性的，并应支持有效沟通，而不是炫耀技术奇迹。就像舞台上有主演和配角，信息发送者也有恰当的角色，其中的人是各种观点的源头，而技术，如机器和软件就像是助手。技术应始终发挥支持作用而不是主导作用。

5.2 合作式的工作

现在信息技术的发展让工作合作变得越来越容易，不论你在广阔世界中的哪里工作，重要的是对于技术的使用要谨慎选择。

5.2.1 虚拟团队

21 世纪的团队可以通过使用互联网视频和音频会议、信息传递、社交媒体和电子邮件进行工作。在过去，分散在地方、国内和国外各办事处的员工之间交流很少，(他们的交流)仅限于年度会议或者临时培训课程。现今，分布在不同地方的虚拟团队，无论是在不同城市、地区，还是在不同国家，都可以进行定期沟通。这意味着企业与企业、部门与部门间的沟通不仅仅存在于领导者之间，也存在于各个层级的员工之间，并且沟通越来越频繁，沟通方式也越来越多。

5.2.2 数字融合

数字融合是指连接手机和网站、社交媒体、信息系统、支付系统等互联网服务。

随着中国电子商务应用日益增多，网站作为企业服务、文化和品牌窗口的媒介作用变得越来越重要。对展示的企业形象、用户友好访问、与其他沟通技术(如社交媒体、电子邮件等)融合的方式，都要做出谨慎的选择，目的是鼓励客户浏览公司网站。要综合运用这些因素去实现成功的商业成果。中国网上购物的发展现状处于世界领先地位，紧跟其后的国家是亚洲的印度和新加坡。同样，由于客户的抱怨能够在社交媒体上分享，所以低劣的沟通会损害组织声誉。

腾讯公司，即社交平台微信(在下文的社交媒体部分会有更详细的阐述)和 QQ 的创造者，最近报告声称中国有 30%的网购者进行冲动消费，在社交媒体上进行产品推荐比传统广告更具说服力。

智能手机与微信支付等服务的数字融合让客户能通过手机上网并有无限选择。集中性商业战略犹如黏合剂，是一种出色的能够抓住客户注意力的商务沟通，引导并建构客户购买经历以达到企业追求的预期结果。企业内部网站也是商务沟通战略日益重要的组成部分。内部网站让员工能够快速、轻松地找到他们想要的信息，并进行内部沟通，员工得到提高，并保证了工作效率。

Airbnb

Airbnb 公司是一个使用互联网和内部网络集合用户的创新型企业，它提供全球在线住宿服务。Airbnb 公司非常成功，在世界各地的很多国家、不同城市和农村地区都可以搜寻到可提供住宿的地方。公司依靠小型私人经营者在家里、公寓或独幢别墅为旅客提供合理价位的住宿，Airbnb 通过其网站和短信服务构建人性化服务，允许客户从网站提供的广泛范围中寻找自己满意的住处，洽谈预定信息和到达安排并对所接受的服务进行反馈。这种反馈是累积的，依据客户对质量、地点及房主的热情程度的反馈对住宿服务进行“星级”评定。所有这些信息为之后的顾客提供细节，以帮助他们做出决定。此外，Airbnb 公司也允许经营者在内部网站提供对客户的反馈信息。这种反馈对其他经营者进行公布，确保优质客户在未来能够受到欢迎。因此，经营者和客户的声誉都是很重要的。这种经营者和客户的即时评估能确保沟通和行为的质量，同时满足了客户和经营者的需求。基于此，Airbnb 公司的声誉得到了强有力的提升。

在上述这些情况下，注意协调内部及外部的商务沟通是 21 世纪企业成功的关键。

5.2.3　社交媒体——微信

由中国腾讯公司开发的微信，自 2011 年引入市场以来，被中国民众广泛地使用，并得到持续发展。据 2016 年《腾讯研究报告》及《微信影响力报告》显示，2016 年微信月用户达 7 亿人。像微信这种社交媒体以其持续和自由的方式，几乎不需要通过记者、政府和组织，在人们交往和分享信息中起着至关重要的作用。

通过提供文本信息，语音通话，传播(一对多)消息，视频会议，视频游戏，共享照片、视频、位置以及支付系统，微信为员工解决业务问题提供了渠道，同时也为其与家人、朋友保持联系提供机会。

2016 年腾讯公司的报告(2016 年《腾讯研究报告》和《微信影响力报告》)中强调，微信在人们的日常生活中的重要性日益凸显。目前，据报道，微信用户有以下特点。

- 每月在微信上支出的费用超过 100 元人民币(占用户 70%)。
- 用微信浏览新闻的人群多于在新闻网站和电视上浏览新闻的总和。
- 每天打开微信超过十次(占用户 61%)。
- 每次打开微信时都会刷新朋友圈(占用户 61.4%)。
- 在公司用微信工作(占用户 40.4%)。

微信软件能为商务沟通和个人沟通提供快速、高效的沟通渠道。腾讯公司研究显示，用户选择使用微信最重要的三个原因分别是：价值(实用性)、兴趣和情感沟通。使用微信是优势与潜在风险并存的。

和很多企业一样，腾讯公司也认识到个人生活和商务活动混用的社交软件存在潜在风险，2016 年，腾讯公司为商务活动推出更安全的服务——微信企业版。72%的官方账户是通过一个商业实体注册的，这充分说明个人生活和公共生活混在一起会使商务沟通存在风险(2016 年《腾讯研究报告》和《微信影响力报告》)。企业运营账户的关键原因是：

- 提高内部管理和沟通效率。
- 改进管理系统。
- 提高公司效率。

为增加内部沟通与合作，必须谨慎并有策略地利用微信软件提供的众多机会。

有效使用微信的指南

(1) 务必认真思考所传递的信息从本质上看是职业的还是私人的。无论属于哪一种情况，恰当的语气和风格是成功的关键。

(2) 如果(信息)是商务用途，要确保使用的语言和信息恰当，以便保护企业声誉和商业安全。避免使用俚语。

(3) 如果(信息)用于私人(交往)，牢记用微信发送的每条信息都代表着你自己。每条信息都在积累个人形象，因此每次按下“发送”键时你的声誉都存在风险。

(4) 发送给一个群体或者个人的信息要具有选择性。与电子邮件一样，如果像轰炸一样发送过多信息，接收者会有一种超负荷的感觉。

(5) 写完一条信息后，要从读者的视角去阅读，确保信息简洁明了且不会冒犯他人。

5.3 使用电子邮件进行沟通

5.3.1 指导原则

在世界范围内广泛使用的电子邮件将继续保持健康的发展。2015 年瑞迪卡提(Radicarti)公司对电子邮件和移动电子邮件使用的研究报告表明，2015 年电子邮件用户数量为 26 亿，预计 2019 年将达到 29 亿，将超过世界人口的三分之一。这意味着现在我们可以与办公室里以及分布在全国甚至世界各地的同事迅速取得联系并解决问题。电子邮件的使用也增加了员工和管理人员的压力，他们每天需要阅读大量的电子邮件，对邮件中提出的要求和问题做出回应要比过去更快速，一天中大部分时间都是在线状态。

使用电子邮件的好处很多，它快捷、相对便宜，无论身处何地都可以和别人互相取得联系，这在以前是很难做到的。电子邮件的易用性增强了我们的沟通能力，因为它为人们提供了与组织内部人员分享想法和意见的沟通渠道，而不仅仅是与直属上级经理进行沟通。例如，维珍集团(Virgin Group，集团业务范围包括航空、音乐商店和其他服务领域)首席执行官理查德 •布兰森(Richard Branson)自豪地宣称他每周会收到 70 封来自公司员工的电子邮件，并通过电子邮件对他们提出的建议和关注的问题进行回复。

然而，电子邮件的易用性在带来机遇的同时也提出了挑战。易用性会产生信息过量的问题，因为发件人能够利用计算机软件的复制、粘贴功能将大量未编辑的文本发送给多人，可以很容易地在列表中添加邮件地址，可能将不太正式的电子邮件与口头交谈混淆在一起。

此外，随着用手机访问电子邮件的用户增多，很多用户用手机不便阅读长段邮件。这些发展趋势给邮件的发件人和收件人带来麻烦。屏幕上大量的文本不便于读者浏览某些重要的信息，读者在阅读开篇几行之后就不会再阅读之后的关键观点了，更糟糕的是有的邮件甚至从未被打开。

下面的案例是一系列电子邮件，其撰写内容是关于大学团队和商务人士为某企业员工培训项目所做的计划和细节安排，具体如下。

第一封信

7 月 10 日

亲爱的陈先生：

我和安今天进行会面，最后确定 8 月份的辅导课程。一切准备就绪。

关于 9 月 13 日的事情，您和小组中的其他成员可以安排发言人并邀请他们吗？我确定卫先生今天已经准备好邀请函。如果 8 月 1 日前告诉我们发言人名单，我可以先大致了解一下。如果 8 月 1 日后告知我们，您可以做最后的名单决定。

如果您组织 9 月份的事情，我可以来安排 8 月 23 日的事情。我正等待员工俱乐部的最后确认。

马莉

第二封信

7 月 15 日

回复

马莉：

感谢您的辛勤工作。辅导课看起来进展顺利。下周的早些时间我会召集会议，安排 9 月份辅导课发言人之事，希望其中包括您和刘先生的名字。

再次感谢！

陈先生

8 月 2 日

几周后，马莉收到陈先生的另外一封电子邮件，信中就马莉还没有安排好 9 月 13 日的事宜表示了关注。马莉回复说，对于陈先生的反应她很惊讶。马莉于是又把她先前发出的邮件又重新发了一遍(第三封信)。

第三封信

8 月 10 日

陈先生：

我将 7 月上旬我们的往来邮件再次转发给你。今天我会安排发出邀请函。

致礼！

马莉

马莉很快收到了陈先生的回复(第四封信)。

第四封信

马莉：

很明显，我曾收到过这封邮件。我努力地从紧张的工作与生活之间寻找一种平衡，但是我还是没有仔细地阅读这封邮件。我很乐意承认这的确是我的错。

陈先生

学习实践

你能发现这里发生了什么吗？很显然，陈先生在 7 月份收到第一封电子邮件时很忙，除了看见第一句话中简单提到对第一个活动的安排之外，其他内容直接忽略了。他没有仔细阅读，以至于没有注意到马莉要求组织 9 月份会面的请求。

这就是电子邮件面临的沟通挑战。如此繁多的电子邮件扑面而来，我们通常并未优先注意到邮件中的细节或者给予其应有的重视。这就是说，我们必须思考对于一项具体任务，电子邮件是否是恰当的传递媒介，我们是否能够将信息的重要性和意图充分传递给收件人。

记住：我们记得 70%的所见所闻，但只能记得 10%的所读内容。

因此，电子邮件的撰写有以下的局限性。

- 邮件包括有限的非口头语言。
- 很难将关键内容突出。
- 邮件不能够像面对面沟通那样可以立即得到反馈和澄清。
- 由于读者工作超负荷或疏忽，有时不阅读邮件。
- 邮件沟通缺少像面对面沟通那样丰富的感官投入。我们只能看。
- 即使添加笑脸等表情符号也不能使电子邮件成为丰富的沟通来源。
- 由于技术障碍，邮件有时无法送达目标读者。

5.3.2 我什么时候不应该发邮件

有许多话题过于敏感，无法通过电子邮件进行讨论，因为如果产生误解将可能产生严重后果。一些不适合通过电子邮件解决的问题如下。

- 处分。
- 等级的矛盾或个人信息。
- 对同学/同事表现出的关心。
- 投诉(抱怨)。

电子邮件中一旦出现这些问题，对话就会变成冲突，建议立刻停止继续发送电子邮件，并与对方进行面对面的对话。

5.3.3 有效使用邮件进行商务沟通的原则

(1) 有意识地选择使用邮件。考虑电子邮件是否是传递特定内容的恰当媒介，也许电话或信函比电子邮件更有效。

(2) 用清晰、醒目的标题抓住读者注意力，使其有阅读邮件的意愿。

(3) 邮件目标明确。

(4) 邮件结构清晰。例如：为了便于一一回复，用数字或者字母将每一内容要点进行编号，运用标题以便快速浏览。同时，在每一内容要点后留出适当空间以便于读者阅读。

(5) 结尾段落列出希望读者能采取的行动。

(6) 以正式的文体行文，使之看上去有商务风格。一些私人化风格也可，但在许多国家，邮件被认为是官方的媒介，在法庭上受法律约束。同时，邮件也代表你所在公司的形象，能够反映你自己，也能够反映公司。所以请避免邮件中含有中伤的或有攻击性的内容。

(7) 谨慎使用表情符号。

(8) 写好邮件后，从读者的角度读一遍。

(9) 考虑所有可能通过抄送或转发收到邮件的人。

(10) 在发送邮件前，再检查一遍。

(11) 比较难写的内容在发送前滞留至少 24 小时。有时，写邮件可以减少对于某种情况的恼怒，但也许 24 小时后，自己希望缓和言辞。

5.4　平衡智能手机和面对面沟通的使用

移动电话的使用日益普遍，像电子邮件沟通一样，使客户和合作伙伴能方便地与我们进行沟通。利用手机进行专业商务沟通时，要注意避免使用私人通信中普遍被接受的缩写和俚语等非正式文体。因为通过智能手机发送的消息往往较短而且忽略细节，你还需要在合适的时间提供更详细明了的信息，确保客户和同事明确了解其内容。

尽管移动电话对我们十分有用，但有时候也会坏事儿。考虑使用移动电话的时机非常必要。例如，在谈话过程中移动电话铃声响起，需要仔细考虑目前的谈话和来电哪个更重要。除非确定电话更重要，否则当打断谈话去接听电话时，一定要考虑这样做会如何影响你与谈话对象之间的关系。

使用移动电话的原则

(1) 考虑沟通的最佳选择是面谈还是电话。

(2) 参加会议或出席演讲时，将移动电话关机或设置为静音。

(3) 不要在会议桌前接听电话。可以到安静的地方接听电话，但最好在会议或者演讲结束后再打。

(4) 在交谈过程中不要查看手机。全神贯注地与你的谈话对象进行交谈。

(5) 打电话时，先要确定对方此时能够或愿意接听。例如，问候之后确认："现在方便和您通话吗？"

(6) 结束电话交谈之前运用积极倾听策略，总结双方已经达成共识的内容。

5.5　实现有效演示

5.5.1　规则和指南

本章第一部分讨论了不能进行面对面沟通时可以使用的其他各种沟通方式。沟通技术的运用可达到有效且高效的沟通效果。然而，在任何时候都要牢记，如果观众要求我们面对面表达观点，选择技术为主的演示(如书面报告或者 PowerPoint 幻灯片)并不是观众所期望的。他们希望你和他们谈谈自己的想法或者建议。他们需要能够展现你个人特质的演示。这可能是因为他们需要了解你及你所在公司和公司员工的特点，或者他们想要提问和阐释观点的机会。不论怎样，这种类型演示的最重要的部分是你，而不是技术。

5.5.2　技术的不当使用

演示者不能让这些潜在的有用的工具及我们可获得的相关技术成为我们努力实现良好沟通的障碍，技术的魅力也不能成为沟通的动力。毫无疑问，技术将支持甚至可能影响或塑造沟通的某些方面，但是要知道，新技术是我们的仆人，而不是主人，这个意识决定我们如何使用新技术。

在准备演讲时，最难决定的是面对众多令人兴奋的技术工具该如何选择。一种选择是运用所有技术，其结果是提供一堆想法和可能性，但是重点不突出可能会让观众漏掉信息。例如，作者曾观看一个演示，演示过程中演讲者一边和观众交谈一边播放视频片段。作为观众，我们当然不知道是应该听他讲还是应该看视频。我的反应是大部分时间听演讲者讲，但是突然间看见屏幕上有趣的东西就开始看视频，从而漏掉演讲者的讲话重点。这对于演讲者来说就错过了一次机会。

尽管如此，我们并不认为技术型演示是无用的。在很多场合，这种类型的演示是很好的选择。我们需要做的是先决定演示的目的和目标，之后依个人演讲风格运用相应的技术完成演示并达到预期目的。

5.5.3　技术的有效使用

一般来说，个人的诚信是有效演示的关键因素之一。演示中可以融入个性特点，因为技术所展现的观念没有个性，可能给观众带来不自在的感觉，将观众与演讲者及其观点隔离开来。相反，演示过程是要把一个“活生生”的个体而不是“冷冰冰”的技术展现给观众，这需要有周密细致的计划。

一个非常有趣的关于选择有效沟通技术的例子是关于 Foxtel 和 Sky 电视台的媒体大亨鲁伯特·默多克(Rupert　Murdoch)的故事。鲁伯特·默多克是世界上规模最大的传媒帝国之一——新闻集团的总裁及首席执行官，他为新闻集团发布了五年发展规划，他的演讲在伦敦现场直播，并通过卫星在纽约、洛杉矶、悉尼实时转播。

默多克广泛运用了新的沟通技术。虽然他可以利用不计其数的媒体机构的专业技能和资源，但他清楚地知道公司的信誉更加依赖于他自己而不是公司本身。针对这种情况，他的演讲内容充满了想象力，经过周密准备，演讲时还有巨大的影视屏作为背景(事实上，在悉尼，他的个人形象在两个全屏屏幕上转播)。

演讲概述了公司下一个五年计划。演讲是在复杂的、极具舞台视听效果的演示中开始的，演示描述了令人激动的未来前景。

默多克将与科幻作家克拉克(C.Clarke)的访谈作为演讲内容的一部分。默多克希望这样能证明自己是开拓者和有远见的思想者，就像科幻作家克拉克在想象新技术方面领先于他所在的时代一样。

(资料来源：McCarthy P, Hatcher C. *Speaking Persuasively: The Essential Guide to Giving Dynamic Presentations and Speeches*[M]. Sydney: Allen & Unwin, 2002.)

有效运用沟通技术不仅可以增强演示的影响力，而且有助于保持演示对观众的吸引力。美国沃顿商学院的研究表明，你所使用的辅助技术可以直接影响观众对你的看法，如果慎重地运用辅助性技术，观众会觉得你比那些没有运用辅助技术的人更加专业。这项研究表明，在演讲中运用可视技术是非常有价值的。沃顿商学院的研究表明，人们能记住：

- 所读内容的 10%。
- 所听内容的 20%。
- 所见内容的 30%。
- 所见所闻内容的 70%。

根据这项研究，下面一些建议有助于达到最好的效果。如运用 PPT 或市场上其他软件制作的演示片，可以从网上下载的或自己创作的图像，由他人或自己创作的视频录像及音乐录音，这些技术的运用都可以增加演示的趣味性。

5.5.4　何时使用可视化支持

有些特定的时候需要运用可视性技术阐明你的观点，也有些时候，可视性技术会分散观众的注意力。

以下建议可帮你决定是否需要使用可视化支持。

(1) 如果将口头表达和视觉表现与文字相配合，繁杂的内容将容易被理解并记住。

人脑不像计算机那样可以容纳许多细节，当你的语言着重强调要表达的重要内容时，图表、清单、表格可以帮助观众将一些重要内容形象化。但是仅仅展示图表或影像是不够的，你还需要将观众的注意力引向图表或影像所要表达的重要内容。

(2) 所有出色的演示都有一个反映主要信息的主题或形象，要为这一主题或形象创造可视性的展示方式。例如，演示的主题为“与顾客合作”，演示过程中可把主题名称与公司的标志同时放在每一页幻灯片的页脚上。或者在每一页幻灯片上注明完成业务活动的特定“团队”的名称，这个图片可以是一只向外伸出的手或小组开会时的情景。

有时用文字描述一些观点是十分困难的，而图像可以迅速引起人们的关注，另外，重复是强调某一观点的微妙而有力的手段。

(3) 照片、录像、录音带有助于将外部世界直观地带入观众的视野中。来源于真实世界的照片、录像和录音带可以帮助观众形象化地理解问题、复杂性和挑战。观众喜欢简短的、影响力强的录像及清晰的图片。这些资源网上有很多，使用这些资源时要标注其来源。

当观众放松或和你一起开怀大笑时，你们之间的关系就增进了一步。幽默会增加亲和力(或增强对观众的影响力)。例如，可以找些插图或是卡通图片吸引观众的注意力，以幽默的方式演示难以理解的内容。

5.5.5 平板演示软件

计算机技术发展的一个最显著的特色就是一系列软件的引入，这些软件使演示的视觉效果更加职业化。

例如，人们经常使用微软 PowerPoint 软件包，利用这个软件包将文本、彩图、相应的图表和剪贴画结合在统一的主题中。然而，在不断发展的沟通技术市场上也有许多其他的软件包。例如，新的无人机技术及其创新软件增加了新颖并令人兴奋的方法，它通过集合人的图像与位置将国内外社区联系在一起。

使用这类软件的灵活性很大，为特定观众制作大量幻灯片后，可以改变幻灯片的内容和顺序来满足其他观众的不同需求。例如，面对一群技术人员的演示需要增加大量的表格和图像，因为如果没有调查结果，他们不会满意，而向专业技术不强的人员演示时，则只需要提供结论性总结。可以删除表格、用其他方法代替表格甚至改变背景来满足观众需求，而不需要重做幻灯片。

像 PowerPoint 这样的视觉支持软件能够通过将辅助性材料和演示结合起来帮助演讲者进一步扩展共享信息。例如，演示时可以链接到网站，访问特定的网站来展示其服务和产品如何运作，然后返回主页，这样就达到无缝衔接的专业化演示。

有了 PowerPoint 这类软件的帮助，可以创建定时放映的幻灯片来配合口头表达，或者在演示产品时设置连续放映的幻灯片。但是，我们建议避免使用这一功能，除非你能确信时间设置得恰到好处。如果设置的时间出错，常常会使演讲者看上去有点儿傻，观众也会因文本与演讲内容不一致而感到困惑。

演示时，必须将注意力集中在与观众的信息沟通上，并将其作为演示动力。使用这些软件的自动设定模板时容易出错，在 PowerPoint 中容易出错的是“自动套用格式”。它试图代替你思考，通过提供一系列演示提纲，帮助构建演示结构，使你开始演讲。

我们建议尽量避免使用这类软件包模板功能，重点要关注演示的特定环境、观众及演示目的，并形成自己的演示提纲。用他人的方法来解决自己的问题会限制自己的创造力，也有可能忽视观众的特殊性。让技术左右演示如同上了公交车后期待司机告知你在哪里下车一样会使你处于被动状态。

使用这种软件进行演示时会带来使观众“麻痹”的危险。如果幻灯片或者文本太多，观众就会打瞌睡，应该避免太过有规律地放映幻灯片及过量信息。如果每张幻灯片讲两分钟并且没有任何幻灯片与观众进行情感联系，观众将失去注意力。

相反，如果通过图像、文本、声音等不同方法创造性地分享观点，会始终让观众保持兴趣。结合互动环节(发放讲义或问答)来改变演示节奏并增加演示多样性。如果帮助观众更好地理解你的想法并激发他们的热情，就能产生让观众更深刻地记住演讲内容的效果。

5.5.6 音乐、视觉工具和背景音

音乐可以增加演示的魅力，使观众回想起一些曾经流行或熟悉的感觉。通过添加背景音和音乐配合演示者的声音使演讲内容增添不少生色。演示开场或结束时，音乐更能吸引观众注意力，使观众对你的观点给予关注。例如，产品演示时使用柔和的背景音乐可以唤

醒那些昏昏欲睡的观众。

切记让视听辅助工具简短且与主题相关。若观众发现所展示的内容不是他们需要看的或想听的，他们很快就会失去兴趣。观众不喜欢浪费时间。

5.5.7 对于使用视听辅助工具的提示

对于使用视听辅助工具的提示如下。

(1) 有选择地使用，使它们尽量简短。

(2) 辅助材料尽可能简单明了。

(3) 务必对所演示的幻灯片或图像进行讨论。不要仅仅通过展示它们，就希望观众能理解相关细节。

(4) 选择有效力的演示方法，而不是那些花费精力、分散注意力的复杂的视觉演示方法。

(5) 确保视频简短并与主题相关。两到三分钟突出重点的视频比长视频更有效。

(6) 能够设置情境或者解释主要观点的视频效果才明显。

(7) 熟悉会场的设备，以便有效使用它们。

(8) 事先演练 PPT 幻灯片。演练要全面，避免出现意外的情况，如网站链接有问题。

(9) 在正式演示前要检查链接，确保链接可用。

(10) 准备一套应急方案以防技术故障。一旦技术出现故障要控制好场面和自己的情绪。切记：演讲的驱动力是演讲内容而不是辅助技术，吸引观众的是演讲内容而不是幻灯片或视频。因此要很好地了解演讲内容。

以下是使用有效文本、视频、图表进行演示的指导性原则。

(1) 确保视觉辅助工具真正有视觉效果，大量的文字会分散观众的注意力。文本最多仅有三到四个观点，用短句或短语表达。

(2) 字体和格式保持整体统一。

(3) 一张图片胜过千言万语。用图表和图像保持观众对主要观点的注意力，使主要观点通俗易懂。图表和图像尽量简单易懂、引人注目。

(4) 保持颜色的协调。为每一演讲设计主题颜色、模式，如果设计简图，仅需要用三种颜色：背景色、标题和要点色以及文本色。对于图表，最多使用五种颜色，太多的颜色会分散注意力，使人眼花缭乱。在浅色背景上使用深色；反之，亦然。

(5) 使用软件功能让图表信息生动起来，逐步显示用数据构建图表的过程。这样，陈述的过程有助于将观众的精力集中在关键内容上。

周密、创新、有效地运用沟通技术可丰富演讲的内容，增强内容的影响力。以上技巧是关于如何在技术创新时代使演示脱颖而出的重要提示。

学习实践

选择有信心的主题准备演讲。做好观众分析(见第 3 章)，同时为特定观众做演示计划。完成这个计划之后，选择其他的观众，例如，更资深或者不同专业的群体，进行演示准备。重复观众分析，调整演讲以满足第二批观众的不同需求。比较两次演讲，你是否满足了每位观众的需求？

阅读以下案例，学习一个团队是如何运用沟通技术进行有效演讲的。

交通规划组正在准备一个关于桥梁发展项目的会议演示。这个项目是关于在陈旧的桥梁边并排建立一座新的桥梁。他们已经提出了创新的解决方案，既有利于交通，又可以满足当地社区希望维持旧桥梁周围钓鱼和娱乐场所的愿望。小组希望通过演示向其他工程师和策划者介绍这一创新方案。

在20分钟的演示中，他们运用了23张文本幻灯片和3张照片。

运用以上所列举的指导原则，我们帮助他们改进支持性技术的运用，通过提出以下问题，我们帮助他们做出更明智的选择。

(1) 你真正想说的是什么，即你的关键内容是什么？

(2) 需要观众了解到什么程度？

(3) 如何向来自全国各地的观众说明项目的情况如何，存在的问题是什么。

(4) 如何向他们说明解决方案是可行的。

小组人员通过回答上述问题形成了演示的整体框架，并逐渐明确了演示目标。他们需要说明这个地方具有的历史意义，应当保持，而交通问题又亟待解决，社区的利益需要满足，同时应该把成本控制在合理范围之内。

他们提出了两个主题："在社区利益与交通问题上寻求平衡"和"管理成本"。围绕这两个主题，他们寻找了许多方法说明这一地区的历史价值、交通的繁杂情况及解决方案的技术问题。他们从当地报纸上找到了1935年发表的关于旧桥梁的报道和照片，运用图像展示旧桥梁及目前桥梁交通情况的状况。这些图像成为此次演讲的动力。

该小组在他们原先准备的23张文本幻灯片中，挑选了支持其关键论点的幻灯片，然后按照每张幻灯片上的内容要点和内容数量的要求来减少每张幻灯片上的内容，在图像上加注一些要点，以增强其影响力。

最后的战略就是在开场和结尾使用设计成功的照片，给观众一个整体的印象。

结果是他们总共使用了19张幻灯片，其中10张照片用来帮助阐述观点、加强论证，而不仅仅是在屏幕上堆砌一系列要点。会议上的演示很成功，许多观众表示很欣赏他们的演示。

本章小结

每位商务人士都可以运用各种沟通技术进行沟通，但挑战是如何最佳地而不是不加选择地利用。沟通技术能够确保良好的沟通效果。然而，只有人们恰当地运用沟通技术，它才会充分发挥作用。沟通技术不能取代有效的沟通计划。不能保证某一种沟通技术会有所帮助。作为战略型沟通者，你要确保自己清楚想要说什么，根据场景选择恰当的技术，而技术用来帮助你以最有效的方式沟通。技术是"仆人"，而不是"主人"。

第三部分

书面商务沟通

第 6 章

管理沟通写作原则

【学习目标】

通过对本章内容的学习，你能够：

- 了解商务活动中写作的重要性。
- 了解一些写作的指导性原则。
- 懂得如何使写作的内容通俗易懂。

引例：当话语产生了伤害

2006 年夏天，中西部的一所大型州立大学正在筹备举办第一届全国特别奥运会，这是一场以智障人士为特色的竞赛。来自全国各地的游客都会来到这里，这个大学小镇计划将城市最好的一面展示给世人。学生报社制作了一份 14 页的全彩旅游指南，并将其作为校园报的插页。不幸的是，他们以畅销书的形式命名其为“为傻瓜准备的某城市(城市名)指南”。(其意是指旅游指南通俗易懂，就是傻瓜也轻易地掌握)。

主编很快就为选择了不敏感的词道歉，同时删除校报的插页，用重新印的新标题内容取代他们。

(改编自：丽莎 · 罗西(Lisa Rossi)，“奥林匹克颁发文件”，得梅因纪事报，2006 年 7 月 1 日，1A,4A)

引例启示：良好的商务与管理写作风格既要与谈话相仿，又不能像那些常常得高分的大学作文和学期论文那样。本章我们将学习如何使写作达到清楚、有效的效果。

沃伦 · 巴菲特(Warren Buffett)以约 420 亿美元的净资产成为《福布斯》全球富豪榜排名第二的富豪，位列微软创始人兼董事长比尔 · 盖茨之后。巴菲特 11 岁时开始投资股票，但在股票暴涨之前全部抛售。这个教训教会他努力学习并仔细分析潜在的投资。结果，伯克希尔 · 哈撒韦(有限)公司发展为世界上最大的控股公司之一。

尽管巴菲特以其选股能力极负盛名，但他在 2006 年因撰写伯克希尔 · 哈撒韦(有限)公司的年度报告，被美国家庭、学校写作的国家写作委员会授予荣誉。巴菲特写道：“不论通过什么途径，你必须把自己的想法投射到他人身上。写作并不容易……但是你会越来越擅长(写作)，我鼓励每个人都写作。”

6.1 口头沟通与书面沟通的不同

演讲与写信或写报告在很多方面有着类似之处。所有的章节关注这一点：当准备演讲时，要有“关注他人”的态度并有实质性重点内容，使读者受益、分析听众、设计幻灯片、避免异议、做好研究、分析数据，以上这些都要与演讲有关联。

发展有效的书面沟通能够使你做以下事情。

- 说明广泛的或复杂的财务或统计数据。
- 说明法律、政策或过程的具体细节。
- 通过澄清事实，将不必要的情绪降至最低。
- 针对手边的问题形成一个永久性的记录。

发展有效的口头沟通能够使你做以下事情。

- 阐明关键主题和内容。
- 利用情感说服听众。
- 使听众关注具体的要点。
- 回答听众的问题，解决分歧，达成一致。
- 修改最初不被接受的提议。

- 得到听众及时的行动和反应。
- 迅速根据听众的需求调整你的信息内容。

口头沟通和书面沟通有许多共同之处。无论采用哪种沟通方式，应该注意以下几项。

- 概述清楚的目标。
- 信息内容必须适合特定的听众。
- 向听众展示他们将如何受益于观点、政策、服务或产品。
- 克服听众可能产生的异议。
- 使用关注他人的态度并有实质性重点内容。
- 用视觉工具说明或强调一些实事。
- 准确指明你希望听众如何思考或如何做。

针对相同听众，口头沟通需要比书面沟通更简单。如果读者忘记某个观点，他们可以重新翻回前面的内容，把相关段落再阅读一遍。在书面写作中，标题、段落的提示和标点符号都可以提供形象的线索帮助读者理解章节内容，允许读者重新回到他们已经忘记或不懂的内容。相反，听众必须记住演讲者所说的内容，他们不记得的内容就遗失了，甚至提问时也要求听众记住那些他们不懂的内容。

6.2　熟练写作的重要性

本书特别强调写作的原因有三点：①当被问及考察求职者什么能力时，经验丰富的商务人士倾向于把写作技巧放在其他沟通技巧之前；②当考虑给谁升职时，他们倾向于写作能力强的人；③用非母语写作面临很大的挑战。因此，对于你来说，作为一个以英语为第二语言的学习者，写作不仅包括语言，也包括用合适的风格和基调使商业文化跨越民族文化这道鸿沟。例如，在对 305 位高管进行的调查中，多数受访者评论指出，不到半数求职者对能够让他们在公司中有所发展的“全球知识、自我导向和写作技能”有足够造诣。随着雇员职位的提升，他们会从事越来越多的知识性工作，这些工作往往要求书面形式的沟通。

我们强烈关注写作的另一个原因是，相比其他种类的沟通，写作更难做好。写作是研究者所谓的“学习媒介”，这意味着它不能提供充足的信息提示、反馈以及面对面沟通或者电话交谈表现的强烈的个人关注点。作者基本没有安全网，他们不能依赖面部表情、身体语言或者声调去弥补他们表达不够清楚的部分。写作中用到的字母、单词、标点等符号与它们表现的东西没有太多关联(除非你认为单词和其命名的声音发音很像，如“嗡嗡声”一样)。用一个个单词描述复杂的现实需要智慧、训练以及预测读者在阅读时的反应能力。

学习实践

回顾本书第 1 章的内容，查阅开头几个段落所描述的雇主看重的技巧和能力。现在，考虑你目前拥有的技能。

用一句话描述你的写作技能。回顾自己最近的一些写作及写作测试结果，列出有待提升的技能。

确定你想改进的写作方面。当阅读本书第 6 章剩余部分、第 7 章和第 8 章的内容时，对需要提高的方面重点关注并练习相关技能。

6.3 劣质写作的代价

来自火星的商务沟通教训

火星气象卫星刚到达火星时就与美国宇航局航天地面指挥中心失去联系。

随后的调查显示，主要问题是由沟通失误导致的软件编程小错误。像许多商业项目一样，火星气象卫星项目涉及范围广、人员多。控制卫星引擎的软件开发人员在英国使用公制测量计算；然而，制造卫星引擎的工程师在美国运用英国测量标准。两个团队都认为他们使用相同的测量标准，也没有尝试核查，别人也没发现这个错误。这个失误使美国宇航局损失了花费一亿两千五百万美元的卫星，白白浪费了一年的努力，同时在公众面前失了脸面。

(资料来源：Source: NASA MCO Mission Failure Mishap Investigation Board. Mars Climate Orbiter Mishap Investigation Board phase report[C], 1999, 11-10.)

学习实践

这个案例告诉你写作面临哪些挑战？

发展出色的写作技巧能够为你增添受雇用能力和吸引力，让你成为成功的商业人士。2004 年，美国国家写作委员会的一项调查发现，写作能力正在成为成功的职业生涯的一个重要要求。在美国大型公司里，有 2/3 受薪员工将写作视为工作的一部分。事实上，80%以上的企业把评估申请人的写作技能纳入招聘的过程，当决定是否提拔员工时，几乎一半企业会考虑写作技巧的因素。

2004 年的一项研究表明，多达 70%的专业员工在工作中需要撰写报告、备忘录和其他信函。遗憾的是，这项研究还表明，很多公司花费 300 万～400 万美元培训员工，提高他们的写作能力。很显然，公司重视写作技巧，因为这对公司发展很重要。

当写作不尽如人意时，你和你的组织会为此付出浪费时间、精力和失去信誉的代价。

6.3.1 浪费时间

首先，要理解劣质的写作所表达的意思需要花费更多的时间阅读。研究表明，人们 97%以上的阅读时间不是花在阅读上，而是花在理解正在阅读的文章上。

其次，劣质的写作要重新撰写。不少管理者发现他们要花很多时间向员工解释如何重写文件。

再次，无效的写作所表达的意思模糊，这样，讨论和决定的时间被没必要地延长。一个组织内的人会有不同的利益和价值取向，但是如果一个方案表达得清楚，至少每个成员都在谈论同一个方案，那么彼此间的差异会很快被发现并被解决。

最后，不清楚和不完全的信息要求读者寻求更多的信息。读者如果有不清楚之处，需要进行拜访或打电话，但这时撰写人不在办公室，那么读者会为此浪费更多的时间，因为读者只有得到回复才可以行动。

6.3.2 浪费精力

无效的信息很少有结果。需要猜测写作人意图的读者，有可能会猜错。读者如果发现信或备忘录无法令人信服或有无礼之处，那么他根本不会按照信上的要求去做。

6.3.3 失去信誉

无论文字本身包含的意思如何，每封信件、备忘录或报告都能使读者建立或破坏对撰写人的印象。

花时间进行正确的写作是建立良好印象的一部分。甚至有些组织接受员工穿着休闲但仍然希望他们的写作显得专业化，没有排印和语法错误。

6.4 规划你的写作

即使有经验的商务沟通者有时也会陷入“灵感”的误区，即相信撰写商务文件的绝好创意直到开始动笔前的最后一刻会光临那些等待、再等待的人。

希望写作令人满意的管理者也必须关注撰写计划，并将其作为写作的第一步。如果没有计划，会导致“书写阻滞”的现象，即文字不“流畅”，让人感到痛苦难忍，这是因为写作中缺少计划。另外，缺少仔细的写作规划会导致混乱且不合逻辑的文本出现。

为了避免这种问题的出现，在开始写作以前，制订一个写作计划是必要的一步。这个计划最好是以记录的形式，但至少是在大脑中考虑过。在计划中，应考虑与写作的六个关键方面相关的六个问题。

- 目的——你希望沟通的是什么？
- 读者——你写给谁？
- 探讨——你将要传递的观点是什么？
- 大纲——如何很好地组织你的观点？
- 细节及实例——如何支撑你的观点？
- 行动步骤——希望读者下一步做什么？

6.4.1 目的——你希望沟通的是什么

为了明白沟通的目的，必须回答下列问题。

- 你沟通的观点是什么？
- 其他人对你完成沟通有什么期待？
- 沟通后希望读者能知道什么？
- 沟通后希望读者的感觉是什么？

- 沟通后希望读者做什么？
- 除听众之外还有什么人会受到沟通的影响？
- 这次沟通的目的不止一个吗？详细说明你希望达到的各种目标。

沟通有不同的目的。你可能是想告知、劝说或描述你的观点。但是，重要的是当向读者进行描述时，一些观点的选择和字词种类的选择都包含说服性的因素。

告知指的是向听众解释某件事情，或者是教他们某些新的东西。这样的写作包括很多活动，例如，对困扰全球计算机用户的千年虫问题作解释，你们部门正在采用的一种新的在线程序，对下一年度的财政预算进行汇报，对两家公司合并的提案，中国企业发展与国际公司合作的机会，有关计划项目进展情况的谈话等。

劝说是指一个或更多的人在一次性的或连续性的互动活动中，去创造、修改、加强甚至改变人们的信念、态度、目的、动机或行为。需要运用说服性技巧的书面沟通形式包括邀请函、信件、报告和电子邮件。

与上述的告知型写作不同，劝说型写作的目的是试图改变读者的信仰、态度或行为举止，或者是促使他们采取某种行动。然而，由于一个人的信仰、态度或行为并非在一夜之间产生，不管你的论点如何令人信服，不可能指望变化会在突然发生。写作者应该考虑的是如何尽可能地让写作更有说服力，以便对读者具有最强大的吸引力。

当信息技术几乎在我们所做、所想的事情上引起了革命之时，它也在企业内引起了动荡。一个企业的智力资本，现在已经成为该企业财富创造的卓越源泉。新的人力管理的挑战来自于对知识型工作的需求。例如，为了更好地利用企业的人力资本，经理必须学会鼓励学习和掌握新的知识。为使结构性的资本(如网络和数据库)，发挥最大效用，企业必须打破传统的组织结构上的界限，让知识和人员流动起来，而且要鼓励所有员工分享彼此的知识。

——弗朗西斯·霍瑞比

学习实践

仔细阅读上述案例。注意这位作者的论点是多么有力。特别注意以下几点。

(1) 有力的词语和短语。

革命；动荡；卓越源泉；知识的自由流动。

(2) 有影响力的长句和短句。

(3) 以读者所要完成的事宜结尾。

鼓励所有的员工分享彼此的知识。

6.4.2 读者——你写给谁

同一信息的读者通常是同质的：他们有着相似的需求和态度。通常读者只是单个人。即使不是单个人，读者也大都是具备相似专业水平及背景知识的人。因此，你能够而且也应该考虑根据读者的需求来发展你的信息。

分析读者的方法之一是“市场分析”，对读者的分析要和对市场的分析一样。分析好了市场，接下来就可以设计你的“产品”。也就是说，要准备为读者量身定制适合他们的信息，就像生产商在决定如何包装产品前必须设计好产品，你也必须在设计信息包装前设计好将要传递的信息。图 6.1 列举了做读者分析时应考虑的问题，以便对读者有清晰的分析。

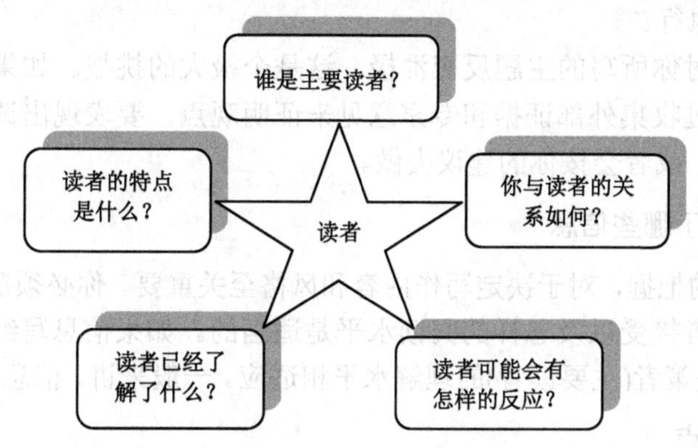

图 6.1　读者分析的问题

(资料来源：Ober S, Newman A. 商务沟通[M]. 7 版. 北京：清华大学出版社，2013.)

1. 谁是你主要的读者

大多数信函的读者只有一个人，极大地简化了写作的挑战。编写专门发送给一个人的信息要比发送给多人的信息容易得多。然而，有时你会拥有不止一位读者。这时，你首先需要明确主要读者(实现你的写作目的的关键人物)和次要读者(那些会读到信息并被其影响的人)。如果你的写作难以满足所有人的需求，那就尽力满足主要决策者的需求。通过询问以下问题对读者进行分析。

- 谁会受到你的(信息)影响？
- 哪些组织、专业、个人的问题或特点会影响读者的反应？

尽管在计划阶段一开始就应该花费时间进行读者分析，但是在整个计划阶段、起草和修改阶段也应该继续对读者进行分析。要不停地思考什么信息对读者来说最重要，并对信息做出相应调整。如果不能满足读者需求，不仅造成信息沟通失败，也会使专业形象受损。

2. 你与读者的关系如何

读者认识你吗？如果读者不认识你，你首先需要通过使用合理的语言表达和足够的证据支撑你的观点，以此来建立个人可信度。信息是写给组织内部人员还是外部人员？写给外部人员的信息通常需要比写给内部人员的更正式，包含更多的背景信息和更少的专业术语。你在组织中的地位与读者有怎样的关系？和上司的沟通对于个人在组织中的成功至关重要。这种沟通通常比与同级或者下属的沟通更正式，表达更民主并传递更多信息。当你和下属沟通时需要有礼貌而不高人一等。努力在提议中树立合作意识和企业所有权。表达赞美或批评时要具体，批评是针对行为，而不是个人。通常在公众场合进行表扬，在私下里进行批评。

3. 读者可能如何反应

如果读者对于你和所写主题的最初反应是积极的，工作就相对容易开展。可以使用直接的表达方式，以最重要的信息开篇，紧接着再提供所需细节。如果读者的最初反应是中立的，用开篇信息获得读者关注，并让他(她)相信你所提供的信息很重要且有道理。确保信息简短、易懂且易于执行。

然而，假设读者对你所写的主题反应消极，这是个极大的挑战。如果读者个人对你表现出不喜欢，最好通过收集外部证据和专家意见来证明观点。要表现出读者可能知道并尊重的人同意你的观点，或者会按你的建议去做。

4. 读者已经掌握了哪些信息

理解读者对主题的把握，对于决定写作内容和风格至关重要。你必须决定需要多少背景信息，术语可否被读者接受以及怎样的阅读水平是适当的。如果信息写给多位读者，多数细节(描写)要与关键决策者(主要读者)的理解水平相适应。一般来讲，信息提供得越多越好。

5. 读者有哪些特点

信息成功或失败经常取决于一些细节，比如对读者说：“你是重要的，我已专门花费时间去了解你”这些带给读者额外的触动。在你提供的信息中哪些涉及读者个人兴趣或者背景特征？读者是无论消息好坏，都喜欢在开端了解重要信息的“冒险主义者”吗？他们对正式性有怎样的期待？信函中直接称呼读者的名字会让读者开心还是反感？最近在工作或家庭中发生的那些好事或坏事可能影响读者对信息的接受程度吗？

读者的文化水平是与读者最相关的因素。不幸的是，即使在发达国家，也必须要问读者的阅读和信息应用能力如何。在美国，答案可能是“不太好”。

美国国家成人文化水平鉴定委员会(NAAL)调查发现，14%的成年人在阅读简单的操作指南时存在困难(比如用药的时候)。12%的人用简单的表格(决定在表格的何处签名)较吃力，22%的人处理数字有困难。此外，NAAL发现5%的成年人是文盲，他们的语言能力达不到评估要求。

总的来说，美国有3000万成年人的阅读和理解水平“低于基准线”，6300万成年人也仅仅达到“基础”文化水平。这给商务写作的人带来挑战。为广大员工或客户提供信息时，你可能不得不使用简短的语句对图形做出阐述。还可以使用其他哪些技巧来保证低文化水平的读者能够理解并会运用这些信息呢？

(资料来源：Kutner M, Greenberg E, Baer J. A first look at the literacy of America’s adults in the 21st century[J]. *National Center for Education Statistics*: 2006, 28.)

6. 探究：为听众提供什么观点

一旦明确信息传递的目的，并且对听众进行了分析，接着便可以为听众设计信息。也就是说，你应该清楚将什么样的信息传递给听众。在许多情况下，这项研究可以是非正式的。例如，寻找过去的信件、咨询其他员工或组织外部顾问；获得销售记录、保单、网站和产品说明等。这种个人调查通常需要专业知识，这可能就是上司指派你处理这个问题的

原因。在其他情况下，你可以做更多正式研究，如进行调查或者实验。实验是科学研究的基本技巧。尽管实验在市场实践中有一些非实验性的应用，但是企业主要还是在实验室使用实验。调查更可能运用于商业，尤其是解决市场问题。在商务中解决营销问题时，更倾向于使用调查研究方法。

在某些情况下，可以使用图书馆或者上网查找所需信息。可能你已经较好地掌握了一些研究的方法。从公开报道中收集所需信息仍然需要其他技巧：比如构建参考书目、引用参考文献、引述、改写等。在任何情况下，你的任务就是熟练地使用各种研究技术收集所需的信息。

写作过程的下一个主要阶段就是对所收集的信息进行解释。理解情境因素，解决写作中面临的问题。还必须解释之前收集的数据，确保能够从中获得适当和足够的信息。研究的结果是形成写作框架和内容的依据。结论应是合乎常理的解决方案，能清晰地应用于解决既定问题。要让读者认为你的想法与他们相关并有益，还应该迎合他们的需要。

7. 提纲：如何更好地安排观点

几乎所有职业商务人士在写作的开始都运用大纲。商务写作的提纲是一个粗略的工作框架，使写作的人能够使其观点具有逻辑顺序。好的大纲会显示哪些要点进行了组合，是怎样的顺序(排序)，以及是怎样的层次结构。

1) 为什么要有大纲

有了提纲，开始撰写时就会很清楚，因为最初的提纲完全能够将主要观点及次要观点按照逻辑顺序规划好。正如建设者要参照设计蓝图一样，撰写人需要参照清楚的提纲有效地完成写作。当提纲中的观点被发展成完整的或部分语句时，艰难的草稿拟写工作已经结束。提纲中主要短语会发展成第一稿中的标题和主题句。通过补充详细内容、例子、定义和说明，你很快可以完成结构性强、具有连续性的第一稿。

2) 大纲的形成

主题一旦选好，接着是根据主题撰写提纲。制定大纲确实要花费很多时间，但是当提笔按照提纲写作时就会发现，前面的努力没有白费。

提纲往往始于一些粗糙的想法，即那些与主题相关，但还没有经过认真思考或检查的内容。然而，这些粗糙的想法是十分重要的，因为它是优秀写作的良好开端。

在构建提纲时，你可以使用任何有助于了解计划内容的逻辑结构的编号格式系统。例如，可以使用常规或者十进制符号系统标记等级。传统系统使用罗马数字显示主标题，用字母和阿拉伯数字显示小标题，如下所示。

传统系统

Ⅰ.一级标题

A.二级(标题)，第一部分

B.二级(标题)，第二部分

1.三级(标题)，第一部分

2.三级(标题)，第二部分

a.四级(标题)，第一部分

(1)五级(标题)，第一部分

十进制系统

1 一级标题

1.1 二级(标题)，第一部分

1.2 二级(标题)，第二部分

1.2.1 三级(标题)，第一部分

1.2.2.三级(标题)，第二部分

1.2.2.1 四级(标题)，第一部分

1.2.2.1.1 五级(标题)，第一部分

即使提纲是基于读者需求而写，也要记住它是你的写作工具。尽可能使用提纲来帮助你写出质量好的报告或信件。

假设你准备做一篇告知型讲话，例如，要谈论电子商务。你已经有了一些想法，如互联网的发展史、互联网上的交易、电子商务及其安全性、网上商务等。你会很快将这些想法记下来，因为你担心会忘了它们。这些想法就是我们所说的“初始想法”。

这些匆匆记下的想法都是好的想法，但它们还不足以形成一个出色的写作所需要的大纲。撰写人现在所要做的是，在两三点初始想法的基础上形成新的想法，然后将这些想法组织起来。事实上，这一过程就像滚雪球。刚开始时，手中只有一把雪，当雪球不断向前滚动时，它越滚越大。

下面是根据假定的有关电子商务的标题所写的扩充式提纲。

1 介绍：互联网与电子商务的发展

2 电子商务的优点

2.1 方便——24 小时服务

2.2 更多的比较不同商店和价格的机会

2.3 更多的产品可供选择

2.4 买卖双方均得益

3 消费者主要关心的地方

3.1 安全

3.2 隐私

3.3 可靠性

3.4 及时性

4 卖方主要关心的地方

4.1 信用及诈骗

4.2 无规可循

4.3 网络销售的成本

5 未来的发展

5.1 所涉各方的共同努力

5.2 制定适当的规则

5.3 更多的有关电子商务的教育

(资料来源：徐宪光，2003. 商务沟通[M]. 北京：外语教学与研究出版社.)

学习实践

选择一个你感兴趣的主题，并拟写该主题的大纲。思考一下大纲是否足够用来写出一篇好文。

8. 细节及实例——如何论证你的观点

需要通过详细资料、实例和故事清楚地说明和支持你的观点。一般来说，详细资料和实例有三种作用。

- 提供信息。
- 验证观点。
- 解释抽象概念。

除非信息包含足够多的经过作者精心挑选的支撑主题和写作目的的事实或数据；否则，它不会具有说服力。但是，事实和数据要求作者要认真挑选。例如，如果你准备提出索赔，应该提供足够的证据，以使收信人知道你的索赔是合理和公正的。回顾第 3 章中的内容，考虑一下什么会使辩论更具有说服力。让我们看看下面的例子。

亲爱的嘉顿先生：

感谢您在 9 月 7 日对 927.96 美元的账目进行核查，我们已经核对了这个账目，余额是 48.84 美元。

你们提到的销售条款是 ROG76。因为你们在 8 月 12 日收到货物，即日起 10 日内你们如果能够付清货款，可以得到 5%的折扣。遗憾的是，这个要求你们没有达到。

嘉顿先生，虽然我愿意对这种情况做特殊处理，但我认为你能够明白这种行为是在处罚那些不具备同样特权的人。

你可能会对随函附上的最新版的产品介绍感兴趣。这些产品将刊登在十月份出版的《塑料工程》杂志上。

您忠实的：×××

（资料来源：Locker K O. *Business and Administrative Communication*[M]. 6th ed. 北京：机械工业出版社，2005.）

这封给嘉顿先生的信是关于嘉顿先生没有满足买卖交易中的一些要求，通知他不能享受折扣，目的是告诉收信人应该为这笔交易承担财务责任。这不是好消息，但是为了让收信人很清楚他需要负的责任，写信人陈述了一些事实和数据，从实际收到的钱的数目到应收钱的数目，从商品分发的时间到支付可以享受折扣的条件。为了使语气更加强势，写信人提醒收信人，对潜在问题的“特殊对待”是公司商业道德中考虑的一个因素。所有这些事实和数据使这封信十分具有说服力。

6.5 让你的写作容易阅读

尽管写作要比口头沟通稍微正式一些，理想的商业和管理写作应该如一个人和另一个人交谈一样。不幸的是，如今很多组织里的写作似乎出自不知名的“官僚者”之手，而不是来自于真实的人。

易读写作方式可以使读者对你的观点反应更积极，有两种方法可以达到易读的效果：①让单独的句子和段落通俗易懂，这样可以只花一点精力去浏览第一段或阅读整个文章；②让文章看起来有吸引力，使用一些标记引导读者进行阅读。

在《商务管理沟通(第六版)》一书中，基蒂·O. 洛克(Kitty O. Locker)提出了几种使写作内容易读的方法。

- 认真选择文字。
- 使写作简短。
- 仔细修改章节。

使写作简单易读的方法如下。

6.5.1 认真选择文字

使用准确、恰当和熟悉的文字。准确的文字是那些能够准确无误地表达意思的文字。恰当的文字传达了你的态度、语气，并且与文章中其他文字相符合。熟悉的文字则容易阅读和理解。

“巨大的”到底有多大

当两个人使用相同文字去表达不同意思时，分歧发生了。

一个潜在的客户告诉洛伊丝·盖勒，他想要为公司举办一个“巨大的”广告活动。洛伊丝·盖勒花三个星期准备了一个预算为50 000美元的广告活动。客户惊呆了。因为他整整一年的预算只有10 000美元。对于这个客户来说，预算5000美元的活动已足够“巨大”。

(资料来源：Horowitz A. Can you hear what I hear[J]. *Selling Power*, 2001, 7/8: 70.)

要想准确，字词的本意必须符合作者想要表达的意思。本意是一个字词字面上的或字典中的意思。多数英语中的词都有一种以上的本意。例如，*pound*这个词，本意是重量单位，可以表示收容迷路动物的地方，也可以表示英国货币单位，或者是动词“打”。

可口可乐公司一年估计花费2000万美金保护它的商标名称，这样*Coke*仅代表可口可乐这个品牌，而不是任何的可乐饮料。

作者误用词汇会带来问题。请看如下案例。

宾夕法尼亚西部是从哥伦比亚转移到费城的。(宾夕法尼亚并未移动，而是一家公司的销售职责转移到费城西部。)

Stiners公司的三大部门在相反方向做好了罢工准备。(三个不同方向不能彼此对立。)

字词也有它的内涵。内涵是与一个字词有关的意思，它表明一个词在什么语境下如何使用。例如，当用“pound”表示“打”的意思时，如果说“the woman pounded the little boy”就不合适，除非她在用一个大圆棍打小男孩。这里“pound”的内涵是指大的重物的敲击，而不是快速拍击或打那个小男孩。这是写作中遇到的挑战。作者必须做到选用字词时，既能表达正确的本意又能包涵适当的内涵，这样表达才有效。

当单词内涵，即它们的情感联结或者感情色彩传达出作者想要表达的态度时，用词就是合适的。很多单词都有赞同或反对、反感或喜欢的内涵。以下第一栏中的单词表示赞同，第二栏中的单词表示批评。

积极词汇	消极词汇
认为	猜测
好奇的	爱管闲事的
谨慎的	害怕的
确定的	固执的

6.5.2　撰写和修改语句

请在大多数时间使用主动语态。“谁做了那些”这样主动语态的语句使写作内容更有说服力，让语句充满活力。这会鼓励读者继续阅读所写的信或者报告。

如果语法中的主语做出句中动词描绘的动作，动词是主动语态。如果主语被施加行动，动词用被动语态。被动语态通常是由一种形式的动词(to be)加过去分词组成。被动语态与过去式无关。

被动语态可以是过去式、现在式或者将来式。

were received	(过去)
is recommended	(现在)
will be implemented	(将来)

要发现被动语态，需找到动词。如果这个动词描述的是主语在做什么，动词是主动语态。如果这个动词描述对主语施加的动作，动词是被动语态。

主动语态	被动语态
客户收到 500 个小部件。	500 个小部件被客户接收。
我推荐这种方法。	这种方法是我推荐的。
国家机构将实施该计划。	该计划将由国家机构实施。

主动语态也能够帮助读者想象当他或她在阅读文章时，他们正在经历着什么。

最初的被动语态形式：

“眼睛检查和视力测试被包含在计划里”。

修改后的主动语态形式：

“这个计划包括眼睛检查和视力测试”。

6.5.3　压缩你的写作

如果用更少的文字来表达相同的意思，写作则不容易出现烦琐冗长的现象。不必要的文字会增加写作时间，让读者厌烦，也会使内容更难以理解，因为在理解写作用意时，读者还要考虑其他多余字词的含义。

举例：

烦琐的表达：在文件中保存这个信息以便将来可以参考。

紧凑的表达：保存信息以便查阅。

为了压缩写作，你可以：

(1) 剔除没有意义或有重复意义的字词。

烦琐的表达：4 月 21 日(星期日)，我通过电话询问两组高年级男生和女生来进行这项调查。根据学生手册，发现他们依然住在学校宿舍。本次调查的目的是找出在学校没有要求的情况下，高年级学生继续住宿的原因，同时明确高年级男生和女生选择继续住宿的原因是否有区别。

更紧凑的表达：4 月 21 日(周日)，我给住在学校的高年级学生打电话，通过电话试图发现和解决两个问题：①为什么学校不要求住宿，他们却依旧住宿；②男生和女生是否有相同的住宿理由。

(2) 用动名词(动词+ing)和不定式(to+动词)形式使句子简短流畅。

(3) 合并句子，剔除不必要的字词。把句子变成主动语态以减少废话。

烦琐的表达：我们建议把过程计算机化是因为它将节省我们获得数据的时间，提供的数据也更准确。

更好的表达：过程计算机化会让我们更快速地获得准确的数据。

(4) 将长句分解成几个不同意思的句子。可以用几种方式改变句型，可以混合使用简单句、复合句和复杂句。简单句只有一个主要从句。

例：本月我们将开一家新店。

复合句有两个主要从句，由连词联结。如果两个从句表意相近，复合句效果最好。

例：我们已经雇用员工，他们将在下周完成培训。

我们希望在新店盛大开幕期间由地方广播电台进行广播，但是 DJ 们都有预约了。

对于句子长度和结构，一般需要考虑这些指导原则。

- 始终要使句子尽量简洁。即使是短句有时也会很啰唆。
- 当主题复杂或全是数字时，尽量保持句子简短。
- 使用长句表明观点是相互联系的，避免使用一系列不连贯的短句，减少重复。
- 将长句和中长句中的单词分块组合可以让读者迅速地掌握信息。
- 使用长句时，把主语和动词放在一起。

6.5.4 撰写及修改段落

多数段落都以主题句开头。好的段落具有统一性，也就是说每个段落只谈论一个观点或主题。主题句表明的是段落的主要意思，为文章提供一个支撑的框架。如果在每个段落的开始都有一个明确的主题句，文章读起来就较容易。如果段落的第一句不是主题句，略读的读者可能会错过要点。好的主题句可以预示段落的结构和内容。

1) 拗口(没有主题句)

2012 财政年度，该公司申请对 319.9 万美元联邦所得税，以及 2008～2010 年度向美国联邦国税局支付的公司所得税 96.9 万美元利息的偿还提出索赔。具体金额不确定的，如果有的话，最终也会收回。

2) 较好的表达(段落以主题句开头)

该公司和美国联邦国税局在是否退税款上并没有达成一致意见。在 2012 财政年度，该公司申请对 319.9 万美元联邦所得税，以及 2008～2010 年度向美国联邦国税局支付的公司所得税 96.9 万美元利息的偿还提出索赔。具体金额不确定，如果有的话，最终也会收回。

当信息是写给新的读者或不得不处理特别棘手的问题时，至少要修改草案三次。第一次针对内容和清晰度：我说的内容全面且清楚吗？第二次检查(段落)组织和布局：我介绍的内容能够让读者易于理解吗？最后一次检查(文体)风格和语气：我是否站在对方角度去思考？最后一定要做拼写检查。

修改文件时，确保从头到尾阅读文件。慢慢仔细地读，查看写的内容，不仅仅是你所“期望”看到的内容。需要添加过渡词句、减少重复部分或者更改词汇以使文档获得形式上的统一。

写作易读小贴士

- 使用友好、简单的语言和谈话式语气。
- 尽量避免行话。如果不能避免，要对行话进行解释。
- 用主动语态。
- 使用简短字词和句子。
- 将内容限制在 3～5 个主要观点，这样使其容易被掌握。
- 分点陈述观点，帮助读者阅读。
- 在浅色纸张上用黑体或深色字体，否则易造成阅读困难。
- 留有较大的间隔。
- 使用最小为 10 号的字体。
- 避免全大写的情况。
- 保持版面简单。

本 章 小 结

书面沟通在商务活动中是个强有力的工具，与口头沟通有很大不同。它是正式的，并留下永久的记录，使你能战略性地表达主要的观点和意图，没有机会根据读者反馈进行修改。从这点看，它是风险较高的沟通形式。书面沟通与口头沟通也有很多相似之处，两者都代表着你留给他人的印象，并可以影响其他人的观点。

作为一个主要商务技巧，本章重点介绍书面沟通。劣质的信件和报告会浪费时间，使努力白费，甚至让公司失去信誉。所以，当计划写作时，需要考虑与写作有关的六个关键方面的六个问题。应该关注沟通目的、读者、观点，以及书面沟通的关键信息，还要确保写作通俗易懂，这一点十分重要，因为写作的目的是传达信息，要求读者根据你的观点采取行动。所有成功的写作都是清楚、简洁的，小心谨慎地选用字词，组织好段落以达到沟通的目的：分享信息、激发读者采取适当的行动。

第7章

通　　信

【学习目标】

通过对本章内容的学习，你能够：

- 了解商务书信的格式和类型。
- 明确写作目的和读者。
- 了解如何将写作风格与内容要求相符。
- 知道如何在信函中表达“肯定”和“否定”。
- 知道如何撰写商务沟通中的简短信函，如说服性信函、推销信函、备忘录。

引例：传播癌症消息

肿瘤学家，那些专攻癌症治疗的医生，有着最艰难的工作，就是传递负面消息。这些医生经常告诉病人，他们面临着一场需与病魔进行艰难的抗争，抗争结果或许几乎没有希望，死亡可能迫在眉睫。

一些医学院现在强调须培养学生学习如何向病人，特别是那些患有癌症的病人传递坏消息。这些医学课程增加了一些课程，训练学生可以通过口头和非口头的交流方式传达负面消息，其中一些学校还利用由学生扮演病人的角色扮演方法进行训练。医学院的学生必须将无法接受的诊断结果通知“病人”扮演者，并适当处理“病人”的反应。一些研究表明，向病人传达坏消息的方式对他们的整体健康有显著影响。

美国临床肿瘤学学会(American Society of Clinical Oncology)开发了一本小册子，作为医生与患者进行正面交流的另外一种资源。当病人得知自己得了癌症时，这有助于他们了解自己的选择。这样可以改善他们的生活质量，最大限度地利用他们人生的剩余时间，并做好临终关怀计划。该协会认为，目前只有不到40%的患者与医生讨论过他们的选择。

(改编自道恩·萨加里奥，“医生要学会以一种亲切、深思熟虑的方式传达病情。”得梅因纪事报，2006年10月17日，E1,E2；“肿瘤小组提倡临终关怀的坦率。”得梅因纪事报，2011年2月8日，6A.)

引例启示：针对负面信息，我们必须传达的基本信息是负面的；我们能够预料到观众会感到失望或愤怒。有些工作需要传达比其他工作更多的负面信息。客户服务代表、员工代表和保险代理人都必须经常性地说“不”。负面信息也是商务和管理沟通的重要组成部分。在这一章中，我们将会了解通过不同写作方式撰写负面信息，如何构建消极信息的不同部分，以及如何通过语气提高负面信息的有效性。

7.1 产生积极效果的写作

麦克斯·艾略特的回信

亲爱的莫利先生：

我们已收到您12月3日的投诉并记录下所投诉的内容。经过对事实的审查，我很遗憾地通知您我必须拒绝您的要求。若您阅读保修手册，就会发现您购买的是上限800磅的轻负载产品。您应该购买重载产品。我很遗憾，这个失误对您造成了伤害，相信您了解自己的处境。希望我们将来可以继续为您服务。

为了给本章做好准备，你再次扮演麦克斯•艾略特的上级即小企业经理的角色。当你复查麦克斯上述的回复信函时，会发现尽管这封信的内容在努力地阐释问题，但信函中出现的沟通缺陷会影响公司的效益。这类信息会传递给公司内外的人，会影响人与人之间的关系，很大程度上决定了经营的成功与否。劣质的写作或者不友好的信息会产生严重的负面效应。上述麦克斯的回复信息就是一个例子。在这则信息中能发现的不只是可读性问题，文字也不礼貌，并没有体现对读者的关心，语言呆板、不得体又不友好。总的来说，这给读者留下了回信者和企业对良好人际关系需求漠不关心的坏印象。本章将说明如何避免这种印象。

7.1.1 清晰且积极的沟通效果的重要性

企业内的书面沟通首先需要清晰。内容清晰是多数商务写作的首要目标，尤其是组织内的沟通。因为这类写作大部分内容并未涉及读者私事，通常可就事论事地进行沟通。主要目标是快速、准确地传达信息。

对于组织外部读者，优秀的商务写作既要表述清晰又要建立良好商誉。当你想要信息更加私人化，那么需要关注的不仅仅是沟通信息。尤其在与外部人员沟通时，主要目标是建立并维持良好关系。写给公司客户的电子邮件或信件就是这种沟通的实例。

几乎在所有写作中都应该努力达到的效果就是为企业建立良好的商誉。明智的商界领袖明白大众对企业的看法会影响企业的成功与否。

他们同样了解大众的想法受到商务沟通中人际交往的影响。信息中体现商誉并不仅仅出于商务原因。它还是我们大多数人都希望在与人交往中达到这种效果。为了建立良好商誉，我们所说的话和所做的事友好而礼貌，可建立良好的人际关系。事实上，这属于商业行为，是良好商务礼仪的重要部分。

7.1.2 强调“你”的感受而不是“我”的感受

从读者出发撰写信函是建立良好商誉的又一技巧。不论你准备的信息是什么类型，从读者出发即关注读者的兴趣。写作中强调读者角度，强调“你”和“你的”，而不是强调“我”和“我的”，这种态度不仅仅是对第二人称代词的使用，还是良好商务沟通实践的基础。

作为商务书信的撰写人，必须关注读信人的感受，尤其私人信件更是如此。为了使读者产生共鸣，必须关注读者的需求而不是自己的需要，我们称之为“关注收信人”。以下例子说明了“关注写信人(关注我自己)”和“关注收信人(关注对方)”的不同之处。

我将有关已出售的电脑配件的相关信息寄给你。

——关注“我”的感受

你将收到整套的有关新电脑的详细内容及可选附件的性能和价格的说明书。

——关注“收信人”的感受

除了现金支付租金方式以外，政策规定禁止外部组织使用我们的内部设施。

——关注“我”的感受

对外部群体出租内部设施的政策能使我们为客人提供全方位的服务。

——关注“收信人”的感受

7.1.3 运用热情，友好的语气

家长、孩子或者成人的状态

20世纪50年代，心理学家艾瑞克·伯恩(Eric Berne)研究出被他称之为“交互分析”的人际关系模式。事实证明，这个模式非常有用，至今仍然很受欢迎。

这个模式的核心思想是，在我们与他人(甚至是自己)的交往中，人们表现出三种角色中的一种: 家长、孩子或成人。

家长状态是高高在上、溺爱、养育、责备、批评或者惩罚的。

孩子状态是无拘无束、情感自由、顺从、抱怨、不负责任或者自私的。

成人状态是理性、有责任、体贴和灵活的。

值得注意的是，一个人所表现出的“自我”会导致他人扮演互补位置的角色。这样，“家长”的行为模式会诱导对方采用“孩子”的行为模式；反之，亦然。而“成人”行为模式会使对方也采用“成人”的行为模式。

无论是内部还是外部商务沟通，努力做到“成人—成人”间的交互模式。你的礼貌和专业的态度，也会收获读者的礼貌和专业。

商务书信中的语气是成功的关键。语气代表着撰写人对读者和主题的态度。关注读者感受的方法之一是在信中表现出热情、友好的语气。这里我们建议可以通过两种技巧将热情、友好的语气传达给读者。

1. 人和事相比，要更多关注人的感受

尽量多关注人的感受。在下面的例子中，主管试图称赞一位员工完成的出色报告。注意一下，信息的重点是报告的内容而不是人的感受，因此显得空洞、冷淡。

描述一：“退休金计划的可选方案”描述了四种常用的退休金计划，每种都有利有弊。报告根据公司具体的需要对计划进行了评估。报告是清晰而有序的。

注意，在如下的描述中，当管理者关注的是人而不是物品时，则听起来好得多。

描述二：玛丽，谢谢你在“退休金计划的可选方案”中的出色表现。你清晰而有序地分析了四种可供选择的方案，这有利于公司做出最佳决策。

如果只是关注客观事物，你的称赞往往是针对客观事物而不是人，读者很难对一个事物表现出关心，但是一旦你的关注点转移至人时，就体现了人文的关怀，会得到更多的积极回应。

2. 关注感觉和事实

除了关注人要比关注事物更多以外，还有一种方法可以增加和强调热情、友好的语气，就是在告诉读者事实的同时说明你的感受，但是下列感受出现在商务书信中通常是不合适的。

(1) 关于你个人生活的感受。

(2) 个人关于公司、同事、客户或任何与你共事的人的负面感受。

(3) 任何关于读者或读者同事的消极的感受。

(4) 一些强烈的感情，如爱、恨、气愤或恐惧。

相反，你应该表达自豪、尊重、高兴或满意的情绪。

切记：商务写作犹如面对面的商务会议，要让人赏心悦目。

7.2　商务书信可读性格式的重要性

你是否曾读过冗长的、不间断的内容、突然分成片段的信件或者文章？商业读者要读的信息太多而不能耐心地阅读这种文章。如果确实想要读者读你所写并且了解你的想法及所传达的信息，那必须注意信息的一个重要元素——写作的格式。不要让读者对你的写作格式产生反感。

撰写人有责任对格式做出选择。几十年前，你可能可以依靠秘书或者打字员给文档排版，但随着功能齐全的计算机的广泛使用，使得可读性格式的设计更多地成为撰写人的责任。除了涉及平面设计师的项目，你应该决定信息的主要格式。使用什么类型和大小的字体，什么类型的标题？会使用一些排版方式突出重点吗？如何编号或者排列项目符号列表？文档应该包含标志、文本框、图片或图表等视觉元素吗？在这些问题上做出明智决定不仅会增强读者的阅读动机，而且可以使读者迅速理解信息的要点和结构。

7.3　标准商务书信的组成

现代商务书信读起来要比过去友好得多。现代书信的撰写人和读者都认识到不仅商务书信的表达很重要，激发读者理解信的内容并付诸行动同样重要。另外，现代商务书信比过去的更简短，现代商务书信也要求比过去更加有吸引力，出现的错误也更少。

现在你已经熟悉了商务书信书写的语气及展示的风格，你还要进一步了解商务书信的每个组成部分，并可以自信地使用它。下面是一封标准商务书信的每个组成部分，其中有一些是书信中必须包括的部分，有一些是应该包括的内容，还有一些是可选择的内容。

- 信头(或回信地址)　(必须包括)
- 日期　(必须包括)
- 封内地址(收信人地址)　(必须包括)
- 主题　(应该包括)
- 指定收信人　(可选择)
- 称呼　(必须包括)
- 信的正文(信的内容)
- 结束敬语　(必须包括)
- 签名　(必须包括)
- 最后声明　(可选择)
- 附言　(可选择)

7.3.1 信头

信头展现的是公司希望展现的形象。知道写信者是谁有助于读者决定是否阅读信的内容。商务书信的信头经常是表明公司名称、公司标志或两者皆有。信头包括公司地址、城市名称、州的名称、公司的邮政编码、一个或多个电话号码、传真号/电传号/电报地址。

7.3.2 日期

将日期写在回信地址后空两行的位置，然后在日期和封内地址间再留出两行的距离。当你写信时，要切记：

(1) 在表达日期时不要将字母和数字混用(不要使用 Feb.2nd 这种格式)。

(2) 不要仅仅用数字表达日期(如 8/21/16 或 9-27-16)。

(3) 如果月份只有 5 个或更少的字母，不要用简写(标准的缩写如 Jan.，Feb.，Oct.等可用)。

(4) 不要用不常用的缩写或不常用的序列表示日期。

7.3.3 封内地址

封内地址是指收信人地址，最好是写明公司具体人员的名称。如果没有收信人的名字，可以通过打电话或与该公司员工交谈了解有关信息。写明 Ms、Mrs、Mr 或 Dr 这样的称呼。女性的称呼可以用 Miss、Mrs 或 Ms。如果不清楚女性最适合的称呼，则使用 Ms。通常人们不会在意你使用的头衔比他们实际的头衔高。在写地址时，按照该国的格式要求进行书写。对于国际地址，在最后一行用全部大写的英文撰写国家名称。封内地址在写信人地址的下一行，或者在日期下方的 1 英寸或 2.5 厘米处开始。不论使用何种格式，都要用从左边开始对齐。

在封内地址写上收信人的全名。当你不知道收信人的名字时，可在封内地址和称呼中都使用工作头衔。例如：

Director of Marketing
Victory Products, Inc.
300 Buena Vista St.
Ft. Worth, TX 46839
UNITED STATES OF AMERICA

7.3.4 主题

主题句简明扼要地描述信的主要内容，是能够引起人们注意的一个重要机会，让收信人相信，阅读这封信对于他们很重要。因此，主题的表达要清晰、简明。在主题句的前后分别留有两行的空行，可以放在封内地址和称呼之间。在正式书信中，商务人士有时会用缩写的“Re:”代替“Subject”。

7.3.5　指定收信人

如果直接给公司写信，可以通过指定收信人明确收信人的姓名、职位或部门名称。使用指定收信人的目的是确保信函能直接地送到正确的人或部门，它经常被放在封内地址之后。

7.3.6　称呼

商务书信中人们经常称呼与其通信的人为“Dear”，尽管有时两者之间的关系还没有达到这一步。称呼必须与封内地址中第一行提到的人一致，如果不清楚收信人的姓名，就用封内地址中的职位名称作为称呼。

使用与封内地址中相同的人物名字，包括头衔。如果认识对方，并且常常以名字称呼他，这时仅用名字作为称呼也是可行的(例如：Dear Lucy)。在其他情况下使用头衔和全名，后面跟着冒号作为称呼。称呼后留一空行。

如果不清楚收信人的性别，使用没有性别的称呼，例如：“To whom it may concern”或“Dear Sir/Madam”，也可以使用对方的全名作为称呼。

7.3.7　信的正文

信的正文包含将要传达的信息。信的编排可以帮助你让读信人一眼就注意到你的信。在结构上要清楚地表现出信的开头、中间和结尾。信的开头部分只用一两句话，使读者一目了然。同样，结尾也应易读。

商务书信的每一段应保持简短(不超过 5～6 行)。

列出清单，这样确保重要的内容没有被遗漏。《管理沟通》一书的作者阿瑟・H.贝尔(Arthur H. Bell)和戴尔・M. 史密斯(Dayle M. Smith)建议：信的正文要做到“六个C”。

(1)　综合性(complex)：使用事实、论点、例子和详细内容充分证明你的观点。

(2)　连贯性(coherent)：以富有条理和逻辑的方式将信中的观点贯穿起来。

(3)　简明性(concise)：用最少的字词表达意思。

(4)　具体性(concrete)：用通俗易懂的语句让读信人对所表达的信息有具体的认识。

(5)　信服性(convincing)：有逻辑性地安排信的正文，使读信人能够理解并相信所表达的内容。

(6)　体谅性(considerate)：用热情、友好的语气，站在读信人的立场，关注读信人的需要。

7.3.8　结束敬语

这是最后一次表达敬意的机会。在正文后留两行空行，写上最适合的结束语，如“Sincerely”或“With best wishes”。但是，怎样才知道商务书信中何时使用比“Sincerely”更热情的结束语呢？在很大程度上，跟着你的感觉走没错。当衡量你的感觉时，切记以下建议。

(1) 给新的客户或不认识的人写第一封信时经常是用保守的结束语，如“Sincerely”。初次通信，用热情的结束语会被认为是虚伪的表现，因为读信人没有根据来判断你的感觉。

(2) 商务书信如用名字开头，如“Dear Jenny”，可用比“Sincerely”更热情的结束语。事实上，用 Sincerely 作为结束语，让读者感觉你本来写的是一封温暖的私人信件，但选择了相当传统的、态度模糊的结束语。

结束敬语应当与称呼配套使用。下面是几组常见的配套使用的称呼和结束敬语。

(正式地)

Dear Sir(s)	*Yours faithfully*
Gentlemen	*Truly yours*

(非正式地)

Dear Mr. Henry	*Yours sincerely* (或 *Sincerely yours*)

7.3.9 签名

你的全名、职位名称打印在你的签名之下，所以签名可以体现个人风格，一种掩藏在签名之后的隐含意思。同时，签名不必总是和信中打印的一模一样。记住：签名要让你愉快，并且看起来自然、自信。

7.3.10 最后声明

最后声明经常出现在商务书信的结尾，并在签名之后紧靠信函的左边缘。撰写人将这些声明放在信的结尾，这样可以告诉读者这封信还抄送给了谁。

7.3.11 附件

附件简单记录书信中包含的传统事项。当读信人将信归档时，附件的说明是与书信有关的材料的永久记录。

7.4 关于信的格式与字体

撰写商务信函时，一定要特别关注信函的格式和字体。最常用的商务书信的版式是平头式。使用这种格式，整个信函左对齐，除了段落之间是双行间距，其他都是单行间距。另一种格式是改良平头式。在这种格式中，信的正文左对齐，单行间距。但是，日期和结束语放在本页的中央。最后一种格式是缩排式。它的风格很像改良平头式，但是每段缩进，而不是左对齐。

下面举例说明不同信函的格式。

7.4.1　平头式

在这个常用的格式中，所有部分的书写都从左边开始。段落之间被一或两行间距分开。这是一种比较现代的格式，让人感觉时尚。平头式信件示例如下：

2012年3月16日

黄先生
Nathan路65号
九龙
香港

亲爱的黄先生：

典型的商务书信的第一段通常是说明信的主要观点。以友好的口吻开头，然后迅速转入信的主要意图。用几句话解释目的，在下一段中再提到详细内容。

第二段提供详细资料证实你的意图。可以使用一些背景信息、统计资料或者第一手数据。在正文中以几个简短的段落支持你的意图。

最后，在结尾段落，简要重复你的意图和它的重要性。如果信的目的与职业有关，在信的结尾留下联系方式。如果信的目的是告知信息，要考虑结束语中表达对读者的感谢。

谨上

露西

7.4.2　缩排式

回信地址(如果没有用印有信头的信纸)、日期、签名和结束敬语被移到信的中间。段落是缩进排的，常常距左边空白边缘五个字母空格。这种风格要比平头式显得传统和具有文学性，它要求撰写人更细心和努力。在如今商务中这种格式的使用要比平头式少，部分原因正是如此。缩排式信件示例如下：

2012年3月16日

黄先生
Nathan路65号
九龙
香港

亲爱的黄先生：

典型的商务书信的第一段通常是说明信的主要观点。以友好的口吻开头，然后迅速转入信的主要意图。用几句话解释目的，在下一段中再提到详细内容。

第二段提供详细资料证实你的意图。可以使用一些正式的信息背景、统计资料或者第一手数据。在正文中以几个简短的段落支持你的意图。

最后，在结尾段落，简要重复你的意图和它的重要性。如果信的目的与职业有关，在信的结尾留下联系方式。如果信的目的是告知信息，要考虑结束语中提到感谢读者的时间。

谨上

露西

7.4.3 改良平头式

平头式和缩排式的元素在这种格式中都会出现。回信地址(如果没有用印有信头的信纸)、日期和签名被移至页面中央。信的其他部分沿着左边空白边缘写起。段落没有缩进，改良平头式比平头式和缩排式使用得少，但如果撰写人想追求时尚，同时保持页面的平衡，这种格式是较为实用的。改良平头式信件示例如下：

2012年3月16日

黄先生
Nathan路65号
九龙
香港

亲爱的黄先生：

典型的商务书信的第一段通常是说明信的主要观点。以友好的口吻开头，然后迅速转入信的主要意图。用几句话解释目的，在下一段中再提到详细内容。

第二段提供详细资料证实你的意图。可以使用一些正式的信息背景、统计资料或者第一手数据。在正文中以几个简短的段落支持你的意图。

最后，在结尾段落，简要重复你的意图和它的重要性。如果信的目的与职业有关，在信的结尾留下联系方式。如果信的目的是告知信息，要考虑结束语中提到感谢读者的时间。

谨上

露西

7.5　在信中说“是”和“否”

7.5.1　直率在商务活动中盛行

大多数商务信息采用直接指令。也就是说，信息直接指向最重要的点，然后转移到额外的或者支撑性的信息。沟通是有组织的人际活动的核心。尤其在商务活动中，人们需要知道做什么、为什么做及如何去做。从事任何工作时，人们需要了解他们应该执行的特定的职能，以及执行职能所需要的信息。任何企业在某些方面都有独特之处，因此，每个公司都会形成自己的直接传递信息的类型，包括信息的目的、模式、风格和格式。可为直接传递信息确定特定的基本计划。这里有一个在电邮、传真或者信件中使用不合适的结构的例子。这封信件间接、模糊的开篇会减缓读者的阅读速度。

亲爱的派珀先生：

我们在日报上看见您为 3200 平方英尺的办公空间做的广告。我们对此感兴趣，因此希望获得更多的信息。我们尤其想了解室内布局、年度成本、交通状况、租赁协议时长、升级规定和任何你认为与其相关的其他信息。

如若您提供的信息有利，我们将去现场考察。请尽快回复。

谨上

为了进行直接写作，让读者很好地理解你在信息中想要表达的真正意思，你需要遵循以下建议。

首先，从目标开始。如果你正在收集信息，从发问开始。如果你正在提供信息，从供给开始。无论你的关键点是什么，让关键点引领全篇。把关键点放在前面。但是你可能需要简短的引导信息从而让读者抓住真正的信息。然后完结第一段落，让剩余内容填充细节。

其次，内容覆盖目标的其他部分。可以通过列表或者分段来阐明目标。如果开篇内容提到了所有目标，意味着不需要其他的内容。如果需要额外的问题、答案或者信息，写作需要包含这些内容，系统性地阐述它们。

最后，以建立良好关系结尾。用恰当友好的语气结束写作，就像结束与读者进行面对面的沟通一样。如果选择适合特定场合的词语，这些表明良好信誉的结束语将会得到最佳的读者反应。像“A prompt reply will be appreciated”和“Thank you for your time and consideration”这类常规结尾是积极的，因为它们表示友好的感谢。另外，在信函结尾或者其他位置表达真诚感谢永远都不会错。

7.5.2　发送积极信息

有时对那些不能全部执行的订单不得以要说“不”，但是读者期望听到对订单、请求、邀请说“是”。若客户听到的回答是“是”，他们会珍视公司的参与，给他们的感觉是让他们有自己的选择而不是代替他们做选择。

当写“是”的信时，有简单的四点可供参考。

(1) 信中尽快传递“是”的信息，将所有细节和附加信息留到下一段落。

(2) 让“是”的信息简单化。单独一段陈述“是”的信息，不要与条件、注释、资格放在同一段落里，不要搞得一团糟。

(3) 准确地告诉顾客你所说的“是”的消息是什么，消息要明确。尤其在合同和信用的问题上，明智的做法是准确地表达你可以许诺的和不能承诺的内容。

(4) 销售公司的服务、产品、形象或关系。

1. 一般性询函

一般性询函的格式可按以下方式设计。

(1) 一般性询函通常以询问具体的或一般的问题开始。首先，它可以是被询问的具体问题之一(假设被问的问题不止一个)。由一个问题引出其他问题会更好。例如，如果你的目标是获取前述案例中描述的办公住房信息，你可以从下列语句开始。

你能把在《周一日报》中宣传的办公住房建筑平面图的其他信息给我吗？

信件正文将包含关于这套房的其他具体问题，或者开篇即提出索取信息的要求，具体问题紧随其后。下面这个开篇句说明了如何提出索取信息的一般要求。

能否请你将《周一日报》上刊登的3200平方英尺办公住房的描述发给我？

(2) 充分告知并解释。你应该解释或者提供一些信息帮助读者解答问题。如果对信息没有做出足够解释或者误导了读者，就会使读者需要完成的任务变得困难。在何处以及如何涵盖必要的解释信息取决于你所传达的信息的性质。通常情况下，一般解释性内容放在开头段落的直接请求之前或者之后比较好。把解释性的说明放在任何符合逻辑的地方。

(3) 建构问题。如果询问仅涉及一个问题，就从这个问题开始。如果涉及问题不止一个，就把问题突出出来。突出问题的方法如下：①把每个问题放在单独的句子里；②每个问题构成一个段落；③利用单词(第一、第二、第三等)、数字(1、2、3等)或者字母(a、b、c等)进行排序或者排名以突出所要引出的问题；④使用疑问句。可用如下疑问句突出所要引出的问题：“你能告诉我……？”“一个人能够节省多少……？”

(4) 以合适的方式友好地结束本次信函。一般情况下，和大多数商务信函一样，友好地结束写作也是恰当的书写格式。我们必须再次强调，恰当的结束语是能够带来好的声誉的。记住，结束语也应包括希望得到回复的期限和原因。

2. 一般性回函

一般性回函提供原信函所需信息或者能回应写作者的要求。像原始的询函一样，一般性回函采用直接的方式写作，把“好”消息，即那些能够积极响应的事实放在回函的前面。

当然，需要遵循的重要准则之一是及时回复。你的回复应是有礼貌的。如果你表现得不情愿，你可能会丧失本应通过亲切回应为你个人或者组织赢得的良好声誉。必须使用客观且清晰易懂的语言回答所有明示或者暗示的问题。你的信件可能为读者带来积极的情绪，可以考虑通过适当地加入一些促销信息或者通过暗示组织具有公共精神、高质量产品、社会责任或关心员工等特点来建立良好声誉。

通常，写作者提出的问题之前已经被其他人问过很多次了，这种情况下，常规信函可能是最合适的回应方式。常规信函是发送给不同人的具有标准化措辞的信件。

一般性询函及回函建议

(一)一般性询函

(1) 在第一句或者第二句提出主要要求，在其之前或之后说明提出这些请求的原因。

(2) 提供必要解释及细节。

(3) 用短语叙述每个问题且只涉及一个主题，这样问题更清晰也更易回答。尽可能少提问题，但是如果需要提若干问题，则要将其按逻辑性进行排序。

(4) 如果可以的话，要考虑读者的利益并承诺保密。

(5) 通过表达感激、对要求得到回复的期限做出解释、提供回报或者以其他方式做出个性化、新颖的信函结尾。

(二)一般性回函

(1) 及时礼貌地给予回复。

(2) 在第一句或者第二句中就提出同意对方的请求或提供对方询函所需的信息。

(3) 回答明示或者暗示的所有问题，包括可能有帮助的额外信息或建议。

(4) 如果可以的话，包含不易被察觉到的促销信息。

(5) 考虑使用常见的标准格式的信函。

(6) 说明随信附上的其他任何形式的文件，并在底部插入附件说明。

(7) 使用积极、友好的措辞结束本次信函。

(资料来源：Ober S, Newman A. 商务沟通[M]. 7版. 北京：清华大学出版社，2013.)

从不说“不”

有些文化背景中，说“不”是粗鲁无礼的表现。

日本人喜欢避免直接的冲突。转移话题——甚至完全无关的话题、道歉、沉默，总是比说“不”更可取。

日本商务人员撰写拒绝信函时，以缓冲内容开始，接着是说明原因、表达道歉和感谢。

为了避免说“不”，捷克人和斯洛伐克人可能会说“我们会再考虑”。

在匈牙利，直接对同辈人或年长者说“不”也是不礼貌的。如果某人不想做某事，他会给出一系列的理由直到其他人认识到应该停止询问。

(资料来源：Azuma S. *Rejection Strategy in Business Japanese*[C]. Association for Business Communication Annual Meeting, 1995, Orlando:11,1-4. Ruder C A, Richmond Y. *From da to yes: Understanding the East Europeans*[M]. Yarmouth: Intercultural Press, 1995.)

7.6　传达坏消息

如今，公司建立良好的信誉，留住老客户，赢得新客户不仅通过对订单、请求、调整函和信用证友好地说“是”，必要时也要有技巧地对一些信函说“不”。

传达坏消息是一个领导者需要完成的最困难的任务之一。如果员工和客户的期望与现实不符，会导致不良行为。为减少这种潜在的不良行为，无论员工和客户有多么不情愿听，不好的消息也应该公开、真实地被传达。

有时拒绝一个人的请求也是必要的。消极沟通如拒绝、抵制、回忆和道歉很难组织，然而它们很重要。质量好的拒绝信函可以重建公司信誉以及赢得客户、雇员的善意对待。质量不好的拒绝信函可能导致诉讼。公司管理人员会因消极沟通得到晋升或者被解雇。雇员报告负面的消息则经常被惩罚。

7.6.1 负面消息的目的

负面消息通常有如下几个目的。

1. 主要目的

(1) 给读者带来坏消息。

(2) 让读者阅读、理解并接受信息。

(3) 尽可能维护声誉。

2. 次要目的

(1) 尽可能维护沟通者和沟通者所在组织的良好形象。

(2) 为了减少或者消除同一主题在今后的重复沟通，信息不会给发信人带来额外工作。

通过以下对比例子说明拒绝信息中的间接指令的优势。两封信函都明确传达了拒绝的信息。但是，似乎采用间接指令(拒绝)容易获得读者的好感。

由于采用直接(拒绝)和消极语言，以下并不是一篇质量较好的电子邮件。

> 主题：您寻求捐赠的请求
>
> 卡吉洛西女士：
>
> 我们很遗憾地通知您，我们不能同意您向我们寻求对协会奖学金基金捐赠的请求。由于收到很多寻求捐赠的请求，我们发现有必要对每年的捐赠进行一定的预算。我们今年的预算基金(额度)已经用完，因此我们不能考虑更多的捐赠请求。但是，我们明年可以考虑您的请求。我们对现在无法帮助您深感遗憾，并相信您理解我们的处境。
>
> 马克·斯蒂芬斯

第二个例子巧妙处理了负面信息。它的开篇是关于(文章)主题并持中立态度的。随后他们做了一些解释，清晰并有逻辑性的解释与开篇密切联系。不使用否定词，解释内容可以顺利过渡到拒绝信息。请注意，拒绝时不使用否定词语，表达也很清晰。友好的结束语贴切主题。

> 主题：您对奖学金基金的请求
>
> 卡吉洛西女士：
>
> 您努力地为协会有需要的孩子建立奖学金基金的做法是值得赞扬的。我们期待您为

推动这项高尚事业所做的努力取得成功。

在平纳克尔，我们随时乐意为高尚的事业效劳。因此每年一月我们都会做出为此类事业贡献的最大预算。只要基金到位，我们就把它分发给许多值得帮助的群体。由于我们已经制定好今年的捐款预算，我们将把您的组织列在明年考虑的名单中。

我们希望您为改善我市儿童生活所做的努力获得成功。

马克·斯蒂芬斯

7.6.2　拒绝信函的组成

商务活动中经常出现对订单或询价说“不”的时候。但必须记住：在写拒绝信函时，不仅要对订单或询价表明否定的态度，同时还要考虑如何维持消费者对产品的忠诚度。这时，可以参考下列对订单说“不”的方式。

(1) 首先，要有积极肯定的缓冲内容(可以是对订单申请的陈述)。

(2) 明确表明你们可以提供的和无法提供的。

(3) 提供一些你认为对读者有用的解释或说明。

(4) 以友好、感谢的语气结束信函。

1. 缓冲

缓冲是肯定或中性的陈述(不是否定的)，一般放在拒绝信函的开始。缓冲让读者在知道拒绝消息前感受舒服些。

有效的缓冲，必须让读者有个理想的思路框架。不是传递坏消息，但也不是给个肯定的回答，内容自然过渡到信的正文。起缓冲作用的陈述经常是好的消息、事实和事件年历表、附件、感谢和对原则的说明等。

创建有效的缓冲，应该做到如下方面。

(1) 选择目前话题的积极方面。

(2) 赞美读者个人的或者职业的品质。

(3) 关注特别的需要。

(4) 把时间因素作为拒绝的理由。

撰写人通过使用缓冲，使读者做好准备接受拒绝的信息。当然，也不可能完全避免让读者失望的结果。但是，为减轻负面影响而做的努力，能够在暂时的失望之外建立友善的关系。

2. 原因

尽量不要说你不能够做某事。多数否定信息的存在是因为写作者或公司出台了一些政策或否定了一些观点。不要以公司的政策为挡箭牌，读者会认为政策的制定是以牺牲他们的利益为代价而让你们受益。如果可能，说明读者将如何得益于政策。如果他们没有受益，根本不用提到有关政策。

不充分的理由：我不能为你制定一个保险政策，因为公司政策不允许我这么做。

充分的理由：只有当汽车在夜间正常地被送入汽车修理厂，中国人寿保险公司才为汽车进行保险。标准的保险政策覆盖广泛的风险种类和较高的保险金额。有限的政策使中国人寿保险公司的客户享受到最低的汽车保险费率。

如果找不到好的理由，就省略理由，而不是找个不充分的理由。即使有充分的理由，如果有损公司形象，也不用提及。

损害公司形象的理由：因为利润下滑的原因，目前公司不考虑招聘。事实上，这种低谷状态促使公司高层管理人员决定在本月裁员 5%，这个数量也许会更多。

较好的理由：公司目前没有空职位。

下面是一个成功说“不”的例子，同时也维护了公司的信誉，维持了生产力的发展。

最好的拒绝是没有意外

20 世纪 90 年代，福特公司缩小了规模，关闭了古老的雷鸟工厂，解雇了数千名工人。福特公司因事先与员工讨论过这项计划而没有引起工人们联合性的冲突。

福特公司的CEO和美国联合汽车工人协会的副主席每隔一个月进行一次早餐会晤。福特公司汇报一些敏感的信息并寻求联合会的支持。在关闭雷鸟公司前六个月，联合会就已经知道这个消息。联合会经过谈判，使那些调动到其他州卡车工厂的员工获得一大笔津贴。

根据对汽车产业的分析，福特公司面对将要来临的负面消息，真诚地与员工进行沟通，不仅防止了罢工带来的沉重代价，而且也有利于保持员工较高的生产力。

(资料来源：Sexton C. If Ford can do it, why can’t GM[J]. *Business Week*, 1998, 7(29): 36.)

3. 拒绝

将拒绝与拒绝的原因放在同一段落而不是使其单独成段，这样可以使拒绝事实不那么醒目。有时可以暗示拒绝的事实，不要直接说明。

直接拒绝：你不能投保只有一个月的保险。

暗示拒绝：最短的保险期限是六个月。

确保暗示是清楚易懂的。任何消息都有可能被误解，但是过于乐观的和过于悲观的读者尤其不大可能理解拒绝信息。发送拒绝信息的目的之一是坚决否定有关内容。你肯定不愿意再发第二封信告诉对方真正的回答是“不”。

4. 替代方案

如果有可能，给读者一个替代方案或折中办法。这样做有很多原因：

(1) 提供给读者其他达到目标的方法。

(2) 能够证明你的确在乎读者，并且想帮助他们，满足他们的需求。

(3) 当你说“不”之后，重新恢复读者心理上的放松。

(4) 以积极的信息结束，并表明你自己或组织是积极的、友好的且是有所帮助的。

替代方案让读者以一种不会损害你的利益的方式做出回应。让读者自己选择是否需要替代方案，使读者心理上又重新找回放松的感觉。

5. 结束信函

最好的结束语是展望未来。下面是一些例子。

好的例子：拥有本公司的账户，无论你在哪里，无论你何时光临，你都将继续得到 CHARGE_ALL 公司为你提供的服务，享受在中国和海外数百万商店、饭店和酒店中支付费用的方便服务，在上海也可以享受到。

避免虚假的结束语：我们很高兴为您服务。如果将来需要我们的帮助，请联系我们。

7.7　表达否定时使用妥当的语气

语气暗示着作者对读者和主题的态度。如果希望读者明白你的确是认真考虑了他们的请求，这时语气就变得尤其重要。

信的外表和寄信的时间也能传达一种语气。如果信函经过准确和认真地撰写，并且提供了所有必要的细节，这表明你已花费了时间去替读者考虑。明显的拒绝内容的表达说明撰写人没有过多考虑读者的要求。

重要的是要记住，如果信的开头就出现直接的拒绝内容，说明拒绝不需要任何考虑。

要尽量避免使用表 7.1 所示的拒绝语句。

表 7.1　避免使用的拒绝语句

使用语句	原　因
我担心我们不能……	你不是害怕。不要用空洞的语句作挡箭牌
很抱歉我们不能够……	你也许可以接受请求，你只是选择了拒绝。如果你真的对于说“不”感到抱歉，为什么不改变你的策略说“是”
我相信你们同意……	不要假设你能猜中读者的心思

7.8　劝说性信息

劝说是激发他人采取具体行动或者支持一个特别想法的过程。劝说是鼓励他人相信某件事或做一些他或她本来不会做的事情。每天，许多人会试图说服你去做某些事情或者相信某些想法。

当撰写劝说性信息时，你的任务是告诉读者一些事情，并让他们确信你的观点是最合适的一个。这类写作需要认真规划，明确写作目的并对读者做全面分析。

谨记下面列出的撰写劝说性信息时应注意的事项。

1. 决定如何开头

(1) 直接性表达。下列情况下使用直接性表达。

—写给上级的信函；

—读者倾向于客观地倾听你的请求；

—撰写的提议不需要强有力的说服性；

—撰写的提议内容多或者完整；

—你知道读者喜欢直接的表达方式。

(2) 在第一段提出建议，包括简短的理性说明。

(3) 间接性表达。以下情形下使用间接性表达。

—给下属或者同事写信；

—给组织外人员写信；

—需要强有力的说服；

—读者最初反对你的建议；

—你知道读者喜欢间接的表达方式。

(4) 开始内容要能引起读者的关注。

(5) 第一句话要能够吸引读者继续阅读。

(6) 保持开篇句简短且与信息相关，并在适当的时候使内容与读者利益相关。

2. 建立兴趣并证明你的请求

(1) 写作的主要内容要能解释你的请求。为使读者做出明智的决定，提供充足的背景资料和证明材料。

(2) 使用事实、统计数据、专家意见及案例支撑你的建议。确保证据是准确的、相关的、典型的和完整的。

(3) 使用客观、有逻辑性、合理及真诚的语气。避免明显的奉承、感情用事和夸张。

(4) 针对直接或者间接的读者利益呈现证据。

3. 减少障碍

(1) 不要忽视障碍或者你的请求的任何消极因素。相反，要证明，即使考虑那些不利因素，你的要求仍然合理。

(2) 根据主题的位置和篇幅来讨论障碍物。

4. 自信地寻求行动

(1) 在讨论完大部分的益处之后，在信息结尾表明具体请求。

(2) 期望读者采取的行动要明确、简单，用一种自信的口吻，不要道歉也不要找借口。

(3) 以前瞻性说明结束写作，同时继续强调读者的受益。

以下的劝说性备忘录使用了直接性表达，因为信息在组织内部采用上行的传递方式。

有说服力的推销想法的请求

发送至：副总裁艾略特·兰伯恩

来自：营销主管简森·J.彼得森

日期：20××年4月3日

主题：对员工停车场进行再分配的建议

为了表达对占据我们销量近一半的福特汽车公司的支持，我提议员工停车场由拥有福特汽车的员工使用。

福特汽车公司的人员在参观本公司的过程中，穿过我们的员工停车场时发现约有 70%的雇员驾驶他们竞争对手制造的车辆。事实上，福特公司的采购代理上周问我："如果你们不支持我们，凭什么指望我们支持你们？"

此备忘录的目的是请求批准我们的员工停车场仅限福特汽车使用。维保部门估计制造所需标记耗资约 500 美元。

劳动合同要求工作环境变化需要工会批准。然而，我们的工人代表莎莉·玛什告诉我如果对行政部门的停车场实施类似限制，她会批准这项建议。

由于我们下一个经理会议定在 5 月 8 日，我期待(当天)给他们宣布新计划。通过批准这一计划，纽顿将给来访者传达强有力的积极信息。我们对所销售的产品充满信心。

(资料来源：Ober S, Newman A. 商务沟通[M]. 7 版. 北京：清华大学出版社，2013.)

第一段，以介绍建议为开篇，并有简短的理由

第二段，提供必要的背景信息，使内容能平稳过渡

第三段，列出众多理由之后重复建议

第四段，客观叙述存在的明显障碍

第五段，以积极的、自信的内容结尾，会激发公司迅速采取行动

无效的劝说性请求

20××年 1 月 13 日

编辑 谭雅·波拉特女士
自体免疫疾病月刊杂志
十山路 1800 号 B 幢
波士顿，邮政编码 02143

亲爱的波拉特女士：

主题：请求您在多发性硬化症大会上发言

我有一个请求，恐怕还是一个不小的请求。我曾担任一家专业杂志的编辑，知道编辑有多忙，但是我想知道 4 月 25 日您是否愿意飞往华盛顿特区，并在我们第七届年会的闭幕会上发言。

当然，问题是作为非营利组织，我们负担不起您的酬金。我相信，对您来讲这不是问题，但是我们愿意承担您的旅费和住宿费。

与会人员将从您丰富的多发性硬化症知识中获益匪浅，因此我们真心希望您能接受我们的邀请。请于 3 月 3 日前让我知道您的决定，以便我们做其他安排。

如有问题，请电话联系我。

谨上
会议负责人梅·里昂

(资料来源：Ober S, Newman A. 商务沟通[M]. 7 版. 北京：清华大学出版社，2013.)

所用主题过于具体

以直接请求开头，使用第一人称语言并省略重要信息

以自私的态度呈现障碍

给了回复最后期限，但是没有给出合理的理由

以陈词滥调结尾

下面这一劝说性请求使用了间接表达，因为作者不了解读者个性而且需要强有力的说服。

有效的劝说性请求——请求支持

20××年1月21日

编辑　谭雅·波拉特女士
自体免疫疾病月刊杂志
十山路1800号B幢
波士顿，邮政编码02143

亲爱的波拉特女士：

主题：多发性硬化症会议安排计划

您在《波士顿环球报》最近采访中关于“每1 000人中就有一位多发性硬化症患者”的评论引起了我的注意和思考。

（第一段，以收信人的话开篇，以此恭维她）

您对医学事实的专业解释将会让来到华盛顿特区参加年会的与会者们产生浓厚的兴趣。4月25日您作为我们在亚当斯酒店举办的宴会的主讲人，将向200位在场人员阐述您的观点。宴会于晚上7:00开始，您作为宴会嘉宾将于晚上8:30左右开始45分钟的演讲。

（第二段，暗示请求；提供必要的背景信息）

我们将承担您的差旅费。尽管作为非营利组织我们无法提供酬金，但我们给您提供介绍您的杂志以及对全国主要自体免疫组织群体代表阐述您观点的机会。

（第三段，把潜在障碍放在从句中，使它居于次要地位）

我们计划在3月3日即下一期通讯简报中报道您演讲的内容。您可以通过电话告知我们您是否可以参加。将有很多热情的医学研究人员等待聆听您的演讲。

（第四段，以再次申述读者获益结尾）

谨上
会议负责人梅·里昂

(资料来源：Ober S, Newman A. 商务沟通[M]. 7版. 北京：清华大学出版社，2013.)

7.9 推　销　信

对读者需求的敏感度对于推销信而言是十分重要的。潜在的消费者需要知道为什么他们需要购买这种产品或服务，为什么向慈善机构捐助，为什么订购杂志等。撰写者必须提供清楚明白的信息帮助他们理解推销信的内容。

有效的推销信必须通过真实地描述有关信息来打动读者。如果推销信的目的是为了影响读者，那么必须证明它所表明的立场或行动是能够满足读者需求的。读者的需求是广泛的，而且读者常常有一些相互交叠的需求，例如下面的一些需求。

金钱	健康
更多的自由支配时间	舒适
生产力	娱乐
重要性	安全
权利	知识
魅力	期望的技能
朋友	名誉

市场调研是一种测试市场、了解读者需求的有效方法。读者是否意识到你们的产品能满足他们的需求？如果是这样，在推销信的开头便说明你们的产品是如何满足读者需求的。读者还没明白你们的产品能帮助他们吗？如果是这样，在开始的一句或两句话中提醒他们可能曾经遇到的某个问题。

1. 撰写推销信的步骤

一旦已经分析了读者的需求，并能粗略判断他们需要的程度，你可以计划推销信每个部分的写作步骤。这里提供一个简单易记的撰写推销信的方法：S-A-L-V-E-S.

S——激发读者的想象力和好奇心；

A——提供产品或服务；

L——列出客户的获益清单；

V——重视客户可以从中获取的利益；

E——表示感谢和善意；

S——确切表明客户该做什么、何时做。

让我们来详细看看每个步骤。这些步骤可以帮助你撰写成功的推销信。

(1) S——**激发读者的想象力和好奇心。**推销信中的开篇句应该能吸引读者的注意力，并帮助他们对产品或服务有清楚的认识，有意引导他们考虑你的产品或服务。

可以通过下面的方法激发读者的想象力和好奇心。

① “你可以做一些独一无二的事情”，把这句话作为第一句。很少有人会拒绝继续读下去，寻找那些“事情”是指什么。

② 适当的话，提到一个给人们深刻印象的名字，然后建立读者与这个名字的联系。

著名宇航员杨利伟，和你们一样，知道常规眼科检查的重要性。

③ 如果可能，推销信中可以提到当地的人、地方和发生过的事情。

(2) A——**提供产品或服务。**坦率、具体地介绍产品或服务。读者在信的开始已经对产品或服务产生好奇，现在想要满足这种好奇心。首先要为产品或服务做广告。谈谈你要提供的，用具体的名称。如果信的空间允许，提供一至两个具有说服力的例子。

(3) L——**列出客户的获益清单。**能够吸引顾客的是他们得到的利益或产品、服务有什么与众不同，顾客考虑的是你提供的产品或服务是否能满足他们的需求。所以，推销信的这部分要使读者确信在第二自然段中推销的产品/服务是实用的。要利用这次机会证明你的产品或服务能够满足读者广泛的需求。

(4) V——**重视客户可以从中获取的利益**。这时应该解释客户能从你的计划中获得怎样的价值/利益。

(5) E——**表示感谢和善意**。这时应该感谢客户考虑你们的建议，赞扬对方的公司或表达友好的意愿。毕竟，目前为止读者已经随着你的思路浏览了推销信的大部分内容。这些恭维对于你来说可能不必要，但对于读者来说却是极其感兴趣的部分。有时结束语事关重大，可以引发具体的行动。

(6) S——**确切表明客户该做什么、何时做**。最后，以清楚、具体的方式告诉读者需要他们做什么和何时做才能得到前面提到的利益。保持乐观的态度。

具体行动的说明常常包括以下内容。

- 行动方式(电话、出席或访问)；
- 一个具体地址、电话号码、具体时间(目前、将要或以前)；
- 如果读者按照你说的去做了，可能得到最终利益。

通过运用 S-A-L-V-E-S 方法，你一定能撰写出成功的推销信。

学习实践

通过以上介绍的 S-A-L-V-E-S 方法，尝试撰写一封推销信。想一想它是否能满足读者的需求，是一封成功的推销信。

2. 如何使你的推销信看起来丰富多彩和有吸引力

推销信是一种既有效果又有效率的促销产品和服务的途径。但是，多数推销信都被消费者视为垃圾，扔进垃圾桶。其原因有很多。消费者被推销信搞得晕头转向，因为他们不能辨别推销信的目的到底是什么，如何从产品或服务中受益。而且，阅读推销信占用了他们大量的时间。所以，引起他们的关注并维持这种关注是十分重要的。

为什么多数推销信的命运都如此不幸？原因之一是它们令人厌烦、俗气、沉闷的信封。所以设计一个独一无二的信封，抓住消费者的眼球是让消费者关注的重要的第一步。这里有一些句子可以放在信封表面，也许会让消费者打开信封，阅读其内容。

(1) 注意！里面的东西将改变您的命运。

(2) 内附样品。

(3) 里面有最特别的礼物。

也许你很幸运，因为消费者对阅读你的推销信感兴趣，那么你可以继续做一些努力吸引他们的注意力。

(1) 和推销信一起，附上一些小玩意儿。

(2) 提供一些赠品如免费券。每个人都喜欢免费的午餐。

(3) 以特别的内容开头，如问题、轶事或有趣的故事。若你提出问题，多数读者会回答它，并继续阅读推销信的剩余部分。

为了缩小写作者和客户之间的差距，有的人会使用虚伪、晦涩的字词或句子。写作者可能想拉近他们与客户之间的关系，但是事与愿违，因为诚信被丢失，写作者的可信度被

客户怀疑。不要使用一些像“革命性的”“难以置信”或“让人惊骇”之类的词，因为它们听起来过分夸张，会降低你的信用度，甚至会给你们的关系带来负面的影响。

应该注意推销信的长度。一些专家建议推销信应该不超过一页纸。也有一些人认为如果在第一页能够吸引住客户，那么在第三页或第四页就可以成交了。无论客户的观点如何，推销信必须强调能提供给客户的是什么，而不仅仅是产品或服务。一旦清楚、完全地列举出你们所提供的产品/服务及其优势，那么信就可以结束了。

请参考以下案例。

阅读下面来自植物展览公司 Sandra Lanson 的推销信。运用上面提到的建议，思考效果好的推销信的特点。你认为这封信是否有效？为什么？

按照 S-A-L-V-E-S 撰写的推销信

4982 Brooks, Suite 4 Toledo, OH 43606 (419)555-9046

1999 年 4 月 10 日

大卫·詹金斯先生
区域经理
Coleberry 财务服务公司
Wall 大街 324 号
托莱多，俄亥俄州 69587

亲爱的詹金斯先生：

S 你希望午餐后能够将公园——树木、鲜花和灌木带回办公室吗？

A 植物展览公司能够将你的愿望变成现实。我们可以为你们的办公室和接待处开展租赁和维护灿烂的热带植物的业务。每天花费不到两美元，可以让你们置于郁郁葱葱的喜林芋属植物丛中，或者将你掩盖在象草香蒲园中。

L 这些植物会让你们的业务活动变得更加愉快和有效益。

V 客户会欣赏你们的创意，赞美你们的品味，可爱的植物使业务空间变得温暖起来。快乐的客户会消费更多、更频繁。

V 员工的跳槽现象会大幅度地减少。员工会逐渐认为办公室是个有吸引力、有魅力的地方。

E 作为在托莱多名列前茅的财务服务公司，你们的声誉会因在一个健康、有吸引力和令人印象深刻的办公环境上的少量投资而得到进一步提高。

S 现在立刻拨打电话给玛西(555-9049)，可以得到免费的办公室植物装饰分析材料。在你们方便的时候，她会来到办公室，快速完成她的工作，她提供的装饰理念会让你们眼花缭乱。如果你们愿意，随邮件附上我们最新的彩色产品目录。

祝好。

桑德拉 • L.兰斯东

营销总监

附件：“你们的预约单目录”(回邮明信片)

(资料来源：Bell A H, Smith D M. *Management Communication*[M]. New York: Wiley, 2009.)

销售信函清单

一、准备阶段

(1) 尽可能掌握较多的有关产品、竞争对手和消费者的信息。

(2) 选择最能体现产品与众不同的特征作为销售主题。

二、赢得消费者关注

(1) 让销售信函开头简短、有趣、有新意。避免明显的、有误导性的不相关陈述。

(2) 选择以下任何一种方式开头：反问句、发人深省的语句、不寻常事件、当前事件、奇闻轶事、直接挑战或一些类似的吸引方式。

(3) 开头引入核心销售主题。

(4) 如果信函是对客户询问的反馈，首先要对询问表示感谢，然后再介绍核心销售主题。

三、建立顾客对产品的兴趣及购买欲望

(1) 使产品介绍自然而然地接在引人注目的语言之后。

(2) 说明产品功能，而不仅仅是简单地描述产品的特点。向消费者展示他们将如何从每一产品特征中获益。让消费者构想拥有、使用和享受产品的画面。

(3) 使用包括系列行动计划、积极和客观的语言。提供令人信服的证据来支持你的主张，包括具体事实和数据以及单独的产品评论等。

(4) 全文始终强调核心销售主题。

(5) 把价格放在次要位置。用简短措辞、长句或讨论消费者获益的句子来陈述价格。

四、鼓励消费者采取行动

(1) 明确期望消费者采取的且易于实现的行动。

(2) 自信地询问，避免犹豫的表达方式，如“如果您愿意”或者“我希望您同意”。

(3) 鼓励消费者迅速地采取行动。

(4) 以提醒消费者的利益来结束信函。

7.10 撰写有效的备忘录

备忘录是在公司、俱乐部或其他组织内传递信息的一种重要沟通方式。它仅次于电话，在世界范围内大多数的商务活动中，备忘录(不论是通过打印稿还是通过电子邮件传递)是主要的组织内部沟通方式。备忘录包括问询信、评论、回复、公告、政策说明、统计信息、提示、授权及其他日常事务中主要的沟通。

备忘录是一种组织内部的沟通方式，使用的每个单词都有助于建立你在公司内部的身份。虽然并不是每份备忘录都是一张“晋升票”，但你的写作确实会加速或阻碍你的职业发展。在第6章中提到的美国国家写作协会的研究表明，半数以上的美国公司在提拔员工时，会考虑写作技能这个因素。在中国，多数企业在招聘新员工时，要求应聘人员要有较好的沟通能力和技能。这里有一些原则可以帮助你写一份有效和高效的备忘录。

(1) 使用肯定的语句。肯定的语言会产生正面的效果。

(2) 有效的内部沟通包括完整的信息，而不是部分信息。

(3) 无论是简短的内部沟通，还是发往公司外部的较长文件，写作风格和格式都同样重要。

一份备忘录通常是关于一个主题。如果有两个以上主题，就写两个备忘录。并不是所有能说的话都能写成书面形式。就像 memo 这个词本身是 memorandum 的缩写一样，备忘录中的信息应该言简意赅、直奔主题。

备忘录不是寻宝图。不要在备忘录中营造出一种悬念或亲密感而忽视了你的信息。尽量让信息清晰，然后可以添加任何你想添加的社评或个人的评论，以增加备忘录的温暖和亲切感。写给组织内客户的备忘录，应该始终保持一种礼貌的态度。用一些语句如“十分感谢”“很抱歉，我不能……”或“我十分感谢如果……”等。

1. 备忘录的格式

以下是典型的备忘录格式。需要记住的是，备忘录有别于信函，因为它仅仅是在组织内部进行的沟通。

> **备 忘 录**
>
> 写给：大卫·J. 卡普兰，主席
> 来自：拉里·哈斯，公共关系部
> 时间：2016年6月3日
> 主题：五月份植物安全委员会会议
>
> 我们于3月30日召开环境影响委员会会议已经达成一致意见，将在5月12日再次会面。我现在要求双方提供会议议程和会议建议……

2. 总结订单确认函及其他感谢信的结构

订单确认函是为了让订购商品的人知道订单的状况。大部分订单确认函是例行公事，仅仅说明货物何时发运。企业通常接受订单形式，有时也用书面文件形式。订单确认函可以达到建立公司良好信誉的目的。

你写的第一封致谢信可能是求职面试信。你一旦被录用，将会有各种可能需要对别人进行感谢，会谈后发送感谢信，当有人帮助过你或送给你礼物，当别人的努力让你受益匪浅，当你想对客户表示感谢，或者某人捐赠时间或金钱给予你的组织或支持组织的事业时。各种需要发送感谢信的可能很多，发送真诚的感谢信是促进商誉和建立您和您的公司专业形象的很好路径。

撰写订单确认函和感谢信，你可以按照下面的建议。

(1) 采用直截了当的写作方法，首先向读者就某件特定的事情表示感谢。

(2) 继续表示感谢，或者提供进一步的信息。

(3) 运用积极的和智慧的语言说明模糊的订单或延期交货。

(4) 如果可以的话，达到次要目标(如转售或达到相互理解)。

(5) 以与主题相适应的美好祝愿结尾。

本章小结

本章讨论了商务书信中最重要的书面沟通格式和种类。通过选择的文字及其在文中的运用，甚至信头、信笺的选择，你都在向读者树立企业和自己的形象。读者很大程度上是根据信件判定公司是否友好、开放、有效率、有组织性和公平。

对于一些简短的商务沟通形式，如备忘录、执行摘要和电子邮件，你仍然需要遵循一些清楚、准确、有力的职业技巧和方法。你应该记住如下内容。

(1) 并不是所有能说的事情都能写在书面形式的文件里。

(2) 书面沟通中，肯定性语言能够产生正面的效果。

(3) 有效沟通传送的信息是完整的，而不是部分信息。

(4) 写作风格和格式对于简短的内部沟通文件和较长的企业外部沟通文件同样重要。

第8章

提案、报告和商业计划书

【学习目标】

通过对本章内容的学习，你能够：

- 理解提案和商业计划书的重要性。
- 了解提案和商业计划书的组成结构。
- 懂得如何撰写提案、报告和商业计划书。

引例：证据是对商业最好的证明

戴夫·拉温斯基(Dave Lavinsky)是职业咨询公司 Growthink 的联合创始人，建议小企业业主谨慎地撰写商业计划书，因为投资者将根据计划中显示的信息对公司的潜力进行评估。

具体地说，戴夫建议客户在商业计划书中所列举的证据是对公司实力的最佳验证(最好的客户服务，最好的质量)。他建议企业业主在商业计划书中引用第三方研究或提供其他具体证据。例如，如果一家公司认为其产品的市场呈指数级增长，它应该引用一些独立的研究结果来证实这一说法。同样，如果一家公司在商业计划中声称它拥有最优秀的员工，那么该计划应该描述相关人员的资格和经验等细节。

商业计划中提供充分的证据将使公司在投资者眼中显得更加可信，从而增加了公司融资的机会。

(选自：戴夫·拉温斯基.“ 商业计划书的读者再也不相信夸张的宣传.”，商业周刊：小企业，2009 年 3 月 20 日， Http://www.businessweek.com/smallbiz/tips/archives/2009/03/business_plan_r. html.)

引例启示：在工作场所，很多工作都是例行公事，或者是由别人专门指派的。但有时你或你的组织会考虑利用新的发展机会，而且你需要为那项工作写一份建议书。一般来说，提案是专门为那些比常规工作时间更持久或成本更高，与常规工作有很大的不同，或者比常规工作产生更大的变化的项目而创建。在这一章中，我们将学习如何有效地写提案。

提案或者商业计划书为商务人士提供了一个表现出色或创造影响力的绝佳机会。提案或商业计划书的完成需要运用所有的劝说技巧和能力论证有关论点，选用最合适的语言表达清晰、准确的内容。总的来说，为实现有效沟通，只有认真对读者进行分析才能完成令读者满意的提案或商业计划书。

8.1 撰写提案

8.1.1 关于提案

提案以不同的形式呈现，从随意的一页纸的备忘录到多卷册、篇幅达上百页的巨著都需要提案。通常提案是一种文件，由某人、某商业团体或代理机构为执行某项工作或为其他人、商业团体或代理机构解决问题而撰写，目的是为执行的任务筹集资金。尽管提案形式不同，但是所有的提案都有一个共同点：都是为执行某项特别的任务或项目而提出建议和要求。

通常提案是应正式的或非正式的要求(RFP)撰写。政府和基金代理机构经常公布正式提案撰写要求。当资金要投入某项研究或需要执行某项任务时，就会公布正式提案撰写要求。正式的 RFP 对已完成的提案提出一些指导方针，告诉撰写人提案书应该包括哪些内容，有时还会规定提案的格式。提案撰写人按照其要求，填写详细内容及项目的费用。遗憾的是，不少有价值的提案没有被通过，原因是撰写人没有遵循有关机构的 RFP 撰写。

提案不同于撰写其他商务性和技术性写作的重要之处，是提案处理的是未来的事情和目前不存在的事情和条件。撰写不存在的事情是比较棘手的，撰写提案面临的更为复杂的困难是提案必须让人信服。提案必须让读者确信有情况需要关注或有问题需要解决，而提案撰写人正是解决这些问题或改变这种局势的最佳人选。最后，撰写人必须面对的是，提案常常是有法律约束力的。

提案有以下特征。

(1) 提案应对未来。

(2) 提案必须说服读者有问题存在，而撰写人能够对存在的问题做些什么。

(3) 提案必须说服读者撰写人是解决问题的最佳人选。

(4) 提案的长短和形式多样化。

(5) 提案经常是有法律约束力的。

(6) 提案一般有下列四种类型：研究性提案、研究与发展性提案、计划性提案、销售性提案。

8.1.2　项目提案

主动提供的提案与征求所得的提案不同，前者通常需要更多的背景信息且更具说服力。由于读者可能不熟悉该项目，撰写人必须提出更多的证据来让读者确信提案的优势。

提案读者通常是组织外人士，这些外部文件格式可以是由征求提案组织提供的一封信件报告、一篇手稿报告，甚至是一份模板报告。如果征求提案组织不提供撰写模板，它将极有可能对提案所需格式作详细的文字说明。

撰写提案时，撰写者需要谨记该提案对撰写者本人和组织具有法律约束力。当提案准确地写出组织将要提供的产品、时间、条件和价格时，它也包含了合同的因素。如果提案被接受，会对组织产生约束作用。

提案是具有说服力的文件，你所学的所有关于说服的技巧在这里同样适用。

(1) 为陈述提供充足、可靠的证据。

(2) 不夸大其辞。

(3) 提供案例、专家声明以及具体事实和数据来支持你的观点。

(4) 使用简单、直白、直接的语言，建议使用简单的句子和主动语态。

(5) 强调读者利益。谨记你在提请求，通常是金钱上的承诺；让读者明白他(她)的回报是什么。

很明显，仅仅有好的想法是不够的。必须清晰又令人信服地呈现想法，这样才能被接受。清晰且令人信服的写作带来的好处远远超出了本项目获得批准的直接目标。一份很棒的提案可以提升你在读者及你所代表的组织中的知名度和可信度。

尽管提案在长度、结构、复杂性和形式上各不相同，但是下列内容是比较典型的。

(1) 背景。介绍正在讨论的问题并探讨为何此问题值得读者深思，提供足够的背景信息说明存在的问题以及可行的解决方案。

(2) 目标。提供详细的有关项目结果的具体信息，详实地讨论读者的付出将有什么回报。

(3) 过程。详细讨论将如何实现这些目标，包括循序渐进地讨论要做什么、什么时间做以及每一部分或者每一阶段的确切花费。

(4) 资质。表明个人、组织及其他参与项目的人均有资质参与该项目。如果可能的话，使用证书或者其他外部证据来支持你的说法。

(5) 申请批准。直接请求批准提案，根据读者的需要，这个请求可以放在提案开始或者结尾。

(6) 支持数据。作为提案附录，补充可能会支持你的论点的相关信息。

学习实践

阅读下面的案例并思考理查德·福尔切尔(Richard Fulscher)提出的读者询问的基本问题：我为什么要聘任你而不是你的竞争对手？你会完成任务吗？

有效的商业计划书采用容易理解的格式撰写所有适合的组成内容。为新业务撰写商业计划书经常被看作是获得面谈机会的必要的苦差事。但是，出色的商业计划书是极好的营销武器，它关注的是团队对项目的说明，把你们和平庸的公司区分开来。

我浏览过大量的管理/租赁提案。它们大多犯有以下同样的错误。

- 信息太有限。只提供含报价内容的小册子。
- 低劣的写作。你饶有兴趣地去阅读，但是读过一遍后，感觉会很厌烦。
- 缺少营销重点。试图告诉所有的人所有的事，但是事实恰恰相反。
- 内容太概括，以自我为中心。关注公司，而没有提到客户的需要和期望。
- 结论过于匆忙。提供一些微不足道的解决方法和一大堆材料，但没有可获得结果的看法。
- 没有“推销”。只提供信息，而不是为公司提供有说服力的论据。

客户需要根据提案在公司之间进行比较，反思他们的选择，比较问题的解决办法。提案要使人信服，让人感觉有实现目标的保证并给人留下深刻印象。你需要在提案中表达对问题的理解、解决的办法并证明你的能力。简而言之，客户的要求是被销售出去。他们要求最基本的问题得到回答：“我为什么要聘用你，而不选你的竞争对手，你能完成任务吗？”出色的提案运用适当的格式提供这些甚至更多的信息。

(资料来源：Fulscher R J. A no-fail recipe: Winning business proposals[J]. *Journal of Property Management*, 1996, 1-2(61): 62.

看看下面的例子，它是一份寻求组织赞助研讨会的提案。

亲爱的索尔女士：

主题：关于商务写作的内部研讨会的提案

我很开心能够和您讨论关于您为 Everglades National Corporation 的工程师的商务写作研讨会提供赞助之事。如您要求，此次提案计划安排两天的研讨会。

开门见山地表明本次通信的目的

一、背景

9 月 4～5 日，我采访了您组织内部的四位工程师并分析了他们的写作样本，他们是训练有素的专业人员，他们深知自己想要表达什么，但有时并不能以最有效的写作方式表达想法……

因此我提议您赞助一场为期两天的“商务写作过程”的研讨会，我将负责组织研讨会。

二、目标

研讨会将有助于工程师们实现这些目标。

(1) 详细说明信息目的并进行读者分析。

(2) 决定写作中应包含的信息及这些内容以怎样的顺序表达。

……

三、程序

随即附上的大纲说明了课程覆盖的范围。研讨会需要有桌椅的会议室、投影仪、黑板或其他书写板面。

两天研讨会的教学费是 2000 美元，外加其他开销。

四、资质

您从所附的数据表中可以看出，我有 15 年的商务沟通经验，口头和书面沟通经验丰富。

五、总结

与工程师们合作的经验告诉我，他们了解有效商务沟通的价值并有积极提升自身的写作技巧的动力。

美好的祝福！

举例说明培训需求的存在

提出可行的建议

具体说明如何实施计划

提供充分的细节，让读者了解计划内容

以开放、自信的口吻商讨费用

只强调来自所附数据表的最相关信息

说明读者如果按照要求做将如何得益

以友好、自信的语调结尾

8.2 撰写报告

8.2.1 报告的定义

有些人认为报告几乎包括任何呈现信息的写作形式，也有人认为最正式的呈现信息的写作形式才可以称之为报告。我们使用处于这两者中间的定义：商业报告是服务于某种商业目的，且对真实信息进行有序而客观的阐述的沟通方式。

我们要认真准备作为有序沟通媒介的报告。因此，需要精心的准备使报告有别于非正式信息的交流。报告的客观性表现为它的无偏见性。报告试图陈述事实，尽可能避免人为的偏见。在我们的定义中，沟通具有广泛的含义。它包含了传播信息的所有方式：说、写及使用图形。报告的基本要素是真实信息，真实信息基于事件、统计数据和其他资料。并不是所有报告都是商业报告，研发科学家、医生、学生和其他人都可以撰写报告。

8.2.2 简短报告

1. 报告的内外环境与目的

简短报告通常不足十页纸，可以一口气读完。任何规模的商业组织都通过这些文件了解两个环境中正在发生的事情、已经发生的或者将要发生的事情。

(1) 内部环境。员工在做什么？做得如何？使用了哪些资源，或者需要什么资源？公司以何种方式扩张或收缩？需要解决什么问题？

(2) 外部环境。客户和公众对公司的认知是怎样的？客户想要从公司得到什么？公司的竞争对手有哪些？如何面对与它们的交锋？

这些问题通过公司内部所有的沟通渠道进行讨论，包括会议、面谈、备忘录和信件。然而，报告会更全面地解决问题，而且比其他形式的商务沟通更正式。

撰写报告的目的可能是告知性的(关于主题的信息)、分析性的(为什么环境已经发展)、说服性的(读者将如何回应)，或者三者相结合的。简短的报告是用来做决定的，所以它包括足够的证据来支持报告中提出的建议。尽管简短报告可以参考其他书面文档，但是不应该只是相对杂乱无章的事实和数字的堆砌。

2. 撰写简短报告的十个步骤

第一步：思考 W-O-R-M。

W(谁/什么)——谁会读这份报告？他们感兴趣的是什么？他们有什么需求？

O(目标)——报告的目标是什么？

R(范围)——报告的范围有多大？描述主题的范围如何？你想解释事实吗？

M(方法)——报告中所用的陈述方法是什么？

第二步：了解读者想要什么，报告撰写者有责任了解读者想要什么。

第三步：头脑风暴式地讨论主题。

第四步：研究报告主题。一旦开始考虑主题，应该知道从堆在桌子上的报告和文件中寻找相关信息。

第五步：整理主要观点。不仅考虑你想要说什么，还要把将每一个部分安排在适当的位置。

第六步：写草稿。

第七步：修改草稿。

第八步：复查草稿的外表形式。

第九步：准备最终文稿。

第十步：有利地呈现报告。

8.2.3 长篇报告

考虑长篇报告的组成要素，首先它通常包含多张被称为“前页”的文前页——标题页、授权书和过渡内容，目录、有时甚至是前言和序，通常是摘要和执行摘要。长篇报告的正文通常是 15 页甚至更多，内容包括附录、法律文书(如果有的话)、尾注、参考书目，也许

还有词汇表和索引。商业长篇报告很少低于 20 页，大多数是相当长的。

在许多方面，长篇报告是简短报告的加长版。可翻阅前边的章节复习简短报告的组成要素。然而，长篇报告很少有长度限制，很容易偏题或者让读者困惑。因此，使长篇报告清晰、可读是非常重要的，尤其要注意段落开头和结尾，利用段落开头和结尾提供摘要、总结及有益的过渡内容。读者不需要费力地读很多句子才能理解信息及其是如何与上下文相联系的。

遵循在之前章节学习到的关于写作风格的建议，并且避免下述的“商务写作的十大致命弊病”。

商务写作的十大致命弊病

1. 没有活力的动词(is, are, were, seems to be)

避免使用：激励创造性思考者是本公司的政策。

替换：本公司促进创造性思考者的发展。

2. 无效动词(被动结构)

避免使用：该账户被处理时十分不仔细。

替换：杰克处理账户时十分粗心。

3. 重点位置不突出

避免使用：这里有两个符合我们需要的金融软件包。

替换：两个金融软件包符合我们的需要。

4. 延长句子长度

避免使用：尽管我们公司中七名公司中层经理反对公司搬办公室的想法，但公司大部分高级职员乐意搬办公室，因为这是一个他们可以生活在阳光地带的机会。

替换：七名中层经理反对我们公司办公室的搬迁。不过，我们的高级职员欢迎这一举措，因为这是一个让他们生活在阳光地带的机会。

5. 名词过度使用

避免使用：公司的统一将有利于建立更有利于偿付能力和盈利能力的安排。

替换：并购公司有助于我们解决钱的问题。

6. 缓慢叠加句子

尝试把主谓宾句型和其他句型混在一起。

例如：令人沮丧的是，杰克写了一份苛刻的备忘录。(-ed 位于主语之前)

7. 段落冗杂

尝试“简单地开始和简单地结束”，在商务信函、备忘录及短篇报告的开头和结尾使用十分简短的段落。

8. 名词堆砌

避免使用：请撰写一篇少数民族发展机会的评估报告。

替换：请撰写一份报告，对少数民族的发展机会进行评估。

9. 间歇性重复

避免使用：我们收到了福利套餐。福利套餐提供了……

替换：我们收到的福利套餐提供了……

10. 有感染力的介词

避免使用：五月份我们在行业杂志上为招聘一位威斯康星子公司的销售部经理刊登了一则广告。

替换：“销售经理”“威斯康星子公司”(将介词短语改为名词/形容词组合的形式)

(资料来源：Source:Bell A H. Nation’s Business, 1984, (11))

8.3 如何撰写商业计划书

8.3.1 商业计划书的重要性

洛杉矶第一商业银行的总裁罗伯特·克鲁莫(Robert Krummer, Jr)说过：“商业计划书是必要的。如果一个人想创建一个小企业但不能写出商业计划书，他/她就会有麻烦。”

为了确定各种各样的危机和潜在的风险：技术风险、市场风险、管理风险、竞争和战略风险和财务风险，商业计划书就成为未来投资者开始尽职调查的出发点。

创业者和投资者试图通过各种会议和讨论为他们的关系和谈判进行定位。各方都在不断思考的问题如下。

- 这些人聪明吗？
- 在这段时间里我们会合作愉快吗？
- 他们能够使企业增值吗？
- 他们有理想的管理团队吗？
- 他们诚实吗？

最有价值的投资者将看到市场如何看待技术或服务、战略、融资和团队的规模及结构方面的弱点甚至是缺陷。他们通过展示自己，为企业带来最深刻的洞察力和专业知识，并为企业带来巨大的价值。

8.3.2 计划不是生意

为一个新的企业描述蓝图、战略、资源和人力资源需求，最好的办法之一是制订一个商业计划。在全球 500 家成长最快的公司中，绝大多数公司一开始就制订了商业计划。没有商业计划，很难从正式的或非正式的投资者那里筹集到资金。

但是计划并不意味着生意。很多给人印象深刻的计划书成就不了一笔大生意，而一些低劣的商业计划反而可能会引来一笔大生意。拥有计划并不意味着生意成功，除非基本的条件已经成熟，加上必要的资源和团队；否则，世界上最好的计划书也没有什么不同。另一方面，商业计划书被认为是一项过程中的工作。计划是个过程，不仅仅是一份计划。商业计划书很难考虑周全，因为计划将受到内部或外部环境的各种变化因素的影响，如资金、人力资源、技术、潜在的危机和机会等。

图 8.1 表明商业计划书仅仅是商业活动过程中的一部分。可以思考一下商业计划书本身的优势和不足，通过内容来判断计划的价值。如果将计划书作为整个过程的一部分，计划书会变得更有价值，因为任何一个出色的计划书如果没有人去实现它，都会是一种浪费。

计划是一个过程，而不仅仅是计划本身。

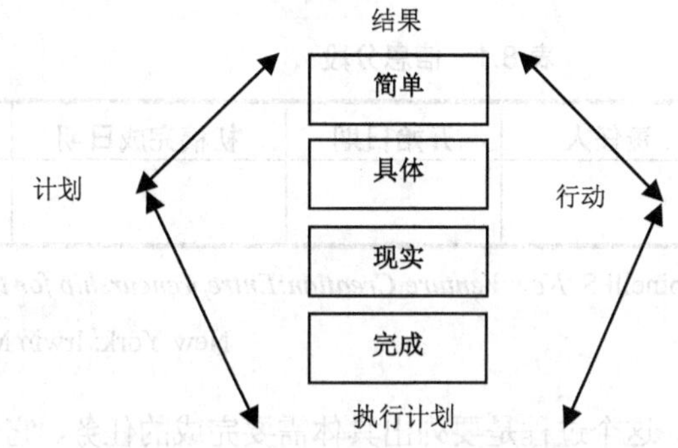

图 8.1　计划过程

8.3.3　准备商业计划书

尽管商业计划书很重要，但是一些企业家在着手撰写文件时仍然行动缓慢。他们认为市场变化太快，以至于商业计划书派不上用场或他们没有时间写计划书。但就像建筑工人没有图纸无法建造大楼一样，满腔热情的生意人没有商业计划书无法开启新的事业。

在准备撰写商业计划书前，务必考虑四个主要问题。

- 你能提供何种产品/服务，能满足什么需要？
- 产品/服务的潜在消费者是谁？他们为什么要从你这里购买产品/服务？
- 如何赢得潜在的消费者？
- 从哪里得到资金开始你的商业活动？

制订商业计划书的团队应该确信他们计划的业务有着极好的市场前景，并且团队拥有实现计划需要的技能、经验、个人目标和价值观。同时，还应该清楚在企业运行过程中会面临的一些最重大的风险和问题、长期受益前景、未来财务和现金流的要求，也要了解运作的时间期限、季节性和设备的位置、营销与价格战略。

1. 分类与整合信息

采用便于管理和有利于写作构思的组织信息的方法是制订有效计划和完成写作的必要一步。按照制订计划的思路，组织信息的一个有效方法是将信息分成不同的部分，例如，一部分关于目标市场，一部分关于行业，一部分关于财务计划等。

每个部分撰写的顺序有所不同，但是有些部分可以同时涉及。例如，一份计划的核心内容是关于市场机遇、竞争和利基市场中取胜的竞争战略的分析，那么，从这部分入手整合信息是明智的选择。而增长率和市场收益计划的主要具体内容会影响企业的财务和实际运营，这部分内容可在后文提到。

2. 采取行动的步骤

撰写计划书时可考虑如下建议。

步骤一：信息分段(见表 8.1)。需要设计一个项目的总体方案，包括优先级、每部分的责任人、计划书初稿完成日期、终稿完成日期。在进行信息分段时，要记住：计划每部分内容的安排要有逻辑性，信息要有连续性。最好是优先考虑市场机会的分析，然后从这里入手，因为这部分内容对整个计划意义重大。

表 8.1　信息分段

部分任务	优先级	责任人	开始日期	初稿完成日期	终稿完成日期

(资料来源：Timmons J A, Spinelli S. *New Venture Creation:Entrepreneurship for the 21st Century*[M]. New York: Irwin McGraw-Hill, 2003.)

步骤二：设计整体进度表。这个过程是要列出具体需要完成的任务、它们的优先级、谁为这项任务负责、何时开始、何时结束。将比较大的项目分解成小的、便于管理的部分，这些小的部分也被视为一种任务，这样有助于整个计划的完成。目录必须尽可能具体、详细，检查环节必不可少，可以发现是否有矛盾的内容，是否对时间的估计符合实际。

步骤三：设计行动日历表(见表 8.2)。这是将分段表与任务表进行整合而设计的一个行动日历表。将这两者进行整合设计行动日历表时，要注意一下是否有什么遗漏，是否已经确定什么人能做什么、何时可以做以及需要做什么。

表 8.2　行动日历表

任　务	周　数								
	1	2	3	4	5	6	7	8	9

(资料来源：Timmons J A, Spinelli S. *New Venture Creation: Entrepreneurship for the 21st Century*[M]. New York: Irwin McGraw-Hill, 2003.)

步骤四：撰写计划书。在撰写计划书的过程中，需要对项目单和日历表进行调整。此过程中需要律师(代理人)对计划进行审查，其目的是确保计划书中不存在让人误解的内容及不必要的信息和说明，而且此计划应由一个客观的局外人进行审查。

8.3.4　撰写商业计划书

撰写计划书时应该记住：虽然计划书的重要功能之一是影响投资者，而不是准备一个特别的演讲，你和你的团队仍然需要向自己和其他人证明计划本身的价值，并提出实施计划的办法。首先要从收集信息、做出各种决策、制订计划开始。在计划中简要描述要实现的目标、预计的成本、营销计划和退出市场战略。商业计划书是路线图，说明如何才能成功和如何衡量成功。

以下是一份商业计划书提纲。仔细阅读大纲的内容，会对制订计划有所帮助。这种模板在最初撰写商业计划书时可以节省时间，因为它直接涉及商业计划书应该包括的主要元素。在我们变得更加自信后，可以调整和改变模板里的一些内容。

完整商业计划提纲

Ⅰ. 执行摘要

A. 对商业概念和商业的描述

B. 机遇和战略

C. 目标市场及方案

D. 竞争优势

E. 经济、利益和潜在的收益

F. 团队

G. 贡献

Ⅱ. 行业和企业与其产品或服务

A. 行业

B. 企业及其概念

C. 产品和服务

D. 进入行业和增长

Ⅲ. 市场研究与分析

A. 客户

B. 市场规模与趋势

C. 竞争和竞争优势

D. 预计市场份额和销售情况

E. 目前市场评估

Ⅳ. 商业的经济形势

A. 毛利润及营运利润

B. 潜在的利润及其持久性

C. 固定成本、可变成本和半可变成本

D. 损益平衡需要的时间(月份数)

E. 研究正现金流时间(月份数)

Ⅴ. 营销计划

A. 总营销战略

B. 价格

C. 销售策略

D. 服务和保障政策
E. 广告与促销
F. 分销

Ⅵ. 设计发展计划

A. 发展状况及任务
B. 困难与风险
C. 产品的发展及更新
D. 成本
E. 专利问题

Ⅶ. 生产及运营计划

A. 运行周期
B. 地理位置
C. 设备和改进
D. 战略和计划
E. 监管和法律问题

Ⅷ. 管理团队

A. 机构
B. 主要管理人员
C. 管理层报酬和所有权
D. 其他投资者
E. 雇用及其他协议、股票期权及分红计划
F. 董事会
G. 其他股东，权利和约束
H. 给予支持的职业顾问和服务

Ⅸ. 总进度表

Ⅹ. 关键风险、问题和假设

Ⅺ. 财务计划

A. 实际损益表和资产负债表
B. 副损益表
C. 副资产负债表
D. 副现金流分析
E. 盈亏平衡分析图和计算
F. 成本控制
G. 突出部分

Ⅻ. 建议公司所能提供的支持

A. 财务要求
B. 提供内容
C. 资本

D. 资金的使用

E. 投资回报

XIII. 附录

（资料来源：Timmons J A, Spinelli S. *New Venture Creation: Entrepreneurship for the 21st Century*[M]. NewYork: Irwin McGraw-Hill, 2003.）

现在可以探讨商业计划书中各个重要部分的特点。运用本书前面章节中学到的商务沟通知识和技巧，撰写内容要尽量清楚、简洁、语气适当、具有说服力。总的来说，如果你不能清楚地表达你要做什么，如果你不能回答读者所能想到的所有问题，你的计划就不够全面和彻底。

1. 执行摘要

商业计划书正文中的第一部分通常是执行摘要。摘要内容简短，大约只有一至两页。摘要是对机遇情况的说明，解释机遇为什么存在，谁将实现这个机会，他们为什么能够这样做以及公司如何成功进入行业并进行市场渗透。

摘要对于那些想筹集或借资金发展业务的企业而言是很重要的。很多投资者、银行家、管理者通过关注摘要内容迅速判断投资计划所描述的是否有利可图。所以，除非整个计划很吸引人，否则摘要有可能是整个计划书唯一被阅读的部分。你很有可能没有亲自介绍或讨论商业计划的机会。

我们建议要特别关注摘要内容。它一般包括以下几个细节。

(1) 对商业概念和商业的描述。例如，Outdoor Scene 公司准备生产帐篷。公司业务概念是“成为提供高质量服务和准时交货的户外休闲产品的领头羊”。对概念的描述只用 25 个单词或更少。

(2) 机遇和战略。简要说明机遇是什么，抓住机遇所运用的战略是什么。其内容包括主要事实、状况、竞争者的弱点、行业发展趋势及其他界定机遇的事实和逻辑。

(3) 目标市场及方案。明确和简要说明行业和市场的情况，主要的客户群是谁，产品/服务如何定位，如何满足和服务这些客户群。需要提供的信息有：市场结构、细分市场的规模及增长率或你们瞄准的商机、预计的市场份额、客户的偿还期和价格策略。

下面内容对商业计划内容进行了概述，包括产业、公司和提供的产品和服务。

2. 行业、企业与其产品或服务

通常这部分有三个方面要考虑：行业、企业及其产品/服务。对于行业，简单描述将要运营业务在整个行业中目前的状态和前景。计划中要讨论市场规模、增长趋势和竞争对手、新产品、新进入市场和退出市场的企业以及其他任何可能对企业业务产生积极或消极影响的趋势和因素。

至于产品或服务，介绍将要出售的产品或服务的详细情况以及产品或服务的应用。要重点强调产品/服务的独一无二的特点及其如何创造或增加显著的价值。也要突出表明目前市场上的产品/服务与你将要提供的有何差异。

正如我们前面提到的，市场分析是整个计划中最重要的部分。正是通过这个部分让读者相信你有取得成功的机会。

3. 市场研究与分析

因为市场分析不仅重要而且是计划中其他内容的基础，所以建议从这部分内容开始做准备。这部分内容主要包括以下方面。

(1) 客户。要研究产品/服务的目标客户和潜在客户，说明每个细分市场中主要的购买者是谁、在哪里、是否容易赢得消费者。如果目前已有了发展较好的业务，谈一谈目前的客户并讨论新产品/服务的销售趋势。

(2) 市场规模与趋势。解释目前市场的总规模，未来五年内你们在细分市场或地区市场中拥有的市场份额，来描述未来三年内产品/服务在总市场中潜在年增长率，并回顾先前市场发展走向。其他影响市场份额增长的主要因素也要提及，如行业趋势、政府政策等。

(3) 竞争和竞争优势。指出目前市场中主要竞争对手是谁，确定竞争对手的长处和不足，进行以市场份额、质量、价格、性能、交货时间和其他有关特点为基础的竞争性和替代性产品的比较。重点讨论几个主要竞争对手的情况，为什么消费者从他们那里购买产品/服务，为什么消费者又离开他们。

同时也需要根据客户和竞争对手得到的经济利益，讨论说明你提供的产品/服务目前的优势、劣势及与其他同类产品的差异，以及你的产品/服务创造出的附加价值。解释说明为什么你认为竞争对手是脆弱的，以及你能够在他们的生意中获取一部分份额的原因。

计划中也应该提到财务因素，如财务状况、资源、成本、盈利能力及利润趋势。

(4) 预计市场份额和销售情况。确定将要购买或已经购买产品/服务的主要客户群，讨论未来几年哪些客户会成为产品/服务的主要消费者及原因。根据对产品/服务的优势、市场规模和发展趋势、客户、竞争对手和他们的产品及近几年销售的趋势的分析评估，预测未来三年内，市场份额、单位销售额以及需要的资金。

(5) 目前市场评估。为了评定客户的需求，指导产品改进、新产品开发，制订生产设备发展计划，并指导产品/服务价格，阐述你们将指导如何继续评估目标市场。

4. 营销计划

营销计划是解释如何实现销售预测，包括总的营销战略、价格、分销、促销、广告策略和销售预测。重点是说明将要做什么、如何做、何时做及由谁来做。

(1) 总营销战略。描述具体的营销理念和公司战略，说明在竞争激烈的市场中你们追求的价值链和分销渠道，指出产品/服务是在国际上、国内还是地区进行推广及这样做的原因。必须说明未来营销计划，如计划从与政府的合约中得到对产品开发成本及日常开支的支持。

(2) 价格策略。讨论价格策略，包括产品/服务的价格，比较竞争对手的价格策略。解释产品定价是如何让产品/服务被接受，面对激烈的竞争和产品利润，如何维持和增加市场份额，以及如何盈利。

通过新颖、质量、质保、及时和性能等给消费者带来经济回报和附加价值，证明价格策略及其与竞争性或替代性产品/服务的价格差异是合理的。

解释价格策略，说明它表达了价格、市场份额和利润之间的关系，包括即时付款或批量购买得到折扣的承诺。

(3) 销售策略。销售和分销产品/服务使用的方法，包括销售团队的初始计划和长期计划。价值链和给予零售商、分销商、批发商、推销员的利润及任何有关折扣的具体政策也

是十分重要的，同样要说明如何建立直销团队及建立的比率。如果运用其他媒介，像邮件、杂志、报纸、社交媒体或按商品目录销售，指出具体的销售渠道或工具、成本和通过不同媒介的营销策略期望得到的回报率。

(4) 广告与促销。说明企业将产品/服务送达客户使用的渠道。对于销售产品，要指出预计通过什么类型的广告和促销手段推销产品，以及将使用何种辅助销售手段；介绍活动进度表及促销和广告的大约成本，并说明这些成本是如何产生的。

5. 设计发展计划

接下来是设计发展计划。即产品/服务提供给客户前，对有关设计、开发工作、需要的时间和资金的详细说明。这种设计和开发工作有可能是一些必要的工程工作，如从实验室原型到最终成品的完成、特别工具的设计、员工的选拔和管理、实现服务业务的设备和特别的技术。

发展计划中的“发展”是指目前产品/服务的状况，指出如何改进产品使其适合市场需求，也要说明公司拥有完成发展所需要的能力或专长。同时，解释说明目前能够维持产品/服务的竞争力和维持客户对产品的忠诚度的设计和发展工作。

通过发展计划简要说明已经采取何种步骤去发展业务，以及需要去做的事。发展计划的步骤可以包括以下内容。

(1) 产品/服务如何生产？介绍产品/服务的生产流程。

(2) 产品/服务在开发过程中会出现什么问题？为确保问题被及时发现，这些问题是否已经被列举出？

(3) 谁是供应商？如果一家供货商停止供货，还有其他选择吗？其他供应商的价格、条款和条件是什么？

(4) 采用什么质量控制标准？

6. 生产与运营计划

不论是哪种业务类型，都需要经过产品生产或提供服务的过程。生产与运营计划是对产品生产和服务提供过程的说明。它主要包含以下内容。

(1) 业务的基本要求是什么？考虑土地、设备和办公场所等。如果已经拥有或需要土地、厂房、设备，应该说明其价值或成本，如何融资(如购买或租借)，以及这些因素对业务成功起重要作用的原因。

(2) 何时开始生产产品、提供服务？生产一单产品或一批产品需要多长时间？

(3) 提供产品或服务所需的原材料从何而来？费用多少？和供应商已经洽谈好条件了吗？

(4) 影响生产进度的因素有哪些(如紧急订单、原料短缺)？

(5) 是自制还是购买生产产品和提供服务所必需的材料？为什么？

(6) 如何应对产品或服务的需求波动？是否已经对产品进行了可行性测试(如产品生产过程、产品原型、定价测试)？

7. 管理团队

这部分包括公司的基本信息，公司有多少职员，多少管理人员，其中多少管理者是公司的创始人。你们的团队完善吗？或还有空缺吗？公司结构健全吗？核心成员的岗位描述和职责明确吗？

1) 说明公司结构

公司的组织结构即组织结构图。如果已经有了公司结构图，那么它对企业运转会起到一些积极的作用。如果没有组织结构图，可以用文字描述组织的结构情况。

要清楚地说明岗位的描述情况及公司的主要功能是如何划分的。公司的结构清晰吗？权利分配合理吗？是否包括只有责任没有权利的工作？你们的资源满足组织的需求吗？

2) 列出团队成员及其背景

列出管理团队最重要的成员，以简历的形式描述他们的背景、经历，描述他们在公司的职能。简历附在计划的后面。

3) 讨论管理缺陷

可能管理中有明显的不足，特别是创立不久的公司，但是一些创建时间较长的公司也存在这个问题。例如，对于制造企业，如果没有生产经理就说明管理上存在问题；不能提供服务的计算机公司也会有管理上的问题。要知道界定并明确管理上的不足比假装其不存在要好得多。详细列出因为关键管理职能上的缺陷而导致的团队的弱点。这些不足如何改进？重要的差距如何填补？

4) 管理团队需要考虑的其他情况

适应性取决于公司。应回答下列问题：管理者或职员有“非竞争”协议吗？谁是董事会成员？他们做出了什么贡献？大股东是谁？他们在管理中的角色是怎样的？

8. 关键风险、问题和假设

所有业务都有一定程度的风险，重要的是能够认真思考，列出可能出现的风险。列举出的风险表明你已经意识到风险及能够补救的风险范围。详细写出将如何减少或处理一些固有的风险。记住撰写商业计划书最重要的原因是：它是帮助你开始并管理业务的一个重要工具。随时做到囊括你的商业计划书中各个阶段的所有可能被识别的风险，并确保阅读你的商业计划书的人能够明确地了解这些风险的内容。例如，可以讨论人力资源风险，如找不到技术熟练的工人。坦诚、认真地对待风险，因为预先考虑可以避免许多问题。

考虑以下问题。

(1) 你所在的行业可能存在的风险有哪些？

(2) 如何面对产品或服务需求的下降？

(3) 如何面对竞争者数量的增加？

(4) 产品和服务生产过程中面临哪些风险？

(5) 营销计划中存在哪些风险？

(6) 面临的人力资源风险有哪些？考虑管理团队、顾问和职员。

(7) 如果核心职员辞职怎么办？

(8) 现金短缺怎么办？还有其他策略吗？

(9) 主供应商遇到财务困难怎么办？还有哪些其他供应商？

(10) 产品和服务会有哪些环境风险？它们是否遵守政府、市政府的有关环境方面的规定？

9. 财务计划

财务计划是评估投资机会的基础，需要体现对财务需求最好的估计。财务计划的目的是表明公司的潜力，展示财务计划可行性的时间表。它同时应用财务标杆作为财务管理的运营计划。

1) 损益表

损益表表明一定时期内公司的利润或亏损，包括所有收入、费用和其他成本。和现金流量表一样，每月或每季度出表以便对任何变化做预先管理。现金流量表用于监控业务的现金状况，而损益表是衡量业务绩效的主要财务工具。

想一想企业何时可以达到损益平衡，即在销售量或销售额上总收益与总成本相等。

2) 现金流量表

有句老话“现金为王”千真万确。一言以蔽之，没有现金，业务无法运转。现金流量表是在特定的时间点业务现金量的反应。如果现金流入(收入)高于现金流出(支出)，现金流量为正。如果现金流出(支出)超过现金流入(收入)，则现金流量为负。在准备损益表和现金流量表时，避免以下常见错误。

(1) 过分乐观预测销售增长——大多数的业务增长缓慢。

(2) 忽视了周期性——业务是夏天最忙还是冬天最忙？

(3) 低估随着销售的增长而产生的费用的增长或现金流出。

(4) 假设回款通常发生在30～60天内。

3) 资产负债表

资产负债表是某一特定时间点公司的财务状况，它概括了公司资产、负债和权益，帮助了解业务净值。资产负债表应列出流动资产，如应收账款、存货和现金余额。同时应列出固定资产，如所有物、设备、家具、固定设施和车辆。

流动负债包括应付账款和一年内应付的债务(供应商或债权人)。长期债务包括长期贷款，如抵押、设备贷款或业务贷款。股东的权益由投入业务的固定资金或某人以物主身份进行的业务投资(股本)和留存收益组成。

以下是撰写成功的商务计划书的指导性建议。

不要做的事

(1) 在管理团队中不要出现没有名字的、神秘的人。

(2) 不要出现不明确的、含糊的或毫无根据的陈述说明。

(3) 描述技术产品或制造程序时不要用一些只有专家才能懂的行话，因为这样会限制计划的有效性。

(4) 不要花经费去制作奇异的小册子和精美的演示幻灯片，不要喧宾夺主。

(5) 能够完成销售任务和收回现金时，不要再浪费时间去写计划。

(6) 已经谈妥或有了口头承诺但是账户里还没有钱时，不要假设已经成交了。

建议做的事

(1) 让所有的管理人员参与到商业计划书的准备工作中。

(2) 计划要合乎逻辑、信息全面和通俗易读，尽量言简意赅。

(3) 明确说明关键风险和假设，并说明为什么及如何承受这些风险。

(4) 明确几种可供选择的资金来源。

(5) 清楚说明被提议的交易，物主将如何受益，投资者将如何盈利。

(6) 对那些可以赢得潜在投资者的关注和兴趣的内容要有创造性思维。

(7) 切记：计划不是生意，一盎司“可以做”计划的执行是价值两磅的计划。

(8) 接受能够产生正现金流量的订单和客户，即使那意味着不得不推迟撰写计划书。

(9) 了解目标投资群，了解他们真正需要的和不喜欢的。根据他们的喜好相应地设计计划。

(资料来源：Timmons J A, Spinelli S. *New Venture Creation:Entrepreneurship for the 21st Century*[M]. New York: Irwin McGraw-Hill, 2003.)

学习实践

这里有一份来自 Moot Corp Competition 公司撰写的市场及市场战略文书样本。将这份市场战略文书与本章前面描述的商业计划书的要素进行比较，学习并思考商业计划书中的每个部分所起的作用，当撰写商业计划书时，这些内容将有助于你拓展思路发展自己的战略。

可以访问网站 www.businessplans.org 或者 www.plans.com ，查看更多有效的商业计划书样本。

本 章 小 结

提案采用的是看似能够满足顾客需求的表达方式。有时，顾客对自己的需求不是很清楚，在这种情况下，提案不仅要提出解决办法，而且要描述存在的问题。

商业计划书，更多的是表达一种过程和工作的进展，而不仅仅是计划书本身。商业计划书是一个蓝图和旅行的飞行计划，它能够把想法转化为机遇，清晰地表达和管理风险与对应的收益，而且说明了适合进行风险投资的时机。计划书回答了几个问题：什么、谁、哪里、为什么、何时和多少。但是，计划书并不意味着商业活动，事实上，多数成功的投资活动在实施中没有计划书可以参照，或者参照的也是被认为说服性不强或有缺陷的计划书。这并不能说明计划书是没有用的。计划书对于撰写人来说至少是迫使他们进行适当计划的动力。在撰写商业计划书时，要避免出现下面的问题。

(1) 计划书太长。最好是简洁明了。

(2) 用极少的事实向潜在的消费者证明商务计划书是有价值的。

(3) 没有充分地评估竞争。

(4) 销售期望值和预测是不合理的。

(5) 计划书展示了极少的运营知识。

(6) 财务预算与财务说明中的数据不符。

(7) 商务计划书没有向投资者提供可行的退出市场计划。

参 考 文 献

[1] 马忠宪. 商务英语函电[M]. 北京：科学出版社，2004.

[2] 徐宪光. 商务沟通[M]. 北京：外语教学与研究出版社，2003.

[3] ANGELL D F. *Elements of E-mail Style: Communicate Effectively via Electronic Mail*[M]. BOSTON: Addison-Wesley Publishing Company. 1994.

[4] AVTGIS T, RANCER A. Aggressive communication across cultures: A comparison of aggressive communication among United States, New Zealand, and Australia[J]. *Journal of Intercultural Communication Research*, 2002, 31(3):191-200.

[5] BAILEY E P. *The Plain English Approach to Business Writing*[M]. New York: New York University Press, 1990.

[6] BELL, A H, SMITH D M. *Management communication*[M]. New York: Wiley, 2009.

[7] BRANSON R. *Losing My Virginity*[M]. Sydney: Random House Australia, 2002.

[8] BURKE K. *A Rhetoric of Motives*[M]. Berkeley: University of California Press, 1969.

[9] CAUDRON, Shari. Virtual manners[J]. *Workforce*, 2000, 79(2): 31-34.

[10] GANESH N. A non-essentialist model of culture: Implications of identity, agency, and structure within multinational/multi-cultural organizations[J]. *International Journal of Cross-Cultural Management*, 2015, 15(1):101-124.

[11] GASS R, SEITER J. *Persuasion: Social Influence and Compliance Gaining*[M]. Sydney: Allyn & Bacon, 2003.

[12] GOLEMAN D, BOYATZIS R, McKee A. *The New Leaders: Transforming the Art of Leadership into the Science of Results*[M]. London: Little, Brown, 2002.

[13] HOFSTEDE G. Cultures and Organizations: Software of the Mind[M]. Sydney:McGraw-Hill, 1991.

[14] HOLDEN N, MICHAILOVA S, TIETZE S. *The Routledge Companion to Cross-Cultural Management*[M]. London: Routledge, 2015.

[15] HOLMES P. *Intercultural Encounters as Socially Constructed Experiences: Which Concepts? Which Pedagogies*[M]. London: Routledge, 2015.

[16] LAGERWERF L. Assessing business proposals: genre conventions and audience response in document design[J]. *Journal of Business Communication*, 2002, 39(4):437-481.

[17] LOCKER K O. *Business and Administrative Communication*[M]. 10th ed. New York: McGraw-Hill, 2013.

[18] MCCARTHY P, HATCHER C. *Speaking persuasively:The essential guide to giving dynamic presentations and speeches*[M]. Sydney: Allen & Unwin, 2002.

[19] MCCROSKEY J, TEVEN J. A re-examination of the construct of goodwill and its measurement[J]. *Communication Monographs*, 1999, 66(1): 90-103.

[20] OSLAND J, BIRD A. Beyond sophisticated stereotyping: cultural sense-making in context[J]. *Academy of Management Executive*, 2000, 14(1): 65-79.

[21] RICHARD J. FULSCHER. A no-fail recipe: winning business proposals[J]. *Journal of Property Management*, 1996(5):62.

[22] SAPIR E. *Selected Writings of Edward Sapir*[M]. Berkley: University of California Press, 1949.

[23] THOMPSON P. *The Secrets of the Great Communicators*[M]. Sydney: ABC Enterprises, 1992.

[24] THOMPSON P. *Persuading Aristotle*[M]. Sydney: Allen & Unwin, 1998.

[25] THOMSON K. *Passion at Work*[M]. Oxford: Capstone, 1998.

[26] TIMMONS J A, SPINELLI S. *New Venture Creation: Entrepreneurship for the 21st century*[M]. New York: Irwin McGraw-Hill, 2003.

[27] TRINCA H. Her way[J]. *Australian Financial Review*. 2000:16-19.